Giving Away A Miracle

Lost Dreams, Broken Promises and the Ontario NDP

Giving Away A Miracle

Lost Dreams, Broken Promises and the Ontario NDP

by
George Ehring
and
Wayne Roberts

MOSAIC PRESS
Oakville - New York - London

CANADIAN CATALOGUING IN PUBLICATION DATA

Roberts, Wayne, 1944 -

Giving away a miracle : lost dreams, broken promises & the Ontario NDP

Includes bibliographical references and index.

ISBN 0-88962-554-9

1. New Democratic Party of Ontario I. Ehring, George, 1949- . II. Title.

JL279.A54R63 1993   324.2713'07   C93-094781-9

Published by MOSAIC PRESS, P.O. Box 1032, Oakville, Ontario, L6J 5E9, Canada. Offices and warehouse at 1252 Speers Road, Units # 1&2, Oakville, Ontario, L6L 5N9, Canada.

Mosaic Press acknowledges the assistance of the Canada Council and the Ontario Arts Council in support of its publishing programme.

Typeset by Aztext Electronic Publishing Ltd.

Printed and bound in Canada.

ISBN 0-88962-554-9   PAPER

MOSAIC PRESS:

In Canada:
MOSAIC PRESS, 1252 Speers Road, Units # 1&2, Oakville, Ontario L6L 5N9, Canada. P.O. Box 1032, Oakville, Ontario L6J 5E9

In the U.K.:
John Calder (Publishers) Ltd., 9 - 15 Neal Street, London, England WCZH 2TU

"The growth and development of the NDP must never allow us to forget our roots. Don't give up conviction for success. Don't ever give up quality for quantity. In a movement like ours, we're not just interested in getting votes. We are seeking to get people who are willing to dedicate their lives to building a different kind of society."

Tommy Douglas speaking to New Democrats on the 50th anniversary of the signing of the Regina Manifesto. Regina, Saskatchewan, July, 1983.

Giving Away A Miracle
Lost Dreams, Broken Promises and the Ontario NDP

TABLE OF CONTENTS

Preface

In the spring of 1990, no one thought Bob Rae would be elected premier of Ontario, least of all us. In fact, we were so sure Rae and the New Democrats were dead ducks that even before election day we were well on the way with a book explaining why they faced extinction.

We were wrong. Who wasn't? We faced the music and dumped the manuscript. It was annoying, but, let's face it, it wasn't as bad as being former premier David Peterson.

We've been critics of the NDP for longer than we care to remember. As leaders of the party's left wing through the 1970s and 1980s, we were frustrated by what the party did. What really burned us was what it did not do. But we haven't just carped from the sidelines. Between the two of us, we have managed campaigns, canvassed thousands of households and contributed lots of money and energy — well, mostly energy. We've also written more than our fair share of speeches, newsletters, campaign material and manifestos. George served a brief term as a party vice-president until being ceremoniously dumped, and years as a legislative assistant in the NDP caucus; Wayne watches Queen's Park for NOW magazine. Both of us have also done time in the union movement, Wayne as an assistant to the president of the Ontario Public Service Employees' Union, and George as a public relations officer with the Canadian Auto Workers' Union. Through all of it we tried to keep our sense of humour, which often caused us as much trouble as our politics. We'd rather laugh than switch.

From 1987 through the spring of 1990, we got together for dinner with friends nearly every Friday night at the down-home Gerrard Pizza and Spaghetti House in Toronto's east end. That's where this book — or, rather, the one we threw away — was dreamed up.

Of the regular crowd who met there, most were trade unionists or disgruntled New Democrats. Some had already left the party. We wined, dined and whined about why the party was going nowhere in Ontario. Gluttons for punishment and good Italian food, we analyzed the failures, deplored the stupidities and condemned the hypocrisies of the Ontario NDP. Sometimes it was hard to stomach, but there was plenty to chew over. Wayne always had the nerve to pay his share with his New Democrats Mastercard: a credit-card-carrying NDPer to the end.

In the spring of 1990 we decided to write a book explaining why New Democrats were chronic losers. In September the party brass foiled our plans. Their election in Ontario opened a new chapter in Canadian political history, and meant far more to us than one or two more chapters. Since the election of Premier Bob, we have had to look at things in a way we hadn't thought would be necessary.

This book isn't exactly what it first set out to be, but it is surprising how much the lessons we learned watching them in opposition explain their present behaviour in government.

The election of an NDP government in Ontario has important national implications. Of course NDP governments have been elected in British Columbia, Saskatchewan and Manitoba, but Ontario is a special case. Here is the industrial heartland, some of Canada's best farmland, a mix of mines and forests, a skilled workforce and the self-appointed financial gurus on Bay Street — all close to one of the richest markets in the world.

Ontario's size, wealth and complexity are the acid test of an NDP government's ability to change the economy and deal with the power elite. If the NDP cannot succeed in bringing new social, economic and political relations to Ontario, then there must be something deeply wrong with the party, a flaw so profound that radicals will have to re-think their options. That assumes, of course, that Bob Rae's government will even give the NDP program a chance. You might get better odds at one of his casinos.

Though our analysis is central to the book, we have tried to make readers suffer through as little theory as possible before getting to the gossip and anecdotes that make up most of the book. Some of these incidents have been carefully hidden by the apologists who have written about the NDP before, as if they were writing about stained-glass saints: a little colour, but essentially two-dimensional.

If you are an Ontario New Democrat, you may find yourself in this book, whether you like it or not. You may have heard some of the stories here, but probably not the details. If you're a political junkie looking for a fix on the NDP, you'll like having the lowdown. If you're just trying to figure out who those people now running the show are, then this book will tell you about them and why they behave the way they do.

This book is based on years of personal observation and countless interviews with party activists. Many of those people talked with us, on and off the record, before the party was launched into government. Some of them are now on the government gravy train. We know their jobs would be on the line if we identified them, so they've been left anonymous. At least this book recognizes that the NDP is more than its leadership. But then, this is not the story the leadership would want told.

Introduction

A promise made is a debt unpaid.
— From Robert Service, *The Cremation of Sam McGee*

When he stepped out of the University of Toronto's Convocation Hall into the brisk, sunny afternoon of October 1, 1990, as the new premier of Ontario, Bob Rae carried with him the unpaid debt of many promises. They were not just the promises of a political platform: of public automobile insurance, of a minimum corporate tax, of a ban on "Sunday working," or of employment equity, labour reform, and a healthier environment; he took with him the bright promise of hopeful expectation, shining in the moist eyes of thousands of New Democrats who thought they would never live to see the day.

This was no ordinary change of government. The pages of Ontario history turned a new leaf as the province's first social democratic cabinet was sworn in. Just blocks away on Bay Street, Canada's business elite was worried. But at Convocation Hall the mood was euphoric, with scarcely a hint of the problems, dilemmas and disappointments ahead. A choir of seniors and children sang "Zippety-Do-Dah," "Take Me Out to the Ball Game," and "Side By Side." Not a single person in the crowd or media missed the significance of one verse: "Oh, we ain't got a barrel of money, maybe we're ragged and funny, but we're travelling along, singing our song, side by side."

Like the nearly 2,000 party faithful in attendance that day, the cabinet ministers had tears in their eyes and lumps in their throats, nervously awaiting their chance to change Ontario forever. Their party, at last in power, was about to bring justice to the oppressed, and dignity and equality to the poor and disadvantaged. The New Democrats, who had worked and hoped so long for this day, expected nothing less.

The ceremonial trumpets that announced the entrance of Bob Rae and Lieutenant Governor Lincoln Alexander to the stage of Convocation Hall triumphantly heralded the dawn of a new political era.

Rae promised a new style of government, substantially different from the tired rhetoric of open and honest, and untainted by backroom deals and backdoor bargains. He asked the people of Ontario to judge him by different standards. He offered them a new beginning, and they looked anxiously for it to start.

The government itself had not just a new stripe but a new look: 11 of its 26 cabinet ministers were women, and women held the key portfolios of health, education, social services, environment and energy. The cabinet had only three lawyers, but included several social workers and trade union activists.

Of the 26 ministers, 12 had never served a day in the legislature. The new tourism minister, Peter North, had never been in an airplane, and on his first trip to Niagara Falls a few months later was so excited he couldn't sleep at night. Zanana Akande, the social services minister, may have reflected the incoming cabinet's ignorance of how the bureaucracy worked when she was introduced to her deputy minister, a woman with twenty years' experience in the public service. She told the deputy that she took her coffee with two sugars.

The NDP caucus included many shop floor workers and local union leaders, a truck driver, and a fourth-year political science student, who would be able to teach his professors how government worked. There were a few small business people, including Ron Hansen, who had a vacuum-cleaner company and drove a car with personalized "VACUUM" licence plates. Hansen had achieved some notoriety for having divorced his wife and marrying his former mother-in-law.

The caucus also included Gary Malkowski, the first deaf politician elected to a senior level of government anywhere in North America. His presence symbolized the NDP's representation of people who had been left out of society's mainstream. Though all but one of its members were white, this government seemed to reflect the diversity of people in Ontario better than any in the province's history.

Across Ontario, many people welcomed the change and seemed to take the results of the stunning election upset in stride. Though only about 38 per cent of voters had opted for the NDP in September, 1990, three months later an Environics poll put the government's popularity at 58 per cent.

The NDP quickly made some bold moves.

Before the end of the year, the government announced it was giving land to natives in northern Ontario who had been involved in a lengthy land claims dispute. It decided it could not afford $55 million for Toronto's ballet/opera house, but gave away the property to be used for affordable non-profit housing. It agreed to fund women's clinics to provide no-cost abortions, and increased pregnancy leave provisions. The government also announced that it would provide health care and other benefits to same-sex couples.

But it didn't take long for things to go wrong.

In March, 1991, maverick cabinet minister Peter Kormos appeared as a *Toronto Sun* Sunshine Boy, after complaining about sexism in alcohol advertisements, and was promptly dumped from cabinet.

Other cabinet ministers made mistakes: letters that smacked of attempts to influence judicial decisions on traffic tickets; a patient's name and medical history revealed; allegations of sexual improprieties both old and new. Some of these scandals resulted in actual resignations; others merely drew protracted media scrutiny and opposition attacks, but together they left the impression that the NDP didn't know what it was doing, or that it was just as corrupt or foolish as previous governments. All this took place in its first six months in office.

The *Globe and Mail* soon ran an editorial cartoon showing a tabloid with a series of lurid headlines, including "Amazing Eclair Diet," "Psychic Pooch Levitates House," "Bishop Weds Chimp" and "Possibility Ontario NDP May Go A Full Day Without Blunder."

But it was not to be.

After an initial spate of announcements, many of them right off the Liberal shelf, the NDP bogged down in the legislature, caught up in vicious partisan bickering, and derailed by the gaffes of its ministers.

When treasurer Floyd Laughren brought down his first budget in April, 1991, the deficit zoomed to $9.7 billion, apparently reflecting the NDP's belief that the government should stimulate the economy in poor economic times. While the business community writhed in apoplexy, the chief economist of the Conference Board of Canada praised the budget as a "confidence builder." He noted that new initiatives accounted for only $640 million of the deficit, while the rest reflected ongoing government commitments and reduced revenues. But the NDP had no idea how to sell its budget to the people, and did not even have a public relations person in the treasury ministry at the time.

Though many Ontarians were concerned about the deficit, many others were angry that the government had resorted to the old standby taxes on alcohol and cigarettes to increase revenue and had not raised corporate taxes one thin dime.

Before the year was out, Laughren was already planning billions of dollars in spending cuts. The government also announced it was looking at all of its assets to determine where it could sell them off. Long an article of faith with right-wing governments, privatization was normally staunchly opposed by social democrats. The list of options included GO transit, the Liquor Control Board, land holdings, the SkyDome, the Urban Transit Development Corporation, and others.

Rae chose the first anniversary of his election victory to announce that the government had abandoned public auto insurance. That action, more than any other, symbolized what the party eventually came to stand for. The reversal from such a key position infuriated many party supporters and bewildered people who had not voted for the New Democrats. The NDP, which argued long and loud that it was the party of principle, had shown that even its highest profile policies weren't worth the paper they were printed on. If the New Democrats could sell out on public auto insurance, what else might they renounce?

Before Christmas 1991, the legislature became embroiled in controversy after northern development minister Shelley Martel blabbed at a cocktail party that charges would be laid against a Sudbury doctor for ripping off the public health plan. Even if this had been true, confidentiality requirements meant that she would not have known about it. In the course of the twisted events that followed, Martel tried to get out of the mess by claiming she had lied at the cocktail party, and even took a lie detector test to prove she was telling the truth when she said she had lied at the party. Rae defended her every step of the way.

Then new solicitor-general Allan Pilkey got caught up in a controversy over allegations of gang rape at a training facility run by his ministry. Pilkey, a former Oshawa mayor who hired his golf pro as his ministerial driver, pleaded ignorance, a claim many in the know found easy to accept, considering Pilkey's infrequent visits to his office. Queen's Park insiders quipped that he should follow Martel's lead and take an IQ test to prove he was as stupid as he said he was.

People were not just angry with the government, they were laughing at it. Even New Democrats shook their heads in disbelief.

But still the end was not in sight.

After years of arguing that lotteries should not be used to fund essential government services, the NDP blew the cork off its self-righteousness and announced it would open casinos. It then reversed another major position and decided not to block Sunday shopping. As one government-watcher put it: "The NDP had said you could lose your shirt on Sunday, but you couldn't buy one." Now you could buy one.

Tourism minister Peter North then had a safe-sex, NDP-style affair with a Toronto barmaid by sleeping with the woman without having sex with her. He offered her a job and then withdrew the offer when she told him she was a Tory. "Scandal interruptus," wrote *Toronto Star* columnist Thomas Walkom. Ridicule was heaped on scandal.

Shortly afterward, Rae's communications advisor, John Piper, tried to leak the criminal record of a woman involved in a messy series of charges and counter-charges against former minister Will Ferguson. Piper resigned in disgrace, but it looked as if the government had an enemies list and was trying to smear its critics. The woman was a survivor of sexual abuse, just the kind of victim the NDP was supposed to champion.

As policy reversals and ministerial blunders continued, the government's popularity, which had once stood near 60 per cent, dropped like a stone. In two April, 1993, by-elections, the government received just over 8 per cent of the vote in both ridings — one of which they had held, and the other they had lost in 1990 by fewer than 100 votes.

Long time party backers felt betrayed and many who had voted for the NDP for the first time in 1990, hoping for something new, realized that they were just getting more of the same — or worse — from the New Democrats.

The policy reversals and ministerial scandals were particularly troublesome for the NDP because while in opposition Rae bathed himself in sanctimony. He and the caucus claimed a purity of principle and cleanliness of spirit unmatched by any politician or party in the land. It is important to understand them in this light, because Rae and other New Democrats honestly came to believe their own propaganda. Rae promised a government that would be squeaky clean, free of influence and corruption. The Tories and Liberals, who had suffered the slings and arrows of Rae's self-righteousness, were more than ready to exact revenge when their turn came.

The focus on scandals, no matter which party is in power, commands far too much attention by the media and the public. It diverts awareness from policy issues that need resolution and obscures what governments do, both good and bad. While in opposition, Rae tried to make people associate the notion of "good government" with one free of scandal, instead of emphasizing one that has the integrity to live up to its commitments. To this extent, his government was hoist on his own petard.

The policy reversals that became his signpost were especially damaging because the NDP had so paraded itself as the party of principle. When Liberal solicitor general Joan Smith introduced the Peterson government's bill allowing Sunday shopping in 1988, Rae lamented that she had a different view before joining cabinet. "Those of us who have been involved in politics and watched the wonders of the effects of power on some can hardly be surprised," he said. "...When somebody says one thing as a private member and then turns around as a cabinet minister and says the opposite, I think something is wrong with respect to telling it straight and telling it like it is."

The party faithful soon trotted out a number of excuses to explain the government's poor performance. At the top of the list was the recession. Conventional wisdom had it that bad economic times made it impossible for the NDP to implement its proposals. For a while, most NDP backers bought this line, and faithfully suggested that if only the government had come to office when it had some money, things would be different.

Another excuse was inexperience. The party had never formed the government in Ontario, and was bound to make some rookie mistakes. Rae said it was like trying to learn to play the violin in public. Things would improve as time went on, New Democrats said.

A third excuse was that the New Democrats couldn't do what they wanted because everyone was ganging up on them: the business community, the media, the opposition — everyone was out to get them. This particular brand of paranoia fit well with the NDP's traditional view of itself as the only political organization fighting for the good and the just.

All apologies more than explanations, these three excuses still have a grain of truth. Governments do have more options when the economy is booming than when it is bust. But social democrats have long claimed they would bring fairness and equality to society — which are even more necessary in bad times than in good. And it made no sense to suggest that social democratic policies only worked when the economy was healthy.

As for inexperience, it might justify foolishness but not incompetence; the government's problem was not its inexperience but its inability to learn from experience. Nor could inexperience explain the abandonment of major policies, unless the government was ready to admit that it simply did not know what it was talking about while in opposition.

And while it is true that the pillars of capitalist society have attacked the NDP government, certainly that was to be expected and should have been planned for. The government was caught in the bind of wanting to work with business, and therefore constrained in its willingness to counter-attack. Similarly, it is difficult to argue that media attacks on the various scandals involving NDP cabinet ministers have been worse than they were on Liberals during the Patti Starr affair, for example, which dragged on for two years and brought down a number of ministers. Like all governments, the NDP wants the media to pay attention to its successes and ignore its mistakes, and blames the media for failing to do so.

As this book went to press in the summer of 1993, Rae's government had announced the elimination of 11,000 public sector jobs, demanded concessions from hundreds of thousands of other workers, and passed the first legislation in the history of the province to freeze or roll-back wages in the broader public sector. It had also slashed billions in government spending and cut back benefits to seniors and those on social assistance.

"I don't believe Brian Mulroney would have had the courage to do what Bob Rae has done," the president of the province's largest teacher's federation complained. "Those of us who've been in the NDP for many, many years thought our party would do things differently," lamented retired NDP MPP Mel Swart. "But we've done the same as a Liberal or Progressive Conservative government might do—and perhaps we've even gone further," he said.

Ultimately, the recession, the NDP's inexperience and the attacks it suffered are not the reasons why Bob Rae's government has so badly disappointed its supporters. The problems go much deeper than that. To borrow the title of Canadian singer Luba's song that the party chose for its 1990 campaign, the NDP seems to be actively giving away the miracle of its election.

We will offer examples of the NDP's failure to learn from its past, and its repetition of mistakes that have stunted its growth and limited its vision. Ignoring rebel organizer Saul Alinsky's famous Rules for Radicals, the NDP instead stuck to its own Rules for Reformists, even though until now those rules left it out of the game.

Most earlier studies of the NDP and its forerunner, the CCF, explain why Canada has a radical third party tradition, and use the party's history to discuss its principled stand while in opposition. Now, with the Ontario NDP victory, Canadians have the rare chance to study history to explain to themselves why the NDP does not live up to its principles. The NDP government in Ontario will become the new benchmark for writing on the NDP.

Part One of *Giving Away A Miracle* outlines ten themes that recur throughout the history of the NDP and provides their historical context. These themes — we call them the "ten deadly sins" — are the chronic problems that have plagued the NDP and now shape its performance in government. Part Two covers the decade of Bob Rae's party leadership in detail, explaining how his background has shaped the Ontario NDP and how it influences his style of governing. It examines the party's behaviour during those years and relates it to the ten themes. Part Two explains what makes the Ontario NDP tick and how it burst into government. Part Three provides a brief look at how each of the ten deadly sins has influenced the government's performance.

Giving Away A Miracle is not a history of the NDP. It is an examination of the problems that make it so difficult for the NDP to fulfil its bright promise and support the hope that warmed the hearts of so many people at Convocation Hall that sunny October day.

PART ONE
The Deadly Sins

The Deadly Sins

Ontario New Democrats used to joke that if they ever won an election they would be the first to demand a recount. But when they counted the ballots on September 6, 1990 and Bob Rae's New Democratic Party was swept into office, no one was laughing.

Rae started the campaign far behind Liberal Premier David Peterson, and wasn't given any chance of catching up. Tired and disappointed by his own failure to make a breakthrough, Rae had wanted to spend the summer with his family at his new cottage on his private island in the Rideau, near the place where he spent the happier summers of his boyhood. When the campaign began, Rae himself thought the NDP would be stuck in opposition again, and that he would have to quit provincial politics.

Instead of his cottage, Rae found himself occupying the Premier's Office in the south-east corner of the second floor of the red sandstone Queen's Park in Toronto. The rantings and delusions of politicians there have replaced those of the inmates from the insane asylum that once stood on the same spot. It's a far cry from the quiet islands of the Rideau, where the call of the loon has a different sound.

From that office, just a few blocks from the pillars of capitalism on Bay Street, Rae directs Ontario's first social democratic government. That government, elected by surprise and with high hopes, has run into formidable problems. Some of those problems are not of the party's doing: the recession, its inexperience and its opposition, both inside and outside the legislature. But behind the scenes, buried in the party's history and in the personalities of its leadership, the seeds of its real difficulties were planted. Over time, they have grown to the extent that they seriously hinder the NDP's ability to govern the province. They are the real reasons why the NDP has not been able to deliver.

We have identified 10 major themes that recur throughout the history of the Ontario NDP. They show that the problems the NDP encountered as government began long before the election. Though they are evident before Rae became party leader in 1982, they have continued and deepened during his leadership.

Here's a short version of the NDP's ten deadly sins:

(1) The NDP lacks new ideas and imagination.
(2) The party is intolerant of internal dissent and has no honest review mechanism to learn from its failures.
(3) It distrusts social movements and won't participate meaningfully in coalition politics.
(4) The NDP has a bureaucratic relationship with the labour movement that isolates it from working people.
(5) The party has no down-to-earth economic plan, what we call "lunchbucket" economics.
(6) The NDP has a romantic view of heroic, victimized workers.
(7) It can't connect with Ontario's multicultural community.
(8) It misunderstands the Liberal party and wishes it would go away.
(9) The party hasn't developed a workable media strategy, and is paranoid about the coverage it gets.
(10) New Democrats can't distinguish between their image as a party and the content of their platform.

Throughout the party's history, these ten themes keep popping up. At different times, each has influenced the way the party defined its course; all of them have limited the party's progress. They never dealt with them in opposition; now, in power, they can't escape them.

We begin with perhaps the most surprising shortcoming for a left-wing party: the absence of new, radical or imaginative policies to cope with a dramatically changing world.

1. Ideology without Ideas

No one thought the NDP would do so little so quickly. That's because people thought the NDP was full of ideas — new, fresh and exciting ideas — that are supposed to be the hallmark of a party of the left. But it isn't so. The NDP has more policies than it knows what to do with, but it's a case of ideology without ideas.

Unlike those of other political parties, NDP policies are an open book. Anyone can buy the New Democrats' policy book and read what they think they stand for. NDPers take pride in the fact that they are not like Liberals and Conservatives, whose positions bend with changing political winds and the bent of their various leaders. In theory, NDP leaders are obliged to support the policies of the party.

The NDP wears its policy book like a hair shirt, a tailor-made source of itchy embarrassment there for everyone to see. A product of the party's intellectual frankness, it is something the leadership often runs from, but can't hide behind.

But despite its soup-to-nuts policies, for a party of the left the NDP has a hard time coming up with new visions for a changing world.

It was not always the case. In Saskatchewan, the Co-operative Commonwealth Federation (CCF), forerunner of the NDP, formed the government from 1944 to 1964. Federally, the CCF remained a small band that never came close to power. Yet they defined the political agenda of Canada from the 1930s until the 1970s. Despite fierce establishment opposition, the early CCF helped bring about a national unemployment insurance program, a federal pension plan, and a country-wide health care system. Calling for these programs at the time opened the CCF to ridicule and attack. Today each of these is not only a reality but a "sacred trust."

The CCF also crusaded for the underdog, championing other changes that pushed social and economic equality. In 1937, the party's first leader, J.S. Woodsworth, proposed a federal law to guarantee workers the right to organize. It was such a popular proposal that the federal government finally went along with it in 1944. In March, 1949, the Ontario CCF introduced the first equal pay bill in any Canadian legislature, and in 1951, the Saskatchewan CCF passed such a bill. In Ontario, the ruling Conservatives blocked the legislation, claiming it discriminated against women since no employer would hire women if they had to pay them the same wages as men. Saskatchewan gave full union rights to its public servants a full 20 years before any other Canadian government. Some other early CCF policies included universal day care and salaries for homemakers.

In *Social Democracy in Canada*, historian Desmond Morton calls the NDP "a transmission belt between new ideas and the Canadian political system." If that's so, the transmission isn't automatic. Morton's claim is more true of the CCF than the NDP; the days of championing dramatic social and political change are over.

This is due in large part to an absence of imagination and a lack of commitment to fundamental change. Writing in *This Magazine* in 1982, University of Western Ontario law professor Robert Martin said: "The greatest tragedy of the Ontario NDP today may well lie in its rejection of critical social thought. There was a time when the CCF attracted the best minds in the country....But the ONDP (and the federal party for that matter) are bereft of ideas and have been for years."

Martin blames some of this on David Lewis's fierce battles to rid the party and the labour movement of Communists. "After the overt or covert CP members were got rid of," he says, "it became time to eliminate people who espoused ideas that sounded 'communist.' Soon it became suspect to have socialist or radical ideas. And eventually it became unacceptable to have any ideas at all."

In a 1978 interview with Sandra Gwyn for *Saturday Night*, federal leader Ed Broadbent petulantly dismissed those who criticized the party for its lack of ideas. "Look," he said. "There are only so many hours in the day. There are a million people out of work in this country. If there's one thing that burns me up it's hearing people bitching, 'You're not talking about our concerns.' How the hell can they keep on being so goddamn self-absorbed and self-congratulatory? Why don't all these people with the new ideas — the professors and the poets and the novelists even — start talking about our concerns for a change? Why aren't they right out in front on issues like unemployment? I sometimes wonder if they bloody well care. Well, I do."

Dan Leckie, a former NDP chairperson of the Toronto Board of Education in the 1970s, a long-time activist and organizer, now a policy advisor for the government, asks questions that go to the fundamentals of politics. "What does the public think the purpose of provincial government is?" he wonders. "What does the political left think its purpose is? The left hasn't thought about that role, and how to change it." Prior to the 1990 election, he lamented that "Bob Rae has been leader all these years without improving the quality of the province's political awareness."

A former senior party official admits that "there's an enormous opportunity to reposition on what the role of government should be", but even in his position was uninterested and totally ineffective in helping the NDP raise those questions.

That Rae has failed to raise political awareness is not entirely his fault, of course, though as NDP leader he has the responsibility for the priorities and vision of the party. Since he was elected leader in 1982, there have been enormous political changes throughout the world. It was not just the era of Ronald Reagan and Margaret Thatcher, it was a time of rich new thinking on the environment, feminism, socialism and democracy, human rights, the globalization of the economy and other issues that challenged established political ideas.

In the 1980s, New Democrats seemed powerless to counteract the economic policies of neo-conservatism. The New Right, whose simple but catchy tune seduced countless unthinking followers, had Reagan and Thatcher leading like Pied Pipers. Sociologist John Conway writes that the response of social democrats to the challenge of the New Right has been only to "adopt the position of defending the last half-century of marginal gains, rather than extending those gains into new areas."

The domination of neo-conservative ideas rose at the time of, and contributed to, mass alienation from politics, which were dirty, and from politicians, who were corrupt. Since, according to the right, government gets in the way of one's own success, it is worse than useless. Brian Mulroney's scandal-ridden federal Conservative party only gives grist to the mill. The NDP's inability to confront this trend lends credibility to the notion that "they're all the same."

Two issues dominated the political scene at the federal level in the 1980s in Canada: national unity and free trade. The constitutional issue plagues New Democrats, who keep bending over backwards to find a position on Quebec. For them, the decade began with federal leader Ed Broadbent making a snap personal decision to go along with Prime Minister Trudeau's patriation of the Constitution and entrenchment of the Charter of Rights and Freedoms. As the 1980s ground to a halt, the NDP supported the Meech Lake accord — despite the fact that the deal took power away from native people, women and the federal government itself. The NDP laid in the Meech mud like a lazy carp and swallowed Prime Minister Brian Mulroney's bait — hook, line and sinker. When the question of Senate reform turned into the dealbreaker in the final days before Meech Lake dried up, and after decades of calling for its complete abolition, the NDP leadership opted into a western Conservative concept of Senate reform. Power to the People became Power to the Provinces. The party didn't develop a socialist perspective on national unity issues; if its view differed from those of Liberals or Conservatives, it was hard to know where.

Free trade was the central economic debate for Canada in the late 1980s, but here, too, there were no new ideas from New Democrats. The party opposed free trade but proposed no alternative. It's not as if the few economic policies they had were out to lunch: it's just that they didn't develop lunchbucket economics for the "ordinary Canadian" they claimed they talked to and spoke for. In the 1988 federal election the NDP allowed the Liberals, who should have had no credibility on the issue, to take centre stage.

Economist Abe Rotstein said of the NDP's failure to make free trade a central issue in the election: "It is the great characteristic of the NDP to be unable to recognize nationalism in either official language."

In Ontario, the NDP made public auto insurance the driving force of its 1987 election campaign. This came at the same time that environmentalists were trying to get away from subsidies for cars. But even this wasn't a new idea, since it was CCF policy as early as 1948, and had been implemented by NDP governments in British Columbia, Saskatchewan and Manitoba. The party called for "driver-owned" auto insurance, since the polls said "publicly-owned" and "government-run" were less popular phrases, but lost the advantage of eliminating a costly bureaucracy when it said the plan would be delivered by private insurance agents rather than the provincial government. The NDP was divided on whether or not people injured in auto accidents would have the right to sue, and once in the driver's seat as government, stalled when they tried to get their plan on the road. Ultimately, of course, they abandoned drivers on the roadside.

The NDP also missed the opportunity to make the link between auto insurance and any form of universal accident and illness insurance. Under such a scheme, whenever a person loses the ability to earn an income, either permanently or short term, he or she needs compensation, which the state should guarantee. It shouldn't matter whether a person loses earnings as the result of an accident at home, at work, on a highway, or as the result of an illness. The idea has been around a long time, but even though it could save millions of taxpayers' dollars in simplified government administration, even though it could provide better coverage for everyone, and even though democratic socialist governments elsewhere have brought in such a plan, it never was a priority for the Ontario NDP.

New Democrats were also caught between conflicting pressures on the number one issue of the 1980s: the environment. In calling for tighter regulations and higher fines for corporate polluters, NDP policies are the toughest of the three main parties. But as government, they can't see the forest for the trees. In particular, they have had difficulty advancing a program calling for production and lifestyle changes that would help protect the environment, but that would upset traditional labour support because jobs might be affected.

In Bob Rae's own introduction to the party's 1990 policy paper on the environment, he wrote: "Politicians of all stripes are spouting rhetoric about the environment. The question for the Ontario NDP is....are we ready to become a...party that puts as much emphasis on people's relationships with nature, and our obligation to future generations, as on the distribution of power and income."

In a later chapter we will look at the environmental record of the Rae government, but let's recall his own answer to the question: "If the answer is no, then our policies will only temper marginally the status quo, making it difficult to distinguish our policies from the environmental policies of the other parties. It will be an apparently safer choice, because it will mean fewer changes. But like all safe choices it will mean the party is excluding the possibility of being a real leader in the creation of a new consciousness, a new awareness, a new politics." This is as true for the distribution of power and income as for the environment.

We wonder what such new politics might mean for the NDP. Traditionally, the party has promised more of everything, but still has had a hard time getting workers to support it. Now the left is faced with telling people that there will have to be less, not more, in order to protect our environment and share with developing countries so they don't destroy their resources as we have. New ideas in this regard will be very difficult for New Democrats to grapple with.

These are only a few examples; we will consider more through the course of the book. Once a visionary political movement, the NDP has become a party dominated by grey administrators with polls in their heads but no fire in their bellies. Even as government, they are cut off from people with ideas and from groups that propose new solutions. They have failed to take hold of the new ideas that surround them.

At issue, of course, is why New Democrats haven't promoted new visions and new solutions. There are many reasons: the cautiousness of their leader and their party bureaucracy, their play-it-safe approach to politics, their alienation from social movements and the multicultural community, their ties to labour bigshots, their search for the political centre, their old boy's network and mutual admiration society, and others.

One key to this problem for New Democrats is their long history of an almost pathological need to crush dissent within the party. These dissenters are often the source of new ideas or new approaches to politics, ginger groups that spice debate and stimulate alternatives. But the NDP has shown itself intolerant of dissent, and has suffered a lack of innovation as a result. That's the second of our themes.

The "S" Word: Socialist or Social Democrat?

In the 1987 provincial campaign, while Bob Rae was mainstreeting with federal NDP leader Ed Broadbent and Canadian Autoworkers' Union President Bob White, a reporter asked Rae if he was a socialist. Rae refused to answer. He said he didn't like labels.

The reporter turned to White, who said immediately that he was a socialist, and then to Broadbent, who said, a little more cautiously, that he, too, considered himself a socialist.

Rae was on the spot, but refused to be labelled. He wouldn't admit to "socialist", though that's honest and accurate. Less so is his common claim to be a "social democrat."

"Social Democrat" is a European term. At the beginning of the twentieth century all socialists, including revolutionary Marxists, called themselves social democrats. During the 1920s, "social democrat" took on its modern meaning, and its sense diverged from the more radical "socialist."

Generally, social democrats were nationalistic supporters of their own countries in World War I and of electoral gradualism; socialists were more international, opposed the war and were still given to support workers' revolutions. The descriptions had definite theory behind them, and many of their intellectuals were commissioned to write books, not to take polls, to justify theories and policies.

In Canada, there was no such split, and socialists were generally pacifists who opposed the war but supported the Russian revolution. J.S. Woodsworth, the revered father of the CCF, was such a person.

CCFers were mainly humanitarians who believed in Parliament as the place to make social, political and economic change. By the 1940s they had watered down their radicalism, part of a North American pragmatism that reflected low levels of class consciousness.

The party's own various manifestos reflect this dilution. The 1933 Regina Manifesto called for the eradication of capitalism; by 1956 the Winnipeg Declaration talked about reforming it; and by 1983 the party was reduced to suggesting that "co-operation and mutual responsibility [must] prevail over private gain and competition as the guiding principles of social and economic life."

More recently, it was Manitoba's NDP Premier Ed Schreyer who popularized Canadian use of the term "social democrat" to get off the hook of being called a "socialist" by his right-wing opponents, who use the term only to raise the Red Scare.

But even referring to the NDP as a party of democratic socialists is a misreading of how it functions and an exaggeration of the evolution of its policies. It implies an ideological consistency — that choices have been made according to a coherent set of values, analysis and experiences — that is absent in the NDP.

In fact, the NDP is a party as dependent on polling to determine its ideology and priorities as the Liberals and Conservatives are. Like the others, New Democrats are pure pragmatists, and pollsters are their theoreticians.

2. The No Dissent Party: Democratic isn't the NDP's middle name.

"The whole socialist movement is no more than an exciting heresy-hunt." George Orwell, *The Road to Wigan Pier*

Premier Rae likes to say that the job of government is listening to people. This is ironic coming from the leader of a party that is hell-bent on ridding itself of dissident voices. Run by a small group of hand-picked insiders, there is little attempt at consensus building or honest listening that goes on inside the NDP. The party's lack of listening while in opposition has led to many of the problems it has as government.

Long before labour leaders pushed Ontario NDP leader Stephen Lewis to expel the Waffle from the provincial party in 1972, both the NDP and CCF had been busy rooting out left-wing members who disagreed with the party brass. The Waffle incident was only the latest and most obvious proof that Democratic isn't the NDP's middle name.

The Waffle was the party's effective extra-parliamentary left-nationalist wing, which more than any group before or since sparked NDP debate on fundamental principles. Upstart graduate student James Laxer even forced Stephen's father, David, a party icon, to an embarrassing fourth ballot during the federal leadership convention in 1969. In the process, Laxer outpolled future leader Ed Broadbent and future MP John Harney.

The expulsion of the Waffle showed the party establishment's paranoia in dealing with challenging ideas from its own left wing. This didn't start with the NDP; David Lewis was a notorious red-baiter who loved to root communists out of the party.

Expulsions mark the history of the CCF. In fact, just a few months after the founding of the party, the entire Ontario wing was disbanded by the national executive after the farmers accused the labour section of being riddled with Communists and quit the party. In 1936 the B.C. provincial leader was expelled, and three members of the legislature left with him.

In Manitoba, two MLAs were suspended in 1945 following a vicious smear campaign by Winnipeg MP Stanley Knowles for being too close to the commies; one was later reinstated but expelled again, along with a third MLA, in 1949. The Saskatchewan caucus pressured its leader, Woodrow Lloyd, to resign in 1970, partly because of his identification with the Waffle. At the time, Lloyd was Leader of the Opposition.

In *Love and Solidarity*, his recent photographic history of the CCF/NDP, Cameron Smith carries on this tradition by referring to all leftists as Trots, and by heading a section on the expulsions as "pest control."

In her book on the CCF, *No Bankers in Heaven*, Olenka Melnyk writes that: "The ideological debates, expulsions, suspensions and disciplinary proceedings, which routinely went on in the party, were time-consuming and extremely damaging to its image."

It wasn't just people, but ideas that were often the source of trouble. At the party's 1950 federal convention in Vancouver, David Lewis went to the microphone to demand that pamphlets from the Socialist Party of Britain be removed from the literature table. A fight broke out and the offending literature was whisked away. Books by Marx and Engels were also banned, ironically by the party's education officer, Donald C. MacDonald, who became Ontario CCF leader three years later.

In the early 1950s, Lewis the Elder expelled the League for Social Reconstruction, a think-tank group, from the CCF while the party was considering its presentation to the Massey royal commission on culture. Lewis stacked meetings and drove out activists. One of them was Frank Underhill, principal author of the Regina Manifesto, which gave the CCF its ideological framework in 1933. Underhill quit the CCF over the incident, and in a parting shot described the party as "a sect whose leaders are mainly interested in maintaining at all costs their own authority within the sect."

The NDP has continued to stifle, discredit, isolate or expel its internal critics. When the left is sufficiently organized, as it was with Ontario's Campaign for an Activist Party in 1986, the party bosses feel compelled to smash it, rather than find a constructive role for its energy. By 1990, this had led to the virtual extinction of organized dissent within the NDP and the self-imposed exile of many of its left-wing members out of the party and into the social movements concerned about the environment, women's issues, peace, poverty or senior's issues, or into the labour movement. It also restricted the talent pool available to the incoming NDP government, because many of the best and brightest were either unwilling to align themselves with a Rae government, or were automatically excluded by those doing the hiring as known dissenters.

Many progressive New Democrats still carry a party card but are more comfortable working with single-issue groups they can contribute to, rather than bashing their heads against the brick wall of the NDP establishment. Not only are their energy and ideas more welcome elsewhere, but they enjoy the more supportive atmosphere. They are less likely to be the objects of attack by an insecure bureaucracy that feels threatened by the spectre of challenge and sees disloyalty lurking around every corner.

With rare exceptions, all debate inside the NDP is thought of as dissent, and all dissent must be eliminated. David Tomczak, former head of the Metro NDP, says that the party brass "has internalized the need for complete control within the party so much they can't see new events. It's not a left-right thing; they're afraid of unleashing forces they can't control and might sweep them out.

"The one thing they've been good at," Tomczak says, "is killing the left. But by making everything left versus right, a test of the leadership, they've sucked the life out of the party."

The role of the labour leadership in stifling dissent has been crucial. Their ready assistance may be due in part to the circle-the-wagons atmosphere of movements that consider themselves under the gun. Harvey Wyers, a former member of the NDP provincial executive and an activist in both the party and the Steelworkers' union in Sudbury, likens the hardball style to the realities of life on the job. "The party's run on trade union lines," he says. "When it comes to dissent, it's not allowed. You carry the line or you don't get anywhere. When local [union] leaders lose an election, their ass is back in the plant. So you keep power by any means necessary. You smash dissent."

The party's executive, elected at conventions, supposedly represents the membership of the NDP. But in fact the executive is made up of people hand-picked by the party establishment and put on a "slate", which is then offered to convention delegates for election. Rarely does someone not on the slate get elected; even running "against the slate" is frowned upon as a defiance of the delicate equilibrium worked out by the party brass.

Members of the executive thus owe their election and loyalty to the party leadership and feel accountable to it, not to the people they are supposed to represent. The slate process is therefore a powerful method of controlling the incoming executive before and after it is selected. Opposition to dissent is deliberately structured into the party; the free-flow of ideas, internal criticism and pluralism are structured out.

"It's a small-minded party," says a prominent CBC producer once very active with the NDP. "They apply the loyalty test at every step. You don't get to the next step until you pass the loyalty test."

Part of this need to crush opposition, rather than give it a legitimate voice, may be a result of the political left's a-historical sense of urgency. Every issue is critical and must be resolved immediately. Disagreements thus become falsely amplified and frantic, resulting in factions that might not arise if the left gave itself more time. This false urgency may also mean that every dispute must result in a decisive victory.

A martyr syndrome within the NDP also limits dissent. The party centralizes work with a small handful of trusted people and pushes them to the limit to get things done. These few get exhausted and isolated from other points of view. They get so buried with details they lose their critical capacity and any chance they had for a different perspective on what they're doing. Then, after they've spent so much time and energy on a project, some ingrate, usually from the party's left wing, has the temerity to criticize what they've done.

This is treated as a disloyal affront. How dare they attack such hard work? When will they do something to earn the right to criticize?

This martyrdom is the signature of party ownership by a small clique. It sharpens and personalizes criticism that might otherwise be recognized as legitimate and constructive. It facilitates a desire to smash dissenters since their criticism appears to be directed against trusted, hard-working party loyalists.

Those trusted few are like characters in a long-running soap opera. Wyers has been active since 1974 and says "the same clique's still in power. You go away for five months and you haven't missed a thing."

The well-cultivated martyr syndrome is an example of how the personal dynamics of cultism correspond to the party's structural needs, and create their psychological counterpart.

This also leads to another of the NDP's major problems: the lack of a legitimate review mechanism. The party is unable to conduct a genuine evaluation of its performance, its political direction or its priorities. A former party vice-president, now a senior policy advisor, agrees that: "Maybe the party doesn't do as much of that as it should. It tends to quickly move on to what's immediately in front of them."

Like its intolerance of dissent, the party engages in continuing rounds of self-congratulation even in the face of major setbacks. On the night of the 1987 election, when the NDP dropped from 23 to 19 seats and failed utterly to capitalize on the decimation of the Conservatives, Bob Rae stood in front of the television cameras and called the result a "great victory." Even Premier David Peterson, whose Liberals elected the largest majority government in the history of Ontario, was under more control than Rae.

The party comes to believe its own rhetoric, and so even behind closed doors there is no process for saying "We got the bejeezus kicked out of us; what the hell happened?" On the rare occasions when someone in the party establishment is willing to object to bad strategy, condemn stupid tactics or decry incompetence, he or she is dismissed as negative and disloyal.

This dishonesty prevents the party from making changes it needs to make.

The NDP suffers more than the other political parties when it loses energetic people since it relies more heavily on the financial and organizational support from volunteers. But the NDP has gone beyond making its more progressive members feel entirely unwelcome and unwanted. Through the 1980s, by design, it turned its riding associations into membership-gathering and fund-raising machines instead of centres of political activism. The result of this organizational misdirection has been a further erosion of people who are interested in electoral politics as a vehicle of change, since there are few people whose motivation for working in a political party is to sign up new members or raise cash. Many New Democrats remain party members only because there is no other legitimate political party of the left they can move to; the NDP is the only game in town. The party establishment knows this, and takes full advantage of it.

The party brass uses guilt and manipulation to keep people in the NDP. A former member of the party's executive thinks of her years in the NDP as an "abusive relationship. I can't believe I took it. I'm a liberated woman and I like to get fucked on my own terms."

Finally, when the NDP loses its activist left wing, it also suffers from the loss of its innovative ginger group, the spark that often helped keep politics and programs fresh, and the leadership and bureaucracy on its toes. Former Ontario leader Donald C. MacDonald said — perhaps not remembering his leadership years — about the left: "Any progressive party which does not have a vigorous left wing runs the risk of losing its sense of direction and becoming a conservative party that's served its purpose."

A former vice-president laments the death of the left within the NDP, and says since it disappeared, "the party hasn't had a built-in challenge, alternatives to cause people to reassess. There's been no creative renewal."

In the absence of the party's left wing, such a renewal might come from members of the political coalitions that were the hallmark of the 1980s. Yet here, too, the NDP can't work with progressive interest groups and give them a meaningful role inside the party.

3. Out of Step with the Social Movements

During the afternoon of election day, 1990, Bob Rae met with Stephen Lewis, Gerry Caplan, and three other close advisors in the living room of Caplan's downtown Toronto duplex to decide what to do about Toronto's Olympic bid. They knew they were about to win their own gold medal that night. It was the first big decision they would have to make as government.

The Olympic bid was backed by some of Ontario's most powerful corporate heavyweights and was fiercely opposed by a coalition of anti-poverty activists. Though their own campaign had condemned the Liberals' connections to "special interests" — David Peterson was a big Olympic booster — on this one the New Democrats lined up behind the corporations without reservation. Anti-poverty organizer Jan Borovoy says theirs was "the first social movement that the NDP sold out." The first as government, she means, because the selling had been going on for a long time.

The 1970s and 1980s saw the flowering of single-issue politics and the emergence of a number of rainbow coalitions demanding green, black and grey power. Others supported peace, women and employment equity and opposed the Meech Lake Accord, free trade and the Goods and Services Tax.

It's a new "designer politics:" single-issue boutiques that attract activists committed to a particular program of social change. They meet special needs in a narrow niche of the political marketplace, and provide an attractive substitute for department store political parties.

In the 1980s, many progressive single-issue movements blossomed into quasi-permanent coalitions. While the right-wing, neo-conservative agenda of the decade tried to establish barriers between politics and daily life by convincing people their needs were best met and their success was best determined by the marketplace, these coalitions were working to convince people that social and economic problems had political solutions.

Political coalitions are not new to Canada — they led to the first wave of progressive social reforms in the period from 1900 to 1914. The CCF itself was explicitly a coalition, not a party, as its full name, Canadian Commonwealth Federation: Farmer-Labour-Socialist, makes clear.

But coalitions became unpopular in the 1940s, '50s and '60s, partly because so many were seen as commie fronts. It wasn't until opposition to the Viet Nam war coalesced in the late 1960s that coalitions gained a new legitimacy and took off again.

This phenomenon was an adaptation of the community organizing championed by the New Left in the United States. In Canada, the Waffle was perhaps the first to recognize this change in the rules of politics, but even the Waffle wasn't ready for coalition politics except as rhetoric. The Waffle saw the NDP leading extra-parliamentary movements, not working with them.

Political coalitions usually have an extra-parliamentary orientation, and sometimes a "revolutionary inspiration" that still causes unease among the NDP establishment. Lenin argued that revolutionary action depended on a worker-peasant and other alliances; he recognized the need for all oppressed peoples to come together in a way that Marx, who was more focused on a united working class, did not.

In a recent book *Fire in the Americas: Forging a Revolutionary Agenda*, authors Roger Burbach and Orlando Nunez propose that revolutionary action no longer comes from Marx's workers or from Lenin's worker-peasant alliance. Instead, they suggest it comes from another force made up of the middle classes, intellectuals, ethnic groups, social movements and solidarity forces. They argue that the task for leftists is to orient to these movements and for them to build alliances with workers.

But while the emerging political coalitions of the 1980s chanted outside the Ontario legislature, the NDP played its own tune inside. The NDP in the House was rarely a home for the coalitions, though their politics were often brother and sister.

More than the heavy wooden doors of Queen's Park kept the coalitions outside the NDP. John Johnson, a longtime party activist and president of the downtown Toronto riding of St. Andrew-St. Patrick in the 1980s suggests that "Maybe the NDP can't reach out to other groups of protest since it values internal harmony too highly."

The distrust between coalitions and the NDP is mutual. For their part, coalitions often feel they can't trust the NDP because they sense that the NDP is prepared to exploit their issues for short-term political gain without making any long-term commitment to them. It's as if the NDP scavenges the social movements for photo opportunities, supporting them when it suits the party's purpose, but dumping them when party leaders think an issue becomes a political liability. Consequently many of these movements develop no special relationship of trust and common purpose with the NDP.

For years the NDP refused to identify itself with the pro-choice movement, for example. Most of the NDP brass thought that it was politically damaging to do so, and nearly half of the NDP caucus in the 1980s were personally opposed to abortion. Judy Rebick, President of the National Action Committee on the Status of Women, was there from the beginning of the fight over the establishment of free-standing clinics. She says the early choice movement "wasn't working with the NDP because they didn't see the value. This was *the* major social struggle, *the* issue of the women's movement. In the early days, the NDP could have made significant gains with women, but they were too late. When it [would have been] courageous was before [Dr. Henry] Morgentaler was acquitted. Afterward it was different."

Throughout the 1980s there are many similar stories of the NDP's refusal to be a little courageous when it was necessary to build trust or stake a political claim to an issue. Robert Martin wrote in 1982 that "the party has become substantially more election oriented in its political work....[It] has disdained active involvement in local struggles. Not only does this strengthen the perception of the party as aloof and abstract, it denies the party the means of attracting fresh activists with new ideas and new perspectives."

If many social activists mistrust the NDP, the NDP also has a deep mistrust of them. The party is not comfortable with coalition politics unless it can control the agenda. While the NDP might agree with one part of a movement's policy — an end to Cruise missile testing in Canada, for example — the party won't align itself with coalitions whose extra-parliamentary approach to politics and consensus-building style are foreign to it.

Despite its pretensions as a grass-roots party, the NDP is a top-down bureaucracy that does not relate well to organizations whose more egalitarian structures do not mesh with its own. A former leading official with the NDP admits to having difficulties relating to coalitions, saying they have "redefined politics." They don't have the formalities of telephone receptionists, regular business hours or people with the authority to make decisions on behalf of the coalition. "It's not just another group to relate to, but another style," he says.

Some influential party advisors are contemptuous of coalitions precisely because they don't adopt a department store view of social issues. Historian Des Morton, one of the few academics who has worked with the party leadership for many years, dismisses the social movements as simple pressure groups that "don't take responsibility for how it all fits in — an ideal middle-class cop out." Jo Surich, chairperson of the 1981 election planning committee, the election in which the party tried to skirt one of the hottest controversies of the day, gay rights, criticized the party's left for its "general tendency to link itself with every chic social issue which comes along."

But party activist Marg McIntosh laments the fact that people whose first commitment is to a social movement usually can't find a home in the NDP. "The way to build credibility in the NDP is to put emphasis into the party itself," she says. "First you have to show you're a loyal party member and do party-building stuff." She says the NDP is structured entirely for electoral work and against the kind of mass action often advocated by the social movements. There's also no mechanism for the social movements to elect people to the party's councils or committees.

Bob Rae and others in the NDP leadership talk about democracy, but are unprepared to let social movements have any meaningful influence in the development of NDP politics. As David Marquand wrote about the British Labour Party, they see people outside the Legislature "not as an agent, but as a patient." Parliament, not church basements, is where it's at.

Failure to make these links has left the NDP on the outside looking in on some of the most exciting new political ideas in the country. It is the classic but unnecessary and unhealthy division between a political party that thinks change can come only through parliamentary means, and social movements, which think that change comes through the mobilization of people.

But suppose the NDP were to change and offer a meaningful role in its policy-making and structure to people dedicated to the social movements — just as it has to members of the labour movement. How would the labour brass feel about sharing power with a motley collection of people from the social movements they often regard as wackos?

The NDP: Party or Movement?

It's been a fashionable debate on the left for a long time: is the NDP a political party, or is it a movement?

These are symbolic codewords for the initiated. "Movement" is a touchstone for the true believers, who want one; "party" stands for brokerage politics and an effective political machine.

Left-wing NDPers wish that the NDP would be a movement, committed to political education and social activism. It would seize on popular struggles, work directly with people in common purpose, and be the voice inside the legislature for those who are left outside. For example, it would not only help organize tenants, the poor, injured workers, parents and teachers, ethnic minorities, and so on, but would work directly with them to help bring about their goals.

This is where the CCF started. Though it later became as dedicated to electoral politics as the NDP is, the CCF originally had a vision, a socialist commitment to build a new society.

Mildred Fahrni, a founding member of the CCF, was a Quaker, a pacifist and the person who delivered the eulogy, by his request, at the funeral of J.S. Woodsworth. Fahrni said: "Our main aim was not to get control. In those days, we were out to educate people, to win them to a new way of looking at life and the rights of people."

Education was a primary tool of the CCF. In days before radio and television, people travelled miles to hear speeches by CCF politicians. The party printed newspapers in six different provinces, as well as study guides and reading lists. It organized study groups and ran summer schools.

As education and information director for the CCF, Donald MacDonald put in place an extensive program of political education. The party even set up Woodsworth House Publishers in the 1940s to crank out educational materials and party propaganda. It printed *Who Owns Canada?*, a 112-page booklet that listed the top corporations with their interlocking directorships. It sold 50,000 copies.

MacDonald also developed correspondence courses on trade unionism, socialism, agriculture, organizing and education. About 200 members signed up, and sent in their lessons to the national office every other week. MacDonald would correct the papers and send them back.

It also got involved in direct support for people. A famous incident occurred in August, 1935, when Ontario Liberal Premier Mitch Hepburn called single unemployed men "shirkers", and ordered them cut off relief. Within days, they were thrown out of their hostels and onto the streets. According to Melnyk, "The bewildered men milled around aimlessly, waiting for something to happen. Before long, CCF workers began pulling up in their trucks and cars and handing out protest signs, sandwiches and flasks of hot coffee. After wolfing down the sandwiches, most of the men decided to take up the party's offer to feed and house them in CCF headquarters and clubrooms around the city." In two days, Hepburn capitulated.

But by the middle of the 1940s, CCF members could already see a change in this type of direct action. John Smith, a grassroots organizer for the CCF, says once the party merged its CCF clubs into riding associations the election machine became more important than organizing and education. "A close friend of mine in the left wing used to say that the CCF's purpose was to emancipate the workers, one by one. It didn't mean electing CCF members to Parliament, one by one," he says.

The NDP brass has gone all out to build a modern political party, complete with the trappings that entails: sophisticated polling, membership gathering, direct mail fundraising appeals, and a reliance on the media to deliver their message to the electorate.

A movement is grassroots, visionary, educational and organizational. A party is technocratic, professional, pragmatic and opportunistic.

The NDP thinks it is more important to have its elected members sitting on endless legislative committees than organizing in their communities. It puts a higher priority on getting Bob Rae into the legislature than onto the street. New Democrats have lost the fire in their bellies that CCFers had. For a social movement that means malnutrition.

4. Keeping the Labour Brass Polished

The first budget handed down by Ontario's NDP government included a special "gas guzzler" tax on cars with low fuel economy ratings. The tax was implemented without input from the Canadian Auto Workers' Union, which vigorously opposed the tax when it was announced.

Less than two months later, the tax had been "rejigged," according to the CAW newsletter: a nice way of saying the government had had a change of heart. CAW President Bob White said "the industry admitted they could not show how the original tax would cost jobs," and took pride in announcing that this was the first time "that a budget item was changed as a result of our presentations."

Big labour backs the NDP, provides it with money and volunteers, serves as the pipeline of the NDP message to its workforce, and supports the party heavies in internal fights whenever it is called upon to do so. At election time, labour unions provide countless organizers and campaign workers, paid for by the unions. For these reasons, the NDP keeps the labour brass polished.

Although the NDP and the unions claim their legitimacy comes from the rank-and-file, they are top-down in their operation. Their parallel structures enable the two bureaucracies to mesh easily together, make decisions, and carry them out by instinct. Professor Robert Martin says: "The Ontario NDP is not the party of ordinary workers, it is the party of the [union] staff, the...reps. For this reason, the labour movement has not been able to deliver trade union votes for the NDP."

Like identical twins who read each other's minds, heads of unions or the Ontario Federation of Labour have ready access to the leadership of the NDP, and know each other's thoughts. Unlike social movements, which are often painstakingly slow in arriving at a consensus, labour leaders can make snap decisions and count on their organizations to act on them without much need for approval by their membership.

The party brass and labour leaders have an old boy's network relationship. It helps account for the fact that there are so few new faces or new ideas. In a movement that sees itself under attack from so many quarters, they rely on personal bonds and trusted insiders like a Mafia family does; the Mafia, however, are usually better dressed. This creates a huge contingent of yesmen and yeswomen, another factor in their lack of inspiration.

Until negotiations broke down on Rae's "social contract" talks in June, 1993, the labour and NDP bureaucracies were as tight as hand in glove. A more accurate description would show the NDP in big labour's back pocket removing bills from labour's wallet.

Whenever they are called upon, union leaders back the party bosses in any internal party division without regard to the particular issue. This goes to extremes. There have even been times when labour delegates to NDP conventions have been ordered to vote against the very resolutions they had supported at their own meetings. Labour delegates stand up and applaud on command; they are the NDP's trained seals.

Labour support isn't just guaranteed — it comes gift-wrapped. The labour leadership delivers considerable numbers of these loyal delegates to NDP conventions or the party's quarterly provincial council meetings — up to approximately one quarter of those voting.

These delegates, whose expenses and lost work time are normally paid in full by their unions, receive their instructions on how to vote at a "labour caucus" meeting held before any party debate takes place. With few exceptions, labour delegates vote in a block. "Solidarity" is imposed through heavy pressure on the labour members, many of whom are union staff subject to the discipline of their organization. Unions mistake conformity for solidarity, or at least care more about it — a message the party has learned well from them.

In return for delivering the vote at NDP meetings, and as a result of the tightness of their bureaucratic relationship, labour has a tremendous influence on party policy and tactics.

While in opposition the NDP adopted not just labour's position on proposed legislation or specific issues but often allowed labour to dictate the degree of support or opposition. As we will show, this was the case even though there were times when the party had a different point of view, a different tactical approach, or an entirely different set of priorities. There were many times in the 1980s when the caucus had other issues it wanted to pursue but had to take on union demands.

But big labour has always had a working relationship with the governing party, either Conservatives or Liberals. Though they could count on the NDP to deliver their line on labour issues, union leaders knew they had to deal directly with whomever was in power.

Bob Spencer, former NDP chairperson of the Toronto Board of Education, says that unions generally didn't see the NDP as an effective opposition. "The NDP is just a complaints bureau," he says. "Workers don't see the NDP as their improver, let alone as their saviour."

Perhaps an indication of this lack of effectiveness is that labour leaders rarely give up the power they have in their union and the influence they have with government to run for elected office as New Democrats or to take full-time party jobs. Charlotte Yates, author of a doctoral thesis on the United Auto Workers' Union in Canada, says that unionists "don't see the NDP as having any power, so they're happy to leave the leadership to someone else. The unions are realistic in not going for power in the NDP — they have more influence for direct action and control through their union."

This was not always the case. When the Ontario CCF won 34 seats in the 1943 Ontario election — having had none before — nineteen of its caucus were trade unionists. They included the heads of the Steelworkers' and Mine, Mill and Smelter unions.

When it comes to delivering the NDP message to workers, labour acts as a filter for the party. The labour movement couldn't tolerate the Waffle's direct involvement in labour struggles, and by forcing its expulsion won the understanding that the party would consult with unions before it took positions on labour issues. Even during elections, the NDP speaks through the labour brass when addressing workers: appeals to rank-and-file members to support NDPers come in letters from the heads of various unions — not from Bob Rae.

"The party is trapped," says Terry Moore, a former NDP researcher now on staff with the Ontario Public Service Employees' Union. "Unions are its only access to workers. It has no strategy, no tactics, no interest in the day to day struggles with workers. They're two solitudes and they can't step on each other."

Part of this division comes from an understanding that the party and labour revolve in different spheres. Labour has the day-to-day world of the economic marketplace to cope with; the NDP lives and dies in the market-place of politics.

Labour has to negotiate contracts, wage strikes, train activists, fight grievances and arbitrations, and organize new workplaces. Unions bargain changes for workers that directly and immediately affect those workers' lives. Their issues are bread and butter. The decisions they make have an immediacy: do we ratify this agreement?, do we go on strike?, will we win this certification?

Unions conduct the economic struggle; the party does the politics. Often there is a relationship, of course, but there is also an understanding between the two that they have different roles to play. This distinction doesn't exist in the real world, and that poses problems for both labour and the NDP. Labour "contracts out" its politics to the NDP, while the NDP doesn't develop a sensible economic platform.

But despite its nitty-gritty economic experience, the labour movement gets locked into its own orthodoxy and rarely develops imaginative solutions to changing times. At the same time, since the NDP borrows its economic policies from organized labour, when the two have a rare falling out, as they did during the social contract talks, labour leaders have nothing new to offer.

The inability of the NDP to develop a series of economic proposals that make sense to workers, what we call lunchbucket economics, is therefore partly a result of its relationship to the labour movement itself. It has always been a serious problem for the credibility of the NDP.

Labour affiliation and the CCF/NDP

Until the 16,000-member Oshawa local of the Canadian Autoworkers' Union voted to sever its ties with the NDP in the spring of 1993, there was little discussion about the merits of affiliation between organized labour and the NDP. It was taken for granted that affiliation was in their mutual interest. That had not always been the case.

The "federation" referred to in the name Cooperative Commonwealth Federation was farmer-labour-socialist. "Labour" meant small independent labour parties, not unions. In fact, when the CCF constitution was drawn up in Regina in 1933, union affiliation wasn't even mentioned.

For many years the Trades and Labour Congress (TLC), Canada's largest union federation in the 1920s and 1930s, rejected direct political involvement. Throughout the 1930s, after the founding of the CCF, the TLC continued to affirm its opposition to union/CCF ties.

The party's federal secretary, David Lewis, thought the CCF could never become a mass movement until unions affiliated in a big way. In 1937, the national CCF convention called on the party to push affiliation with trade unions. Nothing happened on this front until the United Mine Workers District 26 in Nova Scotia decided to sign up in August, 1938. For the first time, rules had to be made to deal with the issue.

Lewis, who learned first-hand about British labour politics while a Rhodes scholar at Oxford, turned to the constitution of the British Labour Party for guidance. The CCF's new rules required the payment of dues to the party on the basis of numbers of members and adherence to CCF policies. Labour delegates to CCF bodies could not belong to any other political party. These rules were approved at the CCF convention in 1940.

No other affiliations occurred until 1942. By that time, the CCF was growing in popularity and the first Ontario CCF MP had been elected, in the riding of York South, later held by David Lewis federally and Donald MacDonald and Bob Rae provincially. Labour's federations were changing, including the founding of the industrial Canadian Congress of Labour (CCL) in 1940. Interest in union affiliation took off.

Right away the CCF feared trade union domination of the party, and, departing from the British Labour Party system, decided not to allow bloc voting. Ballots were supposed to be cast by local unions voting separately, not by one labour leader who carried proxies from the entire membership. Furthermore, representation would be adjusted to ensure that affiliated union members could not outnumber individual members.

In the Ontario provincial election of August, 1943, the CCF leaped from none to an astonishing 34 seats and formed the Official Opposition. The ruling Conservatives elected just 38 members. Of the CCF's 34 members, nineteen were trade unionists, including Charlie Millard, head of the Steelworkers' union, and Robert Carlin, the Mine, Mill and Smelter workers' pioneer organizer.

Just weeks later, the CCL convention overwhelmingly endorsed the CCF and recommended affiliation of its locals to the party.

At that time many union leaders in Canada were Communists. David Lewis figured the CCF would have to smash the CP influence over unions before affiliation could proceed in great numbers. Communists opposed formal ties with the CCF because they felt the party was only interested in electoral politics, and because the CCF wouldn't grant real power to labour organizations inside the party.

Lewis commie-bashed with a passion that lasted long after they posed any problem for the CCF or NDP. He used whatever allies he could muster, including those south of the border. In *The Unfinished Journey*, his biography of the Lewis family, Cameron Smith recounts that in the famous struggle between the Steelworkers and Mine Mill in Sudbury, Lewis collaborated with the U.S. Labour Secretary to get Mine Mill declared a CP union. Later, he worked with American UAW leader Walter Reuther to get the union in Canada on side in an effort to root Communists out of the United Electrical Workers union. Lewis also used Reuther to get the UAW to endorse the CCF, doing an end run around Canadian UAW director George Burt, who for years tolerated Communists.

In 1944, affiliation with the CCF federally had risen to 100 locals with about 50,000 members, but then stalled. By 1952 it had fallen off to 44 locals with just over 16,000 members. Fewer than 6,000 were in Ontario. Affiliated locals and the party organization had little contact with each other. As the party's electoral fortunes hit the skids, neither labour nor the CCF pushed affiliation until they decided to form the NDP.

To the extent, and for the brief time, that it existed in significant numbers, union affiliation in the CCF was bureaucratic. It did little to bring politics to the rank-and-file members of the locals who joined, and it gave labour very little voice in the party.

In 1956 the newly-formed Canadian Labour Congress called for the creation of a new party. (The CLC was a merger of the industrial-union-based Canadian Congress of Labour and the trade-based Trades and Labour Congress.) Although many CCFers blamed their lack of success on the fact that labour support had been only lukewarm, the CCF brass encouraged the move and was looking for a way to make stronger ties with labour. They also hoped to "liberalize" the CCF by attracting middle-class Liberal supporters, since many party bosses mistakenly thought Liberals were a dying breed. The 1958 Diefenbaker sweep gave them hope that a two-party, Conservative/CCF split would emerge, just as in Britain, the birthplace of socialism.

Other factors supported the push for a new party. Unions had abandoned their militant offensive of the 1940s in favour of slow and steady piecemeal growth through bargaining; this cooled the political scene. The post-war boom turned into a cold-war downturn; the CCF retreated from class politics; and Lewis had a long-standing distrust of farmers, whom he thought were conservative and not too bright.

Cameron Smith also cites a few letters by Lewis that show the Oxford scholar's unflattering attitude to working-class people. On Cape Breton miners in 1938, and their affiliation to the CCF, Lewis wrote: "It will all depend on whether...we can find a dozen men who can be relied on to remain always sober and can be trained into an intelligent consciousness of what we're after." He wrote to his wife in 1939 from Windsor: "Nothing is more tiring than talking about big things to little people."

The CLC and CCF each appointed 10 members to sit on a committee to form the new party. Though they later added 10 more representatives from "New Party Clubs", most of whom were the type of middle-class professionals they wanted to attract, it was clear that labour had more clout than ever in the party.

In 1961, the New Democratic Party was formed and Saskatchewan Premier Tommy Douglas stepped down to become its first national leader. Labour's ties were formalized in representation, financial arrangements and access to NDP leaders. Incidentally, neither the words "socialist" or "democratic socialism" appeared in the NDP constitution or program adopted at the founding convention.

At the outset some people supported a move to give affiliated union members the same rights as individual NDP party members. This was fought by the old CCFers, including Donald C. MacDonald, head of the Ontario party. They argued that it would take the steam out of signing up individuals and would destroy the image of a broadly-based party. Within a few years, both union and NDP brass decided to limit votes at party meetings to regular party members. Nonetheless, affiliation stalled individual membership drives, since workers figured they already "belonged" to the party through their union, and they saw their money go in the form of check-off from their wages.

These days, the merits of union affiliation in the NDP are rarely discussed. Both sides seem satisfied with the arrangement, and from the reasons outlined in the text, it is clear why labour and party bosses are happy.

In 1992, the Ontario NDP had about 200,000 affiliated members, which brought about $150,000 to the party.

But it is still worth asking if union affiliation is good for the party, the labour movement or working people.

Long-time socialist and leading Steelworker staffer Murray Cotterill opposed affiliation to the CCF on the grounds that it would de-politicize unions. Cotterill was national director of the Political Action Committee of the Canadian Congress of Labour in the early 1950s, and as he saw it, unions should form their own PACs and agitate, educate and organize for their own agenda. During elections, the PACs would question each party and inform the membership which party was closest to their interests as workers. In that way, the unions remained free to push their own issues for their own reasons. It allowed members to make up their own minds on which party served them best. Cotterill resigned from the director's post in January, 1952, after losing a battle with David Lewis on the issue.

Neil Reimer, long-time head of the Energy and Chemical Workers' union, now merged with pulp and communications workers, and former chairperson of the CLC's Political Action Committee, is another unionist who opposes bureaucratic affiliation. Reimer agrees that direct affiliation is the result of British influence and the British Labour Party model, but points out that the class base of politics is very much more accepted in Britain than it is in Canada. When the new party was being formed, Reimer argued against direct affiliation because it would be an alternative for going out and getting workers to join the party in their community, and because it would cement a bureaucracy-to-bureaucracy relationship between the party and organized labour.

Affiliation has rarely been used as a tool of class education or mobilization. It guarantees union boss control with little input from rank-and-file members. Despite their fears of British-style bloc voting, the NDP wound up with it anyway, without the direct input from ordinary workers whose check-off deductions sustain the party. The NDP also suffers from the image of being in labour's pocket, but doesn't have the advantage that signing up individual workers would bring. The party doesn't benefit from the good points of unions: collective bargaining

gains, representation on occupational health and safety concerns, standing up for workers' rights in grievances and arbitrations, and others, since
workers see these as quite distinct from the union's relationship to the
party. And since affiliation has been more closely linked to private sector
unions, many people in the growing class of white-collar, public sector
workers were left out of the party. The Canadian Union of Public
Employees and some sections of the Public Service Alliance of Canada
are exceptions.

For unions, affiliation has usually meant a "contracting out" of politics
to the NDP; thus labour becomes a passive partner in political change.
Unions let the NDP play politics for them rather than educating their
own membership in political activism or on particular issues. It has
meant not an increase, but a drop in the politics of the labour movement,
since unions are no longer the vehicle of class politics.

Though local union politics played a big role in the disaffiliation of the
CAW Oshawa local from the NDP in May, 1993, it is important to point
out that the impetus for the drive did not come from workers who
thought the NDP had betrayed them. Instead, it came from some who
were angered by progressive commitments the government made. Once
the ball was rolling, even those workers who were predisposed to support
the NDP felt little enthusiasm for the government, and the disaffiliation
succeeded by a two-to-one margin. Though for the wrong reasons, the
Oshawa move forced other union locals to think about their ties with
the party.

5. Figuring Economic Policies that Add Up

In the first weeks after he became premier, one of Bob Rae's favourite lines
was that he finally got the keys to the car, only to discover that it was an Edsel.

Rae's government did have the misfortune to come to office just as the
deepest recession to hit Canada since the Depression of the 1930s took hold.
Faced with bad economic times, the NDP floundered, dithered, acted like
left wingers in running up a big deficit to try to stimulate the economy and
like right-wingers in selling off government assets. If it looked confused,
that's because it is.

A lot of people think the NDP is out to lunch on economics. That's
because it never developed lunchbucket economics.

Early CCF leaders believed in what's called the "social gospel:" a set of
mainly Protestant religious ideals founded in the early twentieth century that

try to apply the social teachings of Jesus to everyday life. The party's first leader, J.S. Woodsworth, was a Methodist minister. Saskatchewan premier and federal leader Tommy Douglas was a Baptist minister, as was Stanley Knowles, who was elected to replace Woodsworth in Winnipeg North Centre. This is not what is normally meant by "ministerial accountability," but it sure helps account for the party's social righteousness. It is said that the Anglican Church was the Tory party at prayer, and the United Church was the CCF at prayer. At least the NDP comes by its holier-than-thou attitude honestly.

Their fundamental critique of society was based on ethics, rather than a hardnosed economic analysis. In her CCF history, Olenka Melnyk writes that: "To the Christian activist, socialism was a practical application of the social gospel, and the party [was] a kind of religious crusade — or in the words of a 1930s campaign song, the CCF represented 'Christ's Call Forward.'"

This ethical foundation has remained a powerful influence inside the NDP. To this day it forms a key part of the party's analysis of how society works. It's one of the reasons you hear Bob Rae talk a great deal about "fairness," and not "exploitation."

Another large group of early CCFers had a rather traditional Marxist view of society. They were proud of their one-plank socialist platform that brooked no reform. The ethical social gospel critique blended with their understanding that economic relationships between people were based on class.

A third group were essentially British Fabians, the elitist academic tradition behind the League for Social Reconstruction, which published *Social Planning for Canada* in 1935. They were long on pre-Keynesian economic planning and short on practical, everyday economic solutions.

With these three overlapping strains, the CCF developed a collective, class-oriented view of society with an ethical foundation. The CCF thus differed from the Calvinist tradition that stressed individual work and merit that was dominant in the United States.

When the CCF approved the Regina Manifesto in 1933, it could say without flinching that the party hoped to establish a "Co-operative Commonwealth in which the principle regulating production, distribution and exchange will be the supplying of human needs and not the making of profits. We aim to replace the present capitalist system, with its inherent injustice and inhumanity, by a social order from which the domination and exploitation of one class by another will be eliminated, in which economic planning will supersede unregulated private enterprise and competition, and in which genuine democratic self-government, based upon economic equality will be possible."

Over time the economic policies of the CCF and NDP changed considerably. When the party met in Manitoba in 1956, it approved the Winnipeg Declaration. Melnyk writes that by then "the CCF no longer aimed to overthrow capitalism but simply to make it work better by assuring everyone a greater share of material goods and opportunities. The radicals had become reformers. In their attempts to woo middle-class voters, CCF politicians pitched promises of new homes and appliances instead of a New Jerusalem. War and post-war CCF election pamphlets offered tantalizing visions of 'Good Food, Good Clothes, and Comfortable Homes,' not to mention brand-new refrigerators, vacuum cleaners and washing machines."

By the time the NDP was founded in 1961 there was not a single reference to democratic socialism in the party's constitution or platform. In 1983, when the party returned to Regina to celebrate its 50th anniversary, the Statement of Principles approved by delegates never mentioned socialized medicare, let alone socialism. The transformation was complete.

One reason the Ontario NDP didn't present an alternative economic plan is that it never expected to form the government, and was able, as an opposition party, to get away with simply criticizing the government. Except in 1978, when a manufacturing task force examined that sector, the NDP never thought through a specific program to build the economy or revitalize any one industry.

The NDP never attracted entrepreneurs or newly-called "ecopreneurs" who could have provided the party with concrete ideas about how to transform Ontario Hydro, how to help the agricultural sector grow, or diversify the north.

Over the years, as the CCF/NDP abandoned its anti-capitalist beliefs, it failed to do the kind of thinking and hard work to replace that earlier vision.

By trying to appeal to more classes, the party has obviously become less class oriented. Its economic policies have become more mainstream and less left-wing. But increased credibility on economics has escaped the party.

In the 1980s neo-conservative economics swept North America. Capitalist politics was successful in de-politicizing daily life to such an extent that government became not the answer but the problem. Capital talks of "managing" the economy, not "governing" it, and the rap that NDPers couldn't even run the corner store was set in peoples' minds. Hard work and thrift, not government planning, were the keys to individual success. People not only lost hope in the ability of government to ensure their futures but came to believe that government was a sinister force that got in their way.

Faith in the anarchy of the marketplace was at the top of the right-wing agenda. This is one of the main reasons neo-conservatives like to decentralize government and privatize public services — to keep people's minds from a clear focus on the role of government and the purpose of politics itself.

In his critique of NDP economics, *Rethinking the Economy,* James Laxer writes that: "The new conservatism is anchored in the 'new selfishness,' the belief that human beings are fundamentally competitive and self-aggrandizing, and the sooner you equip yourself to face up to your own meanness, the better off you will be. The new conservatism is two parts pop psychology and one part astrology. With it we are abandoning traditional values and heading straight for the ouija board."

Laxer criticized the party in the early 1980s for sticking to Keynesian economics long after the conditions that made it work were no longer operating. He says the NDP's central tenet is "increasing effective demand through the injection of stimulus into the economy." They have ignored the need to develop an industrial strategy that makes sense in Canada's foreign-owned economy, and stuck with the economic ideas of the 1950s.

This may be one reason why New Democrats seemed powerless to confront the neo-conservative juggernaut, and shied away from policies that directly interfered with capital's control of the economy. More and more Bob Rae was talking about the party's belief in a mixed economy, and returning to traditional ethical concerns of fairness.

The party's credibility on economic issues has remained low even among people the NDP most hopes to reach: working-class, unionized, the poor and the powerless.

6. Romancing the Working Class

For years the NDP fought against "Sunday working." Demanding a "common pause day" when families could be together, Rae vowed to crack down on Sunday shopping. After almost two years in office, Rae abandoned both party policy and organized labour, and sold off Sunday shopping.

The party had never complained about all the workers in the tourist, manufacturing and broader public sectors who had long worked on Sundays, nor did it seem to notice that with changing work schedules, the best opportunity many people have to shop is on Sunday. Ironically, working people were among those most in favour of having the option to shop. A Goldfarb poll found that 83 per cent of single parents were in favour, as were 73 per cent of union households, and 69 per cent of women who work fulltime.

In opposing "Sunday working," the NDP clung to its romantic 1930s notion of workers: impoverished, oppressed victims of a hardhearted, ruthless management.

A lot of working people fall into that category, but they're not usually in the unions the NDP works with. Most members of the heavyweight unions that carry the freight for the NDP are well-paid and relatively well-heeled. Their incomes make them less reminiscent of a downtrodden working class than a middle class, with their own homes, cottages, pools, Winnebagos or boats. Their financial concerns are middle class: paying the mortgage, the kid's tuition or the orthodontist's bill, and buying a snowmobile or second car. They feel overtaxed, don't like people on welfare, and worry about holding onto their jobs.

The NDP sends a working-class message to these middle-class families and almost no message at all to the working poor or the unemployed.

As M.J. Brodie and Jane Jenson show in *Crisis, Challenge and Change: Party and Class in Canada*, the CCF was slow to realize that workers were better off after World War II. They compare the CCF to the British Labour Party, both of which moderated their stances after the war to appeal to the middle class. The difference is that by then the BLP had sunk its roots deep into the working class, whereas in Canada the CCF and NDP oriented to the bland middle before they had firmed up support with workers.

Brodie and Jenson say that the NDP "demobilized" its working class constituency by appealing to all disaffected voters. This not only stalled the party's support among working people, but also opened the door for other parties to steal their planks.

After World War II, "Fordism" prevailed in the Ontario economy: mass production based on expensive technology requiring relatively low skills. Because the system depended on people having enough money to buy the goods they made, workers were paid relatively high wages. In order to turn nearly everyone into a consumer, social policy changed from assistance only to the very poor to universal social programs for everyone, supplemented by social assistance for the impoverished. The poorhouse was gone, and the poor consumer was born.

The NDP was set up at the start of the 1960s to woo the growing middle class. New Democrats either abandoned elements of a socialist platform or hid a leftist agenda. They became even less militant than the CCF and gave in to middle-class images.

But the workforce is changing. In the late 1940s, over 60 per cent of working people produced goods. Today, over 70 per cent of jobs are in the service sector. About 90 per cent of job growth since the late 1960s has been service sector jobs, and employment in manufacturing has declined significantly. Since 1975, 40 per cent of new jobs have been part-time. These jobs are generally less well-paid than those in manufacturing.

The new jobs also create a different psychology. People in white-collar jobs don't have traditional blue-collar solidarity. They also don't have a sense that the CCF and NDP fought for them during the Depression and the war, as many industrial workers do. The working class has been re-made in terms of jobs and immigration. These circumstances are very unfavourable for the creation of a class-conscious working class.

Many people have pointed to what is called the "hour-glass economy": growing numbers in the upper and lower classes and fewer in the middle. The results are all around us — BMWs and foodbanks, million dollar homes and thousands of homeless people. It's just the opposite of what you want in society: little at the edges and most people in the middle.

The regular hourly wage for an assembler with one of the Big Three auto makers is over $20 an hour. These are not poor workers. Harvey Wyers, a Sudbury steelworker, has over 20 years' seniority at Inco, and he's in the bottom third of the seniority list. Workers above him on the list make between $50,000 and $80,000 a year as bonus miners, have paid off their homes and put their children through school. They are not the downtrodden, however rough and dangerous their mining jobs are.

Miners are a good example of how the NDP holds out this romantic notion of workers. While rightly ranting about the terrible safety records in mines, the NDP won't touch the system of bonus mining, which institutionalizes greed and pays miners to cut corners. They're risking their own lives, and those of other miners, to make a better buck. But both the union and the NDP know that the workers themselves want it, so they lay off.

The worker-victims the NDP idolizes are mostly well-off middle-class success stories who don't much like to hear — and generally don't believe — the NDP's message of their misfortune.

For the truly exploited worker and the unemployed, the NDP message doesn't get through. The NDP talks to the "working class" through unions, and a great many of these workers don't have a union to begin with. Single mothers, immigrant women in the garment industry, members of ethnic minorities who are victims of racism, low-wage workers in the service sector and many others — including those in the public sector — only hear from the NDP what they get from the media, and that message is seldom delivered and rarely informative.

Neil Reimer, former president of the Energy and Chemical Workers Union, says that "the labour movement is no longer the link with the majority of the working poor, because they have no members there." He says that "unionists are noticeably middle class, the better paid in the community. That spells a difficulty for the union. They're still workers, but how will they identify with workers making $5 an hour?"

The middle-income workers the NDP does get through to are people who are generally not interested in fundamentally changing the system. Usually they are not greedy people demanding a bigger share of the pie, but they want their just desserts. They are ordinary workers, trying to do their best for their families.

A great many Canadians do identify as workers, but they hope that their children will break out of their "class" and move up the social ladder. This is particularly true of many immigrant groups who are looking for a better life for their families in Canada.

Workers dream about getting out of the working class. They have been taught in school that working people are nothing. Television and movies almost never have positive images of workers. Usually the media reinforce the notion of dumb, lazy workers who contribute little to society. Workers don't need to be told that rich is better.

The toiling masses have bought into the idea of class mobility. This is unfortunate, not only because it is largely illusory, but also because it lowers their spontaneous sense of worker solidarity. They lose a sense of working class culture, and downplay the value of the legitimate culture that working people develop.

The road out of the working class is paved with good skills training, but while in opposition the party never developed coherent training proposals that would provide workers with useful, portable skills. In recent years, Liberals and Tories have spoken about creating a "training culture", but their schemes are designed mainly to benefit profit-making corporations through the use of "monkey-see, monkey-do" high-tech innovations that often reduce workers' skills. New Democrats haven't yet made a guarantee of job training and re-training one of their priorities.

Workers also care about security — not just more income, even though higher wages are a hedge against the uncertainty of the boss pulling the plug and a means to a more gratifying lifestyle. That's why medicare is the most popular government program ever devised — it protects low and middle-income people against financial ruin from accident or illness.

The other big security blanket is pensions, but the NDP has thrown a patchwork quilt over workers' fears about living their final years in poverty. New Democrats have never developed any serious proposals for funding and managing public pensions for an aging population.

As government, the NDP will have many more opportunities to talk directly to workers without the filter of their unions. It will reach many people who never heard its message clearly before, or who heard a distorted and manipulated version through the media or from the other political parties. But the opportunity will be lost if the NDP continues to hold to its romantic idea of the worker/victim.

Today's workplace is much different from the factory of the 1940s. Fordism is dead. Current technology allows niche marketing, a global economy doesn't require local mass markets where people earn enough to be consumers, computerized technology doesn't need large markets in order to be profitable, and a service economy doesn't produce goods that need to be purchased. Production in the 1990s is high tech, highly computerized, and assures high unemployment. The workplace mirrors society: there are many highly-skilled, highly-paid workers, and many low-skilled, poorly-paid workers. The free flow of goods and services through free trade is capitalism's latest triumph in defining the supremacy of the marketplace.

Since a world market no longer demands that local people have enough purchasing power to absorb local production, capital doesn't care that many people are thrown on the scrap heap. The new welfare state reflects this with less unemployment insurance coverage and levels of social assistance that leave people in misery. And when the NDP talks about paying more in welfare, it loses the support of workers.

The NDP doesn't want to admit that most of the workers it talks to no longer suffer the same hardships they once did. This problem isn't helped by the fact that salaries of union leaders themselves put them near the top of the heap, and the closest they get to poverty is when they make a speech about it at NDP functions. Travelling by chartered plane instead of in boxcars, and meeting with the prime minister instead of the unemployed gives the labour brass a different perspective on life. They would rather be for the working class than in it. The old fat cat cartoon capitalist had a pot belly and a cigar. Now those are the trademarks of the union leader.

Its mistaken idea of working people is one of the major problems that prevents the NDP from having a new vision of society. Tens of thousands of people without a voice are waiting for the NDP to speak up for them.

Now that the NDP has formed the government, it has a vested interest in class harmony and a particular disincentive in stirring up antagonism between different elements of society. This is bound to lead the NDP away from throwing light on the harsh divisions in Ontario.

7. Sorry, we don't speak your language

When it comes to immigrants, the NDP has missed the boat.

As the party prepared to take office in the fall of 1990, one of its objectives was to hire women and visible minorities for senior positions in the ministerial offices. Because it considered only trusted party insiders for those jobs, it had a very hard time finding minority candidates.

Fran Endicott, whom Rae appointed as Human Rights Commissioner in 1992 just months before she died tragically of cancer, said: "In their first round of recruitment for EAs and policy advisors they looked at the people who are closest to them. And in spite of what their policy says, the people who are closest to them are people who look like them. So they're going to be whiter people. They recruited without paying much attention to the kind of face they wanted to put on the party. The difficulty for me is that the party has to recognize how far apart the top people are from who's in the rank and file."

In its earlier days, the CCF actively reached out to minorities, admittedly mostly white. Though in his early career the sainted J.S. Woodsworth was vehemently anti-Italian and considered many non-Anglo-Saxon ethnic people heathens, the early CCF in general had a laudable record on ethnic tolerance.

In Manitoba, shortly after the approval of the Regina Manifesto in 1933, the CCF translated it into French, German, Hungarian and Ukrainian. The party hired a Ukrainian organizer, and published a Ukrainian-language newspaper for a time.

In 1946, the Saskatchewan CCF introduced a Bill of Rights that prevented discrimination against race, colour or creed, but not gender. It was almost a decade before any other Canadian government would do better. During World War II, Premier Tommy Douglas welcomed Japanese-Canadians who had been thrown out of their west-coast homes to Saskatchewan, and hired a Japanese-Canadian into a senior public service post.

The first native elected to a Canadian legislature was CCFer Frank Calder, a hereditary chief of the Nishgas, elected to the B.C. legislature in 1949.

In the early 1970s, New Democrats made a concerted effort to organize the Italian community in west-end Toronto. By combining culture and politics, as in Europe, the NDP successfully won over important elements of the community. One of the rewards of that effort was the election in 1975 of seven New Democrats, four of them Italian, in that part of the city. It took the Liberal sweep in 1987 to knock off the last of the NDP's west-end Italian members.

Despite the obvious success of organizing with the Italian sezione, the NDP never made it work with other ethnic groups, and even lost the initiative with Italians. Though it has tried to make inroads into the minority communities through its "Ethnic Advisory Committees," the NDP has been unable to make a significant breakthrough with any single group.

Kahn Rahi, executive director of the Access Action Council in Toronto, says: "The NDP is symbolically progressive where they have nothing tangible to deliver. They look for symbolism, but fundamentally there's nothing to back it up."

Immigrant communities are largely powerless. Many are afraid to rock the boat. Some are ghettoized. Louis Lenkinski, who came from the Polish socialist movement and was an active trade unionist and NDPer throughout his adult life, thinks that the NDP "doesn't understand that immigrants out there are competing against tremendous odds, and want a comfortable niche at home."

Rahi says, too, that: "Immigrants want power. They don't just want the NDP to have power." Unlike the Liberals, and to some extent even the Tories, the NDP doesn't appear to understand that immigrants get involved in politics to boost their own power, not the party's. They want connections in order to overcome their isolation, and to play a meaningful role in society. "Italians don't want to join a party of down and outs; they see themselves as up and coming," says Frank Lento, a former organizer in the Italian community.

Many immigrants have a tradition of political activism at home that they want to bring to Canada. One of the largest immigrant populations to Ontario in recent years is from the Caribbean, where there is a history of labour militancy. The NDP offers them no outlet for that energy.

Nor has the NDP done anything to facilitate professionals from other countries being recognized in Ontario. This would be of great interest to many ethnic groups, particularly east Indians.

The NDP is a dour white party that has taken the social out of socialism. The trillium is in its logo, but the wallflower is in its lapel. Lento says young men in Italy used the socialist clubs to find young women and break free from a society with tight parental control. Other immigrant groups also have a tradition of social gatherings with political content. New Democrats get together to stuff envelopes and get home by 9:30. There's an old joke among party youth that Young Tories go to conventions to get drunk, Young Liberals go to conventions to get laid, and Young New Democrats go to conventions to get pamphlets.

Kahn Rahi says the NDP is "obsessed not to alienate the mainstream, so they're very timid about crossing the colour line. The bottom line is that they don't want to say there are two separate communities — white and immigrant, and that the political economy of the ghetto has an important impact on them. The NDP won't go too close to the ghetto."

Some of the reasons that immigrant communities are not attracted to the NDP may be beyond the party's control in the short term, but that should speak to a different method of organizing and making sure there is a role for people to play. It means speaking their language literally and figuratively, at home, at work, and in the community.

As government, the NDP has the power that has eluded them so far in Ontario. The party now has an opportunity to make links with multicultural communities. But to forge those links it will have to overcome its history of reluctance and give minority-group members a meaningful role in the party, and in government.

8. Liberals: Easy to Hate, Hard to Understand

The NDP has never figured out the Liberal party. With a recipe of wishful thinking, political naivete and a large dose of political prejudice, New Democrats have cooked up a half-baked idea of what the Liberal party is all about.

Liberals are the India Rubber Men of Canadian politics, double-jointed contortionists able to assume any position and almost look comfortable doing it. Sometimes they seem a bit embarrassed getting into and out of their various positions, but they do it so often, and with such ease, you never really notice. Cynics would say they can do it because they have no backbone.

As reformers themselves, the NDP cannot admit that the Liberal Party can be reformers too, because that would force them to confront what their own politics should be. This dilemma plagues the NDP. A long-time member of the party executive says New Democrats "hate Liberals. NDPers may hate Liberals more than they hate Tories. They don't compete with Conservatives. They want a two-party system where the Liberals are dead."

The NDP and the CCF before it put the Liberals on the endangered species list, only to discover the hard way that they keep right on breeding. A Liberal will screw a New Democrat or a Tory whenever it suits the purpose.

After the 1945 federal election, considering the surprising strength of the CCF, Liberal Prime Minister Mackenzie King stole many of its platforms. "CCF leaders could do little but gnash their teeth at King's 'programmatic larceny' as his Liberal government cranked out progressive legislation formulated by their own party," Melnyk writes.

Melnyk quotes CCF activist John Smith, who said the party "used to boast that its policies had been taken over by the Liberals, but that wasn't something to be boasting about. I think that it just showed that they [the New Democrats] were Liberals really."

Following John Diefenbaker's Conservative party landslide in 1958, CCF leaders and the union brass thought the Liberals were well on their way to the political scrapheap. They presumed the CCF, or the new party to follow it, would capture the political centre, leaving the Conservatives to pick up the remnants of what few Liberals remained on the right.

In 1961, Ontario NDP leader Donald C. MacDonald issued a statement saying there was a political realignment taking place in the Liberal party. He said many Liberals were frustrated by the business domination of their party and would come to — and be welcome in — the NDP.

But even the withering away of the state in the Soviet Union took place with greater speed than the withering away of the Liberal party.

Through much of its history the NDP has tried to defy the laws of both physics and politics by attempting to occupy space already taken up by the

Liberals. The NDP's attacks on Liberals are often dressed up in a cloak of Marxist rhetoric about the two old parties of capitalism, but its failure to see the difference between Liberals and Tories, or to admit that Liberals are opportunists who will do whatever they think they have to do, is not based on a revolutionary view of society. In fact, New Democrats themselves are political opportunists eager to build a movement of the radical middle. Their inability to understand Liberals amounts to a psychological denial of the reality that there is no room for two middlemen on the same deal.

As a result of this lack of perspective, the NDP underestimated the Liberals in the 1981-85 period, leading up to the Liberal success in the 1985 election. The NDP also underestimated what they would have to do during the 1985-87 Accord period in order to counteract the credit that the Liberals would get.

The Peterson Liberals in 1985, like the Pearson and Trudeau Liberals before them, were ready to make a major shift to the left, however insincere, in order to head off the NDP. Whether it was pensions, Medicare or Petro-Canada federally, or banning extra billing and bringing in first contract legislation and a pay equity bill provincially, the Liberals have shown a readiness to expropriate NDP positions and to act on them as government.

In British Columbia, Saskatchewan and Manitoba, where the NDP has formed other provincial governments, the opposing parties have been more right-wing and incompetent than Ontario Liberals and Tories. This meant the Ontario NDP couldn't just wait for the other parties to collapse in a panic of reactionary government, stupidity or corruption. It was forced to be more distinctive, more "left," in trying to hold on to some territory of its own. In the other provinces the NDP was sucked into the political vacuum in the centre, and stayed there comfortably.

The fact that Ontario Liberals and Tories were competent, professional and moderate also meant that they attracted relatively progressive careerists, who saw that the NDP never had the prospect of governing. These people helped keep the other Ontario parties looking fresh and imaginative, and in the political centre. Now that the New Democrats have won in Ontario, it is possible that some of these middle-of-the-road progressives will find a home in the NDP. If they do, it could mean the party will drift farther to the right. At the same time, it won't help solve the NDP's problem with the Liberals.

9. The Media is the Messenger

"We're all in the habit of getting our information from our political enemies," says the copy soliciting subscriptions for *The Ontario Democrat*, the party's newspaper. "*The Scar, The Stun, The Mop and Pail, Gobble News, Maclaims* — They're good for the comics and horoscopes, but as for straight goods on politics in the country, forget it. If you really want to know what's happening in Ontario, you simply must read the New *Ontario Democrat.*"

It's a measure of how much the party distrusts the media, how it feels beleaguered and hounded by them. The party has an odd love-hate relationship with the media, relying on them to deliver its message, but distrusting them every step of the way. It's especially peculiar, given that the party consciously chose its leader because of his media image.

As the federal party's finance critic Bob Rae became a media darling. That fact is without a doubt the single most important reason he won the Ontario NDP leadership in 1982. His 15-second quips and clever one-liners brought him onto people's television screens, and for a party desperately looking to overcome Michael Cassidy's wooden TV image, Bob Rae seemed too good to be true.

He was the magic solution to the NDP's woes. The party's deep thinkers figured that if Rae became provincial leader, he and the party would become household words, and the party's dreadful image problems would be solved. From the outset it was clear that the party brass thought the best way they could deliver their message was through the mainstream media. It has been the party's view that its problem is that the media doesn't get its message out, not that the people reject the message they get.

Years later, when many Rae backers were disappointed that the party had stalled under his leadership, a lot of them privately admitted that MPP Richard Johnston, Rae's main challenger, would have made a better leader. They said it was because Johnston was much better with the media. So much for that lesson learned.

Since the party's strategy was to get the media to deliver its message, getting Rae into the provincial legislature quickly became an enormous priority. Compare this with Donald MacDonald, who was elected party leader in 1953, and waited 18 months, for a general election, to run for office. Ironically, it was MacDonald who eventually was pushed out to make way for Rae. The party hoped and expected that Rae would be the answer in question period, getting coverage bashing Bill Davis and his Conservative government.

The party bosses never clued in to the fact that as far as media coverage is concerned, Queen's Park is a million miles from the House of Commons. Pierre Trudeau told MPs that 20 feet out of the House they were nobodies, but Bob Rae went all the way to Toronto thinking he would still be a somebody: the golden Midas touch to their political fortune.

Relying on media coverage of question period to deliver your message is like putting all your eggs in one basket after the Easter Bunny has died.

This is especially true in Ontario. According to Graham White and Gary Levy, editors of *Provincial and Territorial Legislatures in Canada*: "Ontario is unique among the provinces in that the political orientation of its populace is primarily national rather than provincial. Ontario politicians must struggle to distinguish themselves and their concerns from goings-on in Ottawa. More generally, since provincial politics often rank below national and municipal politics in public interest, the Ontario legislature probably has the lowest salience of any Canadian legislature."

Peter Oliver, editor of the Ontario Historical Studies Series, describes Ontario as a "have-not province" in terms of provincial history, since everyone thinks in national terms.

This may explain why, with rare exceptions, Queen's Park is not the place for career journalists. Turnover in the gallery is very high, and only a few reporters and columnists have made their mark there. In turn, this may be a reason why there is so little investigative journalism at Queen's Park, and why the Camp Commission could report in 1975 that gallery members were little more than "ministry correspondents".

With the expansion of the Global Television network and the introduction of "electronic Hansard," cable TV's broadcast of the legislative proceedings including question period, Queen's Park is available to a much wider Ontario TV audience now than it was when Rae became leader. But there is still a world of difference between federal and Ontario politics.

Peter Gorrie, a former Canadian Press writer at both the House of Commons and at Queen's Park, says that although the leaders' questions were always covered in Ottawa, in Toronto they did not have the same profile. He and other journalists had to fight for space to include them.

Historian Des Morton wrote that: "Very occasionally, the opposition parties can attract the attention and sympathy of the press gallery at Queen's Park but, for the most part, the opposition members enjoy an obscurity and general unimportance exceeded only by the government's backbenchers."

Question period is good for "news," since it offers short quotes, conflict, drama and potential government embarrassment. But it is not the forum to explain ideological differences or policy. York University political scientist Fred Fletcher points out that question period "provides little...in the way of reasoned argument, long-term perspective or concern with underlying social and economic conditions or conflicts. The philosophical differences among the three parties emerge only rarely in question period." Graham White says question period isn't about getting information, it's a battlefield.

For a party with an apparently different agenda, it is surprising that the NDP would rely so heavily on a forum that wasn't good for ideas, didn't get much coverage, and wasn't high in public interest in the first place. Provincial political news is not as important in Ontario as it is in Saskatchewan or Quebec, and rates in the public's mind near the level of municipal politics.

Nonetheless, while they were in opposition the NDP caucus was starstruck by question period. It was as captivating to them as a child's trip to the candy store. They operated as if there were a provincial media, and as if the most important thing the media ever did was cover question period. An incredible amount of time and staff resources were devoted to this single effort.

While in opposition, NDP caucus members met with party researchers at 9:30 every morning when the legislature was in session to decide what questions the caucus would ask that day. Before going into these daily meetings, everyone involved read the Toronto papers so that caucus members could figure out what was worth asking the government. Questions were therefore decided usually on the basis of what the *Globe and Mail* and *Toronto Star* considered important. Following the meeting, researchers were dispatched to try feverishly to dig up information that would allow a caucus member to embarrass a minister with a tricky question. This was clearly not a party with its own agenda.

The most important questions are those asked by the leader, and they are likely to be the only ones that get any coverage at all. Widely recognized as an excellent debater, as leader of the opposition Rae always took the best questions.

Peter Gorrie ran a local paper in northern Alberta at a time when Grant Notley was the sole New Democrat in their legislature. He says that Rae took on so much by himself that it was "almost like covering Alberta where there was only one member of the opposition."

A veteran of the Queen's Park media gallery, Derek Nelson says that although people were impressed by Rae federally, "There's a difference between a guy who can cut a minister to ribbons and a guy who can reflect my vision of Ontario." (One of the gallery's more right-wing members, Nelson aptly describes himself as the type of journalist who "comes down from the hill and kills the wounded.")

Because of the lack of a province-wide media, coverage of question period is inevitably highly biased toward Toronto; the party plays to the city's newspapers and television stations. But between 1987 and 1990, the NDP had just five Metro Toronto area members. Question period did not help out-of-town members develop a profile or raise issues locally.

Oddly enough, the caucus provided little assistance to out-of-town members with their local media. It expected members to do the best they could — even though virtually none of them had experience in dealing with the media prior to their election.

Through the 1980s the NDP ignored opportunities to deliver its message outside the mainstream media. It almost never took advantage of the ethnic media, though their readers and listeners are faithful, and despite the fact that they are a specific target group for the party. When the Peterson government brought in legislation making the Workers' Compensation Board an even more arbitrary organization, the NDP raised strong opposition in the legislature. But they didn't use Italian or Portuguese newspapers or radio shows catering to workers most victimized by the changes to get their message across.

Though the NDP went all out on auto insurance, it never used student newspapers as vehicles to a target audience hardest hit by the companies. The party could have gone after university papers, sending articles, offering interviews, providing information. They might have done the same with alternative publications like Toronto's NOW magazine. But they didn't.

The NDP never made good use of letters to the editor or the production of audio tape clips for radio stations. As opposition they never hired people skilled at orchestrating the media, though they considered it very important.

The party knows well that the mainstream media, for a variety of reasons, is not likely to be a good messenger for its messages. Despite this, the NDP blames them for failing to cover NDP issues in the way that the party would like. In this way New Democrats avoid taking a good look at themselves and at their own media strategy.

10. Container, Content, Image: Old Whine and New Glasses

As they headed into the 1990 campaign, New Democrats worked consciously to change Bob Rae's image. He was no longer the wise-cracking, piano-playing joker of the 1985 campaign, nor the aloof intellectual-with-an-answer of the 1987 campaign. Now Rae was a street fighter, RamBob, a Make-My-Day leader who, from day one, was calling David Peterson a liar.

But the worker's man was dressed in one of the four conservative, dark blue suits he bought the week before the election. Columnist Geoffrey Stevens speculated just days before the vote that if the NDP won, "it will have something to do with a blue suit." Stevens was right in recognizing its importance: "Silly as it may seem," he wrote, "the leader's attire has been a crucial symbol....In it, he can pass unnoticed among the bankers of First Canadian Place, the accountants on Bay Street or the lawyers from Brampton or London, Ont. And that, of course, is the idea."

Rae's blue suit was just the symbol of a new New Democratic Party. Respectable. Mature. Conformist. In the 1990 campaign, Rae benefitted from a change in the way people thought about him. On the other hand, David Peterson suffered from a similar change of opinion.

Prior to the 1990 campaign, Ontarians judged David Peterson as fair, competent, and honest. He, personally, had scarcely been touched by the scandals that plagued too many of his cabinet ministers, a teflon premier to whom nothing stuck. But then things went wrong.

His election call with two years still to run in his mandate was seen as openly opportunistic, in the style of crass politics that people thought was beneath him. Then he resorted to a last-minute tax cut — a sure sign of political desperation — and played to outrageous fears of an NDP victory, even suggesting that children would starve if Bob Rae were elected premier.

Peterson quickly undermined himself by creating an image that ran counter to what people believed of him: no longer fair, nearly non-partisan and above reproach.

These changing impressions of political leaders and their parties are an aspect of politics that Marc Zwelling calls the "content and container."

Zwelling is a former public relations officer for the United Steelworkers who has been around the labour movement and the NDP for decades. He is now a strategist and pollster for public interest groups, and he has tried to take his ideas to the NDP.

His notion of "content and container" is a fresh look at the way groups package ideas for sale to the public.

First there is the *content*, in this case the positions the NDP wants the public to know about. Many of these are popular and go down well with people: no one wants to die on the job, no one should be poisoned by pollution, no one should be homeless, no one should be poor. The NDP develops a program it thinks will address these problems, packages it for sale to the public, and tries to deliver it through the media. The actual content of a great deal of NDP policy isn't a problem for many people, and through polling, the party finds out which of its policies are popular and emphasizes them.

Next comes the packaging and imaging of the content, to create an impression in the public eye. Polling tells the party that "free trade" sounds appealing to a lot of people, but "Mulroney trade deal" sounds awful, so that's what it uses. "Driver-owned" auto insurance sounded safer to some of the electorate than "publicly-owned" or "government-run," so the NDP used that language instead. There are ways of packaging content so it creates a positive and popular impression of the party's message.

Image intimately relates to the leader. "Photogenic" (Robert Redford) and "charismatic" (Kennedy/Trudeau) have been replaced by "telegenic" (Ronald Reagan): someone who comes across well on television. A leader's image is made and remade so he or she looks credible and attractive. Sometimes it's as simple as David Peterson's red tie and contact lenses.

But unlike packaging content, redoing a leader's image usually takes more than makeup. University of Toronto professor Ken McNaught, a leading historian of Canadian socialism and an admirer of Bob Rae, says Rae "still looks like a boy scout. He doesn't inspire confidence like a streetfighter."

Prior to the 1990 campaign, a senior advisor with the Ontario Liberal party said that Bob Rae just didn't come across as sincere on issues affecting workers. "Bob can't lead the party he leads," he said. "He can't go into a tavern and chuck back a beer with the guy who just came up from the mine....He just can't speak for people who make their living by sweat and toil. There's no sense that he breathes the same air as the cause he advocates."

Various attempts were undertaken to "remake" Bob Rae's image, including entirely different approaches in the 1985, 1987 and 1990 campaigns. In the legislature, they tried new glasses, and, in a memorable experiment that lasted exactly one day, contact lenses and a bizarre new hairdo.

Finally, we come to the *container* of the NDP itself, what's beyond the imaging and the content. This is the bottom line, the sum total, that which is *elicited*, and results in the deep-seated impressions people have of a person or a group, the gut feeling they don't have to think about, they just "know." Some of what they just "know" about New Democrats is that they're good on social issues but they can't run the corner store; they're all for big labour and big government; and they're okay as opposition, but not as government.

Whether or not any of this is true doesn't really matter. It's true as long as the public thinks it's true, and these are impressions that have a direct impact on the party's ability to sell its program.

In a stark example, the NDP focused its whole 1987 campaign around auto insurance at a time when people thought they were getting ripped off by their auto insurance companies. Even though the party put together a very popular auto insurance platform and gave it top priority, the issue didn't translate into votes because people still did not trust the NDP to manage the finances. When a party researcher made an unfortunate mathematical mistake calculating insurance rates, it played right into the public's notion that the NDP can't handle economics. It didn't matter that the researcher was forced to resign.

Now in office, New Democrats are being challenged to overcome the negative impressions people have about their ability to run the economy and the government itself. They are being forced to deal with their "container" in a serious way, because the container is more than the content, more than the imaging. This deep-down reality is often true, or at least based on evidence to suggest it's true, and isn't something that gets changed by a better choice of word or a new and different leader.

New Democrats know the public thinks they can't run the corner store.

In opposition, in an attempt to shift public opinion in their direction, their response was to soften their content on economic issues by expressing their belief in a mixed economy and their support for small business, and by accepting corporate contributions. Instead of tackling the difficult task of admitting that they don't have the credibility they need on economic issues, they talked about blanket issues like fairness for ordinary Canadians.

The party personalized the most important economic debate of the 1980s, free trade, by focusing on the unpopularity of the prime minister instead of offering an economic alternative. It showed that it was more concerned with image than substance. The party can keep on watering down its content, but it's the container that leaks.

What it boils down to is that changing their "container" requires hard work. It demands a willingness to look at intrinsic weaknesses within the party and to consider the outsider's point of view. This has been a longstanding problem for the NDP. Through the years in opposition, whenever they failed to make electoral gains they figured that their content was unappealing — in every case too radical. As a result, they watered down that content, trying to whitewash themselves and their image, instead of taking on the difficult task of cleaning up their act.

In the 1990 campaign, people wanted clean government. Peterson seemed opportunistic, scandals had hurt his government, and his last-minute hysteria failed to work. The Tories were saddled by an unknown leader and an unpopular prime minister. The New Democrats came along with a fighter in a blue suit who offered the promise of clean government. They managed to win without having to do the hard work needed to change their "container" because people were ready to take a chance on the party that had never had the opportunity to screw up.

Now in government, the New Democrats are forced to deal with their container.

PART TWO

Chapter One: 1970-1981
Stephen Lewis Leaves His Legacy

> "I learned more in two hours with Peter Barnes than I did in 15 years in the legislature....This is almost the most important thing that's ever happened in my life." — Stephen Lewis, head of the NDP transition team, quoted in the *Globe and Mail*, September 29, 1990.

Like Father, Like Sons: The New Dynasty Party

After 15 years in the Ontario legislature, including 10 years as leader of the NDP, former UN Ambassador Stephen Lewis could say, not with embarrassment but with glee, that he had learned more about the process of government in two hours from a top public service bureaucrat than from all his other political experience. Chilling — and a telling revelation of how little New Democrats understood of the functions of government bureaucracy. It's even more astonishing considering that Lewis was heir to Canada's most dynastic political party and is widely regarded as one of the country's brightest and most perceptive left-wing politicians.

Stephen and his brother Michael, sons of David, grew up on a daily diet of CCF politics. They were spoon-fed socialist rhetoric from an early age.

Stephen, the older of the two, was elected in 1963 at age 26 to represent the new riding of Scarborough West in the Ontario legislature, one of just seven NDP members. Michael, a respected organizer, managed dozens of NDP campaigns, including his brother's, and once held the party's highest paid office as provincial secretary. To complete the circle, one of his sisters, Janet Solberg, was later party president and was very influential during the transition period of the Rae government. Stephen's daughter Jenny is a ministerial assistant. Michael and Janet play important roles later in the NDP story.

From the start Stephen Lewis's oratory dazzled the legislature and gave him prominence and influence beyond his age and experience. In the 1968 NDP leadership contest, Lewis backed Riverdale MPP Jim Renwick against incumbent Donald MacDonald. MacDonald had been CCF/NDP leader since 1953, and Renwick was the stalking horse for those in the party who thought it was time for a change. At the time, Renwick was the party's federal president, a former corporate lawyer who went on to become one of the NDP's brightest and most able statespersons. In his autobiography, MacDonald says that during his leadership bid Renwick "attacked the trade union leadership for their support of me and his campaign became mired in charges and counter-charges." After alienating the labour brass, Renwick was defeated decisively. Lewis learned a valuable lesson.

Lewis's backroom maneuvers with Renwick weren't the only leadership deals he tried to cut in 1968. That same year, the upstart Lewis flew to British Columbia to confront federal NDP leader Tommy Douglas. Lewis asked him to step aside so a younger man, namely Lewis's own father, could take over. Douglas was 64, David Lewis, 60. Douglas politely put the brassy Stephen off.

Just two years later Stephen Lewis himself prepared to challenge MacDonald, whom many in the party considered old hat. Lewis cleverly managed to line up significant labour support, particularly from United Auto Workers' union chief Dennis McDermott, before formally declaring for the leadership, and the close relationship and respect many labour leaders had for Lewis's father definitely helped in this regard. When MacDonald tested the waters himself he found them uninviting, and gracefully resigned as leader.

Lewis now contested the top spot against Peterborough MPP Walter Pitman, and won handily because of overwhelming support by labour delegates. Both Pitman and Lewis believe that Pitman won a majority of votes of delegates from individual ridings. It was the labour brass that put Lewis over the top, and he never forgot it.

As leader, Lewis was successful in drawing attention to social problems that had generally been ignored by politicians and the media. He was passionately concerned about the plight of injured workers, and made issues of occupational health and safety a real priority. Lewis also raised awareness of the dangers of lead and mercury pollution and stressed a number of issues affecting children. His articulate speeches mesmerized Ontarians, and he put the NDP on the map as a party that cared deeply about social issues. But he was never comfortable with economics, and despite his verbal pyrotechnics he was never able to make a socialist vision of the economy catch fire.

Despite the many worthwhile causes that Lewis championed, his years as leader did much to create the ideological "container" that the NDP still has today among the public: good on social issues, bad on economics. In the Lewis era, many of the key party "sins" became consolidated; it was a legacy inherited by Michael Cassidy and Bob Rae.

In the 1971 election, Lewis expected to make big gains. He did not and went into mourning when the party dropped from 20 to 19 seats. MacDonald said Lewis tried to "jolt, not woo" the electorate; Lewis decidedly toned down the rhetoric in his future campaigns.

Lewis had a great opportunity to see how government functioned while in the legislature, especially considering that the Ontario government bureaucracy was fashioned into the modern political state while he was NDP leader. From 1969 to 1971, the province's Committee on Government Productivity (COGP) redesigned the whole face and style of government. Later, Ontario treasurer Darcy McKeough called the bureaucratic reforms "probably the most revolutionary reorganization of any government anywhere in Canada at any period in history."

The COGP put the stamp of the corporate managerial elite on the bureaucracy, modelling its labour relations after the private sector, filling it with professional technocrats, and sustaining it with an elaborate system of boards and commissions. With its emphasis on "productivity," the COGP ended a decade of enormous government expansion in the 1960s — not just in regard to services provided by government, but also by the establishment of the community college system, additional hospitals, educational television, the Ontario Science Centre and other government programs.

Perhaps thinking New Democrats would never be required to manage a state bureaucracy, Lewis seems not to have spent much time learning its intricacies. When the legislation implementing recommendations of the COGP was introduced, NDP members supported it. Lewis said: "The bill doesn't carry with it a sufficient relevance in public terms to get one excited enough to oppose it." When the Rae government took office in 1990 with Lewis as the head of its transition team, it found itself subjected to elaborate on-the-job training at the highest levels.

The party under Lewis does deserve credit for one of its only successful multicultural experiences, the organizing of the Italian sezione in the west end of Metro Toronto, which began in 1973. This grass-roots organizing brought traditionally Liberal Italian voters into the NDP, and paid off handsomely in the 1975 campaign when the party swept west Metro and elected four Italian-speaking NDP MPPs. Though the last of these members wasn't defeated until the 1987 Liberal sweep, the party seemed to forget the merits of organizing in the multicultural community as quickly as it had once learned it.

Toasting the Waffle

In 1969 the newly-formed "Waffle" group of left-wing New Democrats issued a manifesto "For an Independent Socialist Canada." In calling for Canada's economic independence, the Waffle's main themes were nationalism, anti-Americanism, and public ownership. The manifesto argued that economic independence was impossible without socialism. The Waffle excited many New Democrats and generated great interest and controversy inside and outside the party.

At the 1969 federal convention in Winnipeg, the Waffle manifesto was debated beside the aptly-named "Marshmallow Manifesto," a hastily drafted response by David Lewis and former Waffler Charles Taylor. Though the Waffle motion was defeated by almost a two-to-one margin, it shaped the focus of future economic discussions in the NDP for years to come.

Early in 1970, the Ontario Waffle issued its own manifesto, which criticized international unions for being part of the continental problem that prevented Canada from pursuing an independent economic course. For key labour leaders, this criticism was unforgivable, since it was the international Autoworkers' and Steelworkers' unions in particular that formed the backbone of the NDP's labour support. When the Waffle got directly and very publicly involved in support for workers during the closing of the Dunlop rubber plant in Toronto, the labour brass was furious. Labour's understanding with the party had always been that the NDP stayed out of labour's street battles, except when party leaders were invited to appear on picket lines.

The Waffle had not contested the party leadership at the 1970 Ontario convention where Stephen Lewis replaced the retiring Donald MacDonald. Waffle delegates concentrated instead on policy resolutions and promoting their own manifesto. On the Saturday of the convention, a standing vote on approval of the Ontario manifesto was apparently inconclusive, and the party leadership ordered a ballot vote the next day. According to historian Robert Hackett: "Many delegates and at least one MPP approached [UAW head Dennis] McDermott to help halt the Waffle's momentum....McDermott called a meeting of the UAW staff, who then reportedly instructed the 265 Auto Worker delegates to vote against the manifesto on Sunday. They probably made the difference, as the manifesto lost by a 744 to 628 count."

Sensing that the party could not risk alienating his friends in labour, Stephen Lewis moved quickly to try to contain the Waffle and the youth movement in the party that supported it. At the same time, the Waffle realized that getting approval for its more radical policies at conventions was not enough: it would have to challenge the leadership directly.

This Laxer did at the 1971 federal convention, taking on David Lewis. Graduate student Laxer forced the party's elder statesman to an embarrassing fourth ballot, eventually losing 1046 to 612. Along the way Laxer outdistanced MP Ed Broadbent, who had drafted parts of the Waffle Manifesto but then refused to sign it, and Ontario provincial secretary John Harney.

The Waffle fielded six candidates in the 1971 Ontario election, one of whom was Steve Penner. The Penner family has a long history of activism and its links to the Communist Party made NDP officials very nervous. Penner came within 38 votes of victory in Dovercourt riding. Relieved at his defeat, the NDP never asked for a recount.

Shortly after the election, and just two days before the Ontario Federation of Labour's fall 1971 convention, Wafflers issued a pamphlet called "A Socialist Program for Canadian Trade Unionists." It lambasted the union brass, saying that big labour had become "a major institution buttressing private corporate enterprise." It called for "completely sovereign and independent Canadian unions." Union leaders began to call for the expulsion of the Waffle. Several labour heavies, including CLC president Donald MacDonald (not the former NDP leader), its secretary-treasurer, and the Canadian director of the Steelworkers' union all belonged to the Canadian-American Committee, an anti-nationalist group that promoted greater economic integration between Canada and the United States.

In January, 1972, the Waffle Labour Caucus sponsored a conference in Windsor on the Auto Pact. The conference had the support of the Windsor labour council, and though the NDP did not formally endorse it, both Ed Broadbent and provincial labour critic Ted Bounsall spoke at the event. (Incidentally, Bounsall may have been the worst-dressed man in the history of the Ontario legislature. The trousers of his brightly-coloured polyester suits were always several inches too short, apparently the result of shrinkage when his wife at the time would get annoyed and throw them in the dryer.)

Hundreds of area workers showed up to discuss the threatened Auto Pact and its impact on their jobs and community. The conference was praised by the Windsor mayor and by the *Windsor Star*. McDermott refused to attend. The meeting criticized the UAW approach of lobbying and letter-writing as too bland, and called for a one-day work stoppage by Canadian auto workers. McDermott went nuts. This was the straw that broke the camel's back.

It is important to note that many labour activists supported the Waffle, despite the unease of the labour leadership. The Waffle's labour caucus received official labour support for events like the Windsor conference, and drew important party speakers to its functions. The rank-and-file did not turn on the Waffle as the labour brass did.

At the NDP's provincial council meeting in March, 1972, Stephen

Lewis accused the Waffle of being "a party within a party" and got approval for a committee, made up of the party president, its treasurer and Lewis aide Gerry Caplan to study the Waffle. To no one's surprise, they reported six weeks later that the Waffle was "a direct and fundamental challenge to the whole structure, direction, purpose and leadership of the party." They accused it of violating the party constitution, of "messianic fundamental-ism," and of hurting the party's chances in elections — but the report fell short of calling for kicking it out.

That wasn't good enough for the labour brass. At the beginning of June, McDermott, Ontario Steelworkers' head Lynn Williams and OFL president Bill Mahoney met with the father-and-son Lewis leaders and used the ultimate weapon to force their hands: money. They told them, according to the *Hamilton Spectator*, that "unless the Waffle situation was straightened out the unions would withdraw their financial support in the next federal election." The *Spectator* concluded: "Suddenly the issue was not whether the NDP could afford to lose the Waffle but whether it could afford to keep it."

Steelworkers' organizer Bob Mackenzie, now Minister of Labour in the Rae government, wrote in frustration to David Lewis that he was "unhappy, angry, and more than a little disgusted with your arm-twisting in favour of Waffle compromise."

The Waffle began to back off. In May it admitted that it had misused the party name, promised not to do so again and to seek party endorsement for any of its public activities. Historian John Bullen wrote in the *Canadian Historical Review* in June 1983 that "the group retracted its more severe criticisms of the unionists and pledged to lobby publicly for support of resolutions only immediately prior to conventions." This was what the party was looking for, but it came too late.

The final showdown dawned at the June 1972 provincial council meeting in Orillia, the sunshine city where the sun set on the Waffle. Council debated a motion from Riverdale riding presented by Ed Broadbent, but secretly written by historian Des Morton, essentially calling for the Waffle to disband. Morton's personal correspondence, which he provided to a student in the 1970s, makes his involvement clear, although in his books on the NDP in that period Morton never acknowledges his role in this event.

Bob Mackenzie, who had been defeated by Laxer for a spot on the federal executive the previous year, came up steaming, and screamed at Laxer that he would receive a "lesson in gutsmanship today." Stephen Lewis said he wanted "to fight for a free Canada, but without the Waffle forever an encumbrance around my neck." By a vote of 217 to 88, the Waffle was toast.

* * *

What Lewis felt at his neck was not a Waffle albatross, but the sharp knife of the labour brass. He told author Terence Morley years later that "there was an unstated ultimatum from the trade union movement, which weighed very heavily on the party leadership....It was terrifying that the trade union movement should be threatening to tell the party to shove it, that they weren't going to continue to be a part as long as people like [economist Mel] Watkins and Laxer called the shots." He said that Lynn Williams refused any notion of compromise and treated him like he was Inco management.

The refusal of the party to accept the Waffle's deathbed repentance shows that it was its politics, not its structure, that unnerved the leadership. Also, the party clearly felt it had no choice but to heed the demands of the labour brass in going the limit with the Waffle.

The left did not immediately die with the Waffle. Many Wafflers did leave the party in disgust, particularly the Laxerites, some of whom formed the Movement for an Independent Socialist Canada (MISC). Those who stayed were among the Waffle's more revolutionary elements, those who hated social democrats but felt it was right to revolutionize the NDP from within. After deciding to stay in the NDP, one group — which idolized French revolutionaries — chanted for a full twenty minutes, "Ce n'est qu'un debut, continuons le combat!" [it's only the beginning, let's continue the struggle!] The same group jokingly referred to themselves as the "rope caucus" after Lenin's famous statement that "we support the social democrats like the rope supports the hanging man."

According to Sudbury activist and former NDP vice-president Cameron Hopkins, at the party's 1972 convention following the expulsion "a lot of people thought Lewis's first name was Fuck" — since they wrote "Fuck Lewis" on the ballot rather than voting for him as leader. A wild cab driver, Douglas Campbell, running against Lewis, got a respectable vote.

At the 1975 convention, a pamphlet entitled "For a Radical, Revitalized NDP" was published by a number of prominent NDPers. Among the supporters were current federal leader Audrey McLaughlin, Ontario treasurer Floyd Laughren and a number of other MPPs.

Noting that "there is clearly a difference between government and power," the document said that the NDP must first develop a mass base, or even an elected government would be powerless. "Where we have tough, radical policies, shouldn't we unveil them now?" the document wondered. "And where we haven't isn't it time we did? It's not very honest, and it's not even good strategy, to wait till we've 'won' office." The document warned that: "If the New Democratic Party continues its drift towards moderation at elections and conventions — which has the effect of confusing us with Liberals — we shall disintegrate."

At this Stephen Lewis "went nuts," according to one backer. He demanded that they remove the document from the floor. The left was so cowed by the Waffle expulsion that they quietly gave in, and even tried to get back copies that had been distributed.

A "Left Caucus" emerged, but it soon became riddled with vicious infighting and factions. At times it was variously dominated by ultra-left Trots living in anticipation of the workers' revolution, or cautious progressives extremely wary about appearing to be a Waffle-like "party within a party." Denied any influence or practical involvement, it degenerated into a rumpus room for sectarians. Left Caucus, the very name of which insults the leadership of a party that considers itself left-wing, has endured from the mid-1970s, but today is nothing more than a tiny group of disgruntled New Democrats.

One of the important legacies of the Waffle expulsion was that many of the NDP's left-wing activists quit the party, and it has suffered the lack of their ideas and energy. At the same time, many of the left-leaning intellectuals who resigned went into or returned to academic life, where they were cut off from direct contact with workers. The culture of the left, the relationship between left intellectuals and politics, was seriously hampered by the expulsion.

Another key post-Waffle legacy has been that the left often feels a need to be conspiratorial and secretive about its organizing and actions, being careful not to appear to be "a party within a party." The Left Caucus has a mailing list and produces a newsletter, but —especially in the immediate post-Waffle days — was very careful not to sponsor events in its own name or to seem to be acting independently of other "legitimate" party bodies.

Equally important is the fact that the party leadership has been paranoid about dissent and is more anxious than ever to nip any organized left in the bud. Since the days of the Waffle, only token representation by the left wing has ever been allowed onto the party's committees. The Waffle's success, and the reaction it caused, gave party heavyweights the ammunition they needed to shoot down all subsequent organizing on the left, a tradition that still continues — with vigilance.

Another legacy is that since the expulsion, the party has never been able to build a vibrant youth wing.

For its part, the left never learned to use the strength of its numbers to negotiate representation. No way was found to have a serious dialogue with the party, and the post-Waffle left generally remained on the sidelines, reduced to the occasional strong showing at convention. Eventually it all but disintegrated.

Susan Teskey, a former party activist, sums it up this way: "The only time in party history when I recall excitement was the Waffle. They not only threw out the best and the brightest, but also served notice to anyone bursting with new ideas that this was not the place to come. Twenty years later, the party is not identified with any cutting-edge ideas. They're paying the price until this day."

Apres Moi le Deluge

When Conservative Premier Bill Davis called for an election on September 18, 1975, he was anticipating another majority government. But the campaign turned unexpectedly nasty when he and Liberal leader Robert Nixon got into political mudslinging, while the NDP under Stephen Lewis avoided personal attacks and stuck to real issues. Even Davis praised the NDP's 1975 effort, which proved the Tories were vulnerable to a hard-hitting policy-based campaign. The party's main planks were rent control, which appealed to tenants in southern Ontario, and diversification of the economy in the north.

For the first time, the NDP captured the coveted role of Official Opposition, doubling its seats from 19 to 38. Its share of the popular vote, however, increased only two percentage points to 28.8 per cent. The Liberals were inches behind with 36 seats, yet had a much higher 34 per cent of the vote. Davis was saddled with a minority.

The 1975 NDP campaign was one of the few times when the party ran on a "lunchbucket" economic idea: rent controls. NDP candidates and Lewis himself waged a tough fight against the Tories and landlords in southern Ontario on the issue. In the minority government that followed, Davis did indeed introduce the province's first rent control legislation — though it exempted all apartments built after that time. While minority government was no doubt a factor in the decision, Davis was also aware that Prime Minister Trudeau intended to introduce wage and price controls — which came in 1976 — and moved to pre-empt him in this area.

Celebrating the victory, and disregarding the traditional anti-monarchist feelings of socialists, the NDP had buttons made up reading "Her Majesty's Loyal Opposition." Party brass thought the election outcome was a sign of the prediction they'd been making ever since the party's founding in 1961: that the Liberals would eventually disappear and politics in Ontario would polarize into a two-way battle between Conservatives and New Democrats. This was the breakthrough they had been waiting for.

The NDP's sense of loyalty even extended to its attitude toward the government's restraint program, which was the blueprint for a decade of cuts. During the election, Stephen Lewis supported the idea of reduced government spending and proclaimed: "Even I say they have gone too far." The NDP election platform promised cuts in government spending. The effect of this was to lessen pressure on the government to maintain or expand programs; it also helped to bolster the Conservatives' image as effective managers.

This image was further strengthened when, shortly before calling the election, and in an effort to look fiscally responsible, Davis established a commission to review government spending, and appointed former federal auditor-general Maxwell Henderson as its co-chair. When Henderson reported in November, he made 184 recommendations and called for $1.5 billion in cuts the first year and $2.1 billion the next.

Ontario treasurer Darcy McKeough, the other co-chair of the commission, announced he would freeze government programs, cut back on grants to municipalities, charge user fees for some government programs, and reject future cost-shared programs with Ottawa. Direct government employment was cut by 5,000 people over the next five years.

Stephen Lewis, who had once said that asking McKeough to practice restraint was like asking Evel Knievel to park your car, was now in a good position to witness the revolutionary bureaucratic reforms of the Committee on Government Productivity translated into reactionary fiscal reforms of the McKeough-Henderson report.

These changes spelled the end of Ontario government programs to promote social equality, and prepared people to expect less and less from government. They were a blueprint for the next decade of government cutbacks, and marked the beginnings of neo-conservatism.

The state was transforming itself while the NDP remained Her Majesty's Loyal Opposition. Lewis failed to pick up on the significant changes of the COGP and on the implementation of the McKeough-Henderson report. He and the NDP missed the opportunity to talk about how government might be changed to better suit people's needs, how people might become more involved, or how they could be inspired to feel a new sense of ownership of government.

When Davis called an election in 1977, he was anxious to win back the majority government he had lost two years earlier. Aware that he needed to steer his party to the centre, and ready to put on a progressive face to get back power, Davis issued a "Charter for Ontario." In it the Tories made a number of progressive-sounding promises; after their victory they made good on virtually none of them.

In 1977 the NDP wanted only to consolidate its gains, and tried to appear cautious and respectable. Early in the campaign, Lewis made clear the party's objective was simply to hold on to second place. He was a reluctant campaigner, and his right-hand man Gerry Caplan did a lot of hand-holding and arm-twisting throughout the election period.

During the election Lewis backed off the party's positions on increasing the minimum wage and nationalizing resource industries. When asked by

CFTO-TV reporter Fraser Kelly, Lewis couldn't say how fast the party would move to its announced $4 an hour minimum wage, and he expressed his opposition to bringing Inco under public ownership. He said "I can't even see the horizon on that." Lewis suggested that nationalization would not come in his lifetime, even if the NDP formed the government. For the sake of moderation, policy sellouts began long before the NDP came to power in Ontario.

Watching the interview together on television in Sudbury, NDP activist Harvey Wyers said that MPP Elie Martel was so furious that "I thought Elie was going to throw his beer bottle through the TV."

Lewis later told the *Toronto Star*'s Lynda Hurst that he blew the interview: "My mind was elsewhere. I don't know, the south of France. Great time to have your mind elsewhere."

The results of the 1977 election showed that the cautious, moderate route preferred by Lewis was actually the long road to socialism. Instead of continuing on the path to oblivion, the Liberals had held their own. The NDP lost five seats while the Liberals lost two and reclaimed the Official Opposition by the slimmest margin of 34 to 33. Davis was again denied his majority, and Lewis, unwilling to be the head of just the third party again, resigned as party leader just four days after the election.

Years later, Rae's chief aide Robin Sears called Lewis's quick resignation "politically irresponsible," and said it took the party a decade to recover.

Former NDP youth president Gord Cleveland wrote in *Canadian Dimension* shortly after Lewis resigned that in Lewis's view, "the NDP's membership was responsible for the party's loss of seats... 'Silly or indefensible' policies adopted at party conventions caught up with us, Stephen argued. Above all, party leaders must be protected from such mindless radicalism."

Cleveland noted that: "The NDP leadership didn't really try to win the election and didn't want to until they had the party tamed." In his view, the party's election slogan, "Common sense never made more sense than now," was as much an attempt to cool down the party's radical elements as it was an attempt to get votes from the electorate.

Cleveland predicted, accurately, that "there will clearly be an attempt by the party brass at the next convention to free the parliamentary wing from the shackles of policies voted by convention."

Before the leadership convention was held in 1978, the lame-duck Lewis had a major labour dispute to deal with: the well-publicized Sudbury Steelworkers' strike against Inco.

The company used the low world price of nickel and its surplus inventory to justify a contract offer of a meagre 10-cent-an-hour wage increase while demanding concessions in work practices. The Steelworkers' provincial leadership went along with these demands and recommended that workers accept them. In Sudbury, led by Local 6500 President Dave Patterson, the miners rejected the company proposal and the union bosses' recommendation, and walked out.

The *Sudbury Star* held its presses for two hours to get a reaction from the Steelworkers' Ontario division director Stu Cooke, who was at a union meeting in Atlanta, Georgia. The paper ran a banner headline in which Cooke blasted the striking workers. At Cooke's behest, instead of expressing solidarity with the Sudbury strikers, Stephen Lewis denounced them as "Archie Bunkers of the left" for taking on the company while it had a stockpile.

Eight and a half months later, with massive community support, Sudbury workers won the strike against Inco. Patterson was not only re-elected local president by an increased majority, but also defeated Cooke as Ontario division director in the next Steelworker election. In kicking off his campaign, Patterson called Cooke a palace prince, and referred to the leadership as "tuxedo trade unionists." (Forever after branded as a disloyal renegade, Patterson could never get cooperation from the Steelworkers' national office, and relations with the union's top brass were rock hard. Following a concerted anti-Patterson campaign by the Steelworker establishment, co-ordinated out of the national director's office, he was defeated in the next Ontario election by Leo Gerard, now the union's Canadian director.)

The Sudbury Inco strike was important not just for the gains made by the workers after eight months of sacrifice. The strike pioneered the anti-corporate campaign against a company that had ripped off its workers for decades. It showed that the unpopularity of unions could be overcome and a community mobilized in support of workers. Sudbury steelworkers did this without the support of their own union brass; local New Democrats spearheaded the campaign without the support of their own leader.

Although local New Democrats, including the area MPPs, got heavily involved in the strike and the community's support coalitions, Lewis and other party brass didn't dig in with the Inco miners. The provincial party virtually ignored the strike, and offered no tangible support to local New Democrats. Coalition politics was not the leadership's idea of building the party. To Lewis the striking workers would always be Archie Bunkers, yet it was his own bunker mentality that wouldn't let him recognize their determination and the long-term effects of workers taking on bosses (and their own union). Finally, his close ties to the Steelworkers' leadership left Lewis no room to manoeuvre; when they wanted him to oppose the strike, he obliged.

The Sudbury strike showed how party leadership missed a golden opportunity to work with workers and community-based coalitions, but instead, once again, was more concerned with keeping the labour brass polished.

Michael Cassidy and the NDP

In 1978, with the Sudbury strike in full force, the NDP met in Toronto to elect someone to fill Stephen Lewis's shoes, and to try to follow in his footsteps.

The three leadership candidates, all MPPs, were Oshawa teacher Mike Breaugh, Hamilton firefighter Ian Deans and Ottawa economic journalist Michael Cassidy. Cassidy was seen as the long-shot going into the convention, an intellectual too cold to be leader of the NDP. Not a single caucus member endorsed Cassidy. Ironically, the party turned to just the same type of person to replace him four years later.

The fight was expected to be between Deans and Breaugh, with Deans the clear front-runner. The enormously egotistical Deans was so over-confident he went on a Florida holiday just before the convention. Though he routinely won elections by roughly 10,000 votes, he once telephoned one of his lovers the day after an election and whined with disbelief that about 9,000 voters "went out to vote against *me!*"

At the Friday night "bear-pit" session, Breaugh acted more like a stand-up comedian than a potential leader, and hurt his chances badly. The next day Deans caused considerable embarrassment when he was preceded into the convention hall prior to his speech by a parade of kilted men playing bagpipes and sporting Deans-look-alike white curly wigs. This smacked more of the hoopla of U.S. Republican Party conventions than the atmosphere of the NDP, and it put off many delegates.

The labour movement didn't rally behind any of the three candidates; autoworkers' union president Bob White later said this a mistake that his union shouldn't repeat. In any case it gave labour delegates the rare opportunity to make up their own minds, and their votes were split.

Many delegates thought Cassidy's experience with economics would enable him to establish the party's credibility on economic issues the way Lewis had with social questions. He was also the somewhat reluctant choice of the party's progressives, including leading Wafflers, who considered Deans too right-wing and Breaugh too unpredictable. Breaugh was eliminated on the first ballot, and the superior organization of the Cassidy campaign brought him the victory over Deans, who had the support of most of the caucus and party establishment, 980 to 809.

Shortly thereafter, a bitter Deans left provincial politics, was elected as a federal MP, and then accepted a $90,000 a year appointment by Prime Minister Brian Mulroney.

At the end of the convention, a group of Deans's key supporters gathered in his committee room. Deans was devastated, and he and others were crying. After a while, Donald MacDonald said they'd have to pull themselves together and pay their respects to Cassidy. When they did, Steelworkers' Ontario division director Stu Cooke walked up to Cassidy and extended his hand. Cassidy walked right by him. Relations with the labour movement went downhill from there.

The leader of Hamilton Steelworkers' large Stelco local, Cec Taylor, committed the sin of challenging Cooke for the party presidency at the convention. A long-time militant and nationalist rival of Cooke's, Taylor had backed Patterson in the Sudbury strike. Taylor lost by just five votes, and the party exacted its penance. Bob Mackenzie, the Steelworker-turned-MPP, refused to let NDP researcher Anne Forrest work on labour issues, even though she was a labour policy expert, because she was Taylor's partner.

Under Cassidy, the NDP research department, a powerful tool under Lewis, lacked focus and direction and as a result became increasingly independent. The researchers were a highly-qualified team that had a history of working incredibly long hours under enormous pressure from the demanding Lewis. Now they were more free to chart their own course, and they tried to push the party toward more activist positions. In particular they tried, generally without success, to get the party to work with social movements to develop issues and strategy and to work outside the legislature. Researcher Terry Moore was frustrated by their refusal to reach out. "How timid they are," he says. "They're locked into the orthodoxy of debate established by the other parties."

Cassidy's relationship with the caucus and party hierarchy was terribly strained. Neither group had supported him as leader, and neither rallied behind him. In the leader's office, staff even referred to the party's provincial office as "enemy headquarters."

The caucus and party brass tried to assert control. Provincial secretary Penny Dickens hated Cassidy, and did her best to avoid even speaking to his executive assistant, Wendy Baird. Former leader Donald MacDonald set up "Friends of the Leader," a condescending group supposedly created to give Cassidy advice and direction; in fact it was a caucus group designed to exercise power and take the party where they wanted it to go.

There are three structural centres in the party: the leader's office, provincial office and the provincial council. Because of the rift between these structures during Cassidy's leadership, there was less control by party bosses than in the years immediately before or since. As a result, the provincial council was able to exert more influence over the party's operations, especially its spending. According to Cam Hopkins, a party vice-president and executive member spanning the Lewis-Cassidy years, under Cassidy "the party had to meet with ridings before it made its financial plans and get some consensus. Prior to that, the party centre had absolute control. It was a way for the provincial council to impose accountability on the executive." Under Bob Rae's leadership, there has been unity between the leader's office and provincial office, so the countervailing forces so essential to party democracy have diminished.

In 1978, recognizing it had missed the boat by failing to develop a coherent economic strategy, the party called for the establishment of a task force on manufacturing to do just that. In November, 1979, its report, "New Directions for Ontario's Political Economy," was produced. It represented one of the few times the party ventured into a detailed position on economics.

The report condemned the high degree of foreign ownership of Ontario's manufacturing base and the high degree of manufactured goods imported into Canada. "The ownership structure of our industries has led to a system of production which is inefficient, vulnerable to foreign competition, imbalanced towards resource extraction, and weak in opportunities for new employment," the report said. "Without fundamental changes, therefore, the provincial economy will...continue to be afflicted with low growth, high unemployment, and a declining manufacturing sector."

The report also rejected the conventional elements of an industrial strategy. It suggested "improving competitiveness, liberalizing trade, relying on natural resource exports, switching to services in a 'post-industrial' society, and offering government incentives" — all of which were the hallmark of the right's economic strategy through the 1980s.

Its 10,000-word analysis called for more direct government involvement in manufacturing sectors: "Other governments have found it necessary to intervene in their national economies in order to ensure that strategic industrial sectors remain under national control and operate in the national interest." The creation of a Crown Investments Corporation was recommended as "...an essential instrument for making our economy less dependent upon imports of end products through encouragement of domestic industries that can be fully competitive in the manufacturing, resource and service areas." Improved use of efficient new technologies was encouraged as "...the major component of competitive advantage;" increased public ownership in the resource sectors, such as "the provincial equivalent of Petrocan in each resource area [which has a bearing on our manufacturing strategy]" was proposed, and economic and social planning "...in order for...the other tools which we have described to work effectively," completed the package.

The party's left wing criticized the document for not going far enough in calling for nationalization and greater public ownership. The left's most prominent economic analyst, Simon Rosenblum, argued that nationalization was necessary for the provincial government to acquire revenue to use as building blocks for manufacturing. "Given the acceptance of private ownership of major industry, the government has little bargaining power. It either plays ball with the corporations or finds itself faced with a corporate 'investment strike,'" he wrote in a personal critique of the report.

Though the report clearly identified the major problems of Ontario's manufacturing and resource industries and foresaw the direction of the corporate sector in the 1980s, perhaps its greatest flaw was its failure to present an economic vision that hit home with working people. In missing the opportunity to detail "lunchbucket" economic ideas, the report failed to enhance the NDP's economic credibility. It played to people's fears of nationalization and greater government intervention without providing them with practical, alternative ideas that could capture their imagination. The left was equally at fault for its failure to present specific new ideas, and for its reliance on shopworn rhetoric. Debate between the party right and left centred on whether public ownership was "a tool" or "the tool" of economic reform. This religious "a-the-ism" dominated economic debate in the party for years to come.

Crafted into a resolution that passed at the party's 1980 convention, the manufacturing strategy virtually disappeared. The party never took the initiative to develop the specifics that would have made sense to working people. Here, at last, were a set of workable economic ideas, but they died the minute they passed into the resolutions book. It showed that if the NDP couldn't be revolutionary, it could, at least, be resolutionary.

* * *

Throughout the late 1970s, the NDP made occupational health and safety a major political issue. In what is perhaps his finest achievement, Stephen Lewis built this as an issue and kept it on the political agenda with his repeated exposés of unsafe workplaces and passionate speeches about injured workers.

Lewis's harangues, coupled with a famous wildcat strike over miners' safety at Elliot Lake in 1975, forced the Tories to move. Following a royal commission report on mining, in 1979 they introduced Bill 70, the Occupational Health and Safety Act. Behind the scenes in the Ministry of Labour, and heavily involved in the bill's drafting, was deputy minister Tim Armstrong. Armstrong was a former labour lawyer who had worked in David Lewis's law office, had often acted on behalf of the UAW, and as a result had close ties to OFL head Cliff Pilkey and Canadian UAW director Bob White. In addition to the health and safety bill, Armstrong also helped get automatic union certification after bitter strikes at Fleck, Radio Shack and Blue Cross.

Recognizing that stable industrial relations were a key to Ontario's prosperity, Davis hired Armstrong as deputy minister to make sure relations with the labour movement stayed smooth and never got too embittered. The Tories set up the Quality of Working Life Centre in the Ministry of Labour to provide a place for big business, labour and the Conservative government to speak off the record. According to senior corporate and labour lawyer Don Brown, Armstrong held union leaders back "so they weren't as aggressive, weren't as militant as they would be because he was their inside man fighting on their behalf, but Tim was working for the Tories, not the labour movement."

Pilkey and White used Armstrong as their conduit on labour matters with Davis. In fact, their loyalty to Armstrong was so deep that, years later, when the Liberals tried to dump him after a power struggle with the minister, Pilkey and White were there to defend him at every turn. With Armstrong on the scene, labour leaders had direct access to the premier and, because their relations with Cassidy were so bad, they tended to bypass the NDP chief in their dealings with government.

The NDP headed into the 1981 election with a leader few top party people wanted. Michael Cassidy himself acknowledges that there were "significant elements that didn't accept me as leader, and wouldn't stay unless I did astoundingly well."

In fact, the party brass gave up on Cassidy even before the election. The *Globe and Mail* revealed in December, 1979, that labour leaders were already talking to Bob Rae about leaving federal politics to run as Ontario leader. There is no doubt that NDP caucus members and party heavyweights also discussed the possibility of inviting Rae to seek the leadership in late 1979 or early 1980 — a full year before Cassidy ever faced the voters.

The NDP headed into the 1981 election ready to drop the axe. The campaign gave them no reason to change their minds.

Not a Happy Time to be Gay

Bill Davis was anxious to get Stuart Smith and Michael Cassidy off his back and return to the comfortable years of majority government. For the first two years following the 1977 election the Tories were supported in the legislature mostly by the Liberals, and from 1979 to 1981 usually by the New Democrats. Minority government was working, Tory style, which meant hardly working at all. If there was any political energy, it was static electricity.

Then, intending to call an election the following spring, the Conservatives brought in long-awaited amendments to the Human Rights Code in the fall of 1980. Despite the recommendations of the government's own 1977 study, the amendments did not prohibit discrimination on the grounds of sexual orientation. The gay community was unhappy, but not surprised, and both the Liberals and New Democrats said shucks, they were, too. But they didn't do anything about it.

When they prepared the human rights amendments, the Tories tried to make a deal with the disabled community. According to Patti Furman and John Rae, two activists in the blind community, Davis offered to include disabled rights in the Code if they dropped their pressure to include gays as well. They refused. Even though they had a great deal to lose, they stuck to their principles and wouldn't cut a deal that cut out another group.

The failure to include gay rights in the Human Rights Code was just one of the government's attacks on gays that year. Several times it prosecuted the Glad Day bookstore in Toronto for the distribution of allegedly obscene material and twice appealed the acquittal of the gay newspaper *Body Politic* on charges arising from articles it printed.

That same fall, Toronto mayor John Sewell was defeated after he defended the bookstore and newspaper. Sewell also endorsed George Hislop's campaign for alderman, the first declared gay candidate for the post. A *Toronto Sun* headline read "Sewell Embraces Hislop." Hislop lost, too, of course.

The NDP was alarmed by these defeats and nervous about its own support for gay rights. In a letter to a member of the Coalition for Gay Rights in Ontario on November 2, 1979, Michael Cassidy had written: "We share with you a sense of frustration at the delays of the government and we call upon the Premier to bring legislation forward now to make sure the amendments [to the Human Rights Code] include sexual orientation. Our caucus and party remain convinced that amendments must be passed at the earliest opportunity. You may be sure that our caucus will move the amendments and do everything we can to have them adopted if the government fails to act." His stand was based on policy approved at convention in 1976.

Unlike the tough stand taken by the blind community, when the NDP stared principle in the face it blinked. Even though many caucus members condemned the Tories for failing to include gay rights, the party refused to introduce amendments itself. Cassidy said it "was not a priority at this time," and attempted to justify caucus cowardice by suggesting the party's support for gay rights "would become a smokescreen for other issues like housing and equal rights for women." It would be several years before the NDP would find the guts to take on the fight. Though it may have contributed to her losing her Ottawa seat, Evelyn Gigantes forcefully and successfully led the charge for the NDP.

A downtown Toronto municipal ward association voted to censure the caucus for its week-kneed 1981 position, as did the February nomination meeting in the riding of St. George. The St. George candidate, Dan Leckie, also condemned the party. "To be consistent," he said, "the NDP has to get rid of its recent flirting with compromise and stand crystal clear for its principles." The *Body Politic* wrote: "Surely the best way for the 'party of principle' to handle such a situation is to stick to its social, economic and justice policies while pointing out exactly what the PCs are up to. Instead, it's caught jettisoning a party policy which happens to be inconvenient at the moment."

Then the other shoe dropped. In the midst of the election the Metro Toronto Police raided several gay bathhouses, arresting over 300 men, allegedly including a Conservative cabinet minister. A raid of this size in the middle of a campaign could not have happened without the knowledge and support of the provincial attorney general. It was the largest assault on personal liberties in Canada since the War Measures Act was invoked in Quebec in 1970.

In 1970 only the NDP had had enough courage to condemn the federal government for invoking the War Measures Act. But this was 1981. The NDP refused to join calls for a full public inquiry into the raids, hoping the issue would just go away. According to a senior campaign strategist, "they consciously avoided circumstances where the gay issue would arise, and stayed out of ridings with lots of gays."

In an April, 1981 letter, the Ontario NDP Gay/Lesbian Caucus wrote to the provincial caucus: "We cannot flinch from challenging the right-wing reaction which simply begins with a bigoted attack on gays and lesbians and then proceeds to attack school curricula, abortion, childcare, women's rights, unions and everything democratic and decent which this party is fighting to achieve. We had better recognize that New Democrats will continue to be attacked by the Right as long as we are struggling to create and defend a society which respects the dignity of every person...."

A letter from Riverdale campaign manager Robert Shipley to Jo Surich, chairperson of the provincial election planning committee, said: "Attempted avoidance of the [gay rights] issue not only strained against party policy, it cost us many gay activist workers and in the end saved us absolutely nothing at voters' doors since we were openly and viciously attacked on the issue anyway. We feel the party ended up looking as though we were hiding something from many voters. A clear honest statement on gay rights...would have been a better attack."

Shipley and the Gay/Lesbian Caucus understood, and the party didn't, that voters already had a clear idea of where the NDP stood on gay rights. Any attempt by the party to downplay that position only smacked of dishonesty. The NDP confused its message, "gay rights are not a priority right now," with its public perception: "the NDP supports gays". Gay activists deserted the party in droves and other New Democrats were disgusted when the party deserted its policy. Meanwhile, people who were going to avoid the NDP because of its support for gays weren't fooled by the party's soft-peddling of the issue during the campaign.

This is a clear example of the NDP not understanding its "container" with the electorate, and selling out a major grassroots movement that was very open to supporting the party.

1981 Election Night Defeat

As they gathered in the Textile Workers' Union Hall on King Street in Hamilton, Ontario on election night in March, 1981, most New Democrats were anxious but not worried. Like guests aboard the Titanic, they partied, unprepared for the cold reality that lay ahead.

It was no surprise when their own Hamilton Centre MPP Michael Davison lost to Liberal Sheila Copps by almost 3,000 votes. Davison had squeaked by Copps with only a 14-vote margin in 1977, and the egotistical and lazy MPP had badly neglected the riding.

But the faithful troops were shocked as the flickering black and white TV in the corner of the "victory party" brought the news that New Democrats were falling like dominoes right across the province. Beer sales fell off, cheese doodles went uneaten and people went home early.

There was little jubilation for Ontario New Democrats that night. The parliamentary road to socialism had run into another detour.

In the true NDP spirit of boosterism and dishonesty, propaganda from the party's provincial office had led them to believe they were doing okay. Election bulletins from provincial secretary Jack Murray to campaigns sounded like pep rallies for a group of Grade 3 underachievers: "Michael Cassidy is looking good, feeling fine and flying high...." and "Hi there! Hope you're happy in your work. Michael Cassidy says When We Work We Win and When We Win We Work!" Less than two weeks before election day the bulletin named eight ridings not held by the NDP "and many, many others" where the party brass heard "great things." The party's pollster reported "It's there — Go Get 'em!"

Of course, it wasn't going anywhere except down the tubes, and the NDP's slogan, "Go Ahead, Vote New Democrat," sounded like they left out the "I dare you" part. The party didn't win a single one of the ridings where great things had been heard, and the NDP fell from 33 to 21 seats. Premier Bill Davis had his majority government back, and for years to come he would infuriate the NDP caucus with his references to "the realities of March 19th."

In the end, one out of five Ontarians supported Mike Cassidy. That was a much higher margin than among the NDP brass. It would be a mistake to say that they moved quickly following the election to get rid of Michael Cassidy; party bosses had begun to undermine him long before the election was even called.

Following the election defeat, Cassidy became the party's scapegoat. When he resigned three weeks after the election, the collective sigh of relief from the party establishment could be heard all the way to Ottawa, where whiz kid Bob Rae was making his mark as the federal party's finance critic. Former leader Stephen Lewis — sounding too much like King Louis XV — later called Cassidy's years "a bleak interregnum", using a term for a period between two kings — himself and Bob Rae.

The 1981 election debacle and the lessons the party mistakenly figured it learned from the Cassidy years paved the way for the election of Bob Rae as leader. The two main things the party thought it needed were a media star and more middle-of-the-road politics, and it set out to get both.

Cassidy Hops Along

For Michael Cassidy, all the handwriting on the wall from the 1981 campaign must have read like graffiti. "Since we fell back," he says today, "the feeling was that it was my responsibility and I had to go. I reckoned if I hung in, I'd face a very difficult time, so it was better to clear the decks and let the party go forward."

Cassidy knew that Rae was in the wings. He says that opposition to his leadership was "fuelled by the fact that Rae was feeling restive in Ottawa and ready for a go."

A former Cassidy advisor and speechwriter says Cassidy's quick axing shows that "elites are as prone to the presidential syndrome as anyone else. It's easier to fall prey to the need for a new leader than open questions about relations to labour, styles of campaigning or policy."

Cassidy was the party's scapegoat, but the race for leader at least allowed the party to debate its future. Members were annoyed that the NDP had backed down on a principled stand on gay rights. They were frustrated that in 1981 the party had no more credibility on economic issues than it did in 1978.

Members of the provincial council were enjoying the increased power they had won during the years when the party hierarchy was split, and they reacted badly to the self-serving report on the election brought to it by Election Planning Committee chairperson Jo Surich in June, 1981. Surich blamed the party's disastrous showing on everything except the NDP's bad campaign strategy. He even complained about the time the polls closed. He wrote: "It seems that most people believe the support was gone long before the campaign started and couldn't have been recovered so long as the question before the public was 'Who shall run the store?'" Surich thereby dismissed his role, and that of the party leaders, in designing a campaign that might have challenged that perception.

Party members were in the mood for a wholesale review. The powers of council were at their ascendancy, the left was coming together after a few years of internal dissension, and they were getting a hearing, especially since the sell-out of principles in the 1981 campaign hadn't delivered. It looked as if they were about to get their review.

How Many More Years?

At that same June, 1981 provincial council meeting, the party circulated copies of a discussion paper called "The Next Four Years." For a think-piece on the future of the party written by the party establishment, it was remarkably frank. It said that the 1981 defeat "must mark the end of a decade of drift that helped produce it" — a decade that obviously included not just the leadership of Michael Cassidy, but also of Stephen Lewis.

The paper recognized that "riding associations have important political responsibilities and are not just machines for picking up memberships," something the left had been saying for years. It said the grassroots "are a primary source of the activist leadership which must be recruited to renew the executive, party committees and council." It seemed to approve of issue campaigns and educational schools. It even implied that the party had lost its ideological underpinnings when it said that the party needed "a cause to fight for."

Many people agreed when the paper said: "It is difficult to discern any consistent political strategy governing the party's actions in the last 10 years. The result is a party which feels lost, unsure of itself, in need of direction." And there was this prophetic statement: "Any political strategy must be formulated in the light of the fact that governments defeat themselves. This raises questions about the role of the Liberal party in Ontario politics. We must respond to their attempts to undermine our position by pointing out their status as a declining party of opposition and their inability to be a party of government."

A critique for Left Caucus written by Wayne Roberts condemned the proposal as "a series of technocratic household hints rather than a basic reassessment of our direction." He wrote that the document "does not end the drift; it merely gallops off in all directions." Another member of the left wing said that the party wasn't suffering from drift but from a conscious political decision to move to the political centre. He said the party's view of the problem was reduced to "a crisis of its public relations." A third criticism focused on the fact that the party assumed the problem was with its structure, not its politics.

As discussion dragged on, "The Next Four Years" became "The Three

Year Plan for Party Organization." It depended heavily on doubling the party membership to 60,000 by 1985, which would have meant that riding associations would have had to devote more energy than ever into membership gathering. The paper was virtually silent on working with political coalitions or the multicultural community.

In the end, all this rhetoric went for nought. Sparks from the leadership contest short-circuited the debate and the paper quietly died. In February, 1982, the party found a simple, magic solution to its problems, an end to the "decade of drift," a Moses to lead them out of the wilderness into the promised land. His name was Bob Rae.

Chapter Two:
Bonfire of the Vanities:
The 1982 Leadership Race

"I've been called the son of many things, but I'm the son of a professional civil servant." — Newly elected Premier Bob Rae explains his comfortable relationship with government bureaucracy, as quoted in the *Globe and Mail*, September 11, 1990.

Young Master Rae

When former prime minister Joe Clark once described Bob Rae as a silk-stockinged socialist, Rae shot back, "Yeah, I grew up in a log embassy." A good line, and not far from the mark. Rae did grow up in an embassy, and had the family cottage on Big Rideau Lake to retreat to during the summers he spent in Canada. His father, Saul, a career diplomat, had wealth and prestige, and revolved around some of the brightest stars in Canada's post-war galaxy. All this illumination rubbed off on the young Master Rae.

The third of four children, Robert Keith was born on August 2, 1948 in Ottawa. He was still an infant when his family moved to London, England, where his father had been appointed to the Canadian High Commission.

Saul Rae graduated from the London School of Economics, did a doctorate on public opinion, taught at Princeton, and in 1940 wrote *The Pulse of Democracy* with George Gallup. He joined the Canadian foreign service, moved to Ottawa, and was the first allied diplomat in Paris after its liberation. He was Canadian ambassador to Mexico, the Netherlands, the

United Nations and the United States. Rae's mother Lois was educated at Cambridge University, and worked at the National Film Board and the CBC while raising her three oldest children.

Kay Riddell, whose husband was also a career diplomat and at one time UN ambassador, was a close personal friend of Lois and Saul Rae. She described the class of civil servants in external affairs as people with "a high sense of public duty, thinking about a better world, a very conscientious bunch. They rarely had a holiday. Bob would have grown up feeling you don't live for yourself."

According to Susanne Hilton, who was also raised in these diplomatic circles, and who worked with Bob Rae's older brother John on Liberal Jean Chretien's first leadership campaign, the children were known as "dip kids," the foreign policy elite's version of "army brats." The children of career diplomats grew up feeling that duty was more important than ambition. This was a generation of diplomats into nation building, with a strong sense they were a service aristocracy. That attitude was instilled in Bob from an early age. As Charlotte Gray wrote in *Chatelaine*, Rae's "values are bred in the bone; his politics came later."

The Raes returned to Ottawa from England when Bob was four, and in 1956 moved to Washington, D.C. One of Bob Rae's classmates in public school was Julie Nixon, whose daddy went on to become the lying, I-am-not-a-crook president.

Both Bob and John were newspaper boys, and among their clientele in the ritzy part of Washington where they lived were the Nixons and influential Democratic Senator Estes Kefauver. One year they sold a Christmas calendar to Pat Nixon, who gave them 10 pennies. Senator Kefauver paid Bob $20. "Ever since then, I have always felt closer to Democrats than to Republicans," Rae jokes.

Little Bob grew up supporting the other Senators, baseball's perennial losers. There was an old saying about Washington: First in War, First in Peace, and Last in the American League. Prior to becoming leader of the NDP, the Senators were Rae's only experience with losing.

In 1961 the Washington Senators moved to Minneapolis, and, perhaps in protest, Rae's family took off the following year for Geneva, Switzerland. Their frequent houseguests included Canadian diplomats George Ignatieff and Charles Ritchie. Discussions on politics and world affairs were a part of Rae's every-day routine in Geneva, where he was enrolled in the elite International School.

Stephen Gouge, who later became a prominent labour lawyer, travelled Europe when he was 18, and on one occasion stopped in the Canadian embassy in Geneva to read the newspaper. Saul Rae stopped to talk, and ended up inviting Gouge to dinner. He went eight times through the course of the summer, and described young Bob as "the most precocious 15-year-old I ever met. He'd talk about political subjects with more sophistication than I could."

In 1966, Rae returned to Canada and enrolled at the University of Toronto. Impressed with his Geneva training and his A grades at the International School, the registrar placed Bob in second year history, though he was only 18 years old. Right off the bat he was a big man on campus.

A self-conscious young man, Rae considered himself something of an outsider because of his upbringing. He explained this to writer Jeffrey Simpson: "I didn't go to a public high school. I didn't grow up in a neighbourhood. I think there was always a feeling that I had to prove myself in any crowd of people, or else they would somehow feel that I was odd or terribly different."

He had musical talent, and joined the University College Follies — which his father had once produced while at U of T himself. (As a child Saul Rae toured the country as a vaudeville song-and-dance performer with his siblings in an act called the "Little Rae's of Sunshine.") Bob also became friends with Jeff Rose, later president of the Canadian Union of Public Employees (whom Premier Rae appointed his deputy minister of intergovernmental affairs). He also met Hershell Ezrin, who would become chief of staff to Premier David Peterson. It was Ezrin who acted as the point man for the Liberals in the 1985 Accord negotiations, and his acquaintance with Rae undoubtedly helped them relate to each other. At U of T, Ezrin was a Varsity radio disc jockey called Captain Buffalo.

Rae was soon drawn into campus politics, at first in an attempt to stop Dow Chemical from recruiting on campus. Dow made napalm for use in the Viet Nam war, which Rae opposed. This was one of the first serious political disagreements he had with his father, who had served in Hanoi after the withdrawal of the French and supported U.S. policy there.

Rae quickly became a University College representative on the Student Administrative Council (SAC), a member of the President's Council, and one of four students elected to the Commission on University Government (CUG).

Bob Spencer, later president of the University of Toronto student council and chairperson of the Toronto Board of Education, says that U of T president Claude Bissell conceived of CUG as a mechanism to cool out student revolt and head off U.S.-style problems. The student radicals recognized CUG as the university administration's way to co-opt them. Today, Ellie Kirzner, a leading radical of the time, describes CUG as "Uncle Tom all the way."

On the other hand, the more radical students formed the majority of SAC. According to Spencer, "SAC used control words, not dialogue words [as CUG did]. They — CUG leaders, including Rae — had a misunderstanding of power, of the ordinary guy, and were very elitist."

In assessing Rae at the time, Spencer says he "would never do anything activist, anything that would fundamentally challenge the power structure. It's not who he is. His method and operating style haven't changed since the 1960s."

One of Rae's closest university friends, who served with him on CUG, was D'Arcy Martin, now one of Canada's brightest adult educators. Martin reflects on their political activism with this hindsight: "We lost our focus by becoming involved in an intellectual exchange that confused ideology for politics. Bright people who are personally moved by ideas sometimes assume that ideas have a political force in themselves and to win a debate is to win a battle. We won the debate but our base evaporated."

Greg Kealey, now one of Canada's leading labour historians, and then a SAC activist who replaced Rae as university commissioner in 1969, describes Rae as a "tweedy wheelie" who was "into the politics of compromise."

Though a product of the 1960s, Rae was first and foremost, in his own words, "the son of a professional civil servant" who, far from being a campus radical, was from an era of respectable and elitist politics. It is important to understand him in this light today.

In the 1968 federal election, while in his final year at U of T, Rae worked for Liberal candidate Charles Caccia. There are other family connections with the Liberal party: his older sister Jennifer worked for and later dated Pierre Trudeau, and brother John, now a senior executive with Power Corp., managed Jean Chretien's leadership campaigns in 1984 and 1990. Caccia, a political newcomer, was elected in the Trudeau sweep. Rae was critical of the campaign waged by David Lewis, and wrote in the *Varsity*: "The almost unbearable self-righteousness of the NDP was revealed in all its glory when David Lewis claimed that what had really happened in the election was a great Mistake, that the Canadian maiden had been momentarily seduced."

Rae was awarded a Rhodes scholarship, and left Canada to study at Balliol College, Oxford. There he studied and wrote a thesis on Sidney and Beatrice Webb, pioneers of Fabian socialism. The Fabians appealed to Rae because of their gradualist approach to economic change, though he found the Webbs elitist. The Fabians borrowed their name from Roman general Fabius Maximus, who gradually wore down and overcame the onslaught of Hannibal's army by repeated harassment, rather than risk an outright confrontation he knew he would lose. British historian Walter Arnstein describes the Webbs's approach as wanting to "use existing government machinery to forward the cause of economic equality by legislating against poverty and by bringing all major industries under the control of a democratically elected government. They sought no revolution...."

But in his thesis, Rae warned: "The socialism of gradualism can easily become that of accommodation and opportunism." Reminded later of some of the views in his study, Premier Rae quipped to an Oxford audience in November, 1991 that he should "go out and have a look at that thesis — and burn all the excess copies."

After studying the Webbs, Rae started to feel out of touch. "I felt a kind of depression and uncertainty about myself that I had never felt before," he told Jeff Simpson. "It lasted for about a year. I went to a psychotherapist twice a week. I worked as a social worker because I realized that I had to get out of being an academic and start getting involved....I became very awkward, very quiet, very unsure of myself, and very introspective. I was a real perfectionist. I set incredibly high standards for myself. I couldn't make a mistake. It was a case of working out the introspection."

The Rhodes scholarship marked Rae for all time as an intellectual, a description he finds ironic. He told the *Toronto Sun:* "I went to Oxford assuming that I would carry on with the academic life. But I found it frustrating. I wanted a broader range of experience, something more than an abstract discussion of problems. That's why when I hear people describe me as an intellectual because I went to Oxford, I find it funny. It was at Oxford that I discovered that I am not an intellectual."

While at Oxford, Rae was a volunteer in North London, working on a study program for troubled teenagers from British mining communities. This experience helped radicalize him, and show him the value of working directly to help people — quite apart from the rarefied university atmosphere. And yet, despite deploring the elitism he found in the Webbs, Rae already saw himself as something of a father-confessor figure.

He later told journalist Judy Steed: "It was a great experience for me. I realized that advocacy was what I wanted to do. I'd found a vocation. I was useful. I could use my heart and my brain....I wanted to know how other people lived. Clinic work, sitting down with people and listening to them is an absolutely necessary part of political work for me. It's almost like hearing confessions, it's a way of being rooted in what's going on in the world."

Jean Chretien, then minister of Indian Affairs, tried to lure Rae to work in his office, replacing his brother John, but Rae turned him down. "I already knew I was not a Liberal," he says.

He returned to Canada and enrolled in the U of T law school in 1974. But he wanted to carry on with his community work, and served as a paralegal for the Union of Injured Workers and the United Steelworkers union.

Rae attended his first NDP convention in 1975, having joined the party shortly after his return to Canada. There he got to know Broadview (later called Broadview-Greenwood) MP John Gilbert, and when Trudeau appointed Gilbert to the bench a few years later, Gilbert asked Rae to run for the nomination. He agreed.

The nomination fight attracted two other high-profile New Democrats: former Scarborough MP John Harney, later, as Jean-Paul Harney, NDP leader in Quebec, and Kay Macpherson, a feminist and peace activist. Rae won the nomination over Harney by a single vote. In the October 16, 1978 by-election, Rae narrowly defeated his challengers; he was just 30 years old. Rae thus never knew the party as a rank-and-file member; he was at the top right away. His experience was worlds apart from the thousands of party activists — especially women — who spend years doing the grunt work in riding associations, without recognition or influence.

Winning again in the 1979 federal election, Rae became the party's finance critic. Now the media spotlight shone on Rae, and he responded with an apparently endless and effortless stream of 15-second quips. He quickly became a media darling, and a regular guest on CBC radio and television. By NDP standards, this was making it big.

Shooting from the Lip

It took no time for Rae to establish himself as a ready wit. On his very first day in parliament, he referred to the "pre-Keynsian economics coming from the Liberal party opposite and...pre-Cambrian economics coming from the Conservative party to my right."

On one occasion he said of Frank Stollery: "Whenever I listen to a speech by the honourable member for Spadina, I realize why he fought so hard against the introduction of a turkey marketing board. It is because if we did have such an institution, he and many of his colleagues in the Liberal party would be in danger for their lives."

He once referred to then-Tory finance minister John Crosbie as "Newfoundland's gift to 17th-century economics" and to the Senate as "the indoor relief department of the Liberal party."

The finance portfolio may have taught Rae something about economics, but it did far, far more for his career by giving him the image of a media whiz.

Rae always enjoyed reading his own reviews. A *Maclean's* magazine profile written shortly after he became leader quotes school friend Lenny Wise: "One night he phoned me and asked me to read him a story about him in that day's *Toronto Star* because the papers hadn't arrived in Ottawa yet," he recalls. "So, I did. Then he asks me if there was a picture with the story and I tell him 'yes.' Then he wants to know how big it was. Can you imagine?

He was just like a little kid. He really wanted to know how big it was!"

The important aspect of this media attention is that Rae, and many other New Democrats, thought the limelight would follow him no matter where he went. Not understanding the media, they never realized there was an enormous difference between coverage of the House of Commons and the Ontario legislature.

When Rae moved the motion that defeated Joe Clark's Conservative government on December 13, 1979, he was further catapulted into media stardom. The next day, both he and Clark's wife Maureen McTeer passed their bar exams, and it was on to the campaign trail. It's understandable that Bob Rae would not be high on Clark's Christmas card list. Clark once dismissed Rae as "the silver-spooned socialist who, having been nurtured all his life at the rich bosom of privilege, presumes to lecture the rest of us about equality and poverty."

For environmentalists, Clark's defeated budget and Rae's successful non-confidence motion have an ironic twist. The most controversial feature of the budget was its 18-cent-a-gallon gasoline tax — which many environmentalists knew would have resulted in reduced use of cars and trucks. Clark's defeat meant this tax was not introduced.

We're Off to See the Wizard

Handily winning re-election in February, 1980, his third successful federal campaign in just 16 months, Rae — perhaps even more so than leader Ed Broadbent — was truly the party's fair-haired boy. In late 1979, labour leaders and influential party members began privately discussing with him the possibility of his taking over the Ontario leadership, despite the fact that Michael Cassidy had yet to face the electorate.

After the 1981 election defeat, it was clear that Cassidy would have to go. Former provincial secretary Penny Dickens, who had open disdain for Cassidy, called a meeting with Rae that included party heavyweights Gord Brigden, Hugh Mackenzie and MPP Dave Cooke. Rae subsequently met with Cassidy and told him he should resign, though Rae himself had not yet decided to run.

Pressure on Rae increased. Stephen Lewis met with him at least twice in an attempt to get him to run, and Donald MacDonald worked hard to get him to declare.

When Cassidy announced on April 8th that he would step down, a more or less official "draft Rae" movement got underway. It was headed by Marilyn Roycroft, an intense party right-winger who was a former Lewis researcher.

But Rae was not easily persuaded. His wife, Arlene Perly Rae, was pregnant with their first child, and she opposed the move. Broadbent, Tommy Douglas, who was still an MP, and whom Rae greatly admired, as well as Rae's parents, were also against it.

After Rae's daughter Judith was born on August 1st, the three went to the family cottage in the Rideau. They were soon joined by Roycroft, journalist Peter Mosher, and Hugh Mackenzie. Together they convinced Rae and overcame Arlene's reluctance. On September 8, Rae announced his decision.

The Roycroft-Mosher-Mackenzie triumvirate was amply rewarded for their early show of faith. Roycroft managed Rae's leadership campaign and became his executive assistant. Mosher was Rae's first press secretary and married Roycroft. Mackenzie became Rae's first principal secretary. All three eventually fell out of favour and were replaced. But after the NDP formed the government, Mosher became press secretary again, Mackenzie was appointed as executive director of the Fair Tax Commission, and Roycroft was later put in charge of the government's patronage appointments.

Bonfire of the Vanities

Charging that "Ontario has been ruled by one party longer than Poland or Bulgaria," Rae declared his intention to seek the leadership. He said he was running because "I have been asked by many members of my party, and by many Ontarians sympathetic to the goals of the NDP, to accept [the] challenge."

The move to provincial politics was a curious step for Rae. His avowed interest was the federal scene, and he already held the second-highest portfolio in caucus as finance critic. Cassidy thought Rae was "restive." Obviously ambitious, Rae was well aware that Ed Broadbent was unlikely to step down for some time, and that for one Ontario politician to succeed another as federal leader was very unlikely. As Number Two, he was boxed in.

Rae may also have held the view that a breakthrough for the federal party depended on strengthening its base in Ontario, and he may have felt sufficiently challenged by that role.

Once he threw his hat in the ring — the first candidate to declare — party forces lined up solidly behind him. As was typical of the party establishment now fixed on restoring the damage they felt was created by the lacklustre Cassidy years, this was a contest in which they would take no prisoners. They pulled out all the stops to make certain Rae was elected.

In his opening statement, Rae emphasized two "fundamental issues: the quality of human services and fellowship we provide for our citizens, and the future of Ontario's economy."

"We live in a society that treats people like commodities," he said. "The basic truth of our movement is to change that harsh and unnecessary truth....[W]e face a continual struggle against those who would subordinate the claims of the people to the demands of private power and corporate self-interest."

Rae said his economic policy goal was "to emphasize the role that planning and industrial strategy must play in the Ontario of the 1980s. When all the major national and multi-national corporations are planning extensively for their own futures and their own profits, it is vital that the Government of Ontario act on behalf of the people of this province, to protect their jobs and communities."

The fundraising appeal for Rae's campaign was signed by UAW director Bob White and Marion Chambers, a bland party loyalist who would be elected party president at the leadership convention.

In speaking to the Canadian UAW Council on September 12, just four days after Rae's announcement, White recommended that the union endorse his bid. White's recommendations were rejected less often than the Ayatollah Khomeini sent out for spareribs. The endorsement effectively locked up the couple hundred UAW votes that could be expected at a leadership convention.

White implicitly criticized the union's failure to take a position in the Cassidy/Deans/Breaugh race in 1978: "...my role is to lead," White said, "and I want to try and obtain a consensus to support Bob Rae's candidacy. The last time we went to the Ontario leadership convention, we were divided in three or four different groups." That would not happen this time.

Aside from virtually guaranteeing the UAW votes, the important aspect of White's recommendation is that at the time there were no other declared candidates — though it was widely known that Ontario NDP caucus members were testing the waters. White was locking in his members even before anyone else was in the race. It made absolutely no difference to the UAW who else might come along.

In White's autobiography, *Hard Bargains*, he wrote: "The Ontario New Democratic Party held a leadership convention that summer. I'd had some influence in persuading Bob Rae to leave his seat in the federal legislature and run for the provincial party leadership. The UAW people in Oshawa were for Mike Breagh [sic] from Oshawa, but when I got to the convention, I found that almost all the other delegates in the UAW favoured Bob Rae. Rae is an intelligent, articulate, capable man, who has the ability to grasp and explain complex issues."

Though White had described Rae in almost exactly the same words in his report to the council, his memory of the race is a great deal less precise. Breaugh wasn't even in it; he ran for leader in 1978. The convention was in February, not the summer. And White makes himself sound innocently surprised about the union's support for Rae, when, of course, it was the approval of his own recommendation to the Canadian Council that ensured that support.

The United Food and Commercial Workers' Union (UFCW) was similarly locked in to Rae early on. According to a UFCW staff member, one of the union's executives met Michael Lewis, and indicated that he was leaning to supporting MPP Richard Johnston. Lewis told the UFCW officer that Johnston wasn't in the race, which was literally true, since he had not yet declared. The union executive then told Lewis he would endorse Rae, and the union was committed.

On September 24, Johnston declared he would seek the leadership. Johnston had first been elected in April, 1979, replacing Stephen Lewis, for whom he had once been an organizer, as MPP for Scarborough West.

In announcing his candidacy, Johnston, like Rae, attacked the Tories. He called the Conservative government "the greatest problem facing this province." While Rae focused on his economic experience, Johnston stressed social issues, and said he was "concerned that our party no longer speaks on social matters with the credibility it once enjoyed." But unlike Rae, from the outset Johnston signalled his support for public ownership of natural resources, and said that "we must be willing to intervene in other sectors that are crucial to the economic health of the province."

Johnston's stand on public ownership of resources staked his claim with the party's left wing. He further appealed to progressives within the party by emphasizing the need to build a political movement by strengthening the party's riding associations and by reaching out to social movements. "I want to lead a principled party, and I want to lead that principled party to power," he said. "To do that, we must build a political movement the likes of which has not been seen in this province."

In a swipe at Rae's media stardom, Johnston said: "The answer does not lie in magic solutions. Or superhuman personalities. Or million dollar ad campaigns. It lies in work." Johnston was dismissing the notion that Rae's media profile would translate into NDP gains.

He said he looked forward "to working with fellow NDP activists across Ontario in the serious task of building a political movement that is capable of achieving power and worthy of exercising it."

On October 1st, the final leadership candidate, Jim Foulds, announced his intention to run. Foulds, who had represented Thunder Bay since 1971, was clearly the most experienced of the three, and, as a northerner, represented a different constituency. A number of party bosses, including Michael

Lewis, had urged Foulds to run in 1978, but at the time he thought he wasn't ready. Now those same people were all supporting Rae, and Foulds felt betrayed.

Foulds says: "I knew I wouldn't win right from when I entered. I was the establishment's second choice." He also recalls a "strange decision" taken by the provincial executive right after Cassidy stepped down that asked potential leadership candidates not to mount campaigns until after the federal party's convention in June. "They were giving themselves time to recruit Rae," he says. "When I look back on that, I was terribly naive, and just didn't have the right to be that naive."

In his opening statement, Foulds also attacked the Tories, saying that "I do not consider my competitors in this race to be my opponents, because we are all allies in a common cause. My real opponent in this campaign is Mr. Davis and his government."

"It is the duty and the obligation of at least one of the opposition parties to offer the people of Ontario a credible, dynamic and humane alternative to the present destructiveness of Ontario's Conservative government," Foulds said.

Foulds believed in a "clearly-defined program of action" to take to the electorate in the next campaign. He was consistent throughout the race in emphasizing the same four points of his "basic program": expansion of social services, including dental care and the abolition of OHIP premiums; public ownership only where necessary, but including public auto insurance; regional development featuring a "deliberate decentralization of industrial development toward the less developed regions of Ontario;" and "a genuine reform of the taxation system so that there really is a fair redistribution of wealth."

As the leadership race got off the ground, Foulds was painted as the most right-wing of the three candidates — though in many respects he was less conservative than Rae, while Johnston staked out his territory on the left. Rae was clearly the front-runner, the choice of the party establishment and of the labour movement. But unlike the 1978 leadership campaign, when the party brass took a Deans victory for granted, this time they would not let that happen. The bitterness of the race surprised many New Democrats.

That bitterness was not fought out between the three candidates, all of whom took the high road in presenting their platforms to party members. The nastiness of the campaign took shape in the ridings when the Rae camp introduced the use of delegate "slates." At riding meetings where delegates were to be elected to convention, the Rae forces handed out printed lists of people supporting Rae. Instead of riding members voting for individual people running as delegates to convention, as was the custom, they were now presented with teams of people.

Normally, the election of delegates to NDP conventions was a time to reward long-time party activists, those who had done the thankless tasks of administering the riding associations through the years. But this was no longer the case. An article in the Parkdale NDP newsletter entitled "Of Cabbages and Kings" pointed out that "the Rae campaign is a well-oiled machine, and they are nothing if not politically astute. Their analysis told them that in many ridings across Ontario the majority of riding activists and members of riding executives were not breaking their way....It therefore became an essential part of the Rae campaign strategy to run slates in an attempt to bypass unsympathetic local riding leaders. After all, delegate selection meetings could not be allowed to degenerate into a consideration of the personal merits of potential delegates on the basis of riding work, experience in election campaigns and local organizing, and knowledge of party policy. That would play right into the hands of the riding activists Running a slate allows attention to be focused primarily on the single issue of who is supporting whom for leader."

The Johnston campaign was caught off guard — and shocked — when the Rae campaign cleaned up in the downtown Toronto riding of Saint Andrew-Saint Patrick. St. A and P was traditionally a left-wing stronghold with a history of activism. Intensive membership drives in the late 1970s had given it the largest membership in the party, entitling it to more delegates to convention than any other riding. The leadership of the riding unanimously supported Johnston, and his campaign expected to win easily there.

A journalist and former NDPer who was a high-profile Johnston supporter from St. A and P, says: "The Rae people knew St. A and P was a key riding, since it was the largest. They threw in outside organizers and used phone banks [to make sure Rae supporters came to the meeting]. It's not a surprise that insiders win over outsiders. Even though we had the executive, we were outsiders in the party and the insiders used their connections and cleaned our clocks. They'd done it so many times, they knew exactly how to do it."

John Johnson, who was St. A and P membership secretary at the time, remembers the hard feelings when every member of the riding association's executive was shut out. "It was pretty heartbreaking stuff. They didn't even allow the riding president, Stan Kutz, to go." The riding's 1981 election candidate, Dan Leckie, was also defeated as a delegate. The riding association was split apart; many Johnston supporters "didn't talk to the Rae people for two years," Johnson says.

The same tactic was employed elsewhere, especially in the larger Toronto ridings. When the executive of neighbouring St. David's was similarly defeated, six executive members, including the vice-president, secretary, treasurer and membership secretary, resigned in protest. In a letter to their riding president, they wrote on January 21: "We protest against the stacking of the delegate selection meeting to influence the selection of delegates on the basis of who they are supporting for leader, rather than on the broader range of issues to be considered at convention....The delegate selection process, in St. David and in other ridings, has not taken place in the co-operative and democratic manner that has been traditional in this riding and party. The manner in which the selection process has been focused on the leadership issue, ignoring issues of policy and internal democracy, is inappropriate in a democratic socialist party, and in the long run, is very harmful to the party itself."

Foulds says simply that the use of slates "destroyed the feeling about legitimate democracy within the party."

None of this bothered Bob Rae, who dismissed the long-serving members — many of whom had been involved in the party far longer than he had — as "self-anointed activists."

This attitude made relations between camps bitter. Around Christmas time, a ditty circulated through the Johnston campaign:

> You better sell out, you better not shout,
> You better by sly, I'm telling you why,
> Robert Rae is coming to town.
>
> They're making their list, checking it twice,
> If you're not on board, you're naughty, not nice.
> Robert Rae is coming to town.
>
> They know if you've been left-wing,
> They know if you've been right,
> They know if you will rock the boat;
> If you will, you're on thin ice.
>
> The meetings are stacked, the fixes are in,
> Democracy dumped — they just want to win.
> Robert Rae is coming to town!

But the campaign did have its lighter sides.

At one west-Toronto all-candidates' meeting, two young women were seated in the auditorium directly in front Peter Waite, one of the party's most active and outspoken gay members. When one of the women leaned to the other and whispered, "That Richard Johnston's so cute!," Waite said in a mock shriek, "You're telling me! You're telling me!"

After another all-candidates' meeting in late January near Wingham, Johnston, Riverdale MPP Jim Renwick, and their driver Joanne Kirzner got stuck in a fierce snowstorm. Johnston tried for a long time to dig them out, but eventually found it hopeless. Renwick, who had previously suffered a heart attack, stayed in the car while Johnston and Kirzner set out across a farmer's field for help. They had to walk nearly a kilometre through the storm to the nearest light, only to discover that it was a barn, with the farmhouse still some distance away. The farm family had heard on the radio that an NDP candidate was lost, and offered to let them stay the night.

Johnston and Kirzner set out again to get Renwick. When they got back to the car, there he was, with their emergency candle burning, sipping scotch, nibbling cheese and crackers, calmly reading a *New Yorker*. Quintessential, unflappable Renwick.

Finally at the farmhouse, Johnston and Renwick shared a small bed. When he got back to the legislature the following afternoon, Johnston had a raw patch from frostbite on his cheek. He had a lot of fun with the media telling them it was whisker burn he got from Renwick.

As they headed into convention, it was clear that Rae would win a first ballot victory. The insurmountable feature was Rae's media profile. Randall McQuaker, Foulds' northern campaign co-ordinator, felt "It was no use talking to delegates. They had no interest in policy or regions. They were totally won over by Rae's media talents. Bob would get media and that's what the NDP needed."

"The Toronto media loved Bob Rae," McQuaker says. "They liked his jokes, his style, his looks, his everything, his politics being least important. We were up against the party establishment and the media." Foulds, for his part, rightly warned that the media at Queen's Park was very different from Parliament Hill, and that coverage in Toronto was much more difficult to get. He tried to convince New Democrats that wisecracks would get covered in Ottawa, but not in Toronto. His arguments fell on deaf ears.

Johnston campaign manager Peter Hatch knew they couldn't knock off Rae. "So much was locked up before we started," he says. While Hatch was masterminding Dan Heap's surprising defeat of Jim Coutts in the federal Spadina by-election, Rae and Roycroft were already working full time. "Labour support was pretty well gone by the time we started," Hatch says. "We didn't even have a shot at it."

Rae's solid support from the labour movement, which would generate at least one quarter of the delegates, was key. With almost 25 per cent of the votes in his pocket, and the successful use of slates in many ridings, Rae only had to avoid a major mistake, and so his campaign kept him deliberately low-profile throughout the convention. "Bob himself has one characteristic in common with Bill Davis," Foulds says. "They're both no-risk politicians.

They won't make an attempt at something if they're not sure they're going to win."

The story was different for Johnston and Foulds. Both knew by Christmas that they would lose to the Ottawa media star, and kept up bravely through January, talking about their platforms and ways to build the party.

In the Foulds camp, there were rumblings that their campaign wasn't entirely independent of the Rae forces. One of Foulds' key workers strongly believes to this day that Jo Surich, co-chair of the Foulds campaign, was there as a spy for Rae forces, or at least on their instructions.

There was a sense that the Rae forces wanted a three-way race because they feared a two-way, left-right split between Rae and Johnston would get dirty, and Surich wanted Foulds to declare in order to prevent that. "They wanted it to sanitize the race," Foulds' organizer says, "not to sabotage our campaign," because they knew Rae would win on the first ballot.

Foulds himself acknowledges that the party establishment didn't want a polarization, and suggests that that's why he heard "encouraging rumours" about potential support. "It was only after [hearing those rumours] that I found out that the same people who were encouraging me were committed to Bob," he says.

Given the long-standing and close personal relationship between Surich and Foulds, the contention that Surich was a spy is almost certainly untrue. But nonetheless it is indicative of the suspicion and bad feelings the Rae campaign engendered inside the party. Together with the fact that their slates disenfranchised many long-time riding activists, the legacy of the campaign was one where many hard-working New Democrats felt no loyalty to Rae as leader.

There was a real bitterness among many activists toward Rae, and a real distrust on his part toward them. Neither side was prepared to bridge the gulf between them. These feelings lasted for years, and Rae's personality made it difficult for people to warm up to him. The day after his victory, *Globe* journalist Sylvia Stead noted: "Part of the problem in uniting the party and appealing to voters will be...Rae's personal appeal, which is inconsistent. He has difficulty making small talk with people, a trait interpreted by some as cold arrogance. He can also move quickly from being charming and quick-witted to irritable and disinterested."

At convention, the Rae juggernaut rolled on. Not satisfied with an easy victory for Rae, they were intent on capturing the virtually all elected offices in the party executive. They wanted to control all three of the party's power centres: the leader's office, provincial office, and, through the party executive, the provincial council.

Marion Chambers, a Rae loyalist from rural Ontario, was elected party president. She was opposed by Sudbury activist Cam Hopkins, a former vice-president, who had a considerable following on the party left. Thinking that Chambers was ineffective, many delegates who supported Rae nonetheless voted for Hopkins, but he still lost. Michael Lewis was easily elected as provincial secretary. The official slate for executive officers included roughly 20 Rae backers, and, as a token, two or three supporters of both Johnston and Foulds.

The circle was complete. Rae forces controlled the party — but their alienation of the left, and their complete shut-out of other currents in the party, was indicative of their need to crush what they saw as disloyalty. There would be no dialogue with their opponents in the party. The No Dissent Party was at work again.

On Sunday, February 7, the final leadership speeches and balloting took place. The results were predictable: Rae 1,356; Johnston 512; Foulds 232. Rae had won almost 65 per cent of the votes.

When Rae made his acceptance speech, he was joined on the platform by Ed Broadbent. As the cameras zoomed in on the new leader, Broadbent whispered loud enough to be picked up by the open mikes, "You'd better wave, Bob."

Taking New Directions

The 1982 convention was important for more than the election of Bob Rae. In policy terms, just as with the leadership and party positions, the convention represented a triumph of the direction Rae wanted the party to take.

Nuclear energy was one of the key policies the Rae forces wanted changed. In 1980, the party had passed a tough resolution that said that the "construction of four additional reactors at the Darlington [nuclear generating] site is unnecessary and should not proceed." The resolution pointed out that the construction of reactors at the Pickering and Bruce stations then underway would generate sufficient electrical energy for Ontario's needs, and that cancelling the Darlington project would save $5.7 billion. Pointing out that the investment of one dollar spent on insulation "provides four times more energy than the same investment in nuclear electricity," the resolution said that "funds made available by cancellation of the Darlington project should be employed in investment in energy-efficiency technologies and alternative energy industries."

This was too hard a line for Rae and his supporters, particularly those in the big Hydro workers' local, the Canadian Union of Public Employees (CUPE) Local 1000. Other labour delegates, in particular the uranium miners from Elliot Lake, members of the Steelworkers' union, were also vehemently opposed to the party's policy.

In 1982, Rae and his labour backers successfully got the party to water down the tough anti-nuclear stance it had approved two years earlier. They deep-sixed the cancellation resolution and passed a new policy that never mentioned Darlington.

This time, the focus was more on workers and jobs than on energy, and said the party "would phase out or shutdown existing facilities when environmentally-acceptable alternatives are available and economically viable." The true measure of the commitment was found at the end of the resolution, where the party said it "would not implement policies leading to a reduction in employment in the nuclear industry unless and until employees to be displaced are guaranteed the opportunity for alternative employment at comparable wages through measures including fully paid retraining, relocation assistance, full compensation for losses in housing values, and pension portability."

In other words, never.

Another symbolic policy promoted by Rae's backers won a far more narrow victory. They supported a proposal that the party accept corporate donations — an anathema to many CCFers and NDPers. Attempts to win approval for corporate donations had been tried before.

In December, 1976, party president Jim Turk broke a tie at provincial council and cast his vote against corporate donations. Though the division was not strictly along ideological grounds, members of the left wing argued that to receive corporate donations might make the party cautious and fearful of losing its funds. But at the time many party staff, including provincial secretary Penny Dickens and organizer Gord Brigden and a majority of the provincial executive, favoured accepting corporate donations. At that 1976 council meeting, twice the vote came back tied, and Turk used his presidential ballot to prevent donations. "Our side was jumping for joy," Turk says.

On the second day of the council meeting, his wife went into labour and he went to be with her, stepping aside as chair of the council. Dickens engineered a reconsideration of the vote, which lost again. Turk's friend, vice-president Cam Hopkins, burst into the labour room at 4 p.m. to tell him the vote had been defeated. "That's how I remember the day," Turk says.

At the 1982 convention, a rare standing count produced a 670 to 669 vote against donations. Given the closeness of the outcome, the convention chair accepted an appeal allowing another vote after making sure delegates outside the hall were given time to come in. Dozens of UAW members and other labour delegates butted out their cigarettes and burst onto the convention floor. On the second vote, donations were approved. The resolution limited corporate contributions to Canadian businesses with no more than 10 employees, provided they did not have public shareholders and did not engage in unfair labour practices.

Dozens of party members resigned in protest, believing that a socialist party should never accept donations from profits generated by workers. Communications Workers' union staff member Ed Seymour, a burly trade unionist who always put principles ahead of his staff job, was so strongly opposed to taking capitalists' money that he had once cried at the mike when arguing his case. At the 1982 convention, Seymour tore up his party card and asked a friend to give it to Michael Lewis. Feelings ran deep.

Nuclear energy and corporate donations were two of the policies the Rae forces wanted changed, and they were successful. For the most part, Rae himself stayed out of the debates. He knew victory was his and he wanted to avoid antagonizing delegates.

During the course of the leadership campaign, Rae had tried to put a progressive spin on his position, in order to cut off Johnston's support. In his speech prior to the balloting, for example, Rae referred to himself as a "democratic socialist" — a key phrase for party lefties. In his victory speech, however, Rae immediately became a "social democrat," a turn-around as obvious as it was quick.

Rae's ideological adaptability had already been noted in the media. Writing about the young finance critic in the fall of 1980, the *Financial Post Magazine* said: "Precisely because he's a class chameleon, who can adapt his colouring to fit in with bankers, academics and business types as well as trade unionists, university-educated Rae is valuable to the NDP."

But appearances aside, everyone knew Rae flew with the party's establishment wing. Nuclear energy and corporate donations were highly symbolic positions for New Democrats; a third was public ownership.

At the 1981 federal convention in Vancouver, just prior to his decision to enter the leadership race, Rae was the leading force opposing a motion to nationalize financial institutions. Initially, the idea met with some sympathy, because it was a time of runaway interest and mortgage rates, and banks were villains. As then-*Globe and Mail* reporter Thomas Walkom wrote, Rae "played a pivotal role in beating back the NDP's left wing and reaffirming the economic policies of the party establishment." After one of Rae's impassioned speeches, the convention rejected the motion.

During the leadership contest, Rae paid lip service to the notion of public ownership of the resource industry. Speaking to the party's Northern Council in October, he expressed caution, saying "it is important for us to have a sense of pacing and priorities in the implementation of the party's policy [on public ownership of resources]." He conceded that public ownership was not "some abstract theory," and was important "for practical reasons, human reasons, [and] economic reasons."

"Unless we move to public ownership and control," Rae said, "we won't be able to bargain with the world, and build our community. Every time the

Tory government allows another exemption under Section 113 of the Mining Act, they're saying Ontario jobs, Ontario industry, Ontario workers, Ontario communities, Ontario services are less important than multinational profits. It's time they moved over and let someone else drive."

In NDP terms, Rae was now solidly in the driver's seat himself. But once he resigned as MP for Broadview-Greenwood, Rae had nowhere to park.

Chapter Three: 1982-1985: Mr. Rae Comes To Toronto

"It wasn't long after Rae's arrival that the euphoria had turned into charges that he was a 'superficially smart-assed kid.'" — John Coleman, writing on Rae's arrival at Queen's Park in the *Windsor Star*, September 14, 1984.

Musical Chairs

Following Rae's election as leader, caucus members saw their legislative seats become the objects of an elaborate round of musical chairs. They all knew that when the music quit, Rae would be sitting somewhere and one of them would be out of the game. But who?

During the leadership campaign, Rae brushed off challenges to his lack of a seat in the legislature, and had a good democratic line to offer: any New Democrat should have the right to run for leader, he said, not just MPPs. But once elected, his tune changed. A leader had to be in the legislature to make his mark. As *Windsor Star* reporter John Coleman wrote, getting a seat was "paramount among Rae's frustrations" because "caucus members insisted on holding onto their ridings with both hands."

His federal riding of Broadview-Greenwood was in Toronto's east end, and party strategists hoped an east end member would make way for him. All eyes focused on Marion Bryden, from Beaches-Woodbine and Jim Renwick, from Riverdale.

According to people who worked closely with her, Bryden, a Rae supporter, appeared to agree shortly before Christmas to retire if Rae won. But her husband, Ken, a former member of the legislature, talked her out of it. Ken Bryden thought that residents of the riding would revolt at the prospect of a parachute candidate. He thought Rae might lose a by-election.

Bryden also thought Rae would benefit from not being tied down to the legislature. "Having the freedom to get around the province is an advantage," he said. "Being in the legislature asking questions doesn't make much impact. If you're in a small community, you get big press," he noted. He said he "couldn't see the point of the exercise" of forcing a by-election for Rae.

Bryden, a veteran CCFer, thought Rae should hit the road, literally, talking to people and making issues in communities. But Rae was more comfortable in the refined atmosphere of the legislature than making small talk in small towns.

This was just what Donald MacDonald did in 1953 when he was elected CCF leader and did not have a seat. The CCF caucus at the time consisted of just two members, and it was unthinkable that one of them should risk losing his seat, so MacDonald spent his time travelling the province, building the party. Rae was not interested in following this example.

Rae and his people were furious when Marion Bryden backed out of the understanding they thought they had. But as the only woman in caucus, though not a strong women's rights advocate, Bryden had a strong claim on her seat, and the party brass thought it could not push her too hard. It would look very unchivalrous for Rae to force her out. When the music stopped, Bryden was in her seat and Rae was standing around.

Next to be pried from his seat was veteran statesperson Jim Renwick. His Riverdale riding was ideal since it overlapped Rae's federal riding, and was one of the safest seats in the province. Renwick, a Johnston supporter, was not inclined to step aside for Rae, who had told him personally during the leadership campaign that he would not come after Riverdale if he won. Nevertheless, Rae later stood aside while members of the caucus and party put considerable heat on Renwick to retire.

Renwick stood his ground. He told party organizer Gord Brigden and president Marion Chambers that they should have recognized they had a problem when they elected Rae leader. It was up to them, not him, to fix it.

Most of the members of the Riverdale executive were staunch Renwick loyalists and strong Johnston backers still stinging from the Rae campaign's use of slates. Riding officers bluntly let the NDP brass know there would be "all-out war" if they forced Renwick out. They threatened to challenge Rae in a nasty nomination fight and were convinced they could defeat him.

There was a lot of discord in Riverdale, but when the music stopped this time, Rae was left standing and Renwick was still sitting. After winning the leadership in such a convincing fashion, Rae was getting nowhere with the caucus.

Round Three was a short two-step with Tony Grande, a Rae supporter who represented Oakwood in Toronto's Italian west-end. Grande made the case that the Italian community would be annoyed with the NDP if he were forced out for the Anglo leader. The band played on.

On July 6, five months after Rae won the leadership, former leader Donald MacDonald agreed to retire and the music finally stopped. MacDonald represented York South in Toronto's west end, an historic riding once held by the previous Ontario CCF leader, Ted Jolliffe. Federally, it was where CCF teacher Joe Noseworthy had defeated new Tory leader Arthur Meighen in 1942, and was also the riding that David Lewis had represented in the House of Commons. Here, at last, Rae would get his chance.

Incidentally, MacDonald did not leave Queen's Park — he retained his office and staff, and was "hired" as chair of caucus. Though he was entitled to a full pension after 27 years in the house, and drew his salary as a professor at York University, MacDonald was paid from caucus funds — money the staff union argued should be going toward their salaries, not his.

Before making the by-election call, Premier Bill Davis put Rae on hold by waiting until the end of September to set the by-election for November 4th. Rae won easily, his fourth electoral victory in five years, defeating Liberal, and one-time New Democrat, John Nunziata. He was finally on his way into the legislature.

* * *

Bobcita

Shortly after Rae won his seat in York South, an NDP wag wrote a takeoff on the popular musical Evita. Called "Bobcita," it lampooned Rae's quest to make the House his home. "Bobcita" had widespread circulation among Toronto New Democrats and those on the left. Its author, now an elected politician, chooses to remain anonymous.

One of the tunes was called "Don't Cry for Me, Broadview-Greenwood." Another title was "Left-wing Chic." It went like this:
Eyes! Hair! Mouth! Suit! Voice! Style! Glasses!
Movement! Hands! Magic! Glamour! Face! Charisma!
Excitement! Image!

I'm here for the people
They need to adore me
Though really, they bore me,
From my head to my toes,
I need to be dazzling
Not just some dogmatic hick
They must have excitement
Some left-wing chic!

My steelworkers expect me to outshine the enemy — the aristocracy
I won't disappoint them!

I'm their saviour,
That's what they call me
So Lauren Bacall me
Anything goes
I must be fantastic
I have to be left-wing chic
In moderate colours
Just take your pick.

Rae was frustrated at being kept on the sidelines for so long while other caucus members took the lead in the legislature. Widely recognized as an excellent debater, Rae wanted the television lights of question period to shine on him. He won the leadership on the basis of his reputation with the media, and was very eager to strut his stuff. He expected to get good coverage at Queen's Park.

Rae's absence from the legislature was only made the more painful when leadership rival Richard Johnston staged a media coup that fall that brought him a month of sustained coverage, which was unheard of for a third-party New Democrat.

On August 31, Johnston announced that he would live for the next month on the social assistance allowance provided to a single employable man on welfare. To dramatize the deplorable "basic needs" allowance, Johnston took his campaign outside the legislature. As social services critic, he had repeatedly raised questions about inadequate income, shelter allowances and benefits for the poor. Expressing his frustration with parliament,

Johnston said: "The government, the press and even the opposition legislators have not given this issue the emphasis it warrants."

He challenged social services minister Frank Drea to join him in what widely became known as his "welfare diet." Drea refused.

The next day, several television cameras followed Johnston through a supermarket as he bought food on the $56.15 he calculated he would have left after rent and other fixed costs were paid. Newspapers across the province picked up the story. Nearly every day the *Toronto Star* ran a front-page "welfare diet" box, briefly describing what Johnston had to eat that day and how much money he had left. CITY-TV journalist Colin Vaughan took up Johnston's challenge, and tried to make it through the month himself, thus also providing regular coverage.

Johnston got labelled a "hot dog" for his stunt, which he openly admitted was an attempt to get coverage of the issue. But without doubt, people were paying attention — and not just the media. Dozens of poor people wrote or called him with suggestions for cutting costs, with diet and nutrition tips, and with invitations for him to come for homemade soup or chili.

At the end of September, Johnston had lost ten pounds and gained an enormous reputation for caring about people living in poverty. He had eight cents and a few frozen fish sticks left over.

In 1982, concern for the poor was not high on the public agenda. Foodbanks were only starting up, and the media generally ignored poverty issues. Some of Johnston's caucus colleagues worried that his campaign would paint the party as supporting welfare "bums," but they were wrong.

Follow-up stories appeared on local television and in newspapers across the province for months afterward, as the media began to look more closely at the experiences of people in their own communities. Johnston's one-month extra-parliamentary campaign put questions about poverty more in the forefront than a year of questions in the legislature ever would have.

Shortly thereafter, Frank Drea announced a significant increase in social assistance rates.

* * *

If Bob Rae thought getting a caucus member to give up his or her legislative seat was difficult, he had no idea how rough a ride he was going to get from the media gallery once he sat down.

A whiz-kid with the Ottawa media gallery, Rae was convinced that the Toronto media would deliver his message. But political analysts have long recognized the great gulf between coverage in Ottawa and at Toronto, and his star status did not follow him south. Rae and his supporters did not heed warnings from Jim Foulds, Ken Bryden and others that Queen's Park just didn't get the play that the House of Commons did.

In his later years as premier, especially, Bill Davis deliberately low-balled the importance of provincial politics. He recognized that by doing so, he did not raise expectations of what his government should be doing; nor did it generate blame when things went wrong.

The fact is, even with the expansion of the Global television network and with cable TV coverage of the legislature, both of which came after Rae's first years in the House, there still is not an Ontario provincial media. The size of the province, the diversity of its regions, the evolution of locally-owned newspapers, radio and television stations, and the fact of Ontario's emphasis on national politics have all inhibited province-wide media coverage. NDP caucus members privately admitted this at the time, yet still hoped that Rae's profile would transcend the fact. The stardom that Rae failed to generate in Toronto disappointed the caucus and party. "It was a more difficult adjustment than we had expected or counted on," one of Rae's caucus supporters confessed.

In *Out of the Blue*, her account of the collapse of the Tories in 1985, veteran Queen's Park journalist Rosemary Speirs wrote that Rae "soon found that his new job offered less public recognition than life as a federal MP — and a lot of tedious party-building work. He was having less fun, and bearing the enormous weight of responsibility created by the belief that he was the saviour on whose coat-tails everyone else could coast. In fact, Rae had difficulty adapting to provincial politics, where leaders' careers are built on painstaking research that breaks news, not on after-the-fact television commentary, which had been Rae's forte in Ottawa."

While on Parliament Hill, Rae provided a dial-a-clip service to Toronto's popular CBC radio morning show, Metro Morning. He had a standing agreement with the show's producers that they could call him any morning, give him a few minutes' notice, and he would be ready with a quote. Once he became provincial leader, he was frustrated when Metro Morning broke off the arrangement. One of Rae's aides even phoned a Metro Morning producer to complain about the lack of interviews and was told to have Rae call when he had something significant to say.

Individual journalists wanted to take the media-star socialist down a peg, and to show they were as smart as he was. They were not as easily taken in as their parliamentary colleagues; Rae would have to prove himself on their turf. One political analyst attributes some of the Queen's Park media's reaction to Rae as professional jealousy with their more celebrated Parliament Hill counterparts, and says they wanted to prove they were tougher than the Ottawa press gallery. In any case, from Rae's first days in the legislature, he got less coverage than he did in Ottawa, and much of the coverage was negative.

Rae's first press secretary was Peter Mosher, former Queen's Park bureau chief for the *Globe and Mail*. On Rae's behalf, Mosher confronted several reporters whose work the NDP inner circle thought was unfair or inaccurate. This broke one of the cardinal rules of media relations. It also reflected the arrogance Rae brought to the job — the feeling that he was somehow entitled to positive coverage. Similarly, it was a measure of the paranoia of the media that the party had, as if only a conspiracy among journalists would prevent Rae from getting the good coverage he thought he deserved.

Rae was further damaged in the media's eyes when, just three days after he took his seat, he was humiliated by a researcher's mathematical error. He attacked the government for spending $200 for each copy of a health ministry calendar, when the cost was really just $2.00. "It was hardly the kind of performance expected from the federal NDP's finance critic who had been dubbed a 'boy wonder' and 'party saviour,'" John Coleman wrote in the *Windsor Star*. "The sight of Rae shrinking away from insensitive reporters on television that night must have sent shivers up the spines of many party members."

The calendar incident also aroused Rae's suspicions that not just the individual researcher involved, but that the entire research staff — which had unanimously supported Johnston — were out to get him. The research staff were crucial to the Queen's Park operation, and the leader badly needed to have confidence in them. This fiasco undermined that trust.

A researcher of the time says that "Rae made it clear that he saw research as a threat. We were stepping on toes, and challenged caucus members." In his words, they "conceded to allow" Rae to appoint a director of research to oversee the operation, which had run as a collective under Cassidy, but even the director functioned "on our terms," he says. His comments reflect the independence they felt, and which Rae could not accept.

Rae also had a different notion of how the research department was to work. Under Lewis, researchers generally developed issues over the longer term; now, under Rae, the focus shifted more acutely to the one-a-day doses of question period. Whereas Lewis relied on and built sustained attacks on his key issues, Rae adopted a hit-and-run style. After the daily morning question period meetings, where caucus and staff discussed what had been covered in the media, they decided on the day's questions and the researchers were sent off to work up material on that day's media hit. The scatter-gun approach lacked a coherent target.

From the start, Rae the media-whiz had a poor relationship with the Queen's Park gallery, and Rae the Rhodes scholar didn't get along with his research department. It was an ominous beginning.

The Realities of March 19

Whenever the opposition parties criticized Premier Bill Davis for his government's inaction, he took delight in reminding them of "the realities of March 19" — the day in 1981 when he regained his Conservative majority government. The oft-repeated phrase was meant to make sure everyone knew that the Tories were in unfettered control again. The Tories ruled as if by divine right, and their arrogant approach in the legislature between 1981 and 1985 stuck in the craw of New Democrats. It was one reason the NDP couldn't stomach supporting them after the close 1985 election.

The period of dynamic growth in the provincial government was over, brought to its knees by the Henderson report and the restraint budgets of Darcy McKeough in the late 1970s. Now with a comfortable majority, the Conservatives entered into a prolonged period of lethargy. At the same time, the province slid into recession and tens of thousands of workers were laid off while interest rates soared. Cutbacks in the public sector mirrored the loss of jobs in the private sector. The restraint-minded Tories had no intention of using government spending to stimulate the economy, and waited for the private sector to turn things around.

But the economy was not just declining, it was restructuring. In the late 1940s, 60 per cent of workers were in goods producing; by the mid-1980s, 70 per cent were employed in the service sector. In fact, 90 per cent of job growth since 1967 has been in the service sector, a dramatic change that spelled unemployment or lower-paying, non-union jobs for tens of thousands of Ontario's industrial workforce. The proportion of workers employed for fewer than 30 hours a week quadrupled from 4 per cent of all workers in 1953 to 15 per cent by the mid-1980s, and accounted for 40 per cent of all new jobs since 1975. Employment in Ontario's manufacturing sector declined so severely in the early 1980s that it still had not reached pre-1981 levels when the depression of the early 1990s began.

Despite the bad economy and a government in slow motion, Davis and the Conservatives had an easy ride in the first year of their majority mandate. Both Michael Cassidy and Stuart Smith were on their way out, so the NDP and Liberals either had lame-duck leaders or were in the midst of leadership contests. Even when the opposition parties chose their new leaders, they were no match for the experienced and elusive Bill Davis.

In February, 1982, just weeks after Rae's election as leader, the Liberal party chose London Centre MPP David Peterson to replace Stuart Smith, who resigned following his second unsuccessful attempt to bring the Liberals to power. First elected in 1975, Peterson lost to Smith by just 45 votes in the party's 1976 leadership convention, and had soldiered along in the party's right wing in the years since.

In 1982, he won a second-ballot victory over Smith's protege, Sheila Copps. "Both Conservative and NDP observers saw his election as a move to the right for the Liberal party," Graham White wrote, "a shift away from the priorities of Dr. Smith. Some analysts saw potential growth for the NDP on the centre-left." According to Queen's Park journalist Rosemary Speirs, Smith himself suggested that Peterson would "try to be like the Tories and figure that when people get fed up they'll turn to the closest similar party."

Once a light-heavyweight boxer at the University of Toronto, Peterson had not lost his scrappiness, but was at first a political lightweight. Speirs described him as "a nice guy, but no fireball. He was an unsteady performer in the legislature, alternately too soft or too personally nasty." Far from the movie-star image that was crafted for him later, Speirs says "his overall appearance was unimpressive, with his heavy glasses, long black sideburns, petulant mouth, and a five-o'clock shadow. He was no television star, and, beyond that, he was powerless and inept at platform oratory." His 1982 leadership victory "was based on good organization and personal inoffensiveness," she says.

Davis sat back, relaxed, and shifted the gears of the Big Blue Machine into neutral. The government idled. Hydro was going nuclear, but, politically, a person could generate more energy by rubbing a balloon on one's head.

The Battle to Support Abortion Clinics

Political nature abhors a vacuum, and into this one stepped the social movements. Coalition politics, rising from the napalm-scented ashes of the Viet Nam war, took on a new political force in the early 1980s. At the head of the parade were the women's movement and the peace movement, both of which had large numbers of grassroots supporters and which united smaller organizations with a common purpose into broad national coalitions.

The women's movement and peace movement were the vanguard for an array of what some critics labelled "special interest groups." Disappointed by department-store political parties that offered a little of everything but specialized in nothing, organizations mobilized for the rights of gays and lesbians, seniors, visible minorities, the disabled, natives and others. Coalitions demanded protection of the environment and better childcare, and fought against acid rain, nuclear power, free trade and poverty.

They were natural constituencies for the NDP. Most of these coalitions were radically-minded, they were well-organized with thousands of supporters, and they were demanding political solutions to the injustices they encountered. But under Rae's leadership the NDP was unable to overcome its distrust of coalition politics and social movements, which is partly grounded in its fear of communism, the root of many earlier North American movements for social change. The party couldn't make honest efforts to link itself with these forces. Instead, its distrust of their agendas and dislike of their extra-parliamentary direct action found the NDP swimming against these new, major political currents. It left the NDP itself adrift. (Occasionally, elected New Democrats did forge successful links with community activists. At both Toronto's city hall and board of education, municipal New Democrats worked closely with a number of coalitions to their mutual benefit.)

The main struggle among feminists in the early 1980s was for the right of reproductive choice; another key battle was for equal pay. Peace activists wanted an end to the testing of the cruise missile in Canada and the declaration of nuclear-weapons-free zones.

Two elected New Democrats showed a real and ongoing concern with the peace movement's issues: federal MP Dan Heap and provincial MPP Richard Johnston. Both worked hard with peace activists, who reciprocated by donating time, money and supporters to their re-election campaigns. We'll deal with the peace movement in more detail below; here we want to focus on the missed opportunity to make inroads with the women's movement.

In his last year at the University of Toronto, a younger Bob Rae spoke for the affirmative in a debate whose topic was "It should be as easy to have an abortion as it is to have a baby." Years later, his views were more equivocal, when, as leader, Rae attempted to keep the issue behind closed doors.

In the early 1980s, pro-choice activists began to lay the groundwork that was necessary for the establishment of an abortion clinic in Toronto. The Ontario Coalition for Abortion Clinics (OCAC) wanted to build support in the women's community prior to the opening of a clinic so women would be prepared to defend it against the inevitable reaction from the state and from anti-abortionists. By 1982, word was widespread that Dr. Henry Morgentaler would soon open a Toronto clinic.

Morgentaler had been through a long series of expensive trials in Quebec, where despite repeated harassment by the state and after serving time in jail, he was eventually acquitted by juries on three separate occasions. As a result of his acquittals, other abortion clinics opened in Montreal and elsewhere in Quebec; the doctors realized that though they were operating against the law, juries would not convict. Morgentaler and pro-choice activists hoped to achieve the same results in Ontario.

Judy Rebick, who was at the time Morgentaler's chief Ontario spokesperson — and who went on to become president of the Ontario NDP Women's Committee and later of the National Action Committee on the Status of Women — made her first approaches to the NDP over the

Morgentaler issue. She says that even though the right of choice was the key issue in the women's movement, the pro-choice activists were not working with the NDP because they didn't see the point.

In 1982, before Dr. Morgentaler set up his Toronto clinic, the Ontario Coalition for Abortion Clinics (OCAC) approached the NDP Women's Committee for support. At the meeting where this was first raised, the New Democrats sat for a moment in silence. Surprisingly, they looked around the table wondering what to do, because support for private-standing abortion clinics hadn't come up before. The party had a policy dating back to 1971 calling for the decriminalization of abortion, but had not dealt with the specifics of support for private clinics.

It only took a minute for most of the NDP women to realize they should support the OCAC, and they wondered why the issue hadn't been more front and centre before. A pro-choice group of committee members committed itself to seek the leadership of the women's committee at its conference in early 1983. Their goal was to align the NDP with the choice movement and to put the issue of support for Morgentaler on the party agenda.

The women's committee president at the time was Lynn McDonald, who was seeking the nomination to replace Rae in Broadview-Greenwood. McDonald was closely linked to the leader's office and used her position on the committee as a stepping-stone to the nomination. She wanted an acquiescent committee that would not challenge the party. She had low-balled the choice question during her term, and her resistance as chair of the committee only hardened the resolve of the pro-choice activists to make the clinic an issue. They saw it as clearly within the context of the party's commitment to social and economic equality for women.

They were surprised when Rae, personally, as well as his staff moved against them — and lost.

According to Rebick and others involved at the time, Rae's aide Marilyn Roycroft organized a slate of candidates to head off the pro-choice group. The party brass's slate was led by Toronto municipal activist Barbara Hall and included Rae's wife, Arlene Perly Rae. Another person on their team was Marilyne White, whose husband Bob was head of the United Auto Workers' Union.

Here the party establishment made a crucial mistake. Just before Marilyne White was to leave for holiday in Florida, Arlene Perly Rae called her and asked her to run for the women's committee. Naturally, she agreed.

But Rae did not tell her the politics of the situation. The party intended for White to run on a slate blocking pro-choice candidates who wanted the party to be much more active and outspoken on the issue. But White herself was a pro-choice activist, and says the party simply "misread" her. They were trading on her name and her marriage to Bob White.

While on holidays, Marilyne White received a call from Wendy Cuthbertson, the UAW's director of communications, a well-liked and highly-regarded activist for women's rights in the labour movement. Cuthbertson explained to her how she was being used by the party brass. White called Perly Rae and told her how upset she was. She pointed out that Rae hadn't even bothered to find out her position before asking her to run. In the end, they agreed to let White's name stand on the party's slate.

At about the same time, someone from Rae's office called Buzz Hargrove, then assistant to UAW leader Bob White and now president of the autoworkers' union, to try to get Cuthbertson in line. Despite the heavy discipline customary in labour circles, Cuthbertson did not flinch on this issue. She was part of a network of supportive labour women; she also had on her side the fact that the Ontario Federation of Labour convention in the spring of 1982 had already expressed its support for free-standing abortion clinics.

Rebick says the attempt to co-opt Marilyne White and the move to silence Cuthbertson backfired, and "really got labour women charged up." They went into the conference more determined than ever to win.

The pro-choice group's candidate for president of the women's committee was Mary Rowles, then a legislative assistant and the union's chief steward in the NDP caucus — a role that brought her into frequent conflict with NDP caucus management. On the pro-choice slate were Judy Rebick and a number of labour women including — now oddly a member of both slates — Marilyne White. Lynn McDonald derisively and ridiculously referred to the pro-choice activists as "radical lesbian feminists."

At the women's conference where the vote was to be held, carloads of women from Rae's riding of York South arrived just in time for the free lunch, stayed to vote for Rae's slate, and went home. "The thing that surprised us was how open they were about it, bringing all those people from York South," Rowles says. "We didn't mind, except they ate all the lunch."

The pro-choice slate won handily, thanks especially to the votes of labour women. Marilyne White topped the polls. Later that day, when a resolution calling on the party to support the establishment of a clinic was debated, the only person in the room to vote against it was Janet Solberg, sister of Stephen and Michael Lewis.

The experience was instructive for both sides. The party brass, which had always been able to count on labour to do its bidding, learned that labour women did not jump quite as high when asked as their male colleagues did — at least not when it came to women's issues. And the women in the NDP learned that Rae wanted the clinic issue blocked: "It was the single most important issue in the feminist movement and he wanted no part in it," Rowles says.

The pro-choice activists won the battle, but the fight inside the party was just beginning. For years, the Ontario NDP had formally been in support of a woman's right to reproductive choice, but the male-dominated caucus overwhelmingly opposed it. Of the 23 NDP members elected in 1981, 22 were men. The lone woman, Marion Bryden, was a Roman Catholic opposed to abortion. She later changed her view, and took considerable heat in her parish for it. A number of the men were aggressively anti-choice and only two, Jim Renwick and Richard Johnston, were vocally supportive of the choice position.

In 1980 the NDP convention had approved policy that "every woman should have the right to control her own reproductive function," and that "abortion services [should] be available on an equal basis to all women in Ontario." Party policy did not stop fervent anti-abortionists in the NDP caucus — people like Lake Nipigon MPP Jack Stokes (the Speaker of the House), Sudbury MPP Elie Martel, Hamilton MPP Bob Mackenzie and some of the Italian members from west Toronto—from speaking contrary to policy on the issue.

But the existing policy did not mention Morgentaler or private clinics, which was clearly the current issue in the women's community. A very public showdown was bound to come soon over the issue of clinics. Morgentaler's clinic became the litmus test of support for choice, and, by extension, of support for social and political equality for women. It was an ideal opportunity for coalition politics to work, for women outside the party and for the NDP to accomplish their social and political goals together.

In June, 1983, Morgentaler opened a clinic on Toronto's Harbord Street. The clinic faced immediate harassment from evangelical anti-abortionists. Despite having been acquitted three times in Quebec, Morgentaler was still operating outside the law and the public health care system because abortions remained an offense under the federal criminal code.

Shortly after the clinic opened, the NDP women's committee met to plan their actions. "Everyone agreed that we couldn't stay silent," Rowles says. They drafted a press release expressing support. At the time, Rowles was working for Windsor MPP Dave Cooke, and knew how to work the legislative press gallery. "They went nuts" over the release, she says of the party leadership's reaction. "They knew it was an inside job."

Marilyn Roycroft came to Rowles's office and "screamed and yelled," Rowles recalls, until she politely told Roycroft that she had work to do and asked her to leave. Hamilton MPP Bob Mackenzie returned to his office from a fractious caucus meeting, and as he passed Cooke's office he said loud enough for Rowles to hear: "If it was up to me, I'd have her fired." Mackenzie was the party's labour critic and was well known for his support of workers in other workplaces.

On July 5, police arrested Morgentaler and other clinic doctors and shut his Harbord Street clinic. Quite apart from the moral grounds concerning abortion that posed a real dilemma for many people, including New Democrats, support for an illegal clinic proved a real stumbling block for the lawyer Rae. He argued repeatedly that he could not condone illegal acts — though in the past the caucus had supported illegal strikes and backed MPP Ed Ziemba when he was charged after a picket line altercation.

When he finally came to terms with the issue, Rae's view of abortion was based on a civil libertarian view that it was a private matter, and that what went on behind closed doors was not the business of the state. It was similar to his privacy view on another moral question, gay rights. His speech to the party's provincial council in December, 1982 was entitled "Things that Should be Public and Things that Should be Private." The "public" things he referred to were corporate ownership; the private things were gay rights and abortion. "Rae the academic was philosophizing in the abstract when there was a real political struggle going on," Rowles says today.

The day after Morgentaler's arrest, Rae issued a cautiously-worded statement that reflected this behind-closed-doors approach. "What happened yesterday has to concern any of us who think about the fabric of privacy and personal morality in Ontario," he said. "I want to make it clear that I am not protesting an individual arrest or a particular police action. I want to address a different subject: the need to change the law on abortion and to restore rights of privacy and conscience in Canada."

Rae said that abortion should not be a crime, and that "access to abortion should be achieved within the context of the law. We do not condone or advocate breaking the law."

"Those who would make all abortions a crime," he said, "or who would so manipulate the law as to make them virtually impossible in Ontario, are making the fundamental mistake of confusing personal morality and public law. There are a great many people who do not believe in abortion for themselves or their families, indeed who are profoundly opposed to it, but who nonetheless respect a woman's right to make that decision with her doctor. The problem will not disappear with police raids and legal charges," he concluded. "The law is out of step with fairness, and out of step with common sense. The law has to change, and so do governments that fail to respect rights of conscience and privacy."

Rae's tone was a far cry from a much earlier condemnation by Stephen Lewis of Morgentaler's arrest in Montreal. In 1973, Lewis issued a statement at a rally for Morgentaler's defense. "The charges against Dr. Henry Morgentaler constitute a vendetta, executed by the state, against a lonely, brave and principled physician for whom the rights of women are not some pious lip service," Lewis said. "The achievement of justice in this case treads a long, weary road. But it is surely central to the entire struggle for women's rights and as such I am pleased that this demonstration is being held, and I am proud to be associated with it." Lewis's statement laid buried in NDP files, unknown even to the party's feminist activists at the time. Rowles discovered it only after the current struggle was over and sent a copy to Rae.

But the latest Morgentaler arrest, and the galvanized support of party and labour women that followed, forced Rae's hand. Shortly thereafter, Rae spoke at a Queen's Park rally in support of Morgentaler. It was too little, too late. "Rae tried to support choice without mentioning Morgentaler," Rowles says bitterly. "It was a key experience for him, but it was significant only for women in the party. The NDP missed the moment."

While the Ontario charges against Morgentaler wound their way through the courts, NDP women were struggling to get Rae and the party to be more outspoken in support of women's freedom of choice. They were waiting to put specific support for Morgentaler in front of the party at its 1984 convention, and were bolstered by the Ontario Federation of Labour's support for free-standing abortion clinics in 1982. "Labour leaders were responding to the influence of women in their movement," Rebick says. "The women were saying if you represent us, you have to take a pro-choice position. [OFL president Cliff] Pilkey was adamantly pro-choice."

In early 1984, women's committee leaders toured the province talking to party women and organizing for the convention. At the same time, they were working closely with labour and pro-choice activists outside the party.

But Rowles was frustrated by the party's continued refusal to support Morgentaler. "Every time we had a discussion, they had another reason not to support the clinic," she recalls. "It was like dealing with a bunch of Philadelphia lawyers. First they'd say the clinic was illegal, then they'd say it was private; there was always another reason to oppose it."

At convention there was considerable wrangling, but it was evident that a large majority of the delegates supported a strong stand backing Morgentaler. The original resolution put forward by the women's committee was amended to make it even more clear that the party supported the establishment of free-standing abortion clinics and called on the government to drop the charges against Morgentaler and the other doctors. Knowing that the resolution had the overwhelming support of both party and labour women and was bound to pass, the NDP brass knew it could not force a showdown. In the last hours of the convention, delegates approved the resolution. The pro-choice activists had won.

Later that year, Morgentaler was acquitted in Ontario. It was a victory celebrated joyfully by pro-choice activists, but Rae's late conversion failed to win support for the NDP. Rebick remembers it sadly. "Politically, it would have been courageous to do things before Morgentaler was acquitted," she says. "In the early days, the NDP could have made significant gains with women, but they were too late. After the acquittal it was different."

The last chapter in this story was written at the 1986 NDP convention, where Rae himself moved a motion in support of clinics. But by this time he had another motive. At that convention, Rae was busily trying to undermine the appeal of the NDP's left wing to capture the party's elected offices. Ironically, the left's candidate for party president was Judy Rebick; Mary Rowles was running as a vice-president. This time, they lost.

The choice debate was a measure of how the personal was becoming political. As Reaganite and Thatcherite politics of the 1980s tried to depoliticize daily life, the new social movements were successful in trying to politicize what were previously personal issues: abortion, homosexual relationships, domestic violence and child abuse, for example. Rae often seemed uncomfortable with these issues being on the political agenda and with the direct action philosophy of the new left. He was stuck to the old definition of politics being about changing legislatures, not lives.

Give Peace a Chance

The other grassroots coalition at the forefront of social change in the early 1980s was the peace movement. Throughout 1983, MPP Richard Johnston worked closely with peace activists to draw attention to a resolution he had introduced to declare the province a nuclear-weapons-free zone. Known as Resolution One, the intent of Johnston's motion was to ban the manufacture, testing or transportation in Ontario of nuclear weapons and parts that could be used in them.

Already known for his extra-parliamentary manoeuvres, Johnston again moved outside the legislature. Peace activists gathered over 40,000 signatures province-wide on a petition in support of the resolution.

Leading up to the vote on Johnston's resolution, his assistant, Terri Hilborn, organized a week-long series of activities that included a dramatic spoof, Nuclear Potatoes, performed in the legislative assembly building by the Performing Artists for Nuclear Disarmament (PAND). The playwrights included Erika Ritter. It pilloried Bill Davis, who appeared as a Buddha statue with a pipe, Bette Stephenson, with a two-foot high beehive hairdo, Susan Fish and other cabinet ministers for their handling of the too-hot-potato of nuclear disarmament. The Liberals and NDP did not escape attention: Sheila Copps appeared as a cheerleader, and Bob Rae as "the member for Rogers & Hammerstein North." Nuclear Potatoes even garnered a humorous review by the *Globe and Mail*'s theatre critic.

When Johnston's resolution came up for debate in November, 1983, the governing Tories opposed it, very few Liberals voted for it, and it was soundly defeated.

Undaunted, the peace movement continued to organize for nuclear-weapons-free zones over the next several years, winning support in cities and towns across Canada and the western world. They created a political climate that turned voting in support of nuclear-weapons-free zones from a liability to an asset. Thus when Johnston re-introduced his motion in 1986, the governing Liberal party voted heavily in favour. Even a few Tories supported it, and the motion passed easily.

In the years between the two votes, the peace movement changed public opinion to the degree that the Ontario Liberal government would not risk opposing the resolution. Peace activists also became more sophisticated about how to lobby politicians. It was a clear example of how social movements could affect politics, and how they could create a political climate. But only a handful of NDP MPPs saw the weather change. Most continued to rely on stormy moments in question period or in legislative committees.

For the NDP, the years of Davis's majority were "the age of the task force," as one researcher describes it. Frustrated by the lack of action in the legislature, the caucus put together a number of committees to study specific issues: agriculture, the elderly, health and safety, and the North; the party itself established task forces to develop policy on broadcasting, education, Ontario Hydro and others.

The NDP had the right idea — examine the broader scope of issues and develop coherent policies — but it missed being on the cutting edge when it generally failed to include activists from social movements outside the party in its discussions. It was typical of New Democrats to talk to themselves, to rely on insiders, to distrust those on the outside. As a result, the party did not take advantage of the opportunity Davis's slow-motion government afforded them to engage in extra-parliamentary coalition building.

After the caucus task force reports were released amid fanfare at Queen's Park news conferences, accompanied by a series of questions in the legislature by the particular critic, the issues they raised vanished as quickly as they had appeared. Once the party task forces reported to provincial council, the policies they developed just died. There was simply no connection to the world outside the NDP.

The various task forces were all about gathering information for a position, and not at all about building a movement. New Democrats stuck to their long-held view that activists must come to them, and should see the party as their saviour. The NDP wanted this to happen without earning the trust of the movements, which continued to regard the party as opportunistic.

It was bad enough in those areas where the NDP could call upon its own activists, such as the women's movement and peace movement. But in those areas where the party did not have activists — in ethnic communities, and among groups opposed to nuclear energy and among seniors, for example — the NDP's failure to make contacts, forge alliances and build movements left the party on the periphery during a very creative period of extra-parliamentary politics.

Neither Healthy Nor Safe

In November, 1979, Terry Ryan's flaming body was sent flying over a transformer when fumes from the solvent he was using to clean it exploded. Ryan, 23 years old, had his facial bones and jaw broken, was permanently blinded, and lost the full use of his senses of smell and taste. He had been on the job for six weeks.

Ryan was just one of thousands of workers seriously injured on the job every year in Ontario, but his case was different for two reasons. First, the province's new Occupational Health and Safety Act had been passed just the month before; second, his union health and safety rep was Stan Gray.

Gray was a committed workers' advocate and chairperson of the United Electrical Workers Union (UE) Local 504 health and safety committee at the Westinghouse plant in Hamilton, where Ryan worked. The chain of events that Gray unleashed saw his own union side with the Ministry of Labour and with the company; it found the Ontario Federation of Labour supporting Gray against the UE; and it saw Bob Rae dump Elie Martel, the NDP's long-time health and safety critic, because Martel's probing jeopardized the cozy relationship at the top between union leaders and the Tories.

It's an incredible story of union politics and government complicity, and a classic example of how the NDP keeps the labour brass polished. It's also a twisted road that needs mapping.

Back to Terry Ryan. The Ministry of Labour performed a perfunctory investigation of the explosion and absolved the company of any guilt. Doggedly applying provisions of the new law, Gray did his own investigation. It took seven months, but when he was finished, he had 45 pages of material on company negligence and safety violations in handling of the dangerous solvent toluol, source of the fumes that exploded.

He submitted his report to the Ministry of Labour in July, 1980, and one month later the ministry laid 22 charges against Westinghouse and two foremen.

The trial on the charges did not take place until September, 1981. Then, just before Gray and the shop-floor witnesses were to testify, the ministry dropped 20 of the charges and accepted a guilty plea from Westinghouse on the remaining two.

The deal saved the company from damaging testimony and it saved the Ministry of Labour from embarrassing revelations about how inadequate its original investigation had been. The prosecutor even asked the judge to be lenient with Westinghouse, and told him it was their first violation, though the company had been found guilty of another safety offence two years previously. The judge levied a $5,000 fine.

By this time, Gray and other union reps at Westinghouse were on to other complaints, specifically to eliminate dangerous welding and paint fumes. After a number of job refusals (another power of the new Act) and a series of shop-floor petitions, the ministry finally came in to do tests.

First the ministry tested for gases not produced in the arc welding process, and declared the shop safe. The workers screamed, and the ministry came back to do the right tests. This time, the readings were too high, but ministry officials refused to accept them. Tests also showed that the combination of paint vapours was above provincial standards, but then the ministry switched to the wrong guidelines — which were higher — and let the company off the hook again.

A year later, after constant pressure from the shop committee and embarrassing media coverage, Westinghouse installed better ventilation.

By the fall of 1982, Gray and the committee went after the company to switch from leaded paint. Lead had been designated a toxic substance, and readings in the plant showed levels up to 20 times provincial standards. But again the company and the ministry did nothing. A cynic might think a pattern was emerging.

This time, Elie Martel was the spark that ignited a fire.

* * *

Martel held the riding of Sudbury East for the NDP since he was first elected in 1967. He was part of the NDP caucus under Stephen Lewis that brought a high profile to workers' occupational health and safety in the 1970s. The issue was his passion, and as a northerner he had a good understanding of life in the mines and at places like Inco.

Through 1982, Martel put together an advisory committee of health and safety activists, intending to do a tour of the province later that year. The Ontario Federation of Labour was wary; OFL leaders were concerned where all this might lead.

The OFL and the unions tried to load up Martel's advisory committee with their own staff reps — people who would be answerable to their union masters and who could be relied upon to deliver the official line. Even so,

Martel never got the OFL's seal of approval for the tour, and he relied for the most part on people outside official labour circles to help organize the tour and as sources for most of the information that came to light.

John Deverell, whose frequent articles on health and safety for the *Toronto Star* during this period also played a big part in telling the story, calls these sources "Stan Gray's irregulars," after the famous Baker Street urchins who supplied Sherlock Holmes with information. Aside from Stan Gray himself, they included Jim Brophy of the Windsor Occupational Safety and Health Centre (WOSH), a lot of shopfloor rank-and-file members and a few well-placed union staff who cannot be named even today.

At first glance, it seems very surprising that even Martel, with his position and experience, could not count on official OFL co-operation. Surely the Federation considered workers' safety a priority and would be interested in exposing workplace hazards. We will return to this for an explanation below.

In the fall of 1982, Martel took his task force to 10 Ontario communities to hear workers' health and safety problems. News of the lead in the air at Westinghouse became public for the first time at the hearings in Hamilton. Stories of the high lead levels made headlines across the country, and Martel hammered away in the legislature at Tory labour minister Russell Ramsay over conditions in the plant.

By November, with his tour complete, Martel reported in the House on his findings. In some respects, he used the immunity of the legislature to lay allegations at the doorsteps of company officials and labour ministry bureaucrats. (November, 1982, was also the month that Bob Rae won his by-election and was sworn in as the new member for York South.)

Publicity from Martel's tour, his repeated questions in the legislature, and continued shop floor pressure finally forced the minister's hand. In January, 1983, over the objections of senior bureaucrats, Ramsay personally ordered Westinghouse to get the lead out. After months of stonewalling, Westinghouse replaced the paint almost immediately.

That same month, Rae relieved Martel of his responsibilities as health and safety critic, replacing him with Bud Wildman. Martel had not even had time to prepare his written report on the tour. In April, he released "Not Yet Healthy, Not Yet Safe," a devastating critique of workplace conditions around the province. It did not generate much publicity outside an inner circle of activists because he was no longer the critic.

* * *

In December, 1982, after repeated harassment from Westinghouse and intimidation by the Ministry of Labour, Stan Gray laid charges under the Labour Relations Act and the Occupational Health and Safety Act against the company and ministry officials. His complaint claimed that the ministry and the company conspired to cover up a series of safety hazards, and that he had been intimidated and threatened by a ministry official. One incident involved information on high lead levels that Gray gave to Elie Martel, which resulted in Gray's suspension.

In February, 1983, hearings at the Ontario Labour Relations Board began on Gray's charges. As hearings dragged on and his expenses mounted, supporters in the labour movement organized a fundraising drive. In August, the OFL sponsored an appeal for his case. In September, other unions joined the cause. (The final costs amounted to roughly $45,000.)

On the surface, it seems surprising that the OFL would support a maverick activist who didn't even have the backing of his union's leadership. But Gray did have the solid support of the workers in the plant — over three-quarters of them signed a petition demanding that the UE financially support the case Gray launched at the OLRB, and a number of other workers were involved in the case.

In a way, the OFL's financial support for the case came neither on Gray's behalf nor because of the backing of the workers in the plant. The OFL brass had other fish to fry.

The OFL had no use for the UE leadership, whom they considered to be too closely linked to the Communist Party. Since the fight Gray spearheaded was ultimately as much against the UE leadership as against Westinghouse and the ministry, support for the case was a way to undermine the CP-led union. So, in a bizarre twist, organized labour temporarily lined up behind an outspoken dissenter, hoping his continued battles would weaken the UE leadership.

In January, 1984, the labour board handed down its decision. As Carl Kaufman explained in *Our Times*. "The Board's decision substantiates Gray's charges: his health and safety concerns were vindicated, his claims on the threats were upheld, and the Board found these to be objectively intimidating....However, the Board would not award Gray the decision, and this was based on strictly political criteria."

In essence, the OLRB found that although virtually every single one of Gray's allegations was true, the company and ministry actions were consistent with ministry policy of "internal responsibility" and therefore excusable. The charges were dismissed.

(Under the internal responsibility system, management and workers are supposed to resolve their differences without interference by the state. It is not a part of the Act, but it is the key to the ministry's occupational health and safety policy. Most health and safety activists regard the internal responsibility system as biased and inadequate — largely because the powers of the employer and workers are so unequal — and favour more active intervention such as the laying of charges for violations of the Act.)

In hearings at the OLRB, three adjudicators, one each from management and labour, and a neutral chair, decide cases. In this one, former Steelworkers' director Stu Cooke was the labour nominee. Cooke's vote made the decision unanimous. Even knowing that management's nominee and the chair were going to rule against Gray, and therefore that the charges would be dismissed 2-1, Cooke still voted against the workers. As he explained to the *Star*'s John Deverell, "Sometimes you catch more flies with honey than you do with vinegar."

About two months later, Cooke was named head of the WCB's Educational Authority, the branch that controls health and safety training, and which would shortly become the sugar daddy for the OFL's health and safety centre — known by everyone in the business as the Pilkey Institute.

* * *

"The Stan Gray Clause"

As a result of his shop-floor organizing and unflinching determination, the United Electrical Workers brass wanted to shut Stan Gray up. So, of course, did Westinghouse, and he was a frequent target of both the UE and the company.

Westinghouse and the UE eventually negotiated what became known as the "Stan Gray Clause," a provision in the collective agreement limiting the length of service of health and safety reps. Unlike other elected union positions, these reps were appointed by the union's national office; the clause said they could only serve one year, with a possible one year's extension. Gray was its obvious target: they did not negotiate this restriction on other union positions, just for safety reps — and only in the Hamilton-Burlington contract. The clause was such an embarrassment that they removed it when Gray was on his way out.

During the recession in 1982 and 1983, Westinghouse was downsizing and reorganizing its departments. There were layoffs in the plant, but because Gray was a union steward he could not be laid off.

In order to get rid of him, the company transferred — on paper — a number of pro-management workers into his department, giving them a vote for steward. Despite these tactics, after a nasty campaign Gray was re-elected as steward anyway. The very next day, about a month before Christmas, Westinghouse laid off every worker in the department where Gray worked. The company made sure they knew they were laid off because they had elected Gray.

Since he couldn't be laid off, management gave Gray a job sweeping floors.

Finally, back to Rae and Martel, the question of why Martel lost his role as critic, and the matter of organized labour's unofficial position on health and safety issues. It's a position that is often tantamount to selling off shopfloor health and safety.

A career health and safety activist, and an insider during the Martel/Gray affair of the early 1980's, thinks the key is one word: control.

"The OFL didn't support Martel's task force because health and safety is on the back burner," he says. "It's an individual and maverick activity that labour leaders don't control....The control aspect is the key."

He says that labour leaders are always concerned over where health and safety activism might lead. Individual work refusals could be tolerated, but not collective ones. "They wanted to shut down health and safety as an activist function," he says.

The *Star*'s John Deverell adds to the explanation. "To keep up a practical working relationship with employers, [union leaders] have to show that they're in control of the workforce and that the deals they make will stick. The right of individual workers to refuse work and still be paid is a wild card that confronts the employer with unpredictable and possibly very large costs. That really undercuts the value of the collective bargaining deal with the union leader."

Gray puts it a slightly different way. He thinks union leaders sell out health and safety because: "It's part of the deal to enforce labour peace." He says that: "Part of the relationship of unions with the employer and government is that they're selling labour peace in exchange for all kinds of things — some of which are good contracts, some of which are pork chop stuff, some of which are jobs, and some of which are consultation with the big shots. If they don't enforce labour peace, there's no deal. That's what they're selling."

He explains that companies only deal with union leaders and build up a relationship on condition that they enforce peace in the shop. "If they can't do that, all deals are off," Gray says. These deals also encompass the political side, such as contacts with the cabinet, appointments to the Premier's Council, and a raft of formal and informal links. "All that's off if they don't keep the ranks disciplined," Gray maintains.

These motives — the control of shopfloor activists and the selling of labour peace — were behind the move toward joint (management-union) training of health and safety representatives that had already begun in the early 1980s, over the vociferous objections of many union activists including the UE leadership. (The UE was the only OFL union to oppose the joint training and funding proposal.)

Activists argued that it made no more sense for unions to train health and safety reps along side management than it did to train union stewards, negotiators, or grievance officers, etc. with their bosses. To do so was to take the politics out of the situation, and to pretend that management's interests were the same as those of workers.

And there's another reason. Health and safety training is a lucrative business, with lots of money for training and lots of opportunities to reward loyal unionists with appointments. Labour "trades off [union-only] training, which becomes a huge and lucrative pork barrel," one insider says. "So they don't want activists they can't control, and they create a pork barrel, especially when employers fund the system."

He also says that "Elie was attacking the whole system, while [OFL head Cliff] Pilkey was trying to get bucks out of it. Pilkey was working with the Tories and Elie was fighting them, so he [Martel] jeopardized their approach." Windsor activist Jim Brophy points out that "Martel invited health and safety militants to Queen's Park when no one else would talk to them." He says his own centre, WOSH, was on a UAW blacklist for fighting health and safety coverups, but Martel worked with them just the same.

In the clash between Martel and Pilkey, there's a clear winner, and a clear loser.

Martel found himself out of the critic's chair for the one issue that concerned him passionately, and on which he was widely respected and knowledgeable. Sources say that Pilkey went directly to Rae, and that Martel was dumped. Rae didn't even wait for him to complete his report.

The OFL, on the other hand, got $900,000 in funding for its health and safety centre, money from the Wintario lottery that was arranged by the person organized labour considered its inside man, Tim Armstrong.

It will be remembered that it was Armstrong, the deputy minister of labour, who stickhandled the Occupational Health and Safety Act past the Davis government and the labour movement. Armstrong had worked in David Lewis's law office, had represented the UAW legally many times, and was closely tied to Pilkey and UAW leader Bob White. Armstrong was labour's pipeline to Bill Davis, who used him to keep the waters smooth between labour and business. Armstrong also approved labour appointments, so, in tandem with Pilkey, acted as the government's patronage boss.

Gray's charges against Westinghouse and the ministry seemed to point to Armstrong. Pilkey and other labour leaders wanted to protect him. Stu Cooke's vote against Gray at the OLRB showed that big labour was siding with Armstrong in this dispute — despite the financial backing the OFL had given Gray.

"We had Armstrong nailed over a coverup on lead," Gray says. With Martel asking too many questions in the legislature, he was getting too close. "Elie was right, and because of that, they moved him," Gray says.

Gray also recalls a meeting he attended with Rae and Martel to discuss

Gray's charges at the OLRB where "Rae treated Elie like a fool. It was embarrassing," he says. During the meeting, Gray says, Armstrong phoned. Rae took the call, then handed the phone to Martel. Martel left the meeting to see Armstrong. The deputy minister had threatened to sue Martel for libel and Rae ordered Martel to apologize. "Rae humiliated him," Gray says. "He was never the same after that."

In moving Martel out of his portfolio, Rae was doing what the labour brass wanted. More than just bumping Martel, the most effective health and safety crusader the party had since Stephen Lewis, Rae was helping to keep control where labour bosses wanted it — with themselves.

The move toward joint health and safety training was a way to impose discipline on the workers. It helps cool out activists who might otherwise do something labour leaders couldn't control. It also redirects activists toward administrative or bureaucratic positions that get them off the workplace floor, where they can use their experience, activism and organizational talents to mobilize other workers. Finally, joint training was another bargain in the sale of labour peace.

After a suitable period in purgatory, Elie Martel got his job as health and safety critic back. Stan Gray quit Westinghouse in October, 1984 to set up the Hamilton Workers' Occupational Health and Safety Centre with the help of the local Steelworkers' union. Both these moves were a signal of more action to come.

The NDP Underestimates the Liberals

With the Tories in slow motion, the NDP had an opportunity to make political gains, but instead were trapped in their wishful thinking that politics would polarize between themselves and the Conservatives. Most New Democrats underestimated both the effectiveness of David Peterson and the Liberals' willingness to adopt progressive positions.

The Liberals started to prepare themselves for the 1985 opportunity right after Peterson became leader by hiring a number of progressive staff members in key positions. Key among them was Hershell Ezrin, the former University of Toronto disc jockey known to Rae earlier as Captain Buffalo, who became Peterson's principal secretary.

Ezrin was the bull's eye in Peterson's inner circle, a key strategist with considerable influence both before and after Peterson became premier. Ezrin scouted the social movements for capable staff, and wasn't afraid to hire radical and progressive people. As Liberal researcher Gary Gallon put it: "He wanted the best muckrakers he could get," and had Peterson's backing to do it.

Ezrin appointed Tom Zizys, a closet New Democrat, as head of the research department. According to Gallon, who was hired from the environmental movement, Ezrin "didn't care what your political stripe was. 'Think radical' were his words" to describe what he wanted from the people he was looking for. A public affairs lobbyist who watched the Liberals closely says the fact that Peterson hired the radicals "is part of the story, that he attracted them is another part; that he kept them is the real story."

Sensing the Tories were in disarray prior to the 1985 election, the Liberals wanted to make themselves look like they were ready to take over. Gallon says that they "used to cringe" because Rae was a much more able debater than Peterson in the House, but they developed a conscious strategy to overcome that weakness. "We made Peterson and his team look like a potential government, even though Rae looked much better in the legislature," he says. "Peterson always missed the punchline, but we sent out backgrounders to the media, and the media said 'Peterson and his team.'" Unlike the opposition-minded New Democrats, who still acted like an-issue-a-day critics in question period, the Liberals presented themselves as a government in waiting. At the same time, they prepared to outflank the New Democrats.

Former Liberal MPP Eric Cunningham says that "[Premier Bill] Davis had the radical centre the way a squash player occupies the T; the Liberals do it even better." As they approached the 1985 election, the Liberals were getting ready to serve and move to centre court.

* * *

One of the biggest policy and public relations coups the Liberals pulled off was their handling of the Cadillac-Fairview apartment flip. Here was an issue that seemed tailor-made for the NDP, which had fought for and won rent controls in the 1975 campaign. They thought they had a lock on the tenant movement. But after Peterson took hold of the issue, Bob Rae looked like a Johnny-Come-Lately.

In the fall of 1982, almost 11,000 apartment units in Metropolitan Toronto originally owned by Cadillac-Fairview were sold to the Greymac Credit Corp. (an arm of Greymac Trust) for $270 million. The sale involved 26 parcels of land with 65 apartment buildings and was the biggest such deal in Canadian history. The original sale was announced in September, with a closing date of November 5th (moved back from the 16th, because the companies feared government intervention). Late on November 8, Greymac resold the apartments to Kilderkin Investments for $312.5 million, which flipped them the next morning to fifty numbered companies, likely owned by a group of Saudi Arabians, for approximately $500 million.

The sale and re-sales raised serious questions about the stability and regulations of trust companies, and about the ability of the government to control rents in the face of such massive re-financing of apartment units, since a landlord's mortgage costs were legally passed on to tenants. The Tories soon introduced legislation allowing the provincial government to take control of trust companies; they followed up by seizing Greymac Trust, Crown Trust, and Seaway Trust, all of which had been involved in the deals.

But even before the legislature came back into session that fall (when Rae won his seat), the Liberals made headlines for weeks on the issue. They were clearly the beneficiaries of detailed information, much of which came from a professional financial investigator, John Whitelaw.

Whitelaw had offered it to the NDP first, but they turned him down.

When the Cadillac-Fairview sale became public, John Whitelaw approached Dale Martin, then president of the Federation of Metro Tenants' Associations, and offered his expertise. Martin, a New Democrat who later became a downtown Toronto city councillor, suggested that Whitelaw contact the NDP caucus at Queen's Park, which he did.

Unbelievably, the NDP turned down Whitelaw's help; they told him they didn't think the issue would go anywhere. After the first apartment sale was announced in September, the issue died down, but after the November flips, Whitelaw contacted the NDP again. Again they turned him down. Martin says the NDP's refusal of Whitelaw's help was "totally nuts. We couldn't believe it." Instead, the NDP relied on its own research staff, which had little experience in financial investigations and few contacts in financial circles.

Whitelaw went to the Liberals, who quickly offered him a contract to provide them with information on the deal. He wrote about the events for several financial papers, but his deal with the Liberals assured them that he would give them the goods first. Whitelaw was the person brown envelopes and leads were given to.

(The Liberals also hired a team of investigators just to work on this issue. That group included Ann Mason-Apps, a well-known left-wing writer and activist who had applied to work with the NDP and had been rejected.)

Martin says that if the New Democrats had used Whitelaw, "they would have had a clear and unequivocal command of the tenant issue." Instead, Peterson became a tenant spokesperson, plus a spokesperson for those in the financial community who were concerned that lax management was too common. It was, after all, from some high-rollers on Bay Street that Whitelaw's brown-envelope information was coming.

On the media side, the *Globe and Mail* broke the story and kept digging at it. Recognizing that the NDP and his own newspaper were far behind on the issue, a *Toronto Star* reporter suggested to an NDP researcher that they share whatever information they got. The New Democrat turned him down, joking that they were in the position of being "two bums sharing cigarette butts from the gutter."

Rae later admitted privately that Peterson was getting a lot of information, some of it from the trust industry, and blamed the fact that the NDP didn't have too many friends there.

But of course this obscures the real problem: the New Democrats had turned down access to the information, provided by an expert and offered on a platter, because they didn't recognize a big issue when it hit them over the head.

"Until then, the Liberals had no claim on my time," Martin says. "They had no record on tenant matters." He saw the apartment flips as an exciting way to keep the tenant issue alive, and that "a whole front of new issues emerged," but regrets the NDP saw it narrowly, not as one piece of a bigger puzzle. As president of the Tenants' Federation, Martin wrote material on tenant issues that included both Peterson and Rae and he appeared on television with them both.

The failure of the NDP to capitalize on the issue clearly weakened its image as tenant advocates. It also helped "make" David Peterson, as he gained credibility with tenants, the financial community, and the media.

Stories on the apartment flip highlighted rent controls and inadequately monitored trust companies. But the flip was also a sign of another problem — one that most commentators and politicians missed.

The sale showed that Ontario capitalists were abandoning the affordable rental market — a sign that foretold of rental problems in the future. Cadillac-Fairview sold not just to make a profit, but to concentrate its resources elsewhere, particularly in high-rise office towers and shopping plazas across North America. The NDP didn't see this as a tenant issue, and didn't recognize a chance to expose how capitalists make their money.

Martin speculates that the NDP missed the moment on this issue, as it has on many others, because of its opposition mentality. "It may go back to whether New Democrats see themselves capable of government," he said before the 1990 election. "If they have the sense that they have the right to govern, then they would take a broader sense of the issues." Instead, they have a narrow framework of issues that pique their interest, issues usually intended to provide a quick hit. Martin also suggests that the NDP won't spend its time on issues unless there's a quick payback — and that the apartment flip didn't seem like one of those issues.

Finally, there's one last point to make about the NDP's links with social movements, in this case the tenants.

The NDP wanted a close relationship with tenants, and it was clear that New Democrats insisted it be a monogamous one. If tenants were going to play ball with another party, in this case the Liberals, then the NDP considered itself a jilted lover. But the tenant movement, like most of the social movements, is made up of people from the far left to various Tories and Liberals. The NDP had to have loyalty and fidelity; it didn't get it. On the other hand, the Liberals only wanted what they could get from the relationship as long as it lasted.

Waiting for Lefty

The 1982 convention that elected Bob Rae as leader and installed Michael Lewis as provincial secretary brought the leader's office and provincial office together to a degree that they had never been under Michael Cassidy. Now these two power centres worked closely together, exercising uniform control over party operations.

In addition to this new-found uniformity, Lewis brought his considerable talent to the job, something sorely lacking in the provincial secretaries who served during Cassidy's term. Lewis was an organizational whiz-kid, an able backroom boy who had learned well from his father, and who had been heavily involved since his teens in his older brother Stephen's campaigns. By the time he was elected provincial secretary, Michael Lewis was a veteran of campaigns across the country, well-liked and well-respected.

It quickly became apparent that Rae and Lewis intended to centralize power in their offices, turning the party's provincial council into a rubber stamp, and its riding associations into fundraising organizations for the party centre. The ridings would not be centres of political activity but places where membership recruitment and fundraising would have the highest priority. Former NDP vice-president Cam Hopkins quit because there were no longer any negotiations with the ridings over the party's budget. Hopkins says Rae "wanted more resources to fight elections at centre when previously, the initiative was in the ridings." But he and many other riding activists opposed the centralist approach to campaigns, "as if we could ever compete with the corporations," he says.

The most obvious and systematic steps to turn the NDP from a "political movement" to a modern "political party" took place in the first years of Rae and Lewis. The party that they were building would rely on sophisticated polling, huge direct-mail fundraising appeals, and the media to deliver its message. As distinct from a movement, a party is technocratic, centralized, professional, pragmatic, opportunistic and leader-focused. Movements, on the other hand, are generally educational, grass-roots, visionary, organizational and issue-driven.

With these changes taking place, the party's left wing realized it would have to mount a challenge to this centralization of power. Early in 1982, many left-activists, most of whom worked on the Johnston campaign, formed a movement called "For a New Direction." It was process-oriented, rather than policy-oriented — a key shift for the left, which in the past had always addressed itself to debates over hard-line socialist content.

New Directions was concerned primarily with issues of internal party democracy and attempts to reach out to the social movements. The group urged the party to "reach out and be accessible to our supporters and potential supporters: the co-op movement, the gay community, women, the disabled, youth, the unemployed and rank and file working people. We must turn talk into action and we must be there whenever and wherever we are needed."

Though it had the support of roughly a third of the delegates to the 1982 convention, all the candidates it put forward for party positions — with the exception of two who were also on the party's "official slate" — were defeated.

Following the convention, New Directions put together a proposal to eliminate party control over the provincial executive by abandoning the "official slate" drawn up by a select group of party heavyweights, replacing it with nomination by regional representatives at convention. The New Directions proposal would have guaranteed gender parity, assured fair regional representation, and introduced accountability of the executive to the membership.

It brought this idea to the 1984 convention, but Michael Lewis out-smarted New Directions by simply not pulling together the usual committee to draft the "official slate." He made up the list of candidates for office himself, after consultation with a few trusted party insiders. Snookered again, the movement quickly died.

New Directions was significant for more than the fact that it represented an important shift in focus for the left. It was also the first time a broadly-based left wing worked together following the expulsion of the Waffle. But once again, the party could not accommodate its ideas or its advocates.

In years to come, the party adopted an election process very similar to the one advocated by New Directions — but by then the left had splintered into toothpicks of dissent. The election process New Directions had proposed gave more power to the ridings and regions, but by the time it was implemented the left was powerless to take advantage of it — which was precisely why the party centre was prepared to accept it later.

* * *

The party's left wing had not entirely abandoned its commitment to policy development, however. In 1983, the party's Left Caucus devoted a great deal of energy to the preparation of a new manifesto for the federal party. That year marked the 50th anniversary of the founding of the CCF, and the NDP was returning to Regina to commemorate the signing of the Regina Manifesto that launched the party.

Though they celebrated its proclamation, most New Democrats, and certainly the NDP leadership, had abandoned the principles of the famous manifesto and its determination to combat capitalism long before 1983. In particular, they no longer ascribed to its ringing second sentence, which read: "We aim to replace the present capitalist system, with its inherent injustice and inhumanity, by a social order from which the domination and exploitation of one class by another will be eliminated, in which economic planning will supersede unregulated private enterprise and competition, and in which genuine democratic self-government, based upon economic equality will be possible." Its concluding sentence could never have been written about the NDP: "No CCF government will rest content until it has eradicated capitalism and put into operation the full programme of socialized planning...."

For the convention, the party had drafted a new manifesto, called a Statement of Principles. Unlike its 50-year-old counterpart, the new document was long on rhetoric and short on specifics. Critics pointed out that it even failed to mention public health care. It held to the notion of state planning, if not ownership, of the economy: "We reject the capitalist theory that the unregulated law of supply and demand should control the destiny of society and its members," it said. "Society can control its own destiny by planning its future."

No longer looking to eradicate capitalism, the NDP now stood squarely for a mixed economy: "...socialists believe that social ownership is an essential means to achieve our goals. This means not simply the transfer of title of large enterprises to the state. We believe in decentralized ownership and control, including co-operatives and credit unions, greater public accountability, and progressive democratization of the workplace."

The left organized vigorously in opposition to the new statement, and proposed its own Left Caucus Manifesto as a replacement. This manifesto, drafted mainly by the authors of this book, presented a more traditional socialist analysis. It referred to social ownership as "the only solution," and proclaimed that "the half measures of a mixed economy dominated by big business cannot meet the challenge." It advocated sweeping government control: "New Democratic Party governments will replace corporate ownership with social ownership of the major firms in the manufacturing, resource, finance, transportation and communications industries. Only then can we plan for full employment, social equality and economic democracy." The manifesto neatly avoided a discussion of how the state would come to ac -quire these commanding heights of the economy.

Neither document reflected an understanding of the environmental crisis that we face, particularly on a global scale, though both make reference to pollution and waste.

As a drafter of the Left Caucus manifesto and one of the caucus's leaders, Ehring was naturally helping organize the debate in support of the document. This got him into trouble with the autoworkers' union, which he had joined as a public relations officer a few months prior to the convention. First he had a heated shouting match with UAW chief Bob White's assistant, Buzz Hargrove. Then White told Ehring that he would not "speak for, lobby for, or vote for" the Left Caucus manifesto because "the union had decided to support" the party's statement of principles. Ehring's request to know when the union had made this decision, which White clearly regarded as impertinent and insubordinate, was answered simply with an angry "Do I make myself clear?" Ehring learned an important lesson in trade union discipline and saw first hand an example of how White mistook conformity for solidarity.

After one of the most memorable debates in the party's recent history — Rae spoke passionately in favour of the party's document — almost 40 per cent of the delegates supported the Left Caucus manifesto. It was a stunning result, and undoubtedly the biggest showing the organized left had received since the expulsion of the Waffle a decade before. The vote showed the strength of the left and the widespread dissatisfaction with the direction of the party.

Writing in the *Canadian Forum* following the convention, editor John Hutcheson commented that: "The CCF was a cultural movement for equality. It is true that economic questions were central, but a movement that believed that a planned socialist economy would bring about justice, the end of exploitation, and international brotherhood, was a cultural movement which struck deep chords. The NDP still has within its ranks extremely able and dedicated people who have done much to humanize the society in which we live, but it does not now exhibit that sense of purpose."

* * *

The manifesto debate also produced one of the most comical yet pathetic incidents ever to occur at an NDP convention.

Elections for party leader and other officers were to take place the next day. The NDP brass certainly wanted, and anticipated, uncontested support for Ed Broadbent, to show that the party could have a vigorous policy debate and still line up solidly behind its leader.

Perhaps inordinately impressed with the left's showing in the manifesto debate that night, flamboyant and combative Toronto delegate Dale Ritch managed to persuade another Left Caucus member, John Bacher, to run against Broadbent. Left Caucus learned of Bacher's leadership bid only when a frantic Michael Lewis told Ehring about it on the convention floor early the next morning, pleading with him to persuade Bacher to withdraw.

It only took one second to realize that the party's left would have looked ridiculous to mount a challenge to the leader without having organized it — and Bacher himself was a virtual unknown. A number of unhappy and angry Left Caucus activists met with Bacher the minute he showed up on the convention floor, insisting he back out. Unfortunately, by the time Bacher agreed to withdraw, the close of nominations had come and gone; as they were about to inform the convention chair of Bacher's decision, the names of two candidates for leader were announced.

The normally somnolent media leapt to attention, every one of them asking the same question: who on earth is John Bacher?

Dozens of media fanned out across the convention floor of the Regina Agridome to find a person whom none of them would ever recognize. Finally, one camera crew located him and Bacher took off with Dale Ritch, the instigator, in tow.

Bacher high-tailed it across the convention floor, one camera crew at his heels; other reporters joined the chase. The commotion increased as a swarm of media knocked aside delegates to get a look at the man who would be leader. Finding no refuge on the floor, Bacher and Ritch headed for the safest place they could think of quickly: the men's washroom.

They misjudged the determination of the media.

The inside of the washroom was painted canary yellow, and as the TV crews, men and women, forced their way past an overmatched Dale Ritch and went inside, the room lit up like a christmas tree. Two unwitting and innocent New Democrats were standing at the urinals. Startled, one of them turned around to reveal himself to the nation. Bacher hid in a cubicle.

Having watched the comic chase unfold, Ehring hoped to defuse the situation and hurried to the washroom where Bacher and Ritch sought sanctuary. He arrived just in time to witness these events, not knowing whether to laugh or cry. The left was not looking very respectable at the moment.

After a few minutes of negotiation, even the media agreed that perhaps this was not the best place to conduct an interview with a person who was running for leader of the NDP. A hasty deal with the reporters was worked out, and Bacher promised a statement in a few minutes, outside.

Not long afterward, Bacher acquitted himself well with the media, explaining how he had simply hoped to carry on the issues of the previous evening's debate, and to offer delegates an opportunity to vote on their leader, rather than have a simple acclamation. They accepted his explanation, and there was an end to this sorry chapter.

* * *

The surprisingly strong support for the Left Caucus Manifesto at the 1983 convention was a smokescreen hiding the disorganization, fractiousness and sectarian nature of the NDP's left wing in this period. Most of the Waffle leaders had checked out of the party, but their successors were still carrying around their heavy baggage like confused porters.

If the party centre's smashing of the Waffle reflected its paranoia of dissent, the moderate left itself never got over the expulsion and walked on eggshells for fear of alienating party bosses.

The Ontario left had been seriously damaged when six of its leaders quit the caucus in October, 1981. The key figures were MP Dan Heap, former party president Jim Turk, and feminist Kay Macpherson. They resigned because they wanted to avoid organization and permanently-structured confrontation, and to focus on riding work. They saw the Left Caucus becoming bogged down in "abstract policy debates [and the] organizational necessities of a structured left caucus." They raised the Waffle bogeyman by suggesting that this was "a continuation of the sentiment which dominated the Waffle, [and] sees the need for a bureaucratically-structured left caucus which provides an alternative leadership to that of the NDP."

"Since we want to concentrate our energy on political organizing within our ridings and unions," they wrote, "we simply cannot justify the time it takes continually to oppose the undemocratic practice of those within the Ontario Left Caucus who keep pressing for more structure, more meetings, more bureaucracy with less rank-and-file participation."

A response by remaining left caucus leaders showed just how careful the left was about its organizational focus. "Never has any section of the Left Caucus proposed anything even remotely approaching a 'party within a party' strategy,'" they said, and insisted that they were in no way providing an alternative leadership to the NDP. They wrote that "Using the ghost of the Waffle in order to suggest that the Left Caucus has a hidden agenda can only be described as a deliberate attempt to manipulate and scare off Left Caucus members." It is a measure of how careful the left thought it needed to be about itself, and how worried it was about the party centre attacking the left for being an alternate organization.

The left was devolving into a rumpus room for sectarians. In one critique, Wayne Roberts wrote: "If I want to go to a village idiots' convention, I'll go there deliberately, not by mistake when I go to a Left Caucus meeting;" he also wondered if some people might be excluded from caucus meetings not on political, but on psychiatric grounds. It was agonizing to withstand the insufferable diatribes of some of the more socially-challenged participants.

The Left Caucus managed to drive nearly every single woman from its midst with its abstractions and macho, point-scoring sectarianism; they returned to the feminist movement, and every attempt to recruit more left-wing women ended the first time they attended a caucus meeting.

Thus the "organized" left did not contribute to solving the NDP's problems, seldom engaged in meaningful dialogue with the party bosses whom they treated as unregenerate, failed to capitalize on the support it could generate, and lost its activists to the social movements and the labour unions — just as the party did in general. The only people who remained were those with no place else to go, and they liked talking to each other.

And though it was consumed with policy debates, the left also failed to seize the initiative on some of the key new issues of the 1980s, especially the environment.

Of course the party's left wing is mostly to blame for its own incompetence. But the fact is that when the party drove out, smashed, or neutralized its ginger group, it suffered from the loss of their activism, energy, and ideas. Both were the poorer for it.

A Laxer Tiff to Get the Party Moving

On January 1, 1984, James Laxer, the federal party's research director, officially left his job in a blaze of controversy, publicly releasing a report he had prepared for the federal caucus that blasted the NDP's economic policies. The former Waffle leader said that: "The NDP's analysis of economic and social evolution remains locked in the 1950s and 1960s where it had its origins." A wholesale review was necessary: "It is my contention that Canadian social democrats badly need to rethink their positions on the economy, not in minor tactical ways, but from top to bottom. An endless succession of tactical adaptations to the social democratic thought of the past has left the NDP with an economic analysis of little value and an economic program that is a hodgepodge of contradictions and dead-end solutions."

The salvo Laxer fired went to the heart of NDP economic thinking. Because he claimed the NDP had no new economic ideas, and since it triggered a vigorous debate in both federal and provincial sections of the NDP, it's worth examining briefly what he said.

In the fall of 1982, Laxer had urged Broadbent to speak out in favour of deficit control, and when he did so, the federal leader found himself sharply criticized inside the party and from the labour movement. Laxer's days were numbered. He left less than a year later, and completed his contract with the NDP by writing his analysis.

His central thesis was that the party relied too heavily on consumer-led Keynesianism: "The touchstone of NDP economic thought has been the encouragement of consumption rather than production," he said. "In an era in which the nation's productive system is rapidly disintegrating the message is very dated."

"The central idea of current NDP economic thought is that the Canadian economy suffers from a severe case of insufficient economic demand," Laxer wrote. "The NDP's major economic policy idea is this: the Canadian economy needs stimulus to encourage the purchase of goods and services; such stimulus will lead to the rehiring of those now unemployed; once the unemployed have jobs, they too will spend money on goods and services and still more jobs will be created. Since the economy suffers from inadequate demand, the government must act to introduce the badly needed stimulus into the economic system."

But, he continued, the NDP itself cannot decide on the mechanism for this government stimulus: "The NDP rejects some tools of government economic intervention because they could be seen as too radical and could scare off the electorate. It rejects other tools because they seem too accommodating and could turn off party activists. The result is that most of the time the party advocates none of the tools needed in an actual industrial strategy. Instead it leaves the concerns about production where it has always been — in the private sector — while it advocates increasing effective consumer demand."

Former Waffle ally Mel Watkins wrote a sustained critique of Laxer's economic ideas in *This Magazine* in April, saying his report was flawed by "elementary confusion" and "superficial analysis." Watkins complained that what Laxer did was "reduce Keynesian economics to the most simplistic textbook model and then proceed to draw policy conclusions about actual complex economies."

"The flaw is not Keynesianism per se," Watkins wrote. "The problem is the extent of interdependence in the world economy and the need for a clear commitment to buck the system if any national policy is to work. Laxer must come to see that Keynesian policies are not so rigidly constrained, if the will exists, as he claims, for if they are, then so are his proposals. I want to insist that there is room for both, and that the NDP should be pushing both with vigour."

Some in the party welcomed Laxer's criticisms; among them was one-time adversary Stephen Lewis, who called it an "extremely thoughtful analysis," though he said he didn't know "if he's right or wrong," and "wouldn't mind debating some of this." Several federal caucus members publicly welcomed the report, while Broadbent kept mum.

Former federal finance critic Bob Rae called Laxer's attack on the party's policies "totally inaccurate," and disagreed that the party had focused unnecessarily on the issue of insufficient demand. He called the notion that the party was the defender of an economic system in decline a "straw argument." The Ontario NDP's economic researchers, perhaps a bit stung by Laxer's case, sent all caucus members a 16-page, 7,000 word memo that described the report's analysis as "shallow and second-hand." "As is readily evident," they said, "we are not the narrow, reflex demand stimulators criticized by Laxer."

Though he disagreed with much of Laxer's economics, Watkins, along with many others, hit on a real value of Laxer's critique: the fact that it would provoke debate on the economy. Even the *Globe and Mail*, which was not prone to receive either current NDP policies or Laxer's remedies warmly, wrote that "Mr. Laxer's report is said to have made New Democrats wince. If it also makes them think, it will have been worth the wincing." Bill Gillies, a *Toronto Star* editorial writer, said in a column that "Laxer's report may be the first step toward jolting the party out of its self-destructive doldrums."

Watkins lamented: "The economic crisis of the '80s is matched by a political crisis, by an absence of political creativity, a failure of political imagination. No one has any certain answers, whether left, right or centre."

But unlike Lewis's readiness to debate, and Watkins's noting the failure of political imagination, Rae said Laxer's criticism "isn't very helpful," meaning he wished it had not become public. He thus exhibited the chronic problems he has with dissent. He showed he was prepared to foreclose the whole debate on the party's economic policies when he said: "The real target isn't us but is out there."

The internal review that Laxer hoped he would engender never happened, as New Democrats circled the wagons. The federal party complained instead that it expected the report would be used against it in the upcoming election, the contest that swept neo-conservative Brian Mulroney, the most reactionary prime minister in Canadian history, into office.

In his report, Laxer had noted: "One of the most important contributions of radicals, even if they are few in number, is to give a society a valid sense of where power is held. In some ways, that single contribution is worth more than all of the left's legislative programs and electoral efforts. If the left will not tell the people the truth about where power is held, who will?"

By refusing to be drawn into the debate, Rae allowed the Ontario party's poorly-developed economic strategy to remain intact. The NDP continued to rely on the Keynsian mantra, didn't progress beyond the notion of government spending to stimulate the economy, and didn't develop practical "lunchbucket" ideas. The shutting down of Laxer's dissent became more important than listening to what it was that he — and his critics — had to say. When the party came to power in 1990, it had nothing new to offer.

Cardinal Sin

At 2:30 in the afternoon on Thanksgiving Day, 1984, Premier Bill Davis, who knew well where power was held, escorted his wife Kathleen and oldest son Neil into a special meeting of his provincial cabinet. Nearly everyone expected Davis to announce an election for November 22, and this was the last day he could possibly do so. But the highly unusual presence of his wife and son indicated something else was afoot: his retirement.

Ten days earlier, Rosemary Speirs had reported in a front-page *Toronto Star* article that Davis was resigning. The response to her article was a series of swift denials from Davis's close friends and political allies. But the premier just smiled. In fact, he had not yet made up his mind.

On the Sunday before Thanksgiving, during the Davis's traditional turkey dinner at their cottage on Townsend Island in the Georgian Bay—Davis biographer Claire Hoy says it was "between dinner and dessert"—he told his family, simply, "I've decided to retire." They were the first to know; the next day, he told all of Ontario.

Hoy, an unabashed right-wing journalist for the *Toronto Sun*, says that when Davis reached his office that Thanksgiving afternoon, he made two phone calls. One was to Prime Minister Brian Mulroney, who was vacationing in Florida. The other was to Emmett Cardinal Carter, head of the Roman Catholic Church in Canada. Davis phoned to reassure Carter that their deal was still on.

* * *

Bill Davis always agonized over decision-making, sought opinions, took his time, and reached conclusions on his own. But his announcement on June 12, 1984 to extend public funding to the Roman Catholic high school system struck holy terror into his caucus and took even his own minister of education, Bette Stephenson, by surprise. Stephenson was so ticked off that she was the only cabinet minister not to stand and applaud Davis when he made the announcement in the House.

According to Hoy, Davis told his closest advisors at a meeting in May, 1984 called to discuss the possibility of a snap election, that after getting back his majority in 1981, he met with the Catholic hierarchy and "that he had promised Cardinal Carter that during the life of the current government, he would...extend public aid to Roman Catholic separate schools beyond Grade 10 to Grades 11, 12, and 13."

As minister of education in 1971 and then as premier, Davis rejected separate school funding. But over the years he became good friends with bishop and later Cardinal Carter, and now seemed to have made an unbreakable deal with him.

Hoy quotes an anonymous source who was at the May meeting: "Everybody was completely stunned," he says of Davis's decision to extend funding. "He'd done it completely on his own hook. So everybody convinces him he'd better go and see the cardinal and make him understand this isn't the time to do this at the start of a campaign because it could hurt him politically and could drive up sectarian divisions when the Pope was arriving." (Pope John Paul II arrived in Canada in September, 1984, visiting Toronto and Midland, Ontario.)

Hoy says Davis did indeed go to visit Carter, but that the cardinal wouldn't let him off the hook. Hoy's unnamed source says Carter "told Davis he was shocked he'd try to renege on a deal. He said he was a man of his word, a man of honour, and he couldn't believe he would back out. And then the cardinal hit him with the big stick and said: 'If you want to run an election without keeping your word, count on having opposition from every pulpit in every Catholic church in Ontario.' Well, Davis just folded like a three-dollar accordion. That's why there was no election. Nobody will talk about it, but that's what happened."

So on June 12, Davis called an emergency meeting of the Tory caucus just 50 minutes before the afternoon sitting of the legislature and told them he was about to announce the extension of funding. They were, as Hoy says, "flabbergasted." Opposition members of the legislature were just as shocked; both the Liberals and New Democrats favoured full funding, but there had been no signal from the government that they were going in that direction. After Davis made the announcement, all three parties stood and applauded, a rarity in the Ontario House.

Davis denied the events as Hoy described them. Speaking to a select committee of the legislature holding hearings on the funding in 1985, Davis said he never had any deal with Carter, and that "the Cardinal never threatened the first minister of this province." How could he suggest otherwise? Speirs speculates that given their closeness, Carter and Davis may have arrived at a mutual understanding that fell short of a firm commitment from the premier. Whatever the nuance, Davis was leaving a holy mess for his successor.

* * *

For its part, the NDP had endorsed the full public funding of Catholic schools as far back as 1970, and had used the issue effectively in the 1971 and 1975 campaigns when it made breakthroughs with the Italian community in west Toronto. New Democrats argued that both history and constitutional requirements obligated Ontario to fund separate schools. The NDP also felt it was unfair for separate school supporters to pay regular school taxes and then have to pay more for their children to attend Catholic high schools. They won their case in the party that the sons and daughters of Italian and Portuguese construction workers were entitled to the same free, public education that their Anglo Protestant neighbours were.

Once passed, outside of a handful of predominantly Catholic ridings, the policy gathered dust in the party's resolutions book. Through the late 1970s and early 1980s, the issue was almost never brought up.

But when Bill Davis announced that he would extend funding, everything changed. While surprised NDP caucus members rose to applaud, most party members were surprised to learn that it was their policy in the first place. Ironically, it took the Conservative government to agree to implement a long-standing NDP policy before lots of New Democrats figured out they didn't like it. The struggle badly split the party in 1985 and 1986, though it had been on the books for 15 years. As the 1985 election approached, it became the most divisive issue in the party.

It's Miller Time

When Bill Davis resigned, most Tories thought they would sail to another easy victory with whomever the party chose as leader. Polls indicated the Tories had the backing of more than 50 per cent of the population, as high a level of support as they had ever had. After announcing his retirement, Davis called five by-elections for December 13, 1984, wanting to get them out of the way before his successor had to call a general election. The by-election results gave no indication that the Tories were in trouble.

The Tories went into their January leadership convention with four high-profile candidates, all long-serving members of the caucus: Frank Miller, minister of industry; agriculture minister Dennis Timbrell; treasurer Larry Grossman; and attorney-general Roy McMurtry. In a series of behind-the-scenes manoeuvres at the convention—which included Miller delegates voting for Grossman on the second ballot in order to knock off Timbrell—Miller won a close third-ballot victory over Grossman. It was January 26, 1985, and the man from plaid was premier-in-waiting. Bob Rae said: "The Tories have passed the torch to the previous generation."

The Tories were supremely confident of an election victory. "Party pollsters revealed the delegates had made their choices on the basis of who seemed to be the 'nicest guy' and who best reflected their own views, because they believed that the party could win the next election no matter who led the party," said Graham White. "The new premier didn't have to have charisma," Rosemary Speirs wrote, "because neither of the opposition parties looked sufficiently threatening to be taken seriously."

Miller, the wide-grinned used-car salesman from Bracebridge with the plaid jackets hardly seemed the kind of person the Tories would choose to replace the stately Bill Davis. First elected in 1971, Miller was never a big wheel in the Big Blue Machine, despite being health minister and treasurer, as well as holding other portfolios, for Bill Davis. The son of a tool-and-die maker who had died when young Frank was just 13, Miller was as frank as his name, a bright but somehow ordinary man who believed in rags-to-riches success.

Miller had taken a lot of heat for proposing that government could cut expenses by closing several hospitals — a very unpopular move that failed to win support from the Tory cabinet and which forever branded him as a right-winger. As minister of health and treasurer, Miller had also allowed the extra-billing sore to fester.

Just two months after his leadership victory, Miller slipped the campaign machinery into gear and rode into the sunset of the 1985 election, thinking that another tidy Tory majority was just around the corner. Forty-two years of unbroken Conservative rule unfolded behind him. Though Miller was running his first campaign as leader, so were both his opponents, Bob Rae and David Peterson. Only one of them was ready.

Chapter Four: Dealing With The Liberals: 1985-1987

> "...the NDP failed to take Peterson seriously enough when he moved his party onto left-liberal ground and weren't ready for his swift appropriation of the progressive position that Rae had intended to occupy with his moderate NDP platform." — Rosemary Speirs comments on the NDP missing the moment in the 1985 election in *Out of the Blue*.

Don't Shoot the Piano Player

On March 25, 1985, Frank Miller waltzed into the media studio at Queen's Park and confidently called an election for May 2. His party was $2.8 million in debt and had just spent over $5 million on a lavish leadership campaign, but Miller had polls showing his Conservative party with a commanding lead.

Following those polls, most people close to Miller advised him to call the election right away, less than two months after he had been sworn in as premier. In public, Miller promised little change from the Davis rule, a move to reassure those who were concerned about his right-wing views; in private, he moved quickly to reduce the influence of the people who surrounded Davis. Ruling as if by divine right, the Tories fully expected another majority government. In the years following the 1981 election they had become complacent and arrogant, and had quickly ignored the lessons of compromise they had been forced to practice during the minority period from 1975 to 1981.

Miller had barely left the studio when Liberal party workers starting erecting the Liberal backdrop — a bold new logo in traditional Liberal red, with a rising sun foreshadowing the dawn of a new era in Ontario politics. (The sun was quietly removed in 1992 when people joked that it was setting.)

Many Liberal insiders thought the party was running from third place, and David Peterson acted like it. The Liberals had decided they needed to go flat out for the full 37-day campaign, and they were prepared: two campaign buses were parked outside the legislature, engines humming. As soon as Peterson finished his news conference, they were off to his hometown London for a campaign event.

Unlike his uneven performance in the legislature, Peterson came across as polished and competent during the 1985 campaign. Laurentian University political analyst Rand Dyck described him as "a modern, progressive, urban, likeable, young, attractive professional." Throughout the campaign Peterson glad-handed at a frantic pace, and stuck to limited number of issues — job creation, opposition to doctors' extra billing, denticare, sales tax breaks and equal pay. He also proposed to allow the sale of beer and wine in corner stores, an issue that appealed especially to younger Ontarians.

Third into the media studio that March afternoon was Bob Rae, who stumbled out of the starting gate. "Rae admits himself that he wasn't prepared for the campaign," says veteran television reporter Robert Fisher, then CBC TV's Queen's Park reporter. "But they didn't have to bother saying it — it was obvious. They appeared to be completely caught off guard." Two days passed before the NDP campaign got on track, a crucial time during which the NDP appeared indecisive and disorganized — which it was.

The New Democrats had already decided the Tories could not be knocked off, and they were running to become the Official Opposition. They thought Peterson was no match for Rae, who had easily outperformed the Liberal leader in the legislature. This led them to underestimate both his talents and an ideological flexibility that allowed him to get into any position like a yogi. Most New Democrats had forgotten the grittiness of Peterson the boxer and his willingness to fight his way out when he was on the ropes. The NDP also underestimated the value of all the behind-the-scenes organizing the Liberals had been doing — with ethnic communities, for example — since Peterson became leader.

The New David Peterson was a problem for the NDP.

Miller, Peterson and Rae were each in their first campaigns as leader, and they were all out to present an image to the electorate that tried to overcome public impressions of their personalities.

The struggle the Tories faced was to make Miller known to the electorate, for despite his years in the Davis cabinet, he was not well known. He had an image as a used-car salesman from Bracebridge, though he also had a degree in chemical engineering that no one talked about. There were those gaudy plaid jackets, though actually he wore them only once or twice a year, and then to thumb his nose at Bay Street's blue-suited high-rollers. And was he an outspoken, right-wing rural rube, or was he a person capable enough to have had little difficulty grasping the various portfolios he had been handed, including health and treasury?

The Tories went into the 1985 election with an unknown leader, but with a long and stable "container." People thought they were good economic managers and slow but steady reformers, moving at the cautious pace most Ontarians seemed comfortable with. But for many people, Frank Miller did not seem to fit the picture. The recent leadership campaign, in which his rivals played up his right-wing attributes, only made the situation worse. Miller had a hard time living down his reference to himself as the "Ronald Reagan of Ontario," meaning he had good cheer and optimism. He apologized for the remark, explaining that he was not on the far right, but the damage was done.

For his part, Peterson had his image and style remade in the months leading up to the 1985 election. His heavy glasses and long sideburns were gone, his nasty rhetoric was toned down, his most right-wing opinions were moderated, and his most abrasive edges worn off. Part of his image makeover was a trademark red tie and dazzling white shirt for every occasion.

Peterson had been concerned about his television appearance ever since he became leader. In 1983, he casually asked a *Toronto Star* reporter, and prize-winning photographer, for her advice on his looks. She told him that his glasses were a barrier between the viewer and him, and suggested he get rid of them and get contact lenses. "But this is me," Peterson complained. "Then I guess you have to figure out if you want to be premier," she said. A while later he figured it out, and the glasses were gone.

Ever since the legislative session that ended in December, 1984, the Liberals had adopted a calmer and more measured approach in the House. It was part of the party's new style to make Peterson and the caucus appear less antagonistic and wild, more fit and capable of governing.

An example of Peterson's new approach came on December 14, 1984, the legislature's last day before the Christmas holidays. Reflecting on Bill Davis's years in office — it was supposed to be his last day in the House, but Davis didn't show up — Peterson said: "There is gamesmanship to politics. There is organization, fundraising and knocking on doors. However there is the other element of dreams, hopes, aspirations. I believe profoundly it is our responsibility to speak and to plan for the future. There is no other institution in society, except perhaps the church, that has the responsibility of preparing us for the next decade or the next generation."

Long-time Tory Robert Welch was moved to remark: "He was so calm and statesmanlike, I could not believe it was the same person."

Former *Globe and Mail* Queen's Park bureau chief Duncan McMonagle says that he and the press gallery were surprised at how well Peterson performed in the 1985 campaign. He says: "The rap was that he was a small-town bigot with no policy." When *Globe* reporter Rob Stephens, who was travelling on the Liberal campaign bus, said after the first week that the Liberals looked good, "we were all shocked and ribbed him a lot," McMonagle admits. (Stephens was so impressed with the Liberals he ended up working for them. Many of the gallery's reporters took media jobs with the Liberals when they formed the government.)

"David Peterson came across very well on television — poised, sincere, and likeable," political analyst Graham White says. "He had the aura of a man clearly in charge, yet open to new ideas and new political forces; in short, he possessed the invaluable attribute of 'looking like a premier.'"

Feelings toward Peterson had not always been so high, even within his own caucus. In 1984, Liberal MPPs Sheila Copps, Don Boudria, Eric Cunningham and Albert Roy all left Queen's Park to run for the federal party, and Pat Reid and Jim Breithaupt quit politics altogether. The defections to Ottawa and the resignation of Reid and Breithaupt only served to highlight the lack of confidence Liberals had in their leader. According to one former Liberal policy advisor, "there were whispers of a palace revolt" because "the caucus did not see Peterson as a winner." When the Liberals lost two of those four by-elections in December, 1984, their fears seemed confirmed.

Insiders thought Peterson "was friendly and good in coffee clatches, but could never lead in war," the advisor says. As they headed into the 1985 election, the Liberal troops were not enthusiastic. But their leader was true grit.

In the NDP trenches there was uncertainty. Rae's campaign strategists thought the party should run for second place, thinking there was no chance to knock off the Tories, and that to suggest otherwise was unrealistic. Rae himself complained privately that he had never run for second place in his life, but went along. In this case, their cautious campaign showed they missed the huge political change that was unfolding in the province.

As with Miller and Peterson, the NDP was fighting to establish an image for Rae. McMonagle says Rae was torn between being "a goofy, friendly guy and a stern academic theorist." He seemed to be a cold, aloof intellectual who had no fun, so the party tried to warm him up by relying on Rae's talents as a witty song writer. He rode through the 1985 campaign with his portable keyboard on his lap, banging out clever ditties.

The Musical Ride

On the campaign trail, one of Rae's favourite songs was "Frank, They've Turned Your Plaid Suit Blue." Better known in party circles was Rae's medicare song, sung to the tune of "Makin' Whoopee." A few verses went like this:

Another heart. Another hand.
Another liver. Another gland.
There is a reason they like your sneezin.'
They're makin' money.

They're charging you for health care.
They like you feeling worse.
If your appendix is bursting,
Better check your wallet first.

They've got a silver bedpan,
Cheaper model's hard to find.
If my expression's deadpan,
It's still cold on my behind.

The bus was Rae's Musical Ride, but it failed to strike a chord. Because the NDP only had one campaign bus, Rae and the media never had a chance to get away from each other, to let their hair down. The media tired of his singing; on one occasion Rae played and sang virtually non-stop from Cornwall to Toronto and drove everyone nuts. The public wondered if they were being sold an entertainer or a provincial premier.

The party had also tinkered with Rae's looks, trying to make him look older and more responsible. But one CBC producer said Rae "looks like your precocious teenage son, if you have sons who go to private school."

The New Democrats tried to deal with people's impression that Rae was a cold intellectual by portraying him as a witty preppie, but that only played into the real problem of the party's "container:" people did not trust the NDP to run the province. Television pictures of the piano-playing Rae may have served to warm him up, but they did nothing to inspire confidence in his abilities — unless people were voting for a vaudeville performer.

People go to image consultants because they want to change their image without changing reality; it's easier to change hair style than it is to change personality or substance. The New Democrats realized it was easier to alter the image of their leader than it was to deal with their "container," where real problems in the way people perceive them are often based on fact, namely, that they know little about running an economy.

Another part of the NDP's "container" is that it is in the pocket of big labour. In the 1985 campaign, the party tried to deal with that perception by distancing Rae from unions where possible. Terry Moore, an organizer of the leader's tour, says he had instructions to avoid having Rae appear in union halls if there was an alternative. Sudbury activist Harvey Wyers says that the local union executive felt snubbed when Rae refused to meet them at the Steelworkers' Local 6500 hall, and met instead in the President Hotel. "The more 'labour' there was, the less he was at home," McMonagle said. The all-important television would not have footage of Rae cozying up to the labour brass on their own turf.

The outcome of this misguided strategy was not to change the public perception that the NDP and labour were closely linked, because they were and people knew it, but only to make trade unionists angry with Rae and the party. It is hard to imagine there was anything to be gained from people who had no intention of voting for the NDP because of its ties to labour. At the same time, it showed the party's unwillingness to build upon its working-class base and its refusal to treat labour as a positive part of the NDP rather than a liability.

Rae was also personally uncomfortable among the "ordinary Canadians" he was supposed to represent. Robert Fisher reported that Rae's wife Arlene was a much better campaigner than Rae himself, and more at ease with working people during their factory tours. Like Michael Cassidy before him, Rae was terrible at chatting with people.

In the 1985 campaign, the NDP took a giant step toward the centralized, professional, modern political party that Rae, provincial secretary Michael Lewis and the people around them were carefully building. Rae's tour organizers went repeatedly over his route in advance, timing every step, stopwatch in hand.

Though the leader's tour should have run like clockwork, the campaign as a whole was badly organized — its slow start, the silly piano playing, and faulty overall tactics. NDP election strategists missed the signs that the Ontario political scene was changing, and decided to play the campaign as safe as possible. Rae himself certainly knew that change was on the horizon, and said in the legislature in the winter of 1984: "The political mood of this province has begun to shift; that is something I am delighted to see and delighted to note."

Yet unlike the Liberals, who recognized that Miller represented a right-wing shift that presented their party with a political opportunity, for the NDP one Tory was the same as another. The NDP refused to take risks, ran for second place, and worked from strength by protecting incumbents and concentrating on a limited number of potentially winnable seats. They unfolded a very traditional election strategy, but a surprisingly cautious one if they thought change was in the wind.

Political analyst Rand Dyck noted that — despite his piano playing — Rae was low key and often spoke to party groups rather than to the public during the campaign. This in itself was an element of control, of minimizing risks. "If they allowed spontaneity," Wyers said, "some lunatic might break in, a reporter may ask a question. They're afraid to make a mistake. The public is pretty jaded about politicians and see through that."

By the middle of April, it was apparent that the Tories were in real trouble. Things were so bad that even at Tory events the party faithful refused to applaud Miller. It was also clear that the Liberals were picking up their votes. Rae was not the alternative to decades of Tory rule, and, just as damning, his platform was one on which David Peterson could stand with ease. "Rae had attempted to bury some of the old socialist policies that he felt made the NDP unattractive to voters and to place his emphasis on progressive reforms," Rosemary Speirs reported, "But, as he discovered during the election, he staked out ground that could easily be inhabited by David Peterson and his Liberals. Rae ran a principled but uninspired and badly organized campaign at a moment when the province was finally ready to consider real change."

Separate but Equal: Catholic Schools in the 1985 Campaign

There had been no movement on the extension of public funding to Roman Catholic high schools since Bill Davis's June, 1984 announcement. The government had not introduced legislation, though various drafts were said to be in the works.

The five by-elections called in the fall of 1984 gave no hint that the Ontario people were upset at the prospect. But an April Environics poll showed that 45 per cent of Ontarians opposed full funding, while only 42 per cent supported it.

The issue did not become central to the campaign until Toronto's Anglican archbishop Lewis Garnsworthy held a news conference on April 24 to blast the government. He said the government's approach smacked of Naziism and Hitler. His comments were a spark that ignited religious division in the province, setting off a series of charges and counter-charges among political and religious leaders. As Graham White wrote: "The already reeling Tories were again forced into a reactive, defensive position, and their credibility was not aided by public disputes between former Premier Davis and Mr. Miller as to the role played by cabinet, and specifically Mr. Miller, in reaching the decision."

Though all three parties supported the extension of funding, the Tories stood to lose the most because of their traditional support among the large Protestant middle class. Among Roman Catholics, support for the Liberal party ran two to one over the other parties. New Democrats hoped to hold on to their support with working-class Italian and other Catholic voters, but were sharply divided over the issue within the party. The Ontario Secondary School Teachers' Federation (OSSTF), which had influence in the NDP, campaigned for public hearings before funding was extended.

NDP policy dating back to 1970 was based on the so-called "concept of sharing," which called for rationalization of services between the public and Roman Catholic systems. Though practical details were not spelled out in policy, the "concept of sharing" might have meant common use of costly school facilities, such as gymnasiums, libraries, laboratories and computer technology, and possibly joint classroom instruction. Recognizing the validity of constitutional and historical arguments for the extension of funding, some New Democrats argued that the only way to bring this about was to fund the systems equally and insist on shared facilities. Some who opposed the existence of the Catholic system thought that, ultimately, the only way to eliminate it was by forcing joint education. But many New Democrats simply thought the state had no business funding a private and parochial system, especially one that represented the core anti-abortion sentiment in the province, where schools served as centres for teaching anti-choice doctrine, as well as funding and organizing anti-choice organizations and events.

In terms of votes, the extension of funding probably did affect Conservative candidates in 1985 more than those of the other parties. But in terms of the political parties themselves, the NDP likely suffered the greatest division.

For the voters in 1985 who opposed Catholic school funding — perhaps a majority, there was little choice. With all of the major parties on side, there was not even room for a protest vote. In Essex South, the New Democrat finished fourth, behind an independent candidate who ran a strong anti-funding campaign.

The situation foreshadowed the 1987 campaign, when all three parties supported the Meech Lake accord though many people opposed it. Voters were beginning to find such similarity among the parties on major questions. It was no wonder voters despaired that "they're all the same."

OPSEU Sets The Agenda

While the NDP was distancing itself publicly from unions, the Ontario Public Service Employees' Union (OPSEU) was running the most visible campaign in the union's history to raise awareness of the reality of government cutbacks. OPSEU represents over 100,000 provincial public servants and workers in hospitals, community colleges, and government agencies.

OPSEU's political involvement is restrained by the Crown Employees' Collective Bargaining Act (CECBA), which outlaws its direct involvement in partisan politics. In the 1980s, the union waged a number of issue-based, non-partisan campaigns focused on the concerns of its membership and the quality of public services. These included the privatization of parks, overcrowding in jails and psychiatric hospitals, occupational health and safety reforms, and others. OPSEU, unlike most industrial unions, was not tied to the NDP, either through its leadership or in its agenda.

In 1985, OPSEU was in the midst of a serious court challenge by Haileybury College of Mines teacher Merv Lavigne, who had benefitted from the gains negotiated on his behalf by the union, but who objected to the union's use of a small fraction of his dues for political and social purposes. Lavigne was bankrolled by the National Citizen's Coalition, an extreme right-wing organization that trumpets "liberty" but keeps its donors and supporters secret.

Lavigne's suit threatened to undermine the social activism that is essential for the labour movement to articulate its broader goals, and which is a venerable tradition of Canadian unions. Had the courts ruled in Lavigne's favour, which eventually they did not, unions — and not just OPSEU or other public sector unions — would have been unable to use membership money to run public campaigns against free trade, in favour of a woman's right to reproductive choice or improved public pensions, for example.

Considering the restrictions of CECBA and the ongoing Lavigne case, OPSEU could have chosen to keep a low profile during the 1985 election, but the union's new president, James Clancy, wanted to draw attention to t he importance of OPSEU's social involvement. One way to fight Lavigne was to show that the union had a legitimate public role to play. Clancy, who was not an NDP member, did not fit well into the old boy's club of labour New Democrats. His primary goal was not to elect New Democrats but to fight a Tory government committed to cutbacks and the privatization of public services.

Waging a campaign it called "Setting the Agenda," OPSEU spent over $100,000 to whip up its members' enthusiasm for protection from technological change, against cutbacks in social services, in favour of equal pay for women, in opposition to the privatization of parks and other services, and for

the rights of public servants to "blow the whistle" on government misman-
agement or corruption they become aware of in the course of their jobs.

Despite the fact that such a campaign was destined to help opposition
parties, the NDP never understood OPSEU's campaign and tried to get the
union's support in other ways. At a meeting at the Brownstone Hotel in
Toronto, NDP organizers Michael Lewis and Gord Brigden asked Clancy for
desks, typewriters and time off for union staff to work on the NDP campaign. These would have been illegal.

Clancy's assistant, Pauline Seville, also attended the meeting. "They
didn't want us to campaign," she says. "They wanted to control that. We
raised the difficulties around Lavigne as well as CECBA, but the NDP was
asking us to cook the books and endanger the entire union in order to get
some desks and days. The union was keen to fight for the right to be involved
in politics, but donating desks to the NDP wasn't exactly the chosen scenario.
They seemed to think we were using that as a smokescreen. It was even worse
when he [Clancy] hired Wayne [Roberts]. 'It sure makes people talk to have
a Trot on your staff,' they said. It was sure a weird way to ask for stuff."

Clancy rejected the requests made by Lewis and Brigden, and forged
ahead with the union's plan. OPSEU sponsored a series of all-candidates'
meetings around the province, where both the Liberal and NDP candidates
had a chance to shine. The Tories refused to attend, and there was always an
empty chair for their candidate. Clancy would lambaste the government for
its policies and the fact the Conservative party candidate would not participate in the debate.

The campaign was a hit, both with OPSEU's membership and in the
media. Local newspapers, radio and television across Ontario used the
campaign to portray the Conservative collapse. Every meeting drew large
crowds and, outside Toronto, good local media coverage.

The union came to be recognized as a kind of unofficial opposition to the
government. Toward the end of the campaign, when Miller desperately
moved toward the left and announced he would bring in a form of pay equity,
the media went to OPSEU for reaction. Clancy blasted Miller's announcement as "too little, too late."

The OPSEU campaign was a classic example of the NDP's unwillingness
to enter into an equal partnership with the trade union movement. While
Rae was trying to down-play the party's involvement with organized labour,
OPSEU was handing them an opportunity on a platter.

But the NDP just treated the 1985 election as another campaign against
a bad government, with no apparent sense that a dynasty was about to fall.
OPSEU had offered the NDP a genuine parallel campaign that would give
the union the right to name the issues to be put on the public agenda while
the NDP could score points at the all-candidates' meetings, but the NDP

would have preferred the union to release staff. The NDP didn't want a real partnership, it wanted a relation where the party got "stuff" and kept control. In this case, OPSEU was "Setting the Agenda," and the NDP didn't know how best to take advantage of it.

Dead Men Do Wear Plaid

The long-running Tory Dynasty was about to be cancelled. By the end of April the Tories' ratings had collapsed, and there would be no re-run for the man from plaid. Frank Miller had never been able to capture the public imagination or overcome his image as a Reaganite and rural hick. He was not the man for sophisticated Ontario, and for the first time in 42 years, the Tories fell from grace.

On the night of May 2, Miller watched the returns, stunned, in hometown Bracebridge. The Liberals won the popular vote contest, edging the Tories by less than a full percentage point, 37.9 per cent to 37.0 per cent. Rae's New Democrats recovered only slightly from their disastrous 1981 showing, up 2.7 points to 23.8 per cent. The Tories held a slim margin in seats over the Liberals, 52 to 48, with the NDP winning 25, an increase of just two from dissolution.

While the Tories were the big losers, the result was a great disappointment for Bob Rae, who in effect suffered his first political setback at any level. He had confidently predicted the party would win 38 seats and was stung by the results. At the first meeting of the party's provincial council following the election, Rae sat on stage and read the newspaper throughout the discussion on the campaign review, and then complained that the reason he lost was because he wasn't introduced at campaign functions as "the next premier of Ontario." Rae's executive assistant and campaign strategist Hugh Mackenzie prepared an analysis of the results for caucus that was so pollyanna it sounded as if the party had won the election. Typically, the party's analysis hardly went any deeper than that, and once again the NDP denied itself an opportunity for an honest review.

The Conservative party was in real trouble before it elected Frank Miller as its leader, and the blame for its defeat cannot be laid entirely at his doorstep. What surprised many observers was the fact that the Tory collapse appeared so sudden and so complete.

That surprise certainly extended to the New Democrats, who, though they saw change coming, never thought it would be enough to force the Tories from office. Some Liberals, including Peterson and Hershell Ezrin, seem to have sniffed the nosedive that took place once Miller became leader, and positioned themselves better to take advantage of it.

In an unpublished Queen's University thesis, Keith Brownsey argues that the Conservative party's big blue machine was more closely tied into the state apparatus as a government than as a political organization. In the 1980s, the party was decentralizing, with more power going to the ridings — unlike the NDP at the time. Partly as a result of changes to fundraising laws, most Conservative riding associations had lots of money and depended less and less on the party centre for funding. They became increasingly independent. In Brownsey's words, the ridings were now "competing centres of power within the party."

The Tories' enduring strength was based on their power as government, not through the party's ties to the community or through its own riding organizations. They relied on the state as the basis of their power, and so when their support started to collapse among the electorate, there was nothing to prevent the free fall. In effect, what happened to the Tories through the Davis years is the reverse of what is supposed to happen: parties are supposed to capture the state; in this case, the state captured the party. The Conservatives thought and functioned as a government, not as a political party.

In the days following May 2nd, the province's political leaders, their advisors and an entire battery of analysts tried to unravel the political knot the election results produced.

On election night, with his party holding the balance of power, Rae's speech sent signals that the New Democrats were for sale to either the Liberals or Tories. He appeared ready to be seduced by whichever party might offer the better deal. This message made the New Democrats look cynically opportunistic and interested in themselves, not the people of Ontario.

NDP activist David Tomczak, a leader of the Metro Toronto NDP at the time, thinks Rae totally missed the moment. "It was clear that people wanted the Tories out," he said, which was plainly true from the results. "The NDP should have said: 'We won't allow the Tories to form a government and there's no need for a new election. We will propose a program and get the best deal we can for the people of Ontario.'"

But the New Democrats thought they were leaving their options open, and that that route afforded them the best opportunity to work out a deal. At the very least, Rae's response was an indication that the party was surprised by the election's results, as its strategists clearly had not worked out a response in the event of such an outcome. Instead of looking as if he were in the driver's seat, he only looked as if he was for sale.

The New Democrats were perhaps the only players in the game who did not realize immediately that they would have to side with the Liberals. For their part, the Liberals quickly understood that it would have been political suicide for the NDP to prop up the Tories; the only matter at stake was how

an arrangement about Liberal power would be worked out. But David
Peterson was naive about how easy that would be.

Let's Make a Deal

Early on the morning following election day, David Peterson called Bob Rae
and asked him to come on down and make a deal. Rae wondered if the price
was right and said he'd take a few days to meet with his caucus and party, then
talk things over with Peterson.

The two had known each other since the 1960s, when both their families
had cottages nearby on the Rideau. Peterson and Rae were cut from similar
fine cloth — but it was Peterson's family that had radical roots. His father
grew up poor in Saskatchewan and signed the CCF's Regina Manifesto
calling for the eradication of capitalism. Later, he moved to London,
Ontario, where he made his fortune. Since 1982, the two had been bitter
rivals, and Rae was now about to help make Peterson premier. Only the
details needed working out.

The NDP brass was badly split on what to do. Some caucus members
and party heavyweights favoured a formal coalition, others day-to-day
support for the Liberals, and a few, who feared the Liberals, wanted to prop
up the Tories. Rae's preferred option was a Liberal/NDP coalition; some of
the key caucus members including Ross McClellan, Richard Johnston and
NDP house leader Elie Martel shared that view. But when the idea was
discussed in a meeting with the party executive, there was virtually no
support. It is worth pointing out that the debate on coalition did not split
on ideological left/right grounds — there were supporters and opponents of
both views in all camps — but on personal strategic considerations of the
best possible outcome.

Stephen Lewis, already a party icon, thought a coalition was a disastrous
idea that would ruin the party's credibility. Provincial secretary Michael
Lewis also adamantly opposed a coalition. So did oleaginous OFL staff
member Paul Forder, a party vice-president with a long history of obedience
to his masters who was prone to high-decibel fulminations performed on cue.
Forder and Michael Lewis argued long and loud that the Liberals could not
be trusted, and that the NDP should never agree to be part of a Liberal cabinet
where it would be responsible for the government's actions. Both were
graduates of the David Lewis school that taught that Liberals were the NDP's
worst enemy.

Federal leader Ed Broadbent opposed not only a coalition but any
agreement that would bring the Liberals to power. According to Thunder
Bay MP Ernie Epp, most of the federal caucus also strongly opposed a deal

with the Liberals. Federal NDP secretary Dennis Young explained: "We didn't want to see a Liberal renaissance anywhere in the country. We were consciously trying to peel off soft Liberals." He acknowledges that the federal party was hoping to supplant the Liberals as the Official Opposition. After the 1984 federal election, there were just 40 Liberal MPs and 30 New Democrats, and the party's old notion of the disappearing Liberal Party was very much in their minds.

The Sunday morning following the election, Rae met with Broadbent, Autoworkers' union leader Bob White and a handful of other party heavies. White had already told Rae on the phone that he favoured "trying to do something with the Liberals."

In his autobiography, White says that he "played a small part in helping [David Peterson] become premier." Many New Democrats were engaged in countless discussions about the party's possible roles in forming a new government, and White's recounting of how he "saw a way" and single-handedly figured it out is unwittingly hilarious. He writes:

"I bumped into John Sewell, former mayor of Toronto, the next day [after the election]. He said, 'Do you really think there's a chance of getting rid of the Tories?'

"I said, 'I don't know. I've been thinking about it, but I don't know.'

"Later that day I saw a way. The NDP should not prop up the Tories in order to keep a tired government in power. If the NDP supported the Liberals, we could get a fresh perspective that would be good for the system."

A few days later, Rae met with other labour leaders at party headquarters; White did not attend because he was to be at a meeting in Ottawa. He ran into the *Toronto Star*'s John Deverell at the airport, and Deverell asked him what he thought the party should do. White told him the NDP should "dump the Tories," a line that made front page headlines the next day.

Meanwhile, at their meeting, the other labour leaders also narrowly supported some sort of a deal with the Liberals. The next day, they were annoyed to read that White had given his opinion to a reporter at the very time they were meeting to discuss it themselves. It was typical of White, who fiercely expects solidarity, but doesn't always feel obliged to apply those rules to himself.

One of those at the meeting of labour people was Ed Seymour, then a staff member of the Communications Workers' of Canada. He says it was clear that "Rae had already made up his mind," and that the meeting was just pro forma. "Rae is not tuned into the labour movement," Seymour said, "he's tuned into Bob White."

Gradually, New Democrats were coming to the same conclusion that everyone else had already figured out: they would have to support the Liberals in some fashion. Quiet discussions started to take place between senior New

Democrats and Liberals in the days immediately after the election, and before the NDP had decided on its course of action.

One of the Liberal point men was Sean Conway, the young and affable member for Renfrew who was in Peterson's inner circle. He discussed an arrangement with Windsor MPP Dave Cooke, and later at a greasy spoon on Parliament St., with Richard Johnston. The wheels were in motion.

The New Democrats had one major concern: they did not want either the Tories or the Liberals to call a snap election. If that happened, it was clear the NDP would be squeezed out because the contest would be between the other parties to see who would form the government. Their fears of a quick election call were heightened when Frank Miller seemed to speculate that he might force an election over the divisive issue of separate school funding. A crucial feature of any NDP deal with the Liberals would be a guaranteed period of stability in the legislature.

Rosemary Speirs writes that at one caucus meeting, "Rae told his caucus to abandon its dream that the Liberals would disappear and leave the NDP as the alternative to the Conservatives." The NDP concluded that the only way it could overcome the deep distrust of the Liberals that many people in the party felt, and guarantee no quick election, was to force an agreement in writing, one that would bind the two parties. This deal came to be known as an "accord."

The NDP made up a team of MPPs Ross McClellan and Mike Breaugh, and Rae's executive assistant Hugh Mackenzie, to negotiate with the other parties on the text of a deal. This was the price of their support. Interestingly, both McClellan and Breaugh supported a formal coalition with the Liberals — yet, according to a Liberal negotiator, never raised the idea with them formally. NDP house leader Elie Martel, never a Rae favourite, was very bitter when he was left off the team though he, too, supported a coalition. Martel was an old fishing buddy of Bob Elgie's, who was among the Tory negotiators, and Rae thought the two were too close.

The other parties were angry that they were being forced to negotiate a deal, but naturally had to agree to the NDP's process if they wanted support. The Liberals responded with their own heavyweights: Robert Nixon, Sean Conway, Ian Scott and Peterson's principal secretary, Hershell Ezrin. For their part, the Tories picked Larry Grossman, Bob Elgie and party president John Tory.

The first meeting between the New Democrats and Liberals took place on May 13, eleven days after the election. McClellan recalls that the NDP drew up a list of close to a hundred items on which it and the Liberals had the same positions, in the 1985 campaign, which were "whittled down to 35 or 40" before the two sides met for the first time. It did not strike the New Democrats as odd that their platform might be so similar to that of the

Liberals, whom they had always accused of being indistinguishable from Tories. Before the meeting, Peterson told his negotiators not to agree to anything the Liberals had not already promised.

Here, of course, the NDP gave away an enormous opportunity. By having as its starting point only items to which the Liberals had already agreed, the NDP abandoned any attempt to force a Peterson government to adopt new policies. It was a measure of the distrust New Democrats had for the Liberals: getting them to agree in writing to things they had already promised seemed enough of a victory. No new policy items were on the NDP agenda, not even in its initial bargaining position. The NDP certainly had not learned any lessons from its friends in the labour movement about negotiations.

The failure to include new initiatives also meant that the NDP could not release a list of items that the Liberals rejected. That would have allowed the NDP to distance itself from the Liberals, and say to the people of Ontario, "Here are the things the Liberals refused to do. If you want x, y, and z, you need to elect an NDP government."

New Democrats also proceeded to talk with the Tories, though this was essentially a charade and a means to keep up the pressure on the Liberals, as if to suggest the NDP had the possibility of making a deal with Miller's people. The Liberals never took that threat seriously.

Behind the scenes, the NDP was still divided. Many executive members thought the written agreement the caucus was going for was a mistake that would allow the Liberals to take credit for the NDP's agenda. "The accord was a lot of people's second choice," one member of the executive admitted. The considerable tension between the caucus and the party brass lingered even after the deal was signed.

Meanwhile, both Rae and Robert Nixon discussed the constitutionality of their accord with constitutional guru Eugene Forsey, among others. Rae wanted assurances that the deal had at least quasi-legal status, though its real force would be that it was morally binding on Peterson. The best the New Democrats could hope was that if the Liberals reneged on the deal it would cost them at the polls. New Democrats knew that once Peterson was sworn in as premier, there was little they could do to force his hand.

With a little closed-door huffing and puffing, the New Democrats and Liberals finally agreed on a list of measures that a Liberal government would implement. A key to the agreement was the provision that the Liberals would not call an election for at least two years, and that a defeat of a bill in the House, including a budgetary item, would not constitute a question of confidence requiring an election. Rae had the stability he wanted, and Peterson had the job he was after.

Finally, on May 28, the two signed the Accord, formally called "An

Agenda for Reform: Proposals for Minority Parliament." Its final draft was written on the computer in Bob Rae's office. (The Accord text is reprinted as an Appendix.)

The Accord consisted of three "documents:" one list for reforms of the legislature, a second set of "proposals for action first session [sic]," and a third "to be implemented within a framework of fiscal responsibility."

The legislative measures included "legislation on freedom of information and protection of privacy;" the establishment of a number of committees, variously permanent or temporary, including a review of the procedure for public appointments, one on environmental issues, and one to oversee Ontario Hydro; election financing reform; and the introduction of television in the legislature.

The proposals for action in the first session included the implementation of separate school funding; a ban on extra billing by doctors; legislation for equal pay for work of equal value in the public and private sectors; laws to cover first contract legislation for new unions, the designation of toxic substances and language to give workers the right to know about workplace hazards; and reform of tenant protection laws in several areas.

The longer-term proposals included affirmative action and employment equity for women, the disabled and visible minorities; funding for 10,000 co-operative and non-profit housing units; pollution controls; reforms of care for the elderly, of farm financing, of workers' compensation, pensions, and of day care policy; and legislation involving job security, including justification of layoffs and plant closings and improved severance pay.

All in all, the proposed reforms ushered in the most progressive period of change in Ontario history, though there were important gaps. Perhaps the most glaring and significant omission was an end to the construction of the Darlington nuclear generating station, which both the Liberals and NDP had advocated.

Liberal researcher Gary Gallon noted that for all the posturing, his party was very content with what it had agreed to. He recalls Hershell Ezrin's reaction when the deal was done: "He came back laughing after the Accord with the NDP [was signed]. 'They just signed what we wanted to do. We didn't give anything away. There wasn't one thing added. I couldn't believe it; it was so easy,'" Gallon recalls Ezrin saying.

Liberal negotiator Ian Scott, regretting after the 1990 election how difficult the years from 1987 to 1990 had been compared to the Accord years, said that: "Items in the Accord tended to be a superficial cleaning up of old issues. We got the last ten years of Toryism behind us." At the time he was not so sanguine, however, and tried to limit the list. In the House a few weeks after the deal was signed, Ross McClellan quoted Scott when he saw the NDP's list of accord items: "My God, this is the unfulfilled reform program of an entire generation."

In the end, Peterson refused a joint signing ceremony with Rae, and, according to Rosemary Speirs, told a news conference: "I don't want to give you or anyone else the idea that we've formed a coalition. If I am called upon, I will form a Liberal government."

* * *

Though the Liberals had the deal in hand, Peterson still needed to be called upon, and awaited an opportunity to defeat Frank Miller's Tories in the legislature.

On June 4th, Lieutenant Governor John Black Aird read the Conservative government's speech from the throne, a document the opposition and media immediately jumped on as "philosophical harlotry," as Peterson put it. In the media lock-up, reporters joked that the speech had been written by Bob Rae.

Supposedly a statement of the government's general direction, the speech included a list of some 90 initiatives to "honour the mandate for renewal and social progress this assembly has been assigned by the people of Ontario."

These included items few people believed the Conservatives would ever implement, such as employment equity and pay equity in the public sector; legislation on first contracts; pension reform including vested pensions and portability; proclamation of the Spills Bill — which received royal assent in 1979 but had never been proclaimed — and a host of other environmental cleanups. It was clearly a deathbed repentance, as Jim Foulds said, an act of desperation, an abandonment of Tory ideology. Just as clearly, it was window-dressing that Miller knew he would never have to deal with.

As evident as it had been in the months prior to the election, now the differences in approach between the Liberals and the New Democrats became even more obvious. NDP members ranted at the Tories, bearbaiting them in their final days in office. Rae welcomed Tory cabinet minister Bette Stephenson "to this side of the House," said the Ministry of Government Services would provide the Tories with kleenexes over the next couple of weeks, and taunted them to "turn in your keys, fellows."

As the Tories angrily heckled Rae, other New Democrats joined in, and Rae said: "This is fun, Mr. Speaker."

Meanwhile, the Liberals sat mostly quiet through the commotion. They were preparing themselves for more serious times ahead.

On June 18 the Conservative government was defeated, bringing an end to 42 years of unbroken rule. Robert Nixon stood proudly in the House, its longest serving member, wistfully remembering the three short months his father Harry had served as premier, the last Liberal to do so. He recalled that his father had come into the legislature as part of a farmer-labour coalition. "This is an historic day," he said with good reason, "but we should not allow it to be blown out of proportion." He gave credit to the Conservative governments over time for the good things they had done. "We also share in the responsibility to be generous — my very word — and broadminded because of it, to look beyond our differences and to realize that all of us are committed to honest open government with fairness and equity for all," he said.

Ross McClellan spoke for most New Democrats when he admitted that he tasted sweet revenge. "I think this is a great day. The fresh air of democratic change is going to be blowing through the halls of Queen's Park after 42 years of one-party rule, and I think it is a great day for democracy."

McClellan noted that the Conservatives' problem did not begin with Miller; it started in 1981 when they got their majority back. The NDP's anger with the Tories was in part a payback for the contempt and arrogance they had been shown in the years since. "I will never forget the then premier's words about the new realities of March 19," McClellan said. "Then we saw the iron curtain come down and the new ice age begin." The thaw had come.

On June 26, David Peterson and his cabinet were sworn in at an outdoor ceremony designed to indicate an open government without walls. He told the crowd of about 5,000 well-wishers: "This is your day, your government, and your building. Please come in and meet them."

Just a week later, the Liberals presented a throne-speech-like "statement on the resumption of the sitting." Predictably, the new leader of the Official Opposition, Frank Miller, pointed out that the Liberals' speech included only 43 reforms, whereas his had had 90, and moved non-confidence. This angered Rae, who said that although he had intended just to sit and listen, he was compelled to respond. "They still cannot believe they are not the government," he said of the Tories. "They cannot believe that after 42 years nothing has changed. They still think nobody else has the right to have a chance or the right to govern. They think nobody can do it but the Tories because they are divinely guided."

He had leapt to the defence of his Accord partner, doing just what party critics had feared: blurring the lines between Liberals and New Democrats.

* * *

In late 1988, Bob Rae told the *Star*'s Thomas Walkom: "The day after the [1985] election, I knew what the results of the next election would be." He was admitting that he knew that once the Liberals were in power, they would be hard to dislodge. Walkom asked Rae why they didn't support the Tories in that case, and Rae shrugged. The province wanted change, the caucus wanted change, and his personal relations with Miller were not good, he mused.

There will be endless second-guessing about the benefits for the NDP of entering into the Accord with the Liberals. Certainly the enormous Liberal majority in the 1987 election indicates that the Liberals were the beneficiaries of the deal, and the New Democrats, though they were responsible for negotiating the Accord, got little of the credit. Of course we can never know what the outcome would have been had the NDP chosen a different route.

Inside the party, there were many bitter feelings once the Accord was signed. Tension between members of the party executive and the caucus remained high. Many rank and file party members felt shut out of the process, never having an opportunity to participate in discussions about what the party should have done.

Metro Toronto activist David Tomczak said "there was never an open debate on the Accord." He and many others thought the provincial council should have been called together to discuss what the party should do. "The Accord was the ultimate test of their lack of sophistication and ability to discuss," he said. "The question of coalition forces you to the wall in terms of what the party stands for. They opted for the safe approach. It laid bare all problems of the party...and all were found wanting."

Furthermore, the NDP seems never to have even thought to call in the social movements and ask about the most important items on their agendas. If a few leaders from the women's movement or environment movement or ethnic communities, for example, were consulted during the process, it was only because they happened also to be New Democrats. The NDP did not reach out to these groups and ask, "Now we have a chance to get things done. What do you think we should insist on?" Only labour was consulted, of course, because that is where the party's strongest links are.

Maverick NDPer Dale Ritch had buttons printed up marrying the NDP and Liberal logos and reading "Bob Rae, the New Liberals." The buttons immediately became an underground collector's item because, as Ritch said, "everyone wanted a button but few wore one." Ritch says that former provincial secretary Penny Dickens, one of the people who had helped lure Rae from Ottawa, bought a dozen. Party organizer Peter Legacy went to one meeting and found Michael Lewis and Penny Dickens sitting with people from the party's left wing, all of them sporting the buttons. "It was the most incredible thing I ever saw," Legacy said. "These people had ripped each other to shreds for years."

Historian Des Morton thought the Accord itself was good, and said "the province needed it, even if the NDP didn't." Morton thinks the cynicism would have been "devastating" had they backed the Tories. "They knew the

Liberals would look good; getting the deal in writing was the only way to get a piece of the action," he says.

Yet the New Democrats never knew how to take the best advantage of the deal they helped write. In failing to ask for a single item that the Liberals had not already promised, they cut short an opportunity to implement more progressive policies. The NDP was so hung up with its role as opposition it never knew how to play a more dynamic game of influence. Ezrin was right to chuckle that the NDP signed what the Liberals wanted to do, and once having done that, how could the NDP legitimately ask for more?

Rae's reaction on election night and the indecision of the following days shows that the party had never considered the outcome. If it had, it might have been more assertive and, instead of looking like a party on the auction block, might have presented a clear and alternative political vision. Rae could have welcomed the demise of the do-nothing Tories and indicated in public the price of NDP support for the Liberals. If the Liberals had refused to agree with all of their demands — not an unlikely scenario — the NDP could have pictured them as less progressive. New Democrats could have argued that they were getting as much as they could, even if it was not all they would have liked.

On top of that, if they had closer and more legitimate links with the social movements, they might have successfully mobilized those groups for change. The movements could have blasted the specific deficiencies of Liberal legislation and won more than the minimum that was expected from the Accord. Instead, the movements bargained quietly and behind closed doors with the Liberals, and in many cases were co-opted by them in the years following 1985. They made the Liberals look in charge, not inadequate. Even worse, by NDP standards, the social movements — in particular, many different ethnic groups — began a close relationship with the Liberal government. They established connections as insiders that they had never had before.

OPSEU president James Clancy said later that the New Democrats "fronted the agenda and then failed to ensure that they were the bargaining agent for the [social] groups. They turned it over to the Liberals to convene the meetings while the NDP waited outside, and then went after them in the legislature. They hunkered down in Queen's Park and waited for the interest groups to come out of the living room wiping tea and crumpets off their lips. They lost control of the agenda."

Meanwhile, the NDP was caught in a position of voting with the Liberals, for despite the freedom granted to them in the Accord, as well as parliamentary precedent, where the defeat of specific items did not call the confidence of the government into question, the fact is that the NDP seldom voted against them.

To be sure, in the first year or so of the Accord, the press gallery repeatedly made mention of the fact that Rae seemed to be going easy on Peterson. Not surprisingly, Rae denies this charge, but the record speaks for itself.

The NDP caucus felt buoyed following the negotiation of the Accord, largely because it brought down the despised Tories. Some NDP caucus members seemed to believe that the Tories had been defeated more by the NDP's own 25 legislative votes than by the people of Ontario. Nevertheless, caucus members admitted privately that the 1985 election results were a major disappointment. People had turned to the Liberals when they abandoned the Tories, and again the NDP was a bride left at the altar. With the party lacking an honest review mechanism, Hugh Mackenzie could produce a report that made it sound as if the NDP had won the election. Rae could whine at provincial council that he lost because he had not been introduced as "the next premier of Ontario." Down deep, the party knew it had to make some changes, and finally it did.

Tiny Talent Time

When Bob Rae sought a new way to charm the party and the public out of its malaise, he reached all the way to London, England, where former federal NDP secretary Robin Sears could be found serving as deputy secretary of the Socialist International.

One of the press gallery's more erudite television reporters says Rae thought Sears was "some kind of Svengali," referring to the shadowy mesmerist created by novelist George duMaurier in 1894. Lapsing into the vernacular, the same reporter also says, "I don't think I've ever met a bigger prick than Robin Sears."

Svengali, whose name has come to describe a person with an inexplicable and sinister hold over someone, was a fictional character drawn from the experience of Franz Anton Mesmer, the quack physician from whose name we get the word "mesmerize." Mesmer practised his arts in France just prior to the French revolution of 1789, "curing" patients of various maladies by restoring their innate "animal magnetism" through a bizarre use of spells. According to scientist Stephen Jay Gould, when Mesmer performed his wonders, "Bodies would begin to shake, arms and legs would move violently and involuntarily, teeth chatter loudly. Patients would grimace, groan, babble, scream, faint, and fall unconscious."

Robin Sears arrived at Queen's Park early in September, 1985, ready to work his own magic. He was there to cure the caucus and party of its maladies, and he brought with him his own particular brand of mumbo-jumbo.

Rae introduced Sears to a meeting of the NDP Queen's Park staff on the morning of September 11, 1985, a meeting considered so worthy of recollection that the remarks of the leader and his new principal secretary were transcribed and circulated, albeit as CONFIDENTIAL. That transcript sheds light on the personality and style of Sears, and incidentally on the misjudgment of Bob Rae.

Sears "has a real sensitivity on handling personnel problems," Rae told the workers without a hint of irony, "getting a team to work well together. I have some of those qualities but not all of them by far." He went on to say that Sears was there to make changes because "we have...gotten into some bad habits," and "this guy has my 100% support in doing what I'm asking him to do. He is going to make a difference."

And so he did. Sears ushered in a repressive regime that centralized power at his own desk; he belittled caucus, staff and members of the media; he became a one-man Haldeman and Erlichmann jealously guarding access to the leader; he marginalized the talented and influential research department; and he was behind attempts to undercut the collective agreement between the caucus and its workers.

Sears set the tone for his relationship with the staff that morning of September 11 with his very first remarks. "First of all, I want you to know that I will do whatever is humanly possible to live up to your expectations," he said, implying they were considerable and deserved, though few in the room could have had any expectations of him at all. He admonished them for a lack of punctuality, and warned them that "from now on meetings start on time. When a meeting is called for 10:00 the meeting begins at 10:00 even if I'm here talking to the wall."

He said he had "resisted being in a legislative function previously" because "I have not been impressed by the degree to which these staff operations contribute directly to the political advancement of the party. I'm not even sure how directly they reliably contribute to the survival of the incumbent members that are here." To people who had worked hard for many years "in a legislative function" with just those goals in mind, this came as a bit of a let down. It showed, too, that he had a very small understanding of how influential and important those roles were. He was also implying that he personally had been doing much more important work.

Sears said he felt a challenge coming to Queen's Park because of "the circumstances we're in," and suggested that the party would have to learn how to "manage this new experience well." If we fail, he said, "many of us, including me, will be fired because we will have lost sufficient number of members of provincial parliament that our staff budgets will be slashed." He was working his charms.

"It will be from me, ultimately, that the direction of the operations of this office will come at the staff level," he told them, somehow ignoring the fact that members of the legislature assigned work to their staff. "I don't say that because I want to arrogate all authority to myself," he said. Sears then went on to threaten staff with blanket use of the "gross misconduct" clause in their contract that was grounds for dismissal: "I will regard an indiscretion that causes the caucus or the party serious political damage on the part of anybody here, including myself as 'gross misconduct' under the description of that term in the collective agreement."

Then, treating staff like school children, he asked them to "write me 1,000 or 2,000 words about what it is that you do here" and gave them a deadline for their homework. "This isn't a request, by the way, all of those memoranda will be in by 3:00 on Tuesday."

All in all, it was a charming way to begin his rule at Queen's Park.

The spells Sears cast were sufficiently powerful that to this day few people will comment on the record about him, though no-one who crossed his path was left without a strong opinion of him. Caucus members thought he was either brilliant or a fraud. A great many staff members thought he was a conceited, overblown hatchetman. Sears fit a distinction made by Sir Max Beerbohm: "To say that a man is vain means merely that he is pleased with the effect he produces on other people. A conceited man is satisfied with the effect he produces on himself."

One person who worked with Sears in Ottawa, where he was the party's federal secretary beginning at age 24, describes Sears as "arrogant, caught up in own rhetoric, likes to hear himself talk, very aloof." A senior party guru once blasted Sears for his well-known bafflegab and said he "covers up for his lack of formal education by using big words to impress people." (Sears dropped out of Trent University in his first semester. At the time, according to a person who attended Trent, "the only thing you needed to get by at Trent was a pulse" — a good line, if a bit of an exaggeration.) At Queen's Park, his language was described as "baroque;" others said the only school he graduated from was the College of Bullshit-Baffles-Brains. At one point he instructed the researchers, several of whom had graduate degrees, to read Strunk and White's *The Elements of Style*, a guide to clear writing. They were especially insulted that this came from Sears.

Duncan McMonagle, bureau chief for the *Globe and Mail* at the time, says Sears was "widely hated" in the gallery. McMonagle is responsible for nailing Sears with another historical nickname: Vlad the Impaler. The reference was to the legendary 15th century Romanian ruler who had a brutal penchant for impaling his political foes and leaving them to die. Vlad apparently used to dine while listening to their screams, and is the source for the popular mythology that a vampire can be killed by driving a wooden stake through its heart. Friends once gave researcher Graham Murray a wooden cross, garlic strand and a mirror, which he put in his office to ward off vampires. Murray was high on Sears's hit list and was later a victim of Sears's bloodletting. Murray tagged Sears with yet another nickname, Boy Stalin, which caucus staff and media used privately.

A principal source of media contempt for Sears was his appearance on *Dateline Ontario* on October 8, 1986, a CBC-TV show hosted by Robert Fisher. (Fisher has since moved to Global TV, where he does a similar show called *Focus Ontario*.)

On the evening in question, Sears baited Fisher just seconds before going on the air, mocking him for jotting down a comment he wanted to make. "I thought you were more professional than that, Robert," he said. Throughout the show, Sears was condescending and contemptuous of Fisher and the panel of three other journalists. To this day, Fisher says Sears was the most impossible guest he has ever had, and he swore from that point never to have him back on any show he hosted — a promise he kept.

Lorrie Goldstein of the *Toronto Sun*, one of the show's panelists, made reference to the fact that caucus members were afraid of Sears. "Are you aware that when you first came, some of the caucus members were so scared of you that they called you the 'prince of darkness' behind your back?" he asked. "Why do you have this reputation for being so vicious?" When Sears evaded the question, Goldstein tried again: "They say you're warming up, but at the beginning you were like, you know, Darth Vader. I mean it was just like, who is this guy?"

Sears: I think that's what they tell you, Lorrie. They don't tell me that. They don't tell me that.

Goldstein: Well, of course. They're frightened of you. I mean, why is it? Why do they feel that way about you? Aren't socialists supposed to be cuddly and warm?

Sears: Absolutely.

Goldstein: Well, you're not. You're prickly. You come in here, you insult the media. I mean, what's the matter with you?

Sears: I might be a Liberal.

These nasty relations with the press gallery were a serious problem for the NDP, which relied heavily on the media to deliver its message. The party hired Rob Mitchell, who had worked in the real estate section of the *Toronto Sun*, as its new media person, and he tried hard to become friends with members of the gallery. He spent a great deal of time doing damage control necessitated by Sears. The bitterness some journalists felt toward the NDP as a result of their treatment by Sears carried over into their work, and predisposed them to look askance at the party. Mitchell, who has an off-beat sense of black humour that helped him deal with the tensions in the job, was intimidated by Sears and often expected he would be fired.

Sears showed an audacity that is not uncommon in people who are in over their heads, and an unabashed willingness to pontificate on any subject under the sun. When Rosemary Speirs's excellent book on the collapse of the Conservatives was published, Sears wrote two notes to her publisher, berating Macmillan of Canada for the way the book was being marketed. He was good enough to offer them his advice on where it should be placed on the bookshelves.

At the caucus, Sears was also a shameless name-dropper. As a "function-ary" — one of the words he liked to use — of the Socialist International, Sears often had occasion to meet with leaders of socialist parties around the world, and to share his wisdom with them. He often used this name-dropping penchant to try to score points in conversation, saying things like "when I discussed similar matters with Willy Brandt . . ." This irritating habit was never welcome at Queen's Park, where egos are large and fragile. When Swedish prime minister Olaf Palme was murdered in Stockholm, Sears wrote a self-indulgent and maudlin *cri de coeur* and circulated it to caucus and staff. It sounded as if Palme was as close a friend as Sears ever had, a man wise enough to have sought Sears's counsel.

In one sense, as Rae had predicted, Sears managed to bring a team together. The staff and the press gallery were united in their dislike for him. It says a great deal about Rae's judgement of his key staff that he hired and kept Sears on, given how severe and obvious the reactions to him were. The two men were very close, at least up until the 1988 federal election, when labour leaders became very angry with Sears for his role in the campaign and pressured Rae to dump him.

The Defection of David Ramsay

In the 1985 election, NDP candidate David Ramsay defeated the Tories' Eddie Havrot in Timiskaming, a northern Ontario riding that extends around the Temagami wilderness area. Ramsay was ambitious and cocky, a man determined to have a lofty political career.

Ramsay was a newcomer to the NDP, having joined the party in 1983. He was a dairy farmer born in Australia who got involved in municipal politics and had once supported Havrot. In the 1985 election, Ramsay was supported by a number of high-profile local Liberals.

Linda Gavreau, Ramsay's office manager in the 1985 election, says she found it peculiar during the campaign that there were many anonymous donations from Liberals, which were receipted. "There's something not right here," her husband feared. Norm Glaude, a top Liberal lawyer who was later appointed a judge by Premier Peterson, was among those Liberals involved actively in the campaign. (Ramsay met at Glaude's home the night before he defected.) Gavreau says: "We wanted a candidate so we closed our eyes to the facts. We didn't want to think the worst, we thought we were just imagining things."

Just one week after the election, Rene Fontaine, the Liberal MPP for Cochrane North, began to court Ramsay to become a Liberal. Fontaine was the Liberals' only northern member, and as such was certain to be appointed to the cabinet. He knew having more Liberal representation in the north would enhance the party's credibility there. The Liberals also briefly pursued Gilles Pouliot, the NDP member for Lake Nipigon. (Pouliot once told the House that Fontaine had an IQ of 140: 70 in English, and 70 in French. For some reason, Pouliot later apologized. Within a year, Fontaine was kicked out of cabinet over a conflict of interest scandal, resigned his seat, and ran in an August, 1986 by-election that was so trumped up that neither the Conservatives nor NDP bothered to contest it.)

In January, 1986, just seven months after he was first elected, Ramsay began to think seriously about crossing the floor to sit as a Liberal. Ramsay's wife Kathleen, a long-time New Democrat, says she talked him out of it, but the Liberals continued their pursuit. According to Kathleen Ramsay, he discussed this with Sears in February.

In October 1986, Ramsay attended a three-day strategy session of the NDP caucus held in Thunder Bay devoted largely to plans for an anticipated election. Instead of returning home following the meeting, Ramsay went down to Toronto and cleared out his Queen's Park files. Then he went home to New Liskeard and within days held a news conference to announce he was crossing the floor to the Liberals. At the time, Bob Rae was in China.

Environmentalists in the Liberal party both helped persuade him to cross the floor, and to set it up. Owen Smith, a local lawyer and longtime Liberal, played an important role.

Kathy Ingwerson, a local environmental activist, says Ramsay was an opportunist who saw the NDP, which had an electoral machine, as a way to get elected. She supported him when he defected because she saw the NDP as pro-nuclear, and because Ramsay promised he would honour his support for the Temagami wilderness.

At a local news conference announcing his defection, Ramsay said the Accord showed that the Liberal party could be moved to the left. He said he made the right decision for the area and not for his own career, which he thought might be in danger. Ramsay pointed out that the main policies of both the Liberals and the NDP were "very similar," and that he was uncomfortable with the NDP's role of just opposing the government.

He was the first sitting member of the CCF or NDP to cross the floor of the Ontario legislature. But the fact is that Ramsay was a New Democrat in name only. He himself said: "I ran my last campaign as a small-l liberal....It isn't such an abrupt change for people who know me and know how I sit on issues." Jim Morrison, a heritage consultant and a specialist in native issues, was Ramsay's best friend before the defection. Morrison recruited Ramsay to the NDP and says he was never ideologically a New Democrat.

Indeed he was not, and it is a measure of the NDP's 1985 campaign that it neither cared that its candidates were running as small-l liberals, or, worse, that no one could tell. Sears missed this as well. In a note to George Ehring written in March, 1986, Robin Sears says: "Ramsay's conversion was a retrospective conversion. He was an ardent partisan until about Dec. '85, at least in my dealings with him." Sears also wrote: "His treachery was even greater than known. He assured me he was not going the same day he met with Conway. He really is a prize shit, and we all feel a little foolish, I guess."

As duplicitous as his defection was, and as outrageous that he would attend a caucus election strategy meeting just before crossing the floor, Ramsay had a rationale other than his ideological brotherhood with the Liberals. While they were actively courting him, Ramsay says he felt shut out of the picture in the NDP. That may have been his sense, but he cannot have been shut out too far: he was the party's deputy whip. He told colleagues he "felt like he had to make an appointment" to see the leader or his staff, and he commented to staff that he found Sears patronizing.

NDP caucus members were stunned and bitterly resented Ramsay's crossing the floor. It was the occasion for Robin Sears's appearance on Robert Fisher's *Dateline Ontario*.

Fisher questioned Sears about his having apparently gathered clippings from Toronto newspapers about the defection and sent them to Ramsay. Though Sears denied this on the show, he had gleefully told members of the NDP staff that he had done so. The panel of journalists that night did not question Sears about another of his responses to Ramsay's defection: spreading rumours about his marital infidelity.

According to *Globe* bureau chief Duncan McMonagle, when Ramsay crossed the floor, Sears called reporters one at a time and talked about an affair Ramsay was having. "Everybody knew about that — that was pretty low," he says. Sears even invited McMonagle and Fisher to his office so he could tell them a litany of personal information on Ramsay — information they never reported.

But that was not the worst of it. In February 1987, four months after the defection, Bob Rae went on an open-line show on Haileybury radio station CJCT hosted by Rick Stowe, a known New Democrat. Rae was naturally bitter about the whole business, referred to the defection as treachery, and said it was like finding the person you're living with is going out with someone else. This comment was a scarcely veiled hint.

Kathleen Ramsay, who had remained a New Democrat, phoned in to say that some of Rae's statements were very harsh and that he should at least have waited for her husband to be in town to defend himself. Of course Ramsay crossed the floor when Rae was out of the country. She and Rae had an acrimonious on-air conversation, in which he said: "I know things about him even you don't know," and: "There may be a lot of things going on that perhaps Mrs. Ramsay doesn't know either."

At the time, Kathleen Ramsay apparently had not heard rumours about her husband's affair with a prominent Liberal. It was her friend Jim Morrison who finally told her about it — after the radio show.

The defection of David Ramsay is much more than the sad story of a turncoat who never changed suits but just put on a red tie. It should have served as a warning to where the NDP was going with its 1985 campaign that made them indistinguishable from Liberals, and then signed an Accord in which they lost their identity.

Political defectors often pay a price at the polls, but in 1987 Liberal cabinet minister David Ramsay, who received just over 50 per cent of the vote in 1985 as a New Democrat, was returned with 48.9 per cent. Because he was so easily elected as a Liberal in 1987, his defection is also an example of how the party failed to hold its own in an area racked by economic crisis and mass layoffs, an area with a tradition of tough labour action. (In 1919, there was a general strike in Cobalt to back the Winnipeg General Strike, and in 1942 a Kirkland Lake strike started the upsurge toward the Congress of Industrial Organization (CIO) in Ontario.) The NDP couldn't hold its vote in the face of a declining economy and against a political defector.

It is also the story of deplorable media relations from the leader's office — Sears's phone calls and his *Dateline Ontario* appearance — and a lack of control and taste from Rae during his public exchange with Kathleen Ramsay.

Finally, his re-election was a sign that northern environmentalists felt out of place in the NDP, as a number of them aided him in his defection and joined the Liberals afterward. In the 1987 election the NDP ran former MPP Bob Bain, who became so hostile to environmental issues that many of the remaining NDP environmentalists joined the Green Party.

* * *

Ramsay's defection paved the way for a second betrayal, this time by Tony Lupusella, the New Democrat from Dovercourt in west-end Toronto. Following the 1985 election, Ontario provincial ridings were redistributed, which resulted in a re-drawing of the political map in the city. Ross McClellan's Bellwoods riding and Lupusella's Dovercourt shifted boundaries and were merged, with the new single riding, still called Dovercourt, taking up about half of the former Bellwoods.

The party tried to manufacture an appointment for Lupusella so McClellan could run in the new Dovercourt, but Lupusella refused to go. The two fought a bitter nomination fight, narrowly won by McClellan.

Lupusella petulantly and publicly accused Rae of selling him out. He refused to attend the legislature, and, once Ramsay had paved the way, tried to gain acceptance into the Liberal caucus. Premier David Peterson privately admitted he didn't want Lupusella, but in the end argued in caucus that the Liberal party should be open to everyone. The vote to accept him was close.

Lupusella, a staunch activist on behalf of injured workers when he was first elected in 1975, had suffered a serious nervous breakdown just prior to the 1981 campaign. It left him unable to work for almost a year. He always claimed it was a much shorter time, but the fact is that both Michael Cassidy and Rae covered for him over a lengthy period. Recurring depression forced his hospitalization again in early 1986.

McClellan, on the other hand, was a shrewd politician and a man of far greater talent than Lupusella. He was architect and chief negotiator of the Accord, and the party could not afford to lose him. The party was immensely relieved when he won the nomination.

But Lupusella's departure, coming just two months after Ramsay crossed the floor, gave the impression that the New Democrats were coming apart at the seams. It was just one more indication that people saw little difference between them and the Liberals. Rae issued a bitter statement on Lupusella's defection, making scarcely concealed attacks on his stability. Rae said "the pressure of political life has been overwhelming for Tony for some time," and said that he (Rae) had "made every effort to help him through this difficult period." He concluded with a cheap parting shot: "his work on behalf of injured workers and in the Italian community, until recent years, will be long remembered."

Meanwhile, in the legislature, the Tories kept pressure on the NDP by voting against the Liberals while the New Democrats voted with them. Media attention was focused on the new premier, and the NDP had its own Vlad the Impaler making media relations difficult. It was a tough time for New Democrats.

All the Better to See You With

If New Democrats needed a new vision, maybe new glasses for Bob Rae were the answer.

Late in 1986, two women from Rae's staff visited Toronto optometrist Mel Rapp, a well-known maker of individually-designed eyeglass frames, and asked if they could have some samples of frames that might suit Rae. One of Rapp's assistants mentioned to them that she knew someone at Queen's Park, and when asked who, she told them she was television reporter Robert Fisher's sister-in-law.

Rae's staff were immediately on guard, and demanded that she say nothing of this to anyone. They treated the new glasses like a state secret.

Nothing much came of it, and over the Christmas holidays, Cathy Fisher did tell her brother-in-law about it. Fisher mentioned an impending image make-over on the air, and Rae's staff were furious. One of them phoned Rapp and came close to demanding that Cathy Fisher be fired. Rae himself was cooler about it and phoned Rapp to tell him he hoped he would not fire her. Rapp told Rae he had no intention of firing Fisher because she was a more valuable employee now.

The incident is a measure of the media paranoia in Rae's office, and though they never did get glasses from Rapp, they were tinkering with Rae's image. They tried contact lenses — which had done so much for Peterson — but with Rae's pale face, blond hair and thin lips, he looked washed out. His features disappeared and the glasses were back.

Later in 1987, for just one day, Rae appeared in the House with a bizarre pompadour hairdo. "His hair was all puffed up, and if he didn't use a whole bottle of mousse to get it like that, it was at least half a bottle," Robert Fisher says. Rae was wearing a blue suit and bright yellow tie.

Reporters were astonished by Rae's new appearance. So was the NDP caucus. The next day, Rae was back to normal.

The party's problem was not with Rae's image, but with its politics. Still, they were trying new things to get people to pay attention to them. That even included buying a half hour of television time.

In December, 1986, the party aired a show called "Standing Up for Ontario," an NDP promotion and fund-raising gimmick featuring *The Beachcombers* star Bruno Gerussi and author Pierre Berton. In it, they extolled the virtues of the NDP and asked people to call in with pledges on their Mastercard or Visa. The socialist party was resorting to consumer capitalism, and its lead-in on Global Television was *The Wheel of Fortune.*

Gerussi, with footage of British Columbia's stunning landscape behind him, told of the good things the NDP was doing for Ontario. Berton went on about the advances made as a result of the CCF and NDP — such as medicare and pensions — as if the party were championing similar causes then. And the phone numbers flashed across the bottom of the screen.

Dubbed "Bob Rae: The Movie" by the press gallery, it showed Rae deftly raking leaves with one arm while cradling one of his daughters with the other.

Despite the fact that the show did make some money, if the NDP had any luck at all, it was bad luck. Loyal New Democrats — and others — who watched the show at 7:30 p.m., might likely have switched at 8:00 to the

CBC's *fifth estate*. That very night, the *fifth estate* broadcast a segment in which maverick lawyer Harry Kopyto, a bombastic and revolutionary thorn in the side of the NDP brass, described how he found the roots of his socialism at an NDP meeting.

The Liberals Move in on the Movements

From 1985 to 1987, among the more stunning political advances the Liberals made were their inroads with the social movements and with many ethnic communities. The 1980s were the decade when political coalitions came into their own, uniting many of these movements in various political fronts.

For example, the disabled, gays and lesbians, members of visible minorities, seniors and women fought together for human rights. Environmentalists and peace movement activists forged links to make the world not just a safer place to live, but cleaner and healthier. Protecting the planet from nuclear weapons and protecting it from global warming became a common cause. The childcare movement, the choice movement and the labour movement worked together to broaden the social and economic rights, equalities and opportunities for women.

The social movements learned not just to march to their own different drummer but to parade together. In a time of designer politics, when members of every interest group wore their own label on the front of their shirts, coalitions broadened the political perspective. They formed a political bandwagon that the Liberals, at least in Ontario, were the first — and most successful — to jump on.

Modern capitalism has been successful at de-politicizing life to the extent that many people believe governments are elected not to "govern," which implies making choices, but to "manage," which means making technocratic decisions in a world run by the marketplace. Coalition politics, because it is mass action, helps to break down the distance between politics and people's individual lives. Coalitions realized that political action was a real part of finding the solution for the problems they sought to redress.

The rise of mass pressure politics coincides with the growth of "modern" political parties, in which parties either gave away many of their traditional functions or had them taken away from them. The media does their communicating, for example; advertisers replace the party bosses or ward captains of old; the public service or task forces create policy; direct mail replaces the strawberry social as fundraisers. As traditional parties break down, coalitions rise to fill that vacuum. It's one reason they are independent from political parties.

Social movements, by definition, are activist, grass roots and outside the political mainstream. Those that advocate progressive change should have had more natural links with the New Democratic Party than with either of the older ruling parties. Certainly there was, and is, a considerable overlap among activists in the movements and the party. But the NDP's traditional suspicion of social movements as organizations, and its need to control the political agenda, made it difficult for the party to join the parade the movements had formed.

Once in power, the Liberals moved to take advantage of that gap and provide political direction. The Conservatives, whom members of the movements had fought against in one way or another for years, were finally out of office. The Liberals provided the alternative and the NDP was on the sidelines. Of course the Liberals had their own agenda, and were ready and willing to exploit them in their own ways.

The classic example in the Accord era occurred with the tenants' movement.

The Accord required the Liberals to simplify rent controls, extend them to units built after 1975, and block the conversion of scarce rental units to expensive condominiums. The government brought in nine tenant and nine landlord representatives to help them iron out details acceptable to both sides.

The tenants were invited as individuals, not as representatives accountable to tenants across the province. They all had other jobs, little experience with legal technicalities or bargaining methods, and divided commitments. They all wanted strong controls to protect tenants, but they also understood the need for new, affordable housing.

Landlords on the committee had no such problems. They were backed by a $1.6 million dollar war-chest to lobby on rent controls. This was their job, they had the experience, and they suffered no divided loyalties.

Ministry of Housing officials played neutral and mediated between the two groups. They used a classic mediating set-up called the "prisoners' dilemma," says a former manager who was in on the deal.

"It's what police do when they keep two suspects separated. Each prisoner faces a dilemma. What if the other guy breaks down first and incriminates me? So each one starts to blab. Both are worse off than if they had been able to deal together," he says. That's just what Gardner Church, the assistant deputy minister of housing, did. "Then to satisfy both sides, he had to complicate the legislation so neither side would know which came out ahead," the former manager says. Church once boasted to Liberal advisor Sean Goetz-Gaden, himself a former housing activist, that his role in the ministry was to "represent the developers."

Tenants caved in on rent increases that favoured landlords. In return, they got a law protecting rental stock, and a few "deal breakers," such as the promise of 3,000 non-profit units for the disabled.

By posing as neutrals the government pressured tenants to forsake their own interests and act out of social responsibilities that were properly the concern of government. "It was brilliant on their part," says Leslie Robinson, a key tenant negotiator. "Then when they introduced the legislation, they didn't have to take responsibility for it." The deal was a masterful political stroke and textbook case of Liberal success in merging technocratic measures with a bit of participatory democracy.

In the short-term, the deal almost killed the tenant movement. Tenant negotiators were all denounced as sell-out artists by leaders who hadn't been in on the meetings. "It was humiliating," says Robinson, who left the tenant movement for two years after the experience.

But by playing both sides against the middle, the government walked into a predictable problem. Their legislation had no clear unifying thread and eventually came tied together with 97 pages of regulations. "What started as a goal to make the law simpler and more accessible," Robinson says, "made it more convoluted and inaccessible."

Although at first the Liberals had so successfully co-opted the tenants on the committee that anger in the movement was directed at tenant leaders, not at the government, before long the legislation's unwieldy pitfalls revived tenants's organizations. But by then the tenants had formed their links with the Liberals, and that is where they lobbied. Meanwhile, the NDP mindset allowed it to do little more than raise questions in the legislature on the unfairness of the rent review legislation. The NDP was no longer the party fighting for tenants' rights that it had been in 1975. It was also constrained by its unwillingness to denounce tenant leaders.

Just as the NDP missed the value of interventions of outside organizations in the 1985 election, as their preference for getting desks and staff from OPSEU instead of having them run their own campaign shows, they missed coalition politics later. The NDP wants to generate politics, not have social movements play that role. It prefers its politics in the House, not on the street.

Robin Sears was correct, in a way, when he came into Queen's Park and suggested that people's energies were not directed down the right powerlines. The problem was that he and the leadership thought the only thing the party needed was a new transmission system, when what they were missing was the right generator.

In *Fire in the Americas*, sociologists Roger Burbach and Orlando Nunez argue that today's source of political action comes not from workers, as Marx argued, or a worker-peasant alliance, as Lenin thought, but from a third social force made up of middle classes, intellectuals, ethnic and social movements — and a fourth force, solidarity movements.

The NDP, which was formed from the CCF specifically to attract middle-class voters, thinks it will generate its power from that base. It wants to appeal to middle-class guilt and a middle-class sense of fairness. The left outside the NDP, on the other hand, wants for forge alliances and build coalitions like those that were emerging in the 1980s.

Former OPSEU president James Clancy, now president of the National Union of Provincial and General Employees (NUPGE), said: "[The NDP] wants to work through networks, not structures. It's the lazy man's way of organizing. You call up all your friends. It's not going out and building from the bottom." He says that to build these political coalitions, people and organizations must meet to find what they have in common, not what keeps them apart.

A feature of the NDP in power will be whether it plays to the respectability of the middle class, or empowers and tries to forge links with traditionally oppressed or marginalized groups.

During the Accord years and afterward the Liberals brought in a long line of social movements to work with them, sit on their task forces, and make presentations to legislative committees. They invited activists not only to meet with Liberals but to join the party, to change them from within and without.

In addition to hiring staff who were asked to "think radical," as Hershell Ezrin told them, they appointed people with activist backgrounds and political agendas to high-profile government positions. Some of these appointments proved too hot for the Liberals to handle: notably former Toronto mayor John Sewell, who became head of the Metro Toronto Housing Authority in 1986, and human rights lawyer Raj Anand, head of the Ontario Human Rights Commission in 1987. The hiring of Sewell and Anand showed the Liberals were ready to take a chance on change; their firing showed that the Liberals were not ready to take the heat of genuine reform.

Still, the Accord years gave the Liberals the stamp of progressive action. When the NDP never thought of calling in leaders of the social movements to help it draw up items for the Accord, and then watched the movements begin to work with the Liberals, the party lost its reputation as the best vehicle for political change. The movements had moved on.

Ethnic groups also found a place in the Liberal party and government. Kahn Rahi, executive director of Toronto's Access Action Council, and formerly the immigrant outreach coordinator for the Social Planning Council of Metro Toronto, says that power attracted ethnic communities to the Liberals in these years. "Immigrants won't indulge in politics if they don't see power," he says.

Rahi thinks the NDP has never gone much beyond its organizing with the Italian community, and is still a "white bread party." "They haven't really crossed those [colour] lines," he says. "They don't want to be perceived as radical in that sense."

Rae's office hired a staff person to do community relations and, more specifically, ethnic organizing. At this time, members of the party's various "ethnic advisory committees" met from time to time in the third floor caucus room at Queen's Park, often fewer than a dozen New Democrats who came together to express their frustration. They often had to walk past gatherings of a hundred or more Liberals from one ethnic group or another at catered receptions on the second floor.

Monica Woodley, the party's community relations staffer starting in 1987, acknowledges that organizing in the ethnic communities was "very frustrating." One reason was the connection people felt with the Liberals through former prime minister Pierre Trudeau, who had a strong identification in the third world. "Many of them felt that it was because of Trudeau that they were allowed into the country," she says.

A second reason was that immigrant communities were very much into the "party in power." "They came here to better themselves," says Woodley. "They weren't going to associate themselves with us — a 'loser' type. They saw the Liberal party as the way to some sort of achievement."

And she thinks there is a third reason: "Some of them in the immigrant communities came from countries with a very volatile or unstable political situation, and Liberalism represented a kind of middle of the road...that was quite safe. Many felt it was comfortable to be Liberals because they didn't want to be seen as the stirrer-upers of anything as the New Democrats or socialists might have been."

These factors made organizing among immigrant communities difficult, especially so because the NDP, with its suspicion of social movements and unwillingness to participate in coalitions whose agenda it couldn't control, found sharing power with outsiders hard to swallow. It has always been a party of trusted insider loyalists. And yet the ethnic communities were outsiders, untested and unproven, and they would not find easy access to the corridors of the NDP.

The Liberals Operate on the Doctors

In December, 1983, federal Liberal health minister Monique Begin introduced legislation to bring an end to extra-billing by doctors and to eliminate hospital user fees, which threatened the accessibility and universality of Canada's health care system. The new Canada Health Act proposed to deduct from provincial transfer payments the amount of money collected by patient charges. In Ontario, extra-billing by doctors amounted to an estimated $50 million a year.

MPs passed the Act unanimously in April, 1984, and the federal government started to withhold money in July. The Act provided that the provinces would be reimbursed if they banned patient charges within three years. Although the deductions were costing Ontario more than $4 million a month, the most the provincial Conservatives did was ask doctors to comply voluntarily and suggest a gradual phasing-out of extra-billing.

In 1985, both the Liberals and New Democrats in Ontario campaigned against extra-billing, and one of the Accord items high on the list of things to be done in the first session was a ban on extra-billing. The doctors had no intention of taking their medicine lying down. For them it was a bitter pill to limit their income and reduce their status as independent professionals.

At first the Ontario Medical Association refused to believe the Liberals would go through with the ban. In the past, the Tories had given in to doctors' demands by negotiating substantial fee increases that allowed them to maintain earnings that now averaged about $120,000. The Liberals told the OMA that not only would they not renegotiate the fee schedule, but that they had every intention of bringing an end to extra-billing.

On December 19, 1985, Liberal health minister Murray Elston introduced the Health Care Accessibility Act, which banned extra-billing. When the government refused to back down, and when a series of discussions with the Liberals went nowhere, the OMA scheduled a rally at Queen's Park on May 7, 1986 to show their members' defiance. The 3,000 cheering doctors were addressed by new Conservative leader Larry Grossman, who, as Frank Miller's minister of health, had negotiated the last fee schedule — one in which the OMA gloated that it had "wrestled him to the ceiling."

But the Liberals forged ahead and on June 20, passed the Act into law. The government, the NDP voting with them, was forced to invoke closure to get the bill through the Tory opposition.

The OMA responded with a 25-day strike that closed doctors' offices but only a few hospital emergency wards. A *Toronto Star* editorial cartoon showed the doctors as pigs feeding at a trough overflowing with money. In the end, the fed-up doctors caved.

Throughout the dispute, the NDP urged swifter and tougher action on the part of the government. But when all was said and done, the Liberals were seen as fair and tough, and as the champions of accessibility to health care. The NDP were bit players in the dispute with the doctors. The Liberals were implementing what the two parties had agreed in the Accord and got credit for it.

The Mutiny of the Inspectors

When David Peterson formed his first cabinet, he chose Windsor MPP Bill Wrye as his minister of labour. Wrye, a former local CBC reporter, immediately proclaimed himself as the minister *for* labour, letting people know where he stood.

Wrye often seemed well-intentioned on labour issues, but the NDP hammered him in the House. In October, 1985, for example, Elie Martel, back in his role as health and safety critic, and labour critic Bob Mackenzie repeatedly blasted Wrye for the ministry's failure to lay charges against companies under the Occupational Health and Safety Act while labour inspectors simply issued repeat compliance orders. Showing that 4,800 repeat orders had been handed out from a total of 48,000, Martel called the situation "a licence to continue to violate the Act."

In particular, they focused on a Windsor company, Valenite-Modco, a manufacturer of metal cutting tools. The ministry of labour had inspected Valenite many times since 1974, and had issued 29 work orders since then, calling on the company to provide adequate ventilation and clean up its operations. The ministry never laid a single charge or levied a single fine against Valenite. In 1984, one of its workers, Larry Girard, developed "hard metals disease," which causes a fibrosis of the lungs and eventually an inability to breathe.

The situation at Valenite-Modco represented a widespread problem in the province: inspectors issued orders, companies failed to comply, and inspectors issued repeat orders. The legal branch of the ministry of labour rarely prosecuted companies, and almost never laid personal charges against corporate heavyweights, despite the thousands of outstanding orders.

Shortly after becoming minister, Bill Wrye met with his ministry's inspectors and told them that if they had problems getting orders acted on, that they should call him directly. His deputy minister, Tim Armstrong, openly contradicted him during the meeting and told the inspectors to follow standard procedure — which meant working through the ministry bureaucracy that he controlled.

This early confrontation was part of a power struggle between Wrye and Armstrong.

Frustrated by the hammering they were taking in the legislature, the inspectors wanted to show they were doing the best they could, but that they were being thwarted by the ministry's legal branch and by senior bureaucrats. The inspectors set up a private meeting with Wrye and one of his senior aides for May 21, 1986. They were to meet for breakfast at the Park Plaza Hotel, where the inspectors would hand over documents that in their opinion showed a pattern of non-enforcement of their orders indicating ministry obstruction and collusion. Essentially, they were charging that senior ministry bureaucrats were responsible for preventing some charges from being laid, and for refusing to take action on others.

Several days before the meeting was to take place, the inspectors leaked their information to Sandro Contenta of the *Toronto Star*. He promised not to use the information until after the meeting with Wrye had taken place, but the *Star* ran a front-page story on the morning of the scheduled meeting.

On his way to the Park Plaza for breakfast, the ministry aide saw the *Star* headline and immediately knew there was trouble. He met the inspectors briefly in the hotel lobby, told them Wrye could not come because of an emergency cabinet meeting, took their documents and left. At ministry offices, the shit hit the fan. Armstrong was called to Queen's Park to figure out what to do.

OPSEU, the inspectors' union, reacted quickly. The union's long-time and respected health and safety officer, Bob deMatteo, called a news conference that afternoon to demand a public inquiry into the inspectors' charges.

Meanwhile, OFL president Cliff Pilkey was in a rage and phoned OPSEU president James Clancy. Pilkey complained that the union was going after "our guy" — meaning Tim Armstrong. Sources say Pilkey didn't want Armstrong "immobilized" because Armstrong "delivers for us."

For their part, the New Democrats also first called for a public inquiry, but toned down their demand once they learned of the OFL's objection. Any inquiry would do.

Peterson, Pilkey, Armstrong and others all wanted an internal inquiry. Wrye's staff was open to a public inquiry, largely because of their conflict with Armstrong. A public inquiry, with public hearings and the right to subpoena, would have exposed the whole old regime; a private inquiry could be controlled more effectively.

On the day the meeting was to take place, with the inspectors' story splashed in the *Star*, OPSEU delivered a brief to the government, providing details of the charges leaked by the inspectors. Six days later, labour minister Wrye announced a private inquiry, co-chaired by two reliable and conservative insiders. They were Geoffrey McKenzie, a managing partner with Coopers & Lybrand, and lawyer John Laskin, son of the Supreme Court justice, a former counsel to the Royal Commission on Asbestos. In his statement, Wrye indicated that "before making a final determination, we reviewed our approach with...Cliff Pilkey,... [Autoworkers' chief] Bob White,...and [Ontario Steelworkers' head] Leo Gerard...These three leaders of organized labour have fully endorsed the method and approach of this comprehensive, external review." Notably missing from that list was OPSEU president James Clancy, whose union represented the inspectors.

In his response to the minister's announcement, Elie Martel complained: "Nobody from labour is involved. It is two academics — great stuff, lawyers. They know what is going on in the work place," he mocked.

During the behind-the-scenes review that took place, OPSEU provided more details of the cases that in its view constituted a pattern of non-enforcement. The OFL gave no resources or other assistance to OPSEU to help in its case — or to protect its members, the inspectors.

Among the key witnesses was health and safety activist Stan Gray, who by this time was running a workers' clinic based in Hamilton. Gray testified for five days and provided a 59-page written brief detailing 17 cases which, taken together, "indicate the thwarting of health and safety enforcement by senior Ministry of Labour officials," he said.

Martel provided his files to the inquiry, also with evidence to indicate "misconduct" by ministry officials.

The inquiry had just begun when Wrye won the power struggle with Tim Armstrong. In late July, the government created a trade office in Tokyo, and appointed Armstrong as its first agent general. This time, rather than defend him, the Liberals decided to ease him out. Tokyo was about as far away as they could send him.

The *Star*'s Sandro Contenta reported that: "Insiders say Armstrong virtually ran the ministry under the former Progressive Conservative government, unhampered by the minister of the day. But when the Liberals came to power, Wrye, armed with a list of labour reforms from the Liberal-New Democrat accord, tried to put his stamp on the ministry — particularly in the field of workplace health and safety." A lavish going-away party for Armstrong was held at the Harbour Castle Hilton hotel in downtown Toronto that fall. It was hosted by Cliff Pilkey and Bob White.

In January, 1987, the McKenzie-Laskin inquiry reported that it could find no wrongdoing in the ministry. The NDP and labour immediately blasted the report as a "whitewash" and a "coverup." OPSEU and health and safety activists also bitterly condemned it. Even new OFL president Gord Wilson, who replaced Pilkey in the fall of 1986, issued a statement blasting the report.

The report's executive summary indicated that it had little use for ministry critics. And in the competing interests between profits and safety, the inquiry left little doubt where it stood.

"Occupational health and safety provides a ready platform for critics who do not have to bear the responsibility for developing and implementing practical solutions," it said. "Criticism is inevitable;...critics can occupy the 'high ground' in the emotional debate over what constitutes a reasonable and acceptable balance between workplace risk and economic growth."

Labour leaders could be trusted, it pointed out, but health and safety activists had a hidden agenda: "On the labour side, many critics are sincere and committed to working with industry and government to find practical solutions which will protect workers, without jeopardizing industrial competitiveness and employment. At the policy level, the leadership has been constructive. However, within the health and safety sector of the labour movement, other voices are heard.

"At least some members of the latter group are ideologically opposed to cooperative solutions and believe that the system must be changed," the report continued. "They call for an expanded inspectorate, acting not as monitors, mediators and problem solvers, but as policemen using prosecutions as the major tool. Unfortunately, there is evidence that *members of this group have another agenda* and are using occupational health and safety to achieve other objectives. This is particularly destructive, because finding acceptable solutions to workplace hazards depends upon cooperation between labour, management and the regulatory authorities." (Emphasis added.) It lamented "the politicization of health and safety concerns."

The report even took a swipe at the Liberals, implying things were easier in the Tory days. "The visibility of this minority group in the labour movement has been enhanced by the change of government. When in opposition and even now in power, members of the government have, on occasion, sided with those who favour the "big stick" approach to occupational health and safety administration."

McKenzie and Laskin also lamented that business had been quiet. "The strident criticism by some segments of labour has been matched by an unhelpful silence on the part of most employers. The management community has been essentially passive in the public debate...."

Problems in the ministry with regard to enforcement were swept under the rug. With his ministry given a clean bill of health, and with Tim Armstrong in Japan, Wrye planned to move ahead with his own agenda.

The mutiny of the inspectors is an interesting case study of the Liberals, the NDP and the labour movement. By refusing a public inquiry that would have blown open the machinations of an entrenched Tory bureaucracy, the Liberals showed their true colours. Despite the progressive face they put on labour reforms, they had no intention of upsetting the system. Their choice of Geoffrey McKenzie and John Laskin and the absence of labour or health and safety activists on the inquiry team is further evidence that they intended to keep the lid on.

The OFL and other labour leaders wanted to protect their man Armstrong, and so stilled the demands for a public inquiry. Though Armstrong was not its target, OPSEU was not part of the group looking to protect him, either. But all the heat and public exposure of the allegations inside the ministry of labour compromised organized labour's position. Neither Pilkey nor White could go out on a limb to keep Armstrong in place, and the Liberals sawed him off. It appears that in protecting Armstrong from public scrutiny, part of organized labour came down on the side of a bureaucrat instead of injured workers or the labour inspectors.

Finally, the case shows that the NDP's connections to the labour movement kept it from helping to expose the hidden government in the ministry of labour. Elie Martel and labour critic Bob Mackenzie continued to hammer away at Bill Wrye, even calling for his resignation. This was an evasion of the real problems with enforcement inside the ministry, and an echo of labour leaders' support for Armstrong. Martel and Mackenzie might have chosen another tactic, the kind the NDP used against environment minister Jim Bradley, by damning him with faint praise and regretting that he had no influence in government to get the things he wanted done.

The Liberal agenda on health and safety reform became even more obvious after the 1987 election, and provided another classic example of the NDP playing the union leaders' tune. But by then, Peterson moved Bill Wrye out of the labour portfolio and installed North York businessperson Greg Sorbara. He immediately distanced himself from Wrye by making sure no one could mistake him as the minister *for* labour.

Tipping its CAP

Fearful that the party was becoming too closely aligned with the Liberals and hoping to push the NDP in a more activist direction, progressive New Democrats formed the Campaign for an Activist Party (CAP) in the fall of 1985. CAP organized for the party's June, 1986 convention, and became the most widely-supported left-based organization in the NDP since the Waffle.

The story of CAP — its need, its considerable support among party members, and the way it was dealt with by party brass — is from the beginning a story of the party's intolerance of dissent. It also shows how the NDP had lost its roots as a political movement. For all intents and purposes, it also laid to rest the very divisive debate in the party over the extension of funding to Roman Catholic schools.

In the months after the Accord was signed, it became clear to many party members that the NDP was losing not just its separate identity, but also its links with the social movements. The Liberal government was involving leaders from the movements in its consultative process and was even hiring them to its own staff and to positions in the bureaucracy. The Liberals were forging connections and gaining credibility that they never had before.

NDP activists hoped to revitalize the NDP by re-building its foundation as a political movement and sharpening its extra-parliamentary focus. The fact that CAP won the support of a great many rank-and-file New Democrats was testimony to the disenchantment party members had with the direction the party was going. It was also a sign that the party's left was no longer polarizing around traditional left-wing ideological hair-splitting — is public ownership "a" tool, or "the" tool? — but on questions of internal democracy and extra-parliamentary efforts. CAP proved to be the last spice for this kind of ginger group in Ontario.

"If we are going to change society, we must do more than simply elect better legislators," a CAP brochure proclaimed. "The NDP should root itself in the energetic social movements which are fighting for equality, justice, solidarity and peace. By stressing principles and activism, we can sharply distinguish our party from the Liberals in works and deeds and, in so doing, significantly broaden our electoral base."

CAP organized on two fronts by running a slate of candidates for party office and by endorsing a series of convention resolutions chiefly designed to re-orient the party's operations toward grass-roots activism.

CAP endorsed 15 candidates for the party's executive offices, but did not contest the two most important positions, that of leader or provincial secretary. CAP did not try to assert itself as an alternate leadership in that sense; it was content to seek the elected positions that were understood as internal and representative of, and theoretically accountable to, the membership. The fact was that with members of the party's executive being selected for the "official slate" by the party brass, they were never accountable to the constituencies they were supposed to represent.

For party president, CAP ran Judy Rebick. As a person with a long history of involvement in social struggles, she was precisely the kind of candidate that activists were looking for. Incumbent NDP president Gillian Sandeman, a former Peterborough MPP, had announced that she would not be seeking re-election, so when Rebick announced her intention in the fall, she was the only declared candidate for president.

CAP also endorsed a number of other candidates whose backgrounds stressed links with the social movements. Its vice-presidential candidates were Malcolm Buchanan, president of the Ontario Secondary School Teachers' Federation (OSSTF) from 1982-85; Mary Rowles, former president of the NDP Women's Committee; and George Ehring, at this point a party vice-president who had won the position in a surprising upset victory over lawyer Steve Krashinsky, a member of the Lewis clan, in the fall of 1985.

Of the resolutions the Campaign for an Activist Party proposed, the party was especially concerned about one calling for the creation of a "campaigns department" that would "be set up to direct and co-ordinate the establishment of links between the party at all levels and labour, the women's peace, tenants' and housing movements, anti-apartheid, international solidarity, disabled rights and gay and lesbian rights movements, etc. Part of the campaign department's responsibility would be to develop campaigns for all levels of the party and provide resources to the ridings...." The resolution was endorsed by 10 riding associations, and was popular with many delegates.

The other key resolution CAP endorsed was one brought forward by the New Democrats to Preserve Public Education (NDPPE), a group organized to fight the party's policy on the extension of funding to Roman Catholic high schools. Its resolution reversed party policy and opposed funding. The main policy battle at the 1986 convention took place on this question, and stemmed from the on-going sharp divisions in the party on the issue. (See "Separate But Equal" above.)

In the 1985 election, several NDP candidates openly ran against the party's funding policy, which incurred the wrath of the same party leadership that had remained silent for years while many caucus members ran against the party's policy on abortion. Two 1985 anti-funding candidates ran on the CAP slate: Gord Doctorow and Diane Meaghan.

Opposition in the party to the extension of funding crossed ideological grounds and was a serious threat to Rae's position. If the convention overturned the party's support for funding, then as signatory to the Accord, which called for its extension, Rae would have been out on a limb.

The NDP hoped to defuse the situation by sponsoring a conference on public education held in Toronto on February 22-23. But the *Globe's* Robert Matas reported that 31 of 37 speakers were opposed to funding, and that Rae, who told him he was "committed to moving ahead with the decision [to support funding]," could only appeal to the party to support co-operation between the two school systems. The conference just hardened the resolve of the NDPPE and its supporters. A showdown at convention loomed.

As convention neared, the CAP campaign gained strength. Headed into the final weeks, over 200 members had signed a public list of endorsers. This list showed that CAP's support was not limited to a left-wing fringe; it included three vice-presidents of the Ontario Federation of Labour; two future cabinet ministers: Frances Lankin and Tony Silipo; feminist Kay Macpherson; Metro Toronto Councillor Jack Layton, and many riding association presidents.

Party leaders responded by actively organizing against CAP. Early in the new year they approached several high-profile women and urged them to run against Rebick. But her credibility and support among NDP women was so strong that no one was willing to take her on. Some of the women the party approached were quite content to have her elected president.

Eventually, the party persuaded Gillian Sandeman to run for re-election, despite the fact that she planned to be out of the country with her husband for much of the next year. Sandeman agreed, convinced that she was the only person who could defeat Rebick. Party bosses then managed to smear Rebick's candidacy with the allegation that it was she who had challenged the incumbent Sandeman.

On June 5th, Rebick and Sandeman were invited to speak at the Metro Toronto Labour Council. After that debate, in which Rebick scored points arguing for the need to make stronger links with labour and the social movements, more and more delegates started to register for convention. The party understood that Rebick and CAP presented a serious challenge and made an effort to get its people out.

Other moves were in the wind. Robin Sears met with Rebick for lunch, played godfather and tried to persuade her to withdraw as a presidential candidate. Rebick says that Sears promised that if she would "tone down the rhetoric on the abortion issue" and distance herself from her more radical past that he would see that she got a seat on the executive. She told him that there would be no deals.

Sears tried to cut a similar deal with Ehring. Meeting one day in the halls of Queen's Park, Sears told Ehring that if he would quit CAP he would get him a spot on the party's slate of candidates.

When Ehring refused to drop his support for CAP, the party played a trump card. Three male vice-presidents were to be elected — and three women — and the three incumbent men were running again: Ehring; long-serving Ottawa member Simon Rosenblum; and the blustery Paul Forder, from the Ontario Federation of Labour staff. It was virtually unknown that an incumbent seeking re-election would be left off the "official" slate, but the party brass dropped Ehring and prevailed upon Michael Lewis to run against him. An ardent baseball fan, Ehring joked that for the party to bring in such a heavyweight against him was "like being traded for Mickey Mantle."

The popular Lewis had resigned as provincial secretary shortly after the Accord was signed. He begged out of the job, saying that he was burned out from the election and the negotiations, and needed to recharge his batteries. Though that may have been true, it was widely rumoured that he was on the outs with Rae as a result of the Accord.

Lewis was replaced as provincial secretary by Brian Harling, a party vice-president and systems planner at Ontario Hydro. It was Harling's elevation to provincial secretary that created the vice-presidential vacancy into which Ehring had been elected in 1985. Now Lewis was being brought back specifically to knock off Ehring.

The 1986 convention was held in Hamilton on June 20-22. The party leadership had three goals: defeat all the CAP candidates, especially Rebick; defeat the resolution opposing separate school funding; and defeat the resolution calling for the creation of a campaigns department.

The party establishment drafted a last-minute resolution in support of its position on funding, which re-affirmed existing policy and gave the caucus credit for improving the Liberals' proposed legislation on its implementation. In specific, it pointed to protections for teachers' jobs, "open access for all students to both publicly funded systems," and a commitment to improve funding "for all educational institutions."

The legislature was due to vote on the bill in a matter of days, and a reversal at the convention would have been embarrassing and difficult for the party. Many delegates who were inclined to support the party's last-ditch resolution were persuaded not by the merits of the arguments in favour of funding, but by tactical considerations of the position a reversal would put the caucus in.

After a long and bitter debate, the party's resolution passed with about 60 per cent of the vote. It was a narrow victory for such an important issue.

Shortly thereafter, the campaigns department resolution came to the floor. In the debate on the resolution, party brass argued that they could have their cake and eat it, too. Some who opposed the idea made the case that such a department was unnecessary because the party was already doing just what the resolution called for. Others said it was unnecessary because the party did not need to be doing that type of organizing. Louis Lenkinski, an Ontario Federation of Labour staff member, even argued that it "would instill permanent revolution" in the party — a clear attempt to link its supporters to Trotskyism. And party loyalists distributed an unsigned leaflet forbidden by the rules of the convention, attacking the resolution for such disingenuous reasons as "it's not socialism," "there's no political benefit," and "it calls for us to devote scarce resources to movements that have already organized themselves."

Supporters of the resolution pointed to the fact that many labour unions had similar departments or staff members assigned specifically to provide liaison with social movements or organize public demonstrations. (Labour staff were so experienced at pulling off demonstrations that they had a ready putdown for organizations, including the NDP, that couldn't: "They couldn't organize a two-car funeral," labour people would say.) Supporters also argued that the party needed to be involved directly with the movements, or they would lose those links to the Liberals.

But once again the party establishment prevailed, defeating the resolution by about two to one. With these two victories they breathed a huge sigh of relief, and were confident they would defeat Rebick and the other CAP candidates as well.

Rebick admits that when she gave her convention speech, "I never felt so much tension in my life. I said: 'Look at the size of this convention. Who says the left never does anything for this party financially?' No one laughed."

The final vote for party president was decisive: Sandeman 818, Rebick 361. All the other CAP candidates were similarly defeated.

And so the party closed the doors on this brand of activism and on these activists. Secure that the left had been smashed one more time, there was no need to accommodate any of the people who had been defeated or recognize the ideas and forces they represented. Sears's attempt to cut deals with Rebick and Ehring were nothing more than a crude ploy to co-opt them as individuals. The party could quash CAP and its points of view, despite the fact that it had gained a widespread currency among party members.

The intolerance of dissent extended well beyond the defeat of the CAP candidates. Earlier that winter, Michael Shapcott, a constituency assistant for Oakwood MPP Tony Grande, became one of dozens of individual party members to endorse CAP. Though this was certainly his right, Shapcott says he was told "in no uncertain terms that my endorsement was 'not consistent' with my employment." Following a serious dispute with Grande, Shapcott lost his job in a classic case of "you can't fire me, I quit," and was forced to go on unemployment insurance. The New Democratic Party could not tolerate one of its employees endorsing legitimate candidates for party office. CAP subsequently hired Shapcott as its campaign organizer. He went on to become one of the most widely respected anti-poverty organizers in Toronto and a leader of the movement opposed to the Olympic Games.

CAP represented a watershed for the left. It was the last time an organized and broadly-based left wing group tried to build support among significant elements of the party.

Following the 1986 convention, many of the CAP activists either left the party altogether, or remained nominal members but devoted their ideas, energies and money exclusively to the various social movements. The party was happy to see them go, but it was much the poorer for it.

* * *

A footnote to CAP, and a measure of the widespread intolerance of dissent, occurred in the labour movement.

In June, 1986, the independent labour magazine *Our Times* ran a commentary by its editor, Stuart Crombie, on the Rebick candidacy. *Our Times* is a worker-owned cooperative committed to providing a forum for thought-provoking articles and comment on the labour movement. It is one of the few avenues that union members have to reach a broader segment of the labour movement, and though it has occasionally been critical of organized labour, it is a rare positive outlet with a consistently pro-labour point of view.

Though Crombie wrote specifically that "*Our Times* is not endorsing Judy Rebick," the piece did wonder out loud what was wrong with the NDP and why "most union members and working people don't vote for the party."

"By running on a political platform for what has been regarded as an administrative position," Crombie wrote, "Rebick has created the conditions for us to ask serious questions: With the NDP saying all the right things, why are workers not joining and voting for the party in greater numbers? Short of changing the party's program, how can the NDP build a majority?"

Shortly after this article appeared, 55 subscriptions were up for renewal at the Ontario Federation of Labour's June executive meeting. Paul Forder passed around copies of the issue, complaining about Crombie's piece. OFL Secretary-Treasurer Sean O'Flynn recommended that they renew the subscriptions; CUPE Ontario division president Lucie Nicholson countered that the magazine was anti-labour and anti-NDP. (*Our Times* had run a profile of Judy Darcy, who was expected to run against Nicholson in upcoming elections. Darcy became the union's national president in 1991.)

O'Flynn defused the debate by tabling the renewal request, and promised there would be an investigation.

For months the controversy lingered. When Crombie tried to get a table for *Our Times* at the fall OFL convention, a request traditionally granted without fuss, his calls went unreturned. The magazine ended up sharing space with the United Farmworkers.

The Steelworkers' union also pulled its advertisements. An international union, its leaders had been stung by the separation of the Autoworkers' union from their U.S. parent, and were running a soft "What is Canada?" ad complete with four Canada geese. "Our Canada. Let's keep it that way," the ad read. At the OFL convention, Crombie got the cold shoulder from Michael Lewis, who had recently joined the Steelworkers' union staff, and was twice kicked out of the union's "hospitality" suite.

In a meeting with Crombie, OFL president Cliff Pilkey tried to get commitments that there would be no more anti-labour stories, a reference to a November *Our Times* article that described some of the anti-democratic and gangster traditions inside the Seafarers' International Union. When Crombie stood his ground and argued that the magazine needed editorial independence or no one would take it seriously, Pilkey had to agree. At the OFL executive meeting on the eve of the federation's convention, Pilkey pushed the renewals through. Pilkey was stepping down as OFL president at the convention; Crombie wrote a tribute to the outgoing leader.

The incident was a measure of the control the labour movement and the party wanted to exercise. An unflattering article or a column that raised questions about the direction of the NDP were cause for cancelling subscriptions or pulling advertisements from the magazine.

Eventually, cooler heads prevailed, the labour brass admitted the value that *Our Times* brought to the movement, and this sorry attempt to influence the magazine's content was over.

Driving Toward Public Auto Insurance

In 1948, Ontario CCF leader Ted Jolliffe wrote *Planning the Public's Business*, a primer on the party's philosophy of public ownership. Among his list of things a first-term CCF government would bring under government control was automobile insurance.

Jolliffe never saw public auto insurance as a driving force on the road to socialism, just another in the list of items that would be more efficiently run by government. Long before most workers had cars, the CCF believed that by co-ordinating the licensing system with insurance coverage, and by eliminating the profit motive from insurance, drivers and accident victims would be better served.

At its founding convention in 1961, the NDP re-affirmed its belief in government-run insurance and promptly relegated the issue to the back burner. The person who eventually turned up the heat on public auto insurance was Welland-Thorold MPP Mel Swart, who says today that "Whether it's an issue depends on whether there was someone to push it."

Swart became a socialist during the Depression, when his family lost its farm and as a boy he sold milk to neighbours. Swart saw farmers dump their milk because families were too poor to pay for it, and was convinced there must be a better way. He joined the CCF when he was discharged from the airforce in 1946, and says he first debated the merits of public auto insurance in 1967, during one of the many elections he contested before he was first elected to the Ontario legislature in 1975.

Swart sees government-run auto insurance as "a practical thing." "It shows the public the NDP issues aren't developed on Cloud Nine," he says; it's an item that hits people in the pocketbook.

Long a champion of consumer causes, Swart became famous in the legislature for his show-and-tell questions. He would wonder, for example, if a cabinet minister could explain why the Canadian-made toilet paper he held aloft was more expensive than the American-made toilet paper in his other hand, though both were made from Canadian wood. He pushed for a government-financed consumer ombudsman and introduced private member's bills on the subject, but his idea never caught fire.

In 1985, Swart sold the public auto insurance idea to Bob Rae. "It was a way to show we can provide an important service at lower costs," he says. He convinced Rae and other caucus members that it was a good issue for the election, one that people would relate to, a populist measure that had the practical stamp of lunchbucket economics.

As it turned out, in 1985 auto insurance rates took their first big hike in more than a decade, up about 19 per cent on average. Most of that increase was attributable to skyrocketing bodily injury claims awarded by the courts.

The NDP's re-discovery of an old policy had the good fortune to meet with bad news from insurance companies.

The party used the issue in the 1985 election with some success, though it did not become part of the Accord. After all, the Liberals did not agree with public auto insurance. Following the election, the NDP launched a big direct mail campaign, calling the rate increases "highway robbery." As Swart predicted, the measure was immensely popular with NDP members and with the public.

It was also the one big item that differentiated the NDP from the Liberal government.

But while the NDP had a very successful grass-roots issue it could sell both on the basis of "fairness" and lunchbucket economics, the NDP made a few classic blunders that undermined the political advantage it might have gained from the issue. First, it failed to hire professionals to research the insurance industry. Second, it misread how this economic idea would fit in with the party's "container" on economic issues. Finally, the NDP missed an opportunity to connect public auto insurance to a larger scheme of universal insurance coverage.

Political analyst Marc Zwelling showed the party the results of his polls on the issue. They indicated that although a broad cross-section of the public was angry about auto insurance rates, few people were going to vote NDP based on the issue, and few thought public ownership was the answer. People preferred a public "window on the industry," like Petrocan. The greatest anger came from the wealthy, who pay high insurance since their cars are expensive, but who were unlikely to vote NDP, the polls showed.

Both Zwelling and long-time labour staffer John O'Grady urged the party to hire an insurance actuary, someone with an insider's understanding of the industry, to research the issue. But as they had done when they refused the help of a professional during the Cadillac-Fairview apartment flip, they ignored this advice. Instead, they handed the tricky portfolio to caucus researcher Graham Murray, who had no expertise on insurance issues, and who was also responsible for handling the divisive Catholic school funding issue, among many others.

Under the gun from the NDP, the insurance industry was naturally loathe to provide it with information on their rates or profits. Murray had to piece together information from a number of sources, sometimes forced to compare apples and oranges in an effort to develop material. He was panning for gold in a political minefield, and eventually his research bombed.

On April 13, 1987, the NDP held simultaneous news conferences in 10 cities across Ontario, the largest such event it ever held. According to a Canadian Press wire story of the event: "Rae, Swart and other members of the legislature released figures that showed a widening gap between insurance premiums charged by Ontario's private companies and those levied by government-run plans in Manitoba, Saskatchewan and British Columbia." Using figures compiled by Murray, "They said Ontario's average annual premium was about $605 last year, based on amounts charged to motorists by The Co-operators, one of Canada's largest insurers."

Co-operators immediately denounced the figures, saying their average premium was about $450, and that they had given those figures to the party.

Swart attempted to clarify the situation. Canadian Press reported: "The NDP's calculations showed premiums ranged from a low of about $450 based on The Co-operator's statistics to a high of $792 using figures from Ontario's superintendent of insurance, [Swart] said. The average was $606. The numbers were correct, but the average premium was wrongly attributed to The Co-operators."

Maybe so, but the damage was done. At a critical time when the New Democrats were preparing for an upcoming election, they were seen to have blown their math. The mistake played perfectly into the public's belief that the NDP couldn't handle economics. The NDP was asking people to believe that the solution to insurance rate increases was "driver-owned" — government-run — insurance, and here it had apparently gotten its facts wrong. It fit all too well into the party's "container" that it couldn't run the corner store.

A person of integrity, Murray was devastated by his mistake and realized the political damage it did to the party. At the same time, Robin Sears intended to use the incident as a means to fire Murray, who had been a difficult employee and one of his more outspoken critics. Management had gone after Murray before, and they were determined to nail him this time.

Murray was president of the local union representing the caucus workers and understood how important it was for the union to protect workers from being fired for making a mistake. But after several days of tense negotiations he resigned, accepting a severance package with secret terms.

The incident further undermined the already bad relationship between Sears and the staff. Members of the bargaining unit met frequently over the few weeks following Murray's resignation. Many wished he had stayed to force management's hand. They thought that under the terms of the collective agreement, management would have lost an arbitration had they fired Murray simply for making a mistake. Their local president had resigned, and they felt that if the feisty and outspoken Murray had been forced out, it could happen to any of them.

The staff was also beset with internal divisions. At least two union members were widely suspected of being stool pigeons, reporting back to management on the tense private meetings the bargaining unit was holding. At one meeting, as everyone danced around the touchy issue, careful not to open up for fear of being reported to their bosses, Ehring broke the silence and discussed the atmosphere of the negotiations surrounding Murray's resignation. He opened his remarks by saying he knew that what people had to say would be reported to management. In the course of his comments he called Sears a thug.

Later that day, Sears delivered another of his handwritten notes to Ehring, shoving it under his door while he was in the room. Sears wrote to "offer a small piece of gratuitous advice." He said: "As someone who is similarly tempted, by grand occasions, to flights of imprudent rhetoric, may I simply observe — careful of the 'demon hyperbole.' Words such as 'thug' out of context are often boomerangs that come back to haunt. Best of luck."

Sears had proved, of course, that he had spies in the bargaining unit. The next day at another emergency union meeting, Ehring read the note from Sears to the union members. He also read from a note he had sent Sears in return, assuring him that he had used the word "thug" in context. Union members were upset, and relations with management went from bad to worse. Sears, the man whom Bob Rae said had "a real sensitivity on handling personnel problems," was at the centre of the storm.

But even without Murray's mathematical error and the internal crisis that followed, the NDP was not poised to make big electoral gains on the auto insurance issue. Even though it was a rare attempt by the party to promote "lunchbucket economics," Zwelling's polling showed that people did not consider it a vote-determining issue, and the NDP lacked credibility on economics. The party's "container" overrode the populist points the NDP scored.

In philosophical terms, the NDP had dredged up an old idea, and failed to link it to newer ones. Public auto insurance, on its own, boiled down to a "fairness" issue, one where big companies ripped off little consumers.

The NDP's failure of new ideas in this context was no doubt based in part on its opposition mentality. Though the party kept after the issue for months, at a time when the Liberals commissioned study upon study, the NDP used auto insurance as a headline grabber. The more cases it could show where drivers had been hit with huge increases the better. But drivers imagined that the savings they might gain from public auto insurance would have been more than wiped out by a single visit to the body shop or with the deductible on their policy.

Globe bureau chief Duncan McMonagle also thought the NDP approached the issue based on its opposition tactics. McMonagle said later: "In question period there's less scrutiny than in the outside world. They [political parties] get lazy through question period — just enough for a hit and a followup. But that's not good enough when you're up against top companies."

The fact the NDP had an opposition mentality on the issue is also shown by its ambivalence over whether or not accident victims would retain the right to sue under public auto insurance, and by the details on just how public auto insurance would be provided. The efficiency and streamlining that the system assured if insurance were sold along with a driver's licence, and the guarantee that drivers were insured, disappeared if insurance were still sold by private agents across the province.

Some NDP caucus and party members wanted to look at broader questions of social insurance. The NDP might have promoted public auto insurance as part of a universal accident and illness insurance scheme. Under such a plan, people would receive benefits regardless of the cause of an injury or sickness, whether it was caused by an accident at work (covered by worker's compensation), an automobile accident (covered by auto insurance), an accident at home (covered by personal liability insurance) or a debilitating illness (covered by the Canada Pension Plan). It represented real streamlining of insurance coverage and provided a mechanism to avoid duplication and increase dramatically the efficiency of a number of public insurance plans by rolling them into one. Though the NDP studied similar plans in other countries and had its advocates in caucus, it never latched onto the idea.

Similarly, the NDP never connected its public auto insurance plans with broader social initiatives regarding cars: safer roads, drunk driving, more stringent pollution standards, increased public transportation, alternate fuel technology or the like.

Vaughan Lyon, a political science professor at Trent University, says that when New Democrats advocated public auto insurance, "They just tried to tap into a sense of grievance. That just lowered the NDP into the category of tinkering with the system. It's a failure of political imagination, of playing it very safe, and giving up on bringing the public along on more fundamental issues."

The NDP went into the 1987 election with its "highway robbery" campaign in high gear. Some years later, then provincial secretary Brian Harling admitted that the party whipped up the insurance issue for the 1987 campaign because it had to put some distance between itself and the Liberals after two years of the Accord. "For tactical reasons, we had to," Harling says. "Auto insurance saved our ass."

Harling also concedes that: "We did such a wonderful job that people thought that's what it meant to be NDP. It wasn't that big a deal. We made it a big deal."

The NDP used auto insurance as a substitute for real issues about economic direction. It is proof that the party had little new to say that was different from the Liberals. Robin Sears admitted that European socialists ridiculed him for the NDP's gung-ho approach to public auto insurance, mocking that the party certainly was not going after the commanding heights of the economy. Sears defended it by saying they didn't understand the importance of the automobile in North America's independent lifestyle.

Summing up the Accord

The years from 1985 to 1987 were arguably the most dynamic period of political change in Ontario history. Though the Liberals received credit for the popular policies they implemented during that time, the fact remains that they were handed a blueprint through negotiations with the NDP, and they built from it.

The Accord granted much more than Rae's bottom-line of a guaranteed period of stability. It gave the government both an agenda and a timeline, something as useful as the Accord itself.

Governments operate from promises and platforms, and the degree to which they stick to them is a measure of that government's integrity. The Accord's agenda and timeline gave the public a yardstick to measure the Liberals by.

Through those two years, the Liberals showed they could manage a tough agenda that left the NDP with little to say. The NDP was trapped in a bind of me-too-ism, arguing "faster, faster" or "tougher, tougher," but left essentially to agree that the Liberals were doing what New Democrats demanded of them. The Accord spoke for itself. The NDP, as opposition, was uncomfortable saying that it would have done the same things.

But the NDP had no mass base that wanted to go beyond liberalism, and little internal pressure to do so. For reasons we have tried to explain, the party establishment stifled its critics, minimized dissent, and ensured the party's executive was a committee of like-minded and cautious people. It had no challenging new ideas.

The Liberals showed they were willing to be tough-minded, as they were with the doctors. They implemented separate school funding over the objections of a great many Ontarians and despite a powerful lobby by public school boards and public school teachers' federations.

The Liberals' own legislative agenda was far more extensive than the Accord items, and, to be sure, not all of their initiatives were progressive. But at times they demonstrated a willingness to move quickly in new areas. At one point, for example, OPSEU representatives met with Hershell Ezrin, Peterson's chief of staff, to outline the union's intention to refuse to handle South African goods, mostly canned fruit and juices, that were imported for jails and other provincial institutions. OPSEU asked for a joint news conference with the Liberals. The very next day, the Liberal government pre-empted the union by holding a conference of its own to announce that the province would no longer import South African products, including wine.

The Accord era set a standard for future governments to live up to. Both the Liberals from 1987-1990 and the NDP when it came to office afterward have been measured against the progress of those years.

* * *

With widespread anticipation that Peterson would not be tied to the NDP any longer than he had to, by the spring of 1987 all three parties moved into pre-election mode. Inside the legislature the opposition became crabbier; the ministers became less defensive and more aggressive. Peterson spoke less and less about the legacy of Tory governments and more and more about his government's own accomplishments.

Television in the legislature beamed the politicians across the province's cable TV. In preparation for broadcast, the House had been wired, freshly painted, and had lights and microphones installed. Now David Peterson prepared to pull the rug out from under his political opponents.

Chapter Five: The Lost Opportunity: 1987-1990

> "...there is no propensity [among the electorate] to be looking for a new government at this time. But if there were, there is no more inclination to regard the NDP as that alternative than there was prior to the 1985 election." — The NDP considers its 1987 election chances in a confidential election strategy document.

Throw Robin From the Bus

On June 26, 1987, two years after David Peterson was sworn in as premier, the Accord he signed with Bob Rae expired. To no-one's surprise, Peterson called the election soon after, and picked a particularly low-key day to issue the writs: the Friday before the August holiday weekend.

Peterson was running on his record of accomplishments, taken from the program written in Bob Rae's office for which the Liberals took full credit. The Liberals also presented an aura of freshness, openness, fairness and effective management to the electorate.

The NDP election planning committee (EPC) debated running on the Accord. They felt the party had written and negotiated it, after all, and the measures implemented by the Liberal government were popular. But only a handful of NDP EPC members, in particular vice-presidents Michael Lewis and Simon Rosenblum, favoured putting the Accord front and centre in the NDP campaign.

The election strategists abandoned hope of scoring points with the Accord. In deciding not to run on the Accord, the NDP was admitting that it had been unable to share credit with the Liberals, thus acknowledging in an implicit way that those who had said that the route of such close allegiance was fraught with the loss of identity. Just as the party habitually denied itself honest self-criticism, it never had a serious evaluation of the impact of the Accord. The election planning committee suspected, as did all other observers, that the Liberals were destined for a majority government, and they decided that the best they could do was fight for an effective opposition to keep Peterson's team honest.

This opposition mentality grounded their thinking, and the NDP didn't consider or present itself as a party ready to take over the responsibilities of government. Countless NDP staff, once thrust into government, would later lament that "it was so much easier being in opposition."

On the campaign trail, the party ditched the portable keyboard that had been Rae's lapdog in 1985. He had received too much criticism for being a light-weight entertainer, and now the party gave his image another make-over. The NDP brought out Fighting Bob, champion of working people, and gave Vaudeville Bob the hook. The party distributed the corresponding tough photo of Rae, tie loosened, sleeves rolled up. In one poster, a facial scar was obvious. It was easier to deal with Rae's image by turning him into a fighter than to take on the much more difficult task of challenging the set of public perceptions about the party that form its "container."

The party's message, as outlined in a confidential election strategy paper that spring, was that "Ontario trusts New Democrats to fight for the interests of working families at Queen's Park....That's the rallying cry of the NDP as we head into an election in the next several months. It's a theme that's both strategically credible and consistent with the proud and honourable tradition of the party in this province."

But the strategy paper confessed the NDP had real problems: "As [in 1985], the party today has little credibility as a potential Ontario government, or for its capacity as a potential Ontario government, or for its capacity to deal with the province's long-term economic problems."

The party's polling found that "many Ontarians would apparently consider kicking out their Liberal or Tory member in order to elect a fighting New Democrat." So the NDP campaign would "portray the New Democrats as the ones you can trust to fight for working families against the big interests that are beginning to influence the Liberals against the interests of ordinary people."

The party decided to attack these "big interests" behind the Liberals rather than Peterson or the government itself because the latter were too popular. And although the party's masterplan spoke frequently of "working people," the campaign was not class-based; for New Democrats the phrase was virtually synonymous with "ordinary Canadians." Their appeal was as much to the reasonably well-to-do middle class as to blue and pink collar workers. Their class profile was a product of their polling, not of an ideology or principle. It is important to understand the NDP's "radicalism" as mere positioning.

New Democrats confessed to themselves that they did not plan to present an alternative vision or run on specifics: "Our explanation of the chosen issues...should not be designed primarily to convey information, analysis or thoughtful prescriptions," the masterplan said. They admitted they would do their best to avoid the kind of questions they considered "counter-productive:" "are our data accurate? Is our policy coherent? Do we know in substantive terms what we're talking about?" The party of the left consciously and explicitly designed a campaign to minimize ideas. They swapped ideology for image.

In line with its "fighting for working people" theme, the NDP chose a basic formula for all its issues. There would be a villain, e.g. unfair auto insurance companies; a victim: young drivers; a response: gaps in rates don't have to be as great; and a policy: driver-owned insurance will eliminate unfairness. The strategy document suggested that "perhaps the policy is offered later on."

The villain-victim-response formula was geared to delivering a simple, repeatable message. As the NDP's lack of depth on its key issue of auto insurance showed, the formula didn't reflect a coherent analysis of larger social and economic problems such as economic growth in a restructuring economy, rising expectations and the need for a sustainable environment, or public transit in an age of global warming. The formula also did nothing to confront the NDP's chronic dilemma of having little credibility on economic management issues.

As one long-time policy advisor who played a senior role during the election termed it, this was to be a "*sauve qui peut*" campaign — a save what you can election in which the NDP would try to hold its own against a popular government. Under these circumstances, he thinks the campaign strategy was "brilliant."

But Marc Zwelling thinks the NDP missed the boat. "Third-place parties run on protest platforms...," he wrote to his polling clients. "Second-place parties need to turn their attention to their ability to manage government and solve peoples' problems." The NDP would have behaved differently if it had been preparing itself for government. Its incompetence in office is partly a result of the little serious thinking the NDP did previously about governing.

* * *

Robin Sears was the commanding officer of the NDP campaign, and he ran it like a military operation from his bunker at Queen's Park, occasionally venturing to the front lines in person. What he had heard about the 1985 campaign convinced him that it had been too loose, and as a control freak he intended to control day-to-day campaign functions himself.

But Sears was not an experienced campaign organizer, and his stint with the Socialist International in London, from 1981-1985, caused him to miss major political developments in Canada. The NDP's former federal secretary Dennis Young, says: "It was a long time for a political operator to be away. He never got plugged back in."

Sears was also not in the best of health. In the months leading up to the 1987 campaign, he was recovering from one of several operations he needed after badly fracturing his ankle when he fell from a roof in England. (With his leg elevated and in a cast, he used to wheel silently through the red-carpeted corridors of Queen's Park; later a metal cane replaced the wheel-chair, and on his infrequent forays outside his office, his arrival was announced by the menacing click of his cane.) As a result of the operations, Sears reportedly took frequent heavy doses of mind-numbing pain-killers.

Sears kept a tight rein on Rae during the 1987 campaign, and the media commented that Rae did not seem to be having a very good time. He was the fighting friend of the working person, no longer witty and clever but tough and determined.

While Peterson played movie star throughout the election, Rae struggled with his lines. On one mainstreeting tour with federal leader Ed Broadbent and Autoworkers' union chief Bob White, a reporter asked Rae if he was a socialist. Rae refused to answer, saying he didn't like labels. The reporter asked White, who said right away that he was a socialist, and with a little hesitation Broadbent said he was, too. But Rae didn't pick up the cue and realize that use of the term would have little political impact.

This incident became notorious in the campaign as Rae refusing to use the "s-word." Reporters were reminded of the time in 1977 when Stephen Lewis backed off the party's commitment to minimum wage increases and the nationalization of resources. By refusing to deal in a straightforward way with the question, Rae made the "socialist" tag an issue, one that the media pestered him with throughout the campaign. It also undercut his fighter image.

In the tightly-controlled campaign, Rae never loosened up. The media found him edgy and uptight. (It was a common comment during the 1990 election that with Sears out of the picture Rae was finally able to be himself.) But the media that followed Rae's team on the press bus spent much of the campaign annoyed with the way the party was handling them.

Early in the campaign, a serious incident undermined the party's relationship with the media.

Rae was running hard on the auto insurance issue, repeating its villain-victim-response message wherever he went, but was naturally being pressed for more details on its implementation. The party resisted, but eventually realized it would have to flesh out some of its own plan. Sears decided to try to control coverage of its major plank.

To do this, he made what reporters consider an unforgivable mistake. As far as he was concerned, virtually the only campaign coverage that counted was that of the *Toronto Star*. So Sears provided *Star* reporter Bill Walker with a Hamilton hotel room and the party's entire insurance strategy — a major exclusive.

Walker was conspicuously absent from a major Hamilton rally where both Rae and Broadbent spoke. The press corps noticed this, and demanded to know from Rae's press secretary, Rob Mitchell, where Walker was. Mitchell honestly didn't know and told them so. Privately, he "smelled a rat," he says. He asked David Agnew, Rae's executive assistant, what was going on, but Agnew told him "never mind." "I didn't know until I found out the next morning when I got my *Toronto Star* just exactly what had gone down," Mitchell says.

The other reporters all found out at the same time, when the *Star* ran Walker's detailed story on its front page. "When I got on that bus the next morning," Mitchell says, "it was, like, kill me. People were so mad at me it wasn't funny." Later that day, John Valorzi from Canadian Press told Mitchell they knew it wasn't his fault, but that he could pass the word on to Sears that he had instructed his bureau to boycott the story. Other media outlets did the same. Sears's attempt to control the story backfired badly.

Sears, who thought he had nothing to learn, habitually treated Mitchell with contempt and never sought his advice on dealing with the media. Mitchell says that if Sears had asked him about this particular stunt, he would have told him how disastrous it would be. For his part, Mitchell was so angry with Sears that he spoke to him in only a perfunctory way for the entire rest of the campaign. "I felt he seriously compromised my abilities as Rae's press secretary by deliberately keeping me in the dark around crucial events," Mitchell says.

Several reporters who travelled with the NDP during the 1987 campaign confirm that when Sears was rode on the media bus he often drove them crazy, alternately attempting to butter them up with little private chats at his seat, or by being condescending, arrogant or patronizing. The media on the alcohol-free NDP bus had a frequent chant of "No beers, no Sears."

* * *

Some of Sears's behaviour was the stuff of legends.

One day the NDP scheduled an event at a sewage treatment plant on Toronto's lakeshore. The party wanted to highlight safety and environmental issues. This being a hot summer campaign, the plant — which workers called the "shit factory" — smelled unbelievably bad.

Veteran CFRB reporter Hal Vincent's wife had just had a baby, and Vincent returned to the tour that morning and handed out chocolate cigars. During the visit to the "shit factory" that afternoon, reporters noticed Sears standing on one of the walkways over the enormous pools of human waste, eating the chocolate cigar Vincent had given him. "Check out Sears," one of the reporters said, nudging another. "I told you that guy wasn't human."

During the election, Sears often stayed overnight in his Queen's Park office, rather than go home. In the small hours of one morning late in the campaign, Sears ordered the NDP's research director Chuck Rachlis to drive him downtown so they could get the early edition of the newspapers as soon as they came out. Rachlis walked into Sears' office to find him pale and sweating, loud rock music blaring from his expensive stereo system, and his Macintosh computer running a software program displaying colour fireworks.

Trading and Insurance on the Campaign Trail

David Peterson never tried to argue that minority government wasn't working; the Accord years produced a record amount of legislation, much of it progressive and popular. Yet everyone knew that with his government so high in the polls, he would find a reason to call an election as soon as he could.

His excuse was the government's need for a mandate to oppose free trade with the United States, something Peterson said was "a bad deal" for Ontario. Peterson favoured less restricted movement of goods between Canada and the United States, but said that under the proposed agreement "our access to the U.S. market would not be appreciably more secure than it was the day the negotiations got under way."

During the 1987 campaign, he articulated six "bottom line" conditions that were necessary for his support. Obtaining secure access to U.S. markets was one of the conditions. If the deal included gutting the Auto Pact, reducing safeguards for cultural industries, banning subsidies for business development in poor regions, prohibiting continued screening of foreign investment, or excluding safeguards for farm industries, his government would oppose it.

The Liberal government appeared to be considering ways Ontario might do an end run around free trade and thwart some of its elements in the province.

For its part, the NDP was strongly opposed to free trade, both in the legislature and during the 1987 campaign. But apart from adopting language calling for "fair" trade or "managed" trade, and calling for sectoral agreements similar to the Auto Pact, the party offered few specific alternatives to the proposed deal.

Peterson waltzed through the campaign in rolled-up shirtsleeves and his bright red tie. Crowds lined up to shake his hand and get an autograph. The media dutifully reported the premier's widespread popularity and printed pictures of a smiling Peterson swarmed by enthusiastic followers wherever he went. He spent the campaign barbecuing hamburgers for ordinary Canadians while Rae was fighting for them.

Observers thought Peterson looked "new and jazzy." Veteran television reporter Robert Fisher, then CBC TV's Queen's Park specialist, reported that on the campaign tour, people treated Peterson like a movie star. "Campaigning with him was like being on a bus with Alan Alda," Fisher says. "They just wanted to touch him, shake his hand or get his autograph. I've never seen anything like it with a politician," Fisher says.

Attacks by Rae and Tory leader Larry Grossman were small irritations as Peterson's support held throughout the summer. Polls showed that only one in five voters would "never" vote Liberal, and even 60 per cent of those who intended to vote NDP didn't rule out voting for Peterson's team. Meanwhile, about half of the Liberal supporters said they would never vote for either of the other parties. The red-tied tide was reaching the high-water mark.

Throughout the campaign, Peterson suffered only minor annoyances, mainly at Liberal picnics, where OPSEU members went to eat hot dogs and to dog the premier. This campaign followed the union's successful efforts in 1985, and although the 1987 outcome was never in doubt, OPSEU continued to press its agenda for the protection of government services and opposition to cutbacks. Peterson's strategy with the OPSEU members was to offer them a hot dog and ignore them.

The NDP kept fighting: fighting for working people, fighting for families, fighting for fairness. But Peterson, the former boxer, never had to fight back.

Rae's most effective left jab was the auto insurance issue, and he kept pounding away at the unfairness of rates for young drivers, for seniors and for people who were considered first-time drivers if they had no recent driving record. Luckily for the NDP, at about the same time the party was running out of horror stories, the media grew weary of the daily litany of unfairness. Rae kept being pressed for details of how he would implement public auto insurance, but the party ran afoul of the media when Sears gave the *Star*'s Bill Walker exclusive information.

The NDP's plan was not "government-run" insurance, because polls said people didn't like the idea of the government running insurance and didn't trust an NDP government to manage it well, though that is, of course, just what the NDP had in mind. The party called its scheme "driver-owned," which sounded less socialist and more popular, if a lot less clear.

As mentioned above, polls Marc Zwelling provided to the party showed that most people did not consider public auto insurance a vote-determining issue, and the voters most angry about their rates were the wealthy, who were unlikely to vote NDP. Furthermore, the party's credibility on the issue suffered a setback in that spring when it appeared to have its figures wrong.

For months prior to the election, Rae and his colleague Mel Swart repeatedly trumpeted the advantages of efficiency, avoidance of duplication of services and guaranteed coverage if the government sold auto insurance together with drivers' licences. Yet when Rae was pressed late in the campaign about the impact this would have on jobs in insurance offices across the province, he responded by saying that auto insurance would continue to be sold by private agents. He couldn't explain where the efficiency would come from if that were to happen. Even on its central issue, the party left the impression that it didn't know what it was talking about.

Still, the NDP's horror stories on auto insurance made an impact. Three days before election day, Peterson made one of his rare mistakes and said he had "a very specific plan" to deal with auto insurance rates. Though he refused to provide details of his "plan" because there wasn't one, he was too far ahead of his rivals for this to hurt at the polls. Later he would regret this boast when his government was bewildered about what to do.

McMaster University political science professor Henry Jacek noted at the time: "The tide's going out on the Conservatives. So the real threat to the Liberals in the longterm comes from the NDP. The government has to be sensitive to NDP-type issues. That's their real problem over the next few years, and they have to do what they can to neutralize it. They know the NDP's on the right side of the insurance question. That's always worrisome for a government."

Nevertheless, Peterson was on the road to a smashing win, riding a wave of popularity from the dynamic Accord era.

The Great Victory

On September 10, 1987, David Peterson won the greatest electoral victory in Ontario history, capturing 95 of the legislature's 130 seats. The NDP fell from 23 to 19 seats.

The Tories were decimated, winning just 16 seats, their lowest total since the province's first election in 1867. Their popular vote plummeted from 37 per cent in 1985 to 24.7 per cent. Tory leader Larry Grossman lost his own seat and resigned as leader on election night. Just six years earlier, the Conservatives had won 70 seats.

On election night, Peterson was controlled and statesman-like in his remarks to a wildly cheering hometown London crowd. He knew that his government was headed for a big victory, but even Liberal insiders never predicted such a huge majority. "It's not winning an election that counts," he said, "it's how we all use it to serve the great people of this province."

For his part, Rae proclaimed "a great victory" that night, though his satisfaction was hard to fathom. His party lost four seats, including two key caucus members: Evelyn Gigantes in Ottawa Centre and Ross McClellan in Dovercourt. Rae won his own seat by just 433 votes. The party came third in 66 of the 130 ridings, and fourth in one other. The last remaining Italian members from west Metro were defeated, and none of the party's visible minority candidates was elected. There were just three women among the 19-member caucus. The party's popular vote had increased marginally, from 23.8 per cent in 1985 to 25.7 per cent, but this could hardly be considered a step forward in view of the fact that over 400,000 former Tory votes were up for grabs, virtually all of which went to the Liberals.

Polls suggest that the NDP lost support throughout the campaign. A poll done by political analyst Marc Zwelling in May showed the Liberals at 50 per cent, the NDP at 30 and the Tories at 19 per cent. A Goldfarb poll in July had the Liberals at 48, the NDP at 28 and the Tories at 21 per cent. Polling in August by Environics and Angus Reid gave the NDP 27 or 28 per cent, and they finished with 25.7.

Canadian Press reporter Peter Gorrie says the press gallery laughed when Rae proclaimed the "great victory." "It sounded hollow," Gorrie said. "Any time anything went wrong, it was declared a victory."

But the declaration of victory served a purpose. As Zwelling wrote: "For the NDP, if the September election is considered a victory, no further evaluation or change is needed. If it is seen as a defeat, then renewal and change are likely."

A high-ranking member of the party executive admits that there was no reassessment following the campaign. "There was disappointment, but we felt we had done the right thing," he says. An NDP wag commented: "We bloodied the Liberals' boots, they kicked us so hard."

Caucus chair Mike Breaugh admitted publicly he failed to notice the great victory, and wondered out loud about Rae's future. "Look," he said, "he's had a couple of shots at it. He's a young man with a young family. He may consider a career other than politics."

And what of the victory? "There will be some in the party who think it's a great victory," Breaugh said, "but when you come a distant second, that's not winning. I mean when you get your tail kicked this good, there's something wrong."

Breaugh suggested that: "If Bob had a problem, I would say it was that the party put some unreal expectations on him. I mean, having a charismatic and bright young guy as leader is great, but the realm of organization and building the party is more important. The other work was just not done."

But Rae was unrepentant. "Not only am I not discouraged," he told reporters, "but I feel very proud of the campaign we've run."

Most caucus members treated Breaugh like a traitor. For them, his questioning of victory was a loyalty issue, and they circled the wagons around their leader. Instead of honestly evaluating the party's shortcomings, they sought to place the blame elsewhere. Hamilton East member Bob Mackenzie pointed the finger at the media for giving the Liberals a free ride. "The media have given the Liberals a two-year, plus two-month honeymoon in the campaign," he said. "I've never seen anything like it. I think it's the media that should be re-evaluating itself."

But defeated Oakwood member Tony Grande said: "I think we have to re-evaluate our political direction, not just the leadership."

Appearing on Robert Fisher's *Dateline Ontario* one week after the election, Scarborough West MPP Richard Johnston said that he thought Rae's leadership was secure, but that he, too, disagreed with Rae about the victory. "Yes, we have a very different perception on that," he said, suggesting that as leader, Rae was trying "to put the best face on the situation."

"My own sense of the election," Johnston said, "is though that clearly we lost....We were doing better in the polls than we'd ever done before going into a campaign, and we should have been hoping to make some inroads. And we clearly didn't."

Johnston accurately predicted the tone of the upcoming legislative sessions. "...It's very, very difficult for any government of this size not to become arrogant," he said. "They know they're going to win absolutely every vote. So they never have to take into account the opposition's point of view. The opposition knows it's never going to win any votes, and has a tendency, therefore, to become loud, brash and less responsible....The issue of arrogance will be a major issue [going] into the next election."

He also had a word of warning for the Conservatives: "If the Tories get caught very much on the right and [are] unable to move themselves from the right, it may open up a huge area [for the NDP]," he predicted.

Just prior to the party's first caucus meeting following the election, Rae said once again that he had run a "powerful, credible" campaign that "came through the tidal wave as official opposition."

He remained determined, and hinted that he would be reading the caucus the riot act. "People in the caucus are professionals," he said. "They know that our ability to be disciplined and to be united and to be effective is going to have a major impact. I certainly intend to make that very clear to people." He dismissed his critics: "It's a free party; it's a free country."

But it was not a free party for its internal critics, on whom it exacted its penance.

Before the House sat, Breaugh was replaced as caucus chair by Bud Wildman. In a *Toronto Star* article, Rosemary Speirs called this move a "ritual defrocking" and wondered: "When the lettering is gone [from Breaugh's door], will the party have eradicated all disloyal thought?"

She said: "The party would have accomplished more by some serious self-examination."

Speirs went on to ask a series of penetrating questions, ones the NDP should have been asking itself. "What has happened to the links that the NDP forged in the early 1970s with tenant groups, with activists in occupational health and safety and, most importantly, with the immigrant working people of Ontario?" she wondered. "Why has the NDP, the party of ideas, lost its intellectual vigour?" "And, finally," Speirs asked, "how much does conformity in NDP thought have to do with answers to the above questions?"

As the NDP had done so many times before, it did not call into question its campaign strategy, its leadership, its policies or its general direction. Of these, there would just be more of the same.

Zeroing in on Nothing

The Liberal years of majority government following the 1987 election could have been a time for the NDP to regroup, to re-evaluate its broader goals, its direction and its policies. Instead, except in a few areas discussed in detail below, it was a time of drift and pre-programmed opposition-style reaction to Liberal initiatives.

As in the pre-Accord years, the NDP fell back on its old habits of relying on question period to deliver its message, and of using the litmus test of coverage in the *Toronto Star* or *Globe and Mail* to determine if an issue was really an issue or not.

An NDP advisor likens the NDP's opportunity at the time to that of a chess player thinking out moves in advance. "If they had played politics like chess," he says, "they would have planned the Accord, a *sauve qui peut* election and then their opportunity would come if they knew how to capitalize on it. So the real criticism of them is not how they did in 1987 but after."

Yet the party lacked focus. Even on the party's most high-profile issue, auto insurance, which the Liberals handled badly, the NDP was confused in its own message. "Driver-owned" insurance avoided unnecessary bureau-cratic duplication, yet the party said it would be sold through private agents, thus eliminating most of that efficiency.

The NDP also seemed to be putting the issue on the back burner. When Mel Swart, who had championed the issue tirelessly, stepped down in 1988 for health reasons, the caucus gave Swart a set of Ontario licence plates reading "NO FALT," and Rae gave the role of insurance critic to Swart's Welland-Thorold successor, Peter Kormos. Kormos had no experience in the legislature, let alone with the issue, and Swart himself later felt that this indicated the issue was taking on a lower profile because at the time the Liberals appeared to be solving the problem with their rate board.

New Democrats also gave mixed messages about whether they believed in no-fault auto insurance or not, which was crucial because it left open the question of the right to sue. Kormos, a maverick criminal lawyer, believed in the right of accident victims to sue. Most social democrats disagreed, believing that with insurance programs the question of fault is secondary. Generally, social democrats prefer guaranteed coverage to lawsuits, as in the WCB system, where injured workers get benefits but may not sue. An accident victim, in the workplace or on the highway, should be entitled to benefits regardless of fault.

This also made it more difficult for the NDP to make the links between auto insurance and a system of universal accident and illness insurance. There was interest in the party and caucus for the principle of universal coverage, and several caucus members, in particular Floyd Laughren, fought to give the issue greater priority. Yet an attempt to pull together a task force to explore the issue in detail fizzled, and no report was ever prepared.

For the most part, the party drifted, reacting to Liberal initiatives or playing up Liberal "scandals." Individual caucus members pursued their critic portfolios, trying to skewer the inexperienced Liberal cabinet ministers whenever possible. It was difficult to determine what the NDP's agenda was, if it had one, other than to act as opposition.

That lack of focus was apparent to party activists, when they thought about it. One example shows just how obvious that was. In 1988, at a meeting of a dozen labour educators, all of them party stalwarts, they were asked if they could recall what Stephen Lewis's priorities had been. Without hesitation, they listed occupational health and safety, asbestosis, rent review and children's issues. Lewis had not been leader for ten years. "What are Rae's main issues?" they were asked. No one could name a single priority, and they just sat looking at each other.

Their silence was typical. Rae had been leader for almost seven years, and many party activists could not name a single thing that was high on Rae's personal political agenda. Being smart, the tag Rae always wore, is not the same thing as having a vision; having a platform is not the same thing as having an agenda. Developing policy requires more than smarts. It means working cooperatively, having a willingness to promote others' ideas, and letting other people initiate proposals and take credit for them. Having an agenda means sticking to issues even if the *Toronto Star* does not consider them important, educating people on the importance of those issues, and working to create support for your views. Under Rae's leadership, the NDP was a party adrift in a sea of political confusion.

Fighting for Fairness for the Family

In March, 1988, Robin Sears sent the NDP caucus a think-piece called "Welcome to the Nineties" for discussion at a three-day retreat in the Sunday brunch town of Elora. Unwilling to look back at the party's losses in the September 1987 election, Sears had no reservation about his ability to look into the next decade.

In his paper, Sears drew attention to Canada's growing debt and the country's inability to use deficit financing to pull itself out of a recession. "Canada's annual GNP is now less than its accumulated debt," he wrote. "At $30 billion the federal government's debt does not leave a great deal of room for significant growth — as would be required in any major counter-recessionary spending undertaken to fight the next downturn."

Sears ominously predicted the problem the Rae government would later find itself in. "A Keynesian solution to rising unemployment and declining growth would be risky and probably short-lived — even in Ontario," he wrote. "We would not have the capacity to double the deficit to kick-start the economy as was done in the past two sharp recessions."

But after pages of analysis, the document never nailed down an economic approach. Rather than face up to this crisis of traditional NDP policy, Sears capitulated on economics and decided to "metaphor."

"Perhaps it's time we recognized that neither our own people, nor the media feel comfortable having us act in the role of economic policy gurus," he admitted. "...The challenge is to find the focus which marries our social strength to a grit [Liberal] weakness, which has broad popular salience. What we need is a thematic package which unites our economic and social message, not one which places them on competing agendas. A call for [a] change in values which says social justice equals economic success."

"In other words, the family."

Sears wrote: "...for us a focus of 'fairness for families' just seems to fit so many of our natural positions and rhetorical lines."

The family way was picked up by Rae in a March 29 memo to caucus and staff, outlining the theme for the legislature's spring session, whose f-words were: "fighting for fairness for the family."

But critics trashed the family notion as confusing, limiting and exclusive. They pointed to its weaknesses with at least three NDP target groups: women, workers and immigrant communities.

A leading feminist complained that the family theme "drives a nail through women's efforts to define themselves as individuals in their own right." She observed that the party seemed hooked into traditional nuclear families, which left out many people, and which were all too often the settings for domestic violence and male domination.

Though he described himself as a "family person," former Metro Toronto Labour Council president Michael Lyons didn't think it was a good message for working people. Lyons resigned his labour council position so his wife might have more choices and time in pursuing her own career goals.

"Does 'fairness for the family' imply that the wife will go back to the family and kids?" he wondered. "That's the image it creates, even if it's not that they're saying. There's no feeling of community responsibility to it."

Lyons said he preferred a theme that would stress dignity for people. "When I worked for the labour council, I always felt bad that people had no sense of their own worth. It's a terrible feeling, that society can get along without me. And when people have no sense of their own contribution, they don't feel like they're entitled to more benefits. They don't feel: 'We built this country,'" he said.

A similar theme was picked up on by Winnie Ng, an activist in the Asian community and co-chair of the party's ethnic liaison committee. She felt that the family message would not hit home in immigrant communities. "Many immigrants think our present government's as fair as it can be," she said. "We have OHIP, we have a minimum wage, we have human rights. People feel that's the best we can ask for, and they blame themselves for their accent or for not working hard enough." She pointed out that many immigrant families were "just struggling to make ends meet before they can apply to bring in the rest of their families."

"The NDP has to find ways to translate those experiences into a moral language," Ng said. "My sense is that this document is addressed to middle class families that may be in crisis for the first time."

Nonetheless, the brothers and sisters in the NDP caucus left Elora united on their family theme, making orphans of those who felt left out.

The party avoided hard policy and turned to a simple, mushy image approach. There was little dissent at the caucus retreat over the family plan, as it is hard to nail jello to the wall. But because it meant so little to so many, the NDP's family way never took hold, and was dumped unceremoniously, with no debate.

The Sleeping Giant watches over New Democrats in Thunder Bay

It rises enigmatically in Lakehead Harbour in Lake Superior, an enormous, sphinx-like rock formation overlooking Thunder Bay. Locals call it the Sleeping Giant. In June, 1988, it watched as Ontario New Democrats came to town, and its peace was not disturbed.

The June convention was the party's first real opportunity to reflect on its miserable showing in the 1987 election, but that topic wasn't even on the agenda.

Provincial secretary Brian Harling seemed to find little real purpose for the convention, saying that "we hold a convention every two years, whether we need one or not." Though he admitted there was a need for more discussion of basic goals and strategies, "there wasn't the time since the last election to do it in a proper way," he said.

The decision to hold the convention in Thunder Bay, so far away from population centres, was unusual. For most delegates, travel expenses were over $500, supposedly subsidized by the high registration fee, which only made attendance more expensive. In addition, many riding associations were still in debt from the election and not in a position to assist delegates financially. Because of the difficulties of getting their video out of Thunder Bay, several southern Ontario television stations decided not to cover the convention. Even the local CBC station did not have the technology to send signals back to Toronto — it could only receive them — and the party spent about $2,500 in hookup fees.

The Thunder Bay location was an attempt to show that the party cared about the north, and to get local media. But the biggest issue was whether or not anyone would show up. Though most NDP conventions attract between 1,500 and 2,000 delegates, this one drew only about 500. It was a family affair, a guaranteed love-in of party regulars and reliable labour delegates, most of whom had their expenses paid for by their unions.

The quiet Thunder Bay convention was notable for its lack of dissent, a fact that Robin Sears looked on with some satisfaction. "The absence of rancour is less newsworthy but more beneficial," he said, noting that "We don't seek to provide theatre for the media." Though the small size of the convention was a factor in the "absence of rancour," the absence of the party's left wing was more important.

The party's attempts to rid itself of left-wing forces had finally proven successful. Only a hard-core left fringe endured, and even few of them bothered to attend the convention.

Some people regretted the absence of the left. Party vice-president Frances Lankin, for years a bridge between the party brass and its left wing, said that: "Although individuals have influence, there's not a collective left voice. It concerns me that I'm not part of it, and don't have it as a pressure on me."

MPP Richard Johnston, whose leadership bid had been associated with the party's left wing, announced that he would not be running again. He lamented: "We're still responding to the old right with the old answers. The party hasn't been able to develop a gestation process for new ideas, partly because the left's no longer there to do it," he said. "The left, for all its failings, at least was there as ginger and continued to address the issues of the continuing slide into liberalism." Now it was gone.

Like all NDP conventions, Thunder Bay showed that the party was not radical, but resolutionary. Approving 44 new policies was nothing for the party; in fact, that proved to be barely more than half the number (76) passed in 1980. Debating time had also been cut in half, to just seven and a half hours over three days. The rest of the time was taken up with routine reports or guest speakers.

The only resolution to stimulate serious debate was MPP Richard Allen's motion to approve the Meech Lake accord. The party thought it might lose this issue — as had already happened at NDP conventions in British Columbia and Manitoba. Allen couched his remarks in the context of the need to go beyond Meech, but the effect of his motion was to approve Meech as it stood. (See "Meech Ado About Nothing" below.)

Of the 12 speakers on the resolution, nine were elected members, provoking one delegate to complain that the grass roots had not been heard from. Last to speak, making his first appearance at the convention, was Bob Rae. Rae received a standing ovation when he limped to the mike, still pale and just recovering from a painful bone marrow transplant operation on behalf of his younger brother David. The delegates applauded his courage.

In NDP circles, when the leader starts off debate, it is a signal for a strong show of solidarity. When a leader closes a debate, it is a sign that the party fears defeat. Rae began by quoting Marx to the effect that people make their own history but not always in circumstances they choose.

While delegates recovered from his use of the M-word, he elaborated his own version of historical inevitability. Meech Lake was "not a perfect Constitution, but the next human footstep," he said. He supported it, "not with a sense of joy, but in mature recognition that it had to be done because there was no other way."

As a sign of things to come, one of the speakers opposed to the accord was Judy Rebick, who would soon become the president of the National Action Committee on the Status of Women and play such a key role in the Charlottetown constitutional debate.

In Thunder Bay, the vote was three to two to support Meech.

Another vote showed how much the delegates understood authority. On

Saturday, delegates rejected a resolution that called for widening the Trans-Canada highway to four lanes in the north. A majority thought there were better ways to spend the projected $2.4 billion. That night, during a $35 per plate "banquet" catered by Beaver Foods, there was heavy lobbying by northerners to reverse the decision. Thunder Bay-Nipigon MP Ernie Epp had been fighting for a four-laner for almost two years, and supporters argued it would be a major embarrassment to undo his work, right there in his home town.

"It's the same principle as on Meech Lake," one of the delegates said. "The MPs took a position and we had to back them. So tomorrow, we do the same for Ernie Epp." On Sunday, they did.

So the NDP saddled itself with a monstrously expensive policy for the sake of embarrassment. The party stuck to its guns, repeating the position in the 1990 campaign and even after being elected to office.

Standing Ovations, Inc.

At the Thunder Bay convention, delegates sat on their hands when the convention chairperson introduced Robin Sears. Attempting to make light of the underwhelming response, the chair said, "Well, *some* of us like Robin."

Within a matter of days, Sears received a letter from "Standing Ovations, Incorporated," which offered its services to "deliver the sort of thunderous applause that you, as Principal Secretary, feel entitled to receive whenever you are about to lay down the law."

The letter, written by the irrepressible former researcher Graham Murray, whom Sears had forced out a year earlier, said that "Standing Ovations can guarantee that the frenzy of your initial welcome will make the subsequent response to your remarks altogether anti-climactic."

"Let us seed hostile or indifferent crowds with our highly-trained operatives who will shamelessly pretend to be enthusiastic to hear you!" the letter said. "(Some of these people will actually know who you are!)....Call Standing Ovations *now.* The deafening silence you suffered recently in Thunder Bay, if repeated, could prove damaging to your political standing. Authorize us to pay people heavily to attend at your next coming and create an explosion of raucous and insincere approval."

Sears did not respond to the offer, and in less than a year, he was gone.

Despite the 44 resolutions, few new policy initiatives of any consequence were passed in Thunder Bay. Delegates did learn, if they had not been already aware, of a few major initiatives the party was either already in the midst of, or planned to undertake.

These were on universal accident and illness insurance, economic policy, education and the environment. As it turned out, the party's consideration of universal accident insurance never got off the drawing board.

Floyd Laughren, caucus treasury critic, initiated an economic policy review and invited a few dozen academics and economists to submit papers on various topics. A review paper, compiled and edited by professor Isabella Bakker under Laughren's direction, was released in August, 1989. It contained a summary of the diverse papers and was "meant to stimulate thought and encourage the debate and discussion that is necessary to forge new policy resolutions." Altogether, it dealt with 16 topics covering economic restructuring, the transition to a service economy, resource policy, worker ownership, international competition, a national income program for children, and others. The full-length papers were available from Laughren.

This attempt — like the environment and education reviews — was one of the most thorough compilations the party prepared on economic issues. Unfortunately, the review didn't proceed beyond the summary paper. The paper was not in a form that could be approved by the party's council or convention, the issues were enormously wide-ranging, and efforts to bring the various economic topics together into a new, coherent economic policy for the party failed. The review fizzled without analysis or resolution of the issues. As in other key areas, the NDP came to power without having worked out many of these competing economic views.

The education and environment reviews fared better.

At the June, 1988 convention, education critic Richard Johnston released discussion papers on eight separate issues: adult education, anti-racist education, childcare, a special feminist education agenda, finance and governance, job training, literacy and streaming. The papers were specifically designed to review existing policy, provide information on the issue, propose new policy directions, and pose questions or problems on the topic. After convention, they were mailed to over 2,000 party members.

The papers followed a series of public forums, where education activists were invited to discuss particular topics at length. Over the course of the review, hundreds of parents, teachers, students, administrators and interested party members participated in the process. It was very much a grassroots, bottom-up policy review.

Though the "discussion papers" provoked little discussion once they were released, their recommendations were turned into resolutions that were approved at the party's 1990 convention. Among the proposals were a commitment to de-stream high school classes and provide universal childcare in the schools.

Through 1989, a number of activists met to discuss the party's environment policy, and to forge a new awareness among New Democrats of the global environmental crisis. In the fall of that year, they decided to draft a report, which was released in March, 1990.

Called *Greening the Party, Greening the Province*, it, too, provided an in-depth discussion of the issues, including an outline for a sustainable economy and an ecological agenda for the NDP. The paper advocated creation of "a substantial and vital conservation-oriented economy," which would "create fuller employment by shifting to more labour-intensive economic development, and by embracing new technology, encouraging entrepreneurship, and implementing 'green' tax reforms that create a new market for products and services in tune with a sound ecological society."

The report dealt with other issues of transportation, an environmental ventures fund, resource conservation, land use, and global warming.

As an indication of the seriousness of the report, Bob Rae wrote its introduction. "In simple terms," he asked, "are we ready to become a green party, a party that puts as much emphasis on people's relationships with nature, and our obligation to future generations, as on the distribution of power and income, and the more traditional concerns of social democracy?

"If the answer is no," he said, "then our policies will only temper marginally the status quo, making it difficult to distinguish our policies from the environmental policies of the other parties. It will be an apparently safer choice, because it will mean fewer changes. But like all safe choices it will mean the party is excluding the possibility of being a real leader in the creation of a new consciousness, a new awareness, a new politics."

The environment review was some of the most thoughtful re-thinking of socialist policy since the 1950s, pointing a new direction for global problems. Like the education review, it served as a good approach for policy development, starting with a well thought-out document that was circulated widely for discussion.

The environment paper was a green light for the party's 1990 election campaign. For some months, the party's election planning committee toyed with the idea of running a "green" campaign. That notion was abandoned — once again, because of polling. The decision not to run a campaign based on environmental issues showed that Rae was answering his own rhetorical question in the negative.

* * *

Rae's closing speech to the Thunder Bay convention provided a hint of the new direction he was taking as a politician. Personal tragedies were changing him.

Rae was born into a life of privilege, the silver-spooned socialist that Joe Clark made fun of. He never knew defeat; his political successes were strung back to his university days, and he never experienced life in the NDP as a minion. Rae was never a riding activist, an envelope-stuffer, a foot soldier. Soon after joining the party he became a high-profile member of the federal caucus, and he cakewalked to the leadership of the Ontario party. The May, 1985 election, his first as leader, brought him unexpected power and influence through the Accord with the Liberals.

Then on August 18, 1985, his wife Arlene's parents were killed in an automobile accident, the victims of a joyriding youth barrelling down the wrong lane of a country road. Arlene Perly Rae went through a lengthy personal crisis, not unexpected following such a tragedy, and Rae spent a great deal more time at home with her and his three daughters. He frequently left the legislature to be with her. Rae became more introspective, more in touch with his emotions.

Then, around Christmas, 1987, his younger brother David, a New York investment banker, was diagnosed with lymphatic cancer. Just before the Thunder Bay convention, Rae donated bone marrow for his brother, an operation that involved inserting about 200 needles into his rear pelvic bone, and which had to be performed without anaesthesia.

In his Thunder Bay speech, Rae approached class politics from the most personal emotions. He deplored the trend toward a society geared to the rich and famous, when their private affluence is "purchased at the cost of the care and concern we have for each other, the love we have for one another."

"What we owe each other; that is the essence of social democracy," he said. In years to come, he would elaborate on that theme.

Reporting on Poverty

On January 6, 1986, with a growing economy side by side with a growing disparity between the rich and poor, NDP social services critic Richard Johnston asked Premier Peterson to "consider a major review of all the social assistance programs in this province." Without agreeing, Peterson replied that he "would like to hear the member's specific ideas on what the review should encompass."

The next day, apologizing tongue-in-cheek for the delay, Johnston sent an open letter to Peterson and social services minister John Sweeney, detailing what such a review might involve. He suggested a broadly-based task force that "calls for the involvement of the poor themselves," so they could "have their say about what is the reality of being poor in Ontario today."

Such was the spirit of cooperation that by the summer, Peterson agreed to a review — though he chose to announce it when Johnston was on a school-building brigade in Nicaragua.

In July, 1986, Peterson established the Social Assistance Review Committee (SARC) and named former family court judge George Thomson as its chairperson. Johnston had a key, behind-the-scenes role in Thomson's appointment. Using Sean Conway and Peter Barnes, deputy minister in the social services ministry, as go-betweens, Johnston proposed that the government appoint Thomson. The Liberals knew that Johnston would have to mute his criticisms of the government if they agreed. For his part, Johnston was convinced that Thomson would put together a serious and thorough review, and was delighted when he was chosen.

Though still in his forties, Thomson was well-qualified for the job. He had done graduate work at Berkeley, California in the late 1960s, when Berkeley was a hotbed of anti-war and civil rights radicalism. He became a law professor and then a judge. He had also served as an assistant deputy minister in the social services ministry. He and Richard Johnston became friends when Thomson was responsible for drafting a new Ontario child and family services law.

Soon after his appointment, Thomson and Johnston met privately to discuss how the review might work. Johnston suggested that the committee hire the director of the National Poverty Organization, Patrick Johnston — no relation — as its research director, which it did.

The Thomson committee is a case-study in the brilliant use of extra-parliamentary politics. The social services review it undertook was the most thorough and far-sighted approach to social assistance reform anywhere in North America in decades.

SARC put together a series of advisory committees to look into a wide range of problems related to social assistance: minimum wage; delivery and administration; childcare; job training; housing; the disabled. The review committee heard from people in 14 cities and received over 1500 submissions.

When the report was handed down in September, 1988, it contained 274 recommendations for sweeping changes to virtually every aspect of social assistance. The report lifted the veil of secrecy that shrouded the extent of poverty in the province, and put particular emphasis on its blameless victims: the 400,000 children living in poverty, the elderly, the working poor, the disabled and native people. The reforms it proposed were estimated to cost over $2 billion, yet scarcely a whisper of dissent came even from Ontario's right-wing business sector. By showing the costs of the present, dead-end system, they won over the sceptics. It was a tribute to the genius of the report and the way the committee was organized that even its most pernicious potential critics were on side when it was released.

Shrewdly called *Transitions*, the report focused on getting people off social assistance. The goal of the reforms would be to ensure the "transition from dependence to autonomy, and from exclusion on the margins of society to integration within the mainstream of community life," it said.

The focus on transitions "allowed a win-win rather than a left-right" view of reform, says David Thornley, former director of Toronto's Social Planning Council, and a SARC member. Lobbyists mastered the lingo, talking of the short-term "investment" in assistance that pays long-term "dividends," going "from welfare cheques to pay cheques."

It said everyone in society has the right to a level of "frugal comfort" based on the real costs of basic necessities: what the committee called a "market basket definition of adequacy." SARC said a standard of frugal comfort is the precondition to participation in society and the very ability to get off social assistance.

Transitions also called for measures to empower the poor, to increase their options and self-reliance. It called for a complete set of legal rights and an advocacy system that would let welfare recipients challenge decisions of the welfare bureaucracy. It proposed that welfare workers function as advocates for their clients, focusing on "opportunity planning" by providing guidance on available options including job training and other support programs.

It called for income supplements to top up the minimum wage, and for increased shelter allowances to cope with the high cost of housing. It put forward these measures in a context of major changes to housing and labour market policy, denouncing minimum wage laws for having slipped 22 per cent behind the cost of living since 1975. It proposed that the province to take the lead in turning over all public lands for affordable non-profit housing.

The SARC report called for vigorous action from the Human Rights Commission and for affirmative action policies to promote the hiring of women and the disabled.

It wanted a federal tax credit to cover the costs of raising children and a federal insurance program to cover living expenses of the disabled. The committee argued that neither group should be lumped in with other social assistance recipients. They deserve the dignity of access to automatic and universal programs, the report said.

And *Transitions* advocated a system of universal accident and disability insurance to cover people who were unable to earn a living regardless of the cause of their disability.

When the report received widespread acclaim instead of criticism, Thomson attributed it to the fact that "People never saw this information in one place before. People are disenchanted with seeing the foodbanks and homeless excluded from prosperity."

Joanne Campbell, one of the committee members and head of the Social Assistance Review Board, says they were conscious that they had to write a report "that was reasonable and sensible in its approach to staged changes in the system. We didn't set [the government] up for proposals that they couldn't implement."

The report turned some tough and conflicting orders from government into a harmonious package. "All these elements are like the components of a mobile; they are very finely balanced, and shifting one component even slightly will affect the balance and operation of the whole system," it said.

Thomson and the key SARC members deftly turned the various advisory committees into lobbyists once the report was released. They had worked hard to share experiences and ideas before the report was drafted, and now they were enlisted to sell the report's recommendations. Team members knew it was key for the poor to organize behind *Transitions*. They "had the sense that the ball was in their court once we finished," says Patrick Johnston.

The advisory groups, along with the grassroots organizations that delivered the 1500 presentations, gave a head-start to community support. SARC also gave the government a six-month deadline to move on its first phase — a short enough timeline to energize supporters.

Yet the government dithered, and it was almost a year before there were signs that they might be prepared to move on the recommendations.

"It wasn't until this February [1989] that the government realized it was going to take some flak" if it didn't take action, said John Southern, a SARC member active in the blind community. Southern says he felt the tide turning at presentations to the legislative committee hearing presentations on that year's budget. Welfare reformers outnumbered all other lobbyists. At first, they were asked to name a few proposals they would most like to see passed. "They refused to answer," Southern says. "They said 'Implement all of Phase l.' That threw the government. They couldn't break the opposition down. People power worked for a change."

Following the budget presentations came the March Against Poverty, a coalition of the poor, churches and labour, with the backing of the NDP, that arrived on the doors of Queen's Park on April 8. George Thomson marched with the poor to press for government action.

Finally, on May 17, 1989, social services minister John Sweeney announced the beginning of the implementation of Phase 1 of *Transitions*. He topped up $120 million in inflation adjustments in benefits with $300 million in new money for families on social assistance. The first instalment also facilitated the transition to work by allowing people to combine limited wages with benefits.

Peterson hired Patrick Johnston as his advisor on social policy, moving him into his inner circle.

The difference between the Liberals and the Tories was striking. "In the old days of the Conservatives," said John Southern, "we had to stone them to death with briefs. Today, you see people hanging around the doors. The Liberals like to be seen consulting with the public."

By commissioning the Social Assistance Review Committee and by beginning to implement its recommendations, the Liberal government had gained enormous credibility with social movements — not just from anti-poverty groups, but with women, seniors, natives and others. No longer could the NDP claim the moral high ground and exclusive political connection with these progressive movements. In future, the NDP would have to fight along side the Liberals for their hearts and their votes.

* * *

The NDP was actively engaged in the SARC process itself. On January 23, 1987, five NDP caucus members made individual presentations to the committee during its hearings at Queen's Park. Evelyn Gigantes spoke about women in poverty, Bob Mackenzie about changes in labour legislation, Dave Cooke about housing, Floyd Laughren about universal accident and illness insurance, and Richard Johnston about the overview of a new income maintenance system.

Called *Toward a New Ontario,* the lengthy caucus report detailed the party's policies in these areas and tried to synthesize them into a coherent and related package. It was the most systematic presentation on reforms to social assistance the party ever prepared.

Most of the party's proposals were long-standing policies put into a larger context. The party argued for a full employment economy, and said it couldn't come about until work was reorganized by providing for earlier retirement with adequate pensions, shorter work time and better job training. It called for a minimum wage pegged to 60 per cent of the average industrial wage, and for laws to facilitate unionization.

The report pointed out that the majority of the poor in Ontario were women. It called for dramatically improved and less expensive childcare, with more spaces and better wages for caregivers. It also called for an affirmative action hiring program, or employment equity, equal pay, and the judicial enforcement of maintenance orders.

The party's housing program advocated that the Ontario Mortgage

Corporation become a direct lender for the development of private and public non-profit housing. It called for tougher rent controls, assistance to low-income home-owners, protection for existing housing stock, improved emergency shelters and support housing for the mentally and physically disabled.

Perhaps the caucus's most dramatic and far-reaching proposals were those in relation to universal accident and illness insurance. Its brief showed how a family of four whose primary wage earner becomes unable to work would receive a wide range of income depending on the nature or cause of the disability. A compensable accident at work might provide a total disability pension from the Workers' Compensation Board of $1,600 a month, but if the same family had to rely on General Welfare Assistance, it would receive benefits as low as $750.

It called the existing maze of disability benefits slow, adversarial, confusing, expensive and inefficient. In place of the various existing programs, the party proposed "a comprehensive, universal accident and illness insurance program that provides financial stability when illness or injury strike."

"The principle of a universal public insurance program accepts that we, as a society, share a community responsibility to provide financial security to those unable to work because of illness or injury," the caucus report said. "Under today's system, taxpayers' dollars support the administration of welfare, family benefits, WCB, federal programs and private insurance company profits. The system we are proposing would put our dollars into a system that supports the disabled, not administrative costs and profits."

"The centrepiece of an illness and accident compensation scheme is the income replacement or earnings-related compensation," the NDP said. It gave the example of the New Zealand system, which consists of 80 per cent of lost earning capacity to a maximum that covered all but the top three per cent of wage earners. The Ontario WCB maximum rate of 90 per cent provided higher income but was paid to a very low percentage of people unable to work because of a disability.

The NDP had long advocated a system of universal insurance, but in 1987 provided its most fleshed-out look at the issue. It had never been a high-profile plank in the party's election platform, and throughout its preoccupation with auto insurance, the party never made the links to a universal system. In 1987 the party went further than it ever had — or has done since — on the road to universal insurance.

As *Transitions* did one year later, the NDP said its goal was "to get people off social assistance and into jobs." In reorganizing the delivery of social assistance, the party wanted to reduce the number of programs providing assistance and eliminate the different levels of benefit. It wanted the federal and provincial governments to fund the income maintenance system, removing that tax burden from municipalities. The party called for provincial management but local delivery of services.

Many of the NDP's recommendations were picked up by the Social Assistance Review Committee. This was no surprise, since they were similarly being advocated by poor people and the organizations that represented them at the committee hearings.

While SARC continued its work through 1987, the NDP's advocacy of poverty issues took a lower profile after its presentation to the committee. Following the September election, Rae shifted Richard Johnston from his social services portfolio to education, and gave former education critic Richard Allen Johnston's portfolio.

A Scandal a Day Keeps the Issues Away

In the legislature the Liberals quickly succumbed to arrogance and the other parties to loud sniping from the opposition benches. With whopping majorities in the legislature and on every legislative committee, the Liberals took control of the business of the government. No longer the partners in progress, and without an agenda of their own, the NDP fell back on the ad hocery of question period and occasionally resorted to legislative stunts to obstruct the business of the house.

Among the most questionable and destructive of these tactics was the high and mighty position the NDP took with regard to a number of insignificant mistakes by rookie Liberal cabinet ministers, quickly elevating them with the help of the media to the status of major scandal. Repeatedly sounding holier than thou, the NDP treated every lapse of judgement as a cardinal sin. They also used the rules of the House to their advantage to block the government's agenda.

In the spring of 1988, for example, the NDP stalled introduction of the government's Sunday shopping bill by reading petition after petition after petition into the record. The party opposed Sunday "working," as New Democrats wanted to think of it, and was backed heavily by the United Food and Commercial Workers' Union. (The NDP could never explain why it so vigorously opposed Sunday work in the retail sector while not objecting to the tens of thousands of Sunday jobs in the industrial and service sectors.)

The business of government was so disrupted by the NDP's petition-reading that on April 20, treasurer Robert Nixon resorted to the unprecedented necessity of reading the government's budget in the media studio rather than in the legislature.

The next day the NDP requested a recorded vote on the introduction of the Sunday shopping legislation and then refused to answer the bell calling the members to the House for the vote. That stunt lasted four days, until the government agreed to hold public hearings on the bill.

In May, 1989, solicitor general Joan Smith visited a London police station in the middle of the night on behalf of a close friend whose son had been arrested. Debate on that spring's budget was sidelined, and on May 29 the NDP and Tories walked out of the House, demanding release of a police report on the Smith incident. They returned briefly two days later to pass a major spending bill, then shut down the legislature again. On June 5, Smith resigned. She became the fourth Liberal cabinet minister to resign a portfolio, but the first of the majority government period.

Smith's error was foolish but inconsequential — she did not attempt to use her position to influence her friend's son's case — but the NDP behaved as if the solicitor general had committed a felony.

The New Democrats' behaviour, not just concerning Smith but also during other minor incidents, was in part a symptom of the powerlessness they felt. They were playing a macho game of using what little clout they had. It also reflected their lack of serious issues or their own agenda.

In the end, the NDP tactics just served to discredit all politicians in the public eye — something that could only be counter-productive for a party that believed in a greater role for government. The NDP's belligerent attitude to Liberal scandals from 1987 to 1990 also played into a right-wing agenda that made people believe that politics was inherently corrupt, and that government — far from playing a useful role in society — was not an efficient governing or managing force. The NDP was helping make people believe that the real test of "good government" was not its ideas, its policies, its legislation or the capabilities of its members; "good government" was simply one free of scandal. Issues like the growing disparity between rich and poor, the deteriorating environment, or systemic discrimination of the sexes or races took a back seat to the Liberals' petty mistakes and lapses of judgement.

When a legitimate and serious scandal took place later, the Patti Starr affair, the NDP's previous histrionics made them look like the boy who cried wolf.

Any party that vaults into an enormous majority government is bound to have a high percentage of inexperienced members and cabinet ministers. This was true of Mulroney's Conservative government in 1984, Peterson's Liberal government in 1987, and the Rae's NDP government in 1990. The NDP's self-righteousness in attacking the Liberals made the opposition parties want to exact revenge on the mistakes of NDP cabinet ministers later on.

The 1988 Federal Election

Politics in Ontario have frequently been overshadowed by events in Ottawa. For many Ontario politicos, the real action in 1988 was over the Canada-U.S. free trade agreement, fought out in that fall's federal election.

For our purposes, the election is significant for four reasons: first, the NDP's downplaying of free trade during the campaign; second, the party's, and labour's failure to pose an economic alternative; third, labour's role in the Pro-Canada Network and how that helped change labour's relationship with coalition politics and hence with the NDP; and fourth, the unusual public criticism of the party's campaign by its close friends in the labour movement. Most of the key players were influential establishment figures within the Ontario NDP.

At the end of August, the House of Commons passed the free trade deal over the vigorous objections of the Liberals and the NDP. The Liberals then proposed using their majority in the Senate to block the deal. Several prominent labour leaders supported this strategy, though it put the NDP in an awkward spot. To support the move only highlighted the Liberals as the best opponents of the deal and legitimized the Senate, which NDP policy looked to abolish. But to oppose the Liberal tactic seemed to be soft on free trade. The NDP dithered for a few months before coming out against the Senate move.

On October 1, Brian Mulroney called an election for November 21, seeking a mandate to implement free trade, and using the moral authority of the people to block action by the non-elected senators.

For over a year prior to the election the NDP led in the polls, with some predicting the NDP could win as many as 100 seats. The party led in Quebec, where it had never elected a single member. Broadbent was by far the most popular leader.

Perhaps out of wishful thinking, the party seemed not to realize that people were "parking" their votes, waiting for the time when they had to make a real decision about support. But the party's apparent popularity influenced a number of key decisions.

As mentioned previously, the party's elevated status was one of the reasons why many federal New Democrats wanted the Ontario party to avoid formal links with the provincial Liberals in the Accord. They were still clinging to their fond hope of the withering away of the Liberals, and were hoping to supplant them as the alternative to the Conservatives. Three weeks into the campaign, NDP leader Ed Broadbent speculated that Canada might be headed toward a two-party system. Though the NDP was running against the Conservative government, New Democrats saw the Liberals as their main contenders for votes; this left them with a confused view of who the "enemy" was.

For over a year prior to the election, federal New Democrats had talked tough against free trade. But their polling showed that free trade was an issue of economic management, where the NDP had little credibility. Their polling also showed that the people most opposed to free trade were likely to vote Liberal, and the party was afraid of splitting the anti-free-trade vote with them. Perhaps most crucial of all, the NDP wanted to cater to Quebec, where it was high in the polls and where there was considerable support for free trade. This combination of factors led NDP strategists to play down the party's attacks on free trade in the immediate pre-election period and once the election began. In fact, in Broadbent's news conference kicking off the campaign, he made no mention of free trade.

Banking on its high level of popular support, the party tried to be all things to all people. Its 24-page election platform stressed moderation, never mentioning socialism, social democracy, or the vexing and divisive questions of abortion, nationalization or withdrawal from NATO and NORAD. As one party insider put it: "Their message turned to mush;" their TV ads were so soft they came to be called "On Golden Pond."

During the English-language leader's debate, Liberal leader John Turner attacked Mulroney sharply over free trade and set himself up as the defender of Canadian sovereignty. Broadbent's pallid response was interpreted as meek me-too-ism. Turner emerged as the champion of the anti-free-trade forces. Free trade was clearly the defining issue, and the NDP had let it get away.

In *100 Monkeys*, his study of the election, Robert Mason Lee says the NDP missed a glorious opportunity by failing to press its opposition to free trade — which it might have focused in social terms. They were "served a gourmet lunch, and allowed the Liberals to eat it," he wrote.

Party historian Alan Whitehorn wrote in *The Canadian General Election of 1988* that: "In the 1988 election the party drifted to the right to woo the electoral centre. This strategy of trying to outperform the Liberal party in the political centre has largely failed...."

The free trade campaign also showed that both the party and the labour movement had no real alternative to free trade, nor did they give their opposition to free trade a socialist analysis. Despite the enormous combined resources of the labour movement and the federal and provincial New Democrats, they had few concrete economic alternatives and little to say about a restructured Canadian economy.

Free trade did not cause the Canadian economy to become heavily American-owned: that has long been the case and free trade didn't change it. Going back to the days of the Waffle, labour and the NDP rejected anti-American nationalism and now they managed to avoid it as they wrapped themselves in the flag over free trade. Even sectoral agreements like the Auto

Pact, vigorously supported by the party and labour, have only served to facilitate the Americanization of the Canadian economy. The NDP and labour have not seen U.S. ownership as a key issue in the Canadian economy, and the free trade debate did not alter that tradition.

Failing to present a lunchbucket economic alternative, New Democrats and labour abandoned the free trade issue to a simple question of whether the Liberals or NDP were its more credible opponent. On this score, the Liberals won hands down. It is no surprise the NDP had no credibility on economics.

Both in opposition and as provincial governments, the NDP has shown itself to be a paper tiger over free trade, unwilling or unable to combat the deal. It has been even less willing or able to expose the power of international capital. Though complaining that the Peterson government did little to thwart free trade, Rae's government has done even less.

* * *

The third lesson of the campaign showed itself in labour's new relationship with coalition politics.

Long before the campaign started, the Pro-Canada Network was making people aware of the perils of free trade. The coalition formed in 1985 in response to the trade talks, and included labour, churches, women's groups, seniors, peace activists and others. It became one of the largest political coalitions in Canadian history. The labour movement played a key role in the Pro-Canada Network, partly as a cash cow, partly because of its organizational expertise, and partly with its economic research staff.

Perhaps because working people had so much at stake, the labour movement was front and centre in anti-free-trade coalitions, and was happy to participate beside other movements that broadened the critique. Free trade would not affect just workers, it would weaken social and cultural institutions, and labour wanted to fight with these elements to show that its interests were not purely self-serving.

With this experience through the late 1980s, labour lost some of its disdain and suspicion of coalition politics. Labour leaders also came to realize that this was where much of the political action was. By acting as patron and benefactor, organized labour also exerted control over elements of the coalition. Some groups were more cautious than they would have otherwise been, or more readily accepted labour's line because they depended on organized labour for their funding or office space.

In his analysis of the NDP campaign, discussed in detail below, CAW president Bob White talked about coalition politics. "Within the federal caucus and the full-time officials of the Party," he wrote, "there is a suspicion of the social movements. They are viewed as including many small-l Liberals, with no loyalty to electing a social democratic government, and to some extent as being in competition within the NDP for the leadership on certain progressive issues. All of these points have some validity. But they are also beside the point.

"The organization and energy of political mobilization at *all* levels is fundamental to taking on the establishment in this country. If many of the activists in these movements are not yet supporters of the NDP, that's not a problem but a challenge...."

White wanted the party to respect the movements' independence, and to build a complementary relationship with them by holding talks before determining its positions. "The more the NDP views itself as a *social movement*, rather than just an electoral machine, the easier this will be," he said.

White even went so far as to advocate that the NDP establish a "campaign committee" to facilitate participation by New Democrats in social movements, and to help bring about "some co-ordination and joint actions." (Though this is exactly what Ontario's Campaign for an Activist Party had suggested with its "campaigns department" two years earlier, the CAW under White's leadership was among those actively involved in smashing CAP.)

Following the 1988 campaign, others in the labour movement expressed similar support for coalition politics. Officially, labour was coming on side. While the labour movement never saw its own independence fettered by participation in broad-based coalitions and continued to act, organize, and speak out on its own behalf, labour also saw the benefits of broad, co-ordinated efforts. Labour leaders were finally seeing the value of working with the movements.

* * *

The final important result of the 1988 campaign was the labour leadership's unprecedented public criticism of the party. Many labour leaders and working people felt the party sold them out. They wanted and expected the NDP to be front and centre in its opposition to free trade, and when the party low-balled the issue, they were infuriated.

In particular, the labour establishment was eager to scapegoat the three campaign directors, Robin Sears, federal secretary Bill Knight and Broadbent's chief of staff, George Nakitsas. Labour leaders felt these three had not consulted them and they blamed them — perhaps not entirely fairly — for allowing the focus of the campaign to shift from free trade.

In Ontario, the rift provoked a serious falling out between Rae and Sears, as the leader came under pressure from his labour friends to dump Sears.

The two most public critics were White and Gerard Docquier, national director of the Steelworkers' union.

One week after Mulroney was re-elected with a majority government, White sent a seven-page letter entitled "Lost Opportunity" to NDP officers and executive members. His letter quickly found its way into the newspapers. Many party loyalists found his public remarks traitorous.

White wrote as a vice-president of the federal NDP, and as chair of the Canadian Labour Congress' political action committee. He said that the party "never really came to grips with the importance of free trade...," and that the results and strategies of the campaign "are so disastrous that they warrant a full debate within the party." He said: "I've never seen such a level of disappointment and anger among our activists, leaders of the labour movement and candidates..."

He complained that the party gratefully accepted labour's money and people during the campaign, but that "its ideas and leadership are completely ignored."

White made no attempt to conceal his anger. "There are a lot of people inside the NDP who must make up their minds," he said. "Are we going to be a party that tries to finesse our way through, with the thought that we will be a serious contender for the government of Canada, or are we going to be a party that clearly knows the importance of representing working people, that recognizes the importance of the labour movement, not just for its financial support, but for its ideas, and its leadership, as an important part of the success of the NDP. We need to have a long, hard discussion about our future."

A week after White's letter, Steelworkers' national president Gerard Docquier wrote a 14-page letter to the CLC executive council with much the same message. Party stalwart Michael Lewis, a member of the Steelworkers' staff, told *Our Times* editor Stuart Crombie that he wrote the letter on Docquier's behalf. It certainly has the mark of a party insider, and coming from the loyal Lewis, it is a revelation.

"The NDP's failure to play a significant role in the national debate over free trade that was carried on in the campaign was a betrayal of everything that a social democratic party is supposed to stand for in Canada," the letter said. "It is inconceivable that any serious political strategist in Canada could believe it possible to avoid the free trade issue during a seven week election campaign.

"Putting it simply, we didn't campaign in this election. We conceived a (highly suspect) plan. We carried it out. And when it came unglued, we were incapable of responding effectively or appropriately."

He suggested that the impact of the campaign on the relationship between the party and the social movements would be long-lasting. "To use a military analogy for a moment," he said, "the social movement against free trade — dominated by the trade union movement — organized the troops, bought them their uniforms, gave them their marching orders and lined them up — and then the NDP ducked down a side street and left them there. The sense of betrayal of that coalition by the NDP will be very hard felt, extremely bitter, and will take a very long time to go away."

He speculated that "it may be necessary in the future for the trade union movement to fight election campaigns on two fronts. It may be necessary to include single-issue campaigning as an explicit part of the strategy of both the trade union movement and the NDP."

Provoked by the open dissention of such key supporters, the federal NDP put in place an unprecedented review committee, which toured the country. Bob White sent another submission to the committee, acknowledging that "had some of us not expressed our concerns in the manner we did about the last election, we would not even have had this committee."

White's statement touched on a number of themes: the expansion of extra-parliamentary politics in Canada; the need to work with the social movements; the need to turn the party into an organization of creative debate and education; the need to admit that Quebec is a nation within Canada; and the need for the NDP to develop an economic program. These were all things that the party left had advocated for many, many years.

In his conclusion, White rejected the idea that the NDP could gain success by moving to the middle of the road, which he described as "the best place to get hit by trucks coming from both directions."

"As a 'realistic' electoral strategy, this holds no promise," he said. "It blurs the distinction between the NDP and the Liberal [party], inviting voters to stay with the Liberals if they want 'moderation' and inviting the Liberals to make its own pragmatic shift if the NDP makes some inroads.

"Furthermore, the name of the game is not simply to achieve electoral success. It that was our goal, we wouldn't be in the NDP but would find a much easier way to be on the winning side. You cannot sneak in the back door when you want basic change: our enemies won't be fooled; our friends will be confused. The name of the game is to win power for a specific purpose: to carry out the party's program and build a fundamentally different society."

The party's review committee was a glorious opportunity to evaluate where the party was headed. The great number of submissions it received indicated party interest. When their deliberations were over, the committee submitted a report to the party's federal council.

The report was nothing but a shopping list of bureaucratic recommendations about process and committees, that were, as one insider put it, "anything but substance." For this reason, the report was initially rejected by the council. Then, when attention turned to the leadership race, the council approved the report and quietly put it on the shelf.

* * *

Before leaving the federal election, we cannot let the criticisms by White and Docquier pass without remark. Both of their critiques are substantively accurate. But they also cover up their own roles in the campaign.

Though neither of the labour leaders was among the small group making day-to-day campaign decisions, they cannot have failed to notice that the party started low-balling free trade long before the election was called. The shock and dismay they express over the party downplaying its opposition to the trade deal does not correspond to the influence they have in the party nor to their close relationship with Ed Broadbent.

Furthermore, both the CAW and the Steelworkers are guilty of playing down the politics of the campaign in their own messages. White took considerable pride in the fact that in October, 1987, his union spent $392,000 to publish a two-page ad opposing free trade in 44 daily newspapers across Canada. It was later turned into an eight-page booklet for CAW members. The ad and booklet did not once mention the New Democratic Party. They did not accuse the Liberals of being dishonest in their opposition. They did not suggest that working people should vote NDP to oppose the deal.

The Steelworkers' union sent a letter to all its members near the start of the campaign. The original draft of the letter contained a political message that the Quebec director of the union objected to. As a result of his objection, the union dropped the politics from the letter — to both its francophone and anglophone members. The letter that went out made no mention of the NDP.

The party's two most public labour critics, and others, had themselves been responsible for messages that were politically non-partisan. While publishing good anti-free-trade information, they drew no distinction between the Liberals and the NDP on the issue. The CAW's and Steelworkers' own anti-free-trade information helped prepare the ground for the Liberals to usurp the trade issue.

Though this issue was mostly federal in its jurisdiction, its key players were part of the Ontario NDP establishment and their views were important for the party. As the economy slumped further at the time when the New Democrats came to office, partly as a result of free trade, the Ontario NDP government did little to combat either the impact of the agreement or of U.S. ownership of the economy. Its lack of economic alternatives became increasingly apparent, and labour had little to offer.

Appearances are Deceiving

Peterson made symbolic gestures against free trade. In June, 1988, his government introduced three bills that flew in the face of the trade deal. One gave Canadian companies preference when the province licensed health facilities. Another allowed Ontario Hydro to export power only if it was surplus to Canadian needs. A third supported Ontario's wine industry through a surcharge on imported wines. In November that year, the Liberals introduced legislation making it illegal to ship large quantities of water out of the province without specific permission.

But for all his talk prior to the 1987 election, Peterson did little about free trade once the deal came into force at the start of 1989. His appearance as an opponent of free trade — and his lack of action on the issue later — mirrored his government's approach to other issues.

On the surface, the Liberals appeared to take a reform approach in a number of areas. But the reforms went no deeper than the surface.

The Liberals accomplished this political sleight of hand by making changes at senior levels of the public service, by announcing a number of progressive appointments that gave the appearance of a commitment to political change, by continuing to make inroads with social movements and ethnic communities, and by establishing a battalion of task forces that marshalled hundreds of recommendations to government. They looked like a government committed to reform, which was just what they wanted: to look like one.

They started this approach in the Accord years, but moved into high gear once the minority brake was off.

The Liberals gave many career bureaucrats a golden handshake with their Voluntary Exit Opportunity. The Liberals hoped to get rid of dozens of aging Tory functionaries but ironically, much of the deadwood stayed, while those with other choices took the money and ran. In some respects, the idea backfired.

On the day after the new cabinet was sworn in in 1987, the Liberals appointed nine new deputy ministers and shuffled 11 others. Within a few months, they made a total of 24 changes at the deputy minister level and hundreds of lower-level managerial moves in the ministries. Of the new deputy ministers, eight were women, including the first-ever woman deputy in treasury, and one of the men was a native, the first such appointment outside the Northwest Territories. This was Ontario's version of the Quiet Revolution, a bureaucratic shake-up, as the Peterson government positioned people who had the power to make change without making noise.

Among the first and most surprising of the Liberal appointments — made back in 1986 — was former Toronto mayor John Sewell as head of the

Metro Toronto Housing Authority, overseeing provincial public housing in the city. Sewell had lost none of the determination he showed on Toronto City Council and as mayor. As Thomas Walkom wrote in the *Toronto Star*, his appointment was "a signal that the Liberals were transforming themselves from a doughty, right-of-centre party into one serious about urban problems." In the short time he survived, Sewell did much to sweep out the cobwebs of a paralysed system. We'll return to him below in connection with the Patti Starr affair.

On December 10, 1987, the Liberals appointed Raj Anand as chief commissioner of human rights. Anand was a labour and human rights lawyer who promised to make the Human Rights Commission an active combatant in fighting racism and discrimination. He took the job on the understanding that the commissioner would be no more Mister Nice Guy. Like Sewell, he lasted long enough to become unwelcome, but no longer than it took for the Liberals to find an excuse to get rid of him.

Anand was just 32, a young man for such a job. He was a superstar law student, and had practised with the firm in which Attorney-General Ian Scott was a partner. He went on to make his legal reputation with his work for OPSEU.

Anand's parents came to Canada from New Delhi when he was a baby; they were among the first Indian families to settle in Montreal. His father was an engineer, his mother a university professor, and he was urged to succeed. Like most immigrants he sought acceptance in a new world, but unlike many he stepped on toes and condemned racism in his new home. In his law practice, his favourite target was the provincial government. At the time of his appointment, Anand was on retainer by the Ontario Public Service Employees' Union to charge the Ministry of Housing for racist management practices.

In choosing Anand, the Liberals chose to feed a hand that would bite them and they knew it. They passed over a host of Liberal stalwarts and government insiders who would have made life easy for them, and they cannot have expected Anand to become a quiet critic once he was on the inside.

Like many of the other outsiders and upstarts they placed in socially delicate posts, Anand was needed to establish credibility for an agency that had none. Anand took the Liberals at their word when they said they wanted reform. That took a lot of them by surprise.

Anand arrived at the Human Rights Commission only to find that the commissioner's office wasn't even in the same building. He solved that bit of discrimination by moving himself into an empty meeting room over Christmas. True to his word, with little money, staff or government support, he began to turn the commission into an actively anti-discrimination vehicle, no longer content to wait for complaints to be lodged. It was his own impatience that drove him out of a job.

Shortly after Anand took office, the commission had a hand in a six million dollar equal-pay settlement for female cleaners employed by the Brampton Board of Education, the largest such settlement in Canadian history. The commission also awarded $293,000 in damages to employees at Majestic Warehouse, and made the company agree to feature people of colour in its advertisements. It offered public support for government critics, most notably native people on a hunger strike for educational rights, immigrants objecting to the federal government's refugee bill, and injured workers opposing changes in worker's compensation.

Under Anand, the commission submitted a brief to the committee holding hearings on the Meech Lake accord, claiming provisions of the deal violated human rights; it was the only government agency in the country to make such a report. The commission also supported women's groups that opposed Meech Lake.

The old commission had no public relations department, no unit that conducted policy and research, and no unit that specialized in systemic discrimination. Anand changed that. And when he hired seven new managers to fill seven functions and expand the commission's operations, he ran afoul of his enthusiasm.

The downfall of Raj Anand really started on March 1, 1989, when he appeared before a committee of the legislature to criticize Bill 162, the government's proposed changes to the Worker's Compensation Act. No Ontario human rights commissioner had ever done that before, and none has since. He pointed out how the proposed law discriminated against workers on the basis of their age and shortchanged those in the construction industry.

The government's reaction to his appearance stripped the veneer off its image of reform.

Insiders claim that prior to Anand's presentation, labour minister Greg Sorbara asked him: "What will it take to get you not to make this presentation?" Not being for sale, the new commissioner had nothing to offer.

Shortly thereafter, on May 2, during a statement in the legislature, Sorbara called the commissioner's presentation "shameful." Then, starting on May 5, the *Toronto Star*, thought of by many as the "government's newspaper", ran a series of front-page stories accusing Anand of lily-white hiring practices in his seven new top appointments.

The accusations were first made six months earlier on CBC radio by Gerry McAuliffe, but received little attention at the time. (The NDP government later hired McAuliffe as its "issues manager," a professional-sounding term for "spin doctor.") People wondered if their new play on the *Star*'s front pages had anything to do with the fact that Sorbara's executive assistant was married to a *Star* editor. If not, the brief three-day gap between Sorbara's condemnation of Anand and the re-appearance of the story in the paper was certainly coincidental.

The new-found accusations created a storm of controversy, both in the legislature and in minority communities. Legislators demanded an inquiry; some wanted Anand's resignation. On the street, ethnic communities felt sold out — again. Human rights lawyer Charles Roach even called for the abolition of the Human Rights Commission.

Rae was quick to join the chorus of those asking for an inquiry into the commission's hiring practices. Had he checked the facts first, he would have learned that one-quarter of commission staff were visible minorities. Of a top management team of nine, two, including Anand, were from visible minorities. Another four were white, but from minority ethnic groups. All but two had a wealth of experience in the human rights field. Five of the six people reporting directly to Anand were from disadvantaged groups.

At last the Liberals had found the excuse they needed to get rid of Anand. His main potential supporters, the minority communities, had abandoned him, and that opened the door for the Liberals to show him out. Anand resigned on June 2, 1989. A report commissioned by Peterson concluded that there were hiring irregularities but "there was no evidence of discrimination, favouritism or competition rigging in the hiring process." But by then, Anand was already gone.

In October, a legislative committee began an inquiry into goings-on at the commission. Here the New Democrats failed to pick up on the commission's retreat from Anand's pro-active stand that was evident by that time. Details of the post-Anand retreats were reported in NOW magazine, but conspicuously escaped attention in the *Toronto Star*, which had done so much to undermine Anand, or from the NDP.

As committee hearings opened, NDP MPP Mike Breaugh missed the significance of the fact that the Liberals were suffering a crisis of legitimacy over the commission and the fact they had forced Anand out because he was making waves. Breaugh treated it as any other inquiry and said to the committee: "I really do not have much of an inclination, to tell you the truth, to listen to everybody's complaints about another government agency. There are lots of those around."

Employment equity — ostensibly the source of Anand's downfall — had not improved at the commission, and there was nothing forthcoming from the NDP on that count. This alone suggests that the government's attacks on Anand were nothing more than an excuse to be rid of him.

During the committee hearings, the NDP seemed confused about two basic elements of human rights administration: first, whether the commission could legitimately act as both advocate and adjudicator; and second, the degree of its independence from the government. On the first point, Breaugh wondered out loud if responsibility for determining if the Human Rights Code was broken should rest not with the commission but with the courts — as if advocacy for human rights is contrary to judging whether the code had been broken in individual cases.

On November 22, NDP MPP Ed Philip observed that "in an attempt to get the heat off themselves, the Liberals burned Raj Anand at the stake;" but he failed to pick up on that theme. The committee hearings went out with a whimper and the Liberals were off the hook. Once again, they had a Human Rights Commission that faded into the background.

The NDP failed to pick up on the significance of the events surrounding Raj Anand's dismissal. The Liberals were in retreat from human rights reform, preferring a quiet Human Rights Commission that waited for cases to be dropped on its doorstep, and that did not interfere in government legislation or support government critics. The Liberals did indeed "burn Anand at the stake," and the NDP saw the smoke but missed the fire.

The Anand case shows the party didn't have an agenda for human rights. Once again, the NDP was responding ad hoc to a series of events, without a program of its own.

Swinging on a Starr

One week short of the first anniversary of their big majority win, the Liberals made a mistake that eventually led to their undoing two years later.

On September 3, 1988, housing minister Chaviva Hosek fired John Sewell as chair of the Metro Toronto Housing Authority. The sequence of events that followed came to be known as "Pattigate," a series of scandals that reached into the premier's office, burned the teflon coating that protected Peterson and seriously damaged the government's credibility. It also lifted the veil that hid the government's bent on privatization. If the defeat of the Liberals in 1990 can be traced to a single event, it is the firing of John Sewell.

This is not the place to recount the sordid details of Pattigate, but to consider how the NDP reacted to the scandals and information that flowed from it. Some background is necessary.

Appointed in 1986, Sewell tried to institute a number of reforms at the province's public housing projects in Toronto. He hired an architect to try to make the properties more attractive and to design ways to increase the density of existing projects while protecting the greenspace. He hired on-site superintendents at the buildings to solve immediate problems — something that seems natural enough, but which had not been the case. As a result of a paralysed central administration before Sewell's time, for example, getting simple repairs often took weeks, adding to frustration, annoyance and expense.

Sewell wanted to expand public housing and disagreed with a federal-provincial task force that recommended selling off government-owned land in Moss Park to private developers, and wanted instead to upgrade the public housing there. He also opposed attempts to contract-out MTHA services to private companies. On both these positions he ran into opposition from his minister of housing, and from one of the MTHA board members, Patti Starr.

Sewell learned that the development conglomerate Tridel, owned by members of the Del Zotto family, was awarded an MTHA contract which they then subcontracted to a numbered company they owned to avoid hiring union labour. He protested, Starr leaked the file to her friend at Tridel, Elvio Del Zotto, who just happened to be the president of the Ontario wing of the Liberal party.

Starr also promoted a Tridel company to build non-profit and seniors housing. Sewell also resisted this, and Starr publicly criticized him for it.

These moves immediately drew attention to the fact that Starr had two provincial appointments, because she was named chair of Ontario Place after the 1987 election. That doubling-up is not supposed to happen.

Hosek wanted Sewell out. She saw him as irresponsible, someone who made promises he couldn't deliver on. Hosek told authors Dan Rath and Georgette Gagnon: "He was throwing hand grenades into a place where, if your constants were not properly managed, you could end up having racial warfare."

But Hosek had been warned against firing Sewell. Attorney-general Ian Scott, for one, said that Sewell was "an icon, that means a little gold-tinted god, and you don't screw around with them." Nevertheless, on September 3, a Saturday, she swung the axe and the head of the MTHA rolled. Hosek phoned Sewell at 2:45 p.m. to inform him; 15 minutes later she held a news conference to announce his firing.

On September 20, Colin Vaughan, who had served with Sewell on city council in the 1970s, wrote: "If you want to know how out of touch David Peterson is with Toronto, look at John Sewell. The premier doesn't understand how Toronto works, what its aspirations are, and what people's feelings are....I heard several of Sewell's arch-enemies rising to his defence like you wouldn't believe. They said to a man Peterson has made the biggest political mistake of his life." The next day, *Globe* columnist Michael Valpy wrote: "Sack Sewell — as premier David Peterson and his housing minister Chaviva Hosek have done — and you slap Toronto."

Rae sent an open letter to Peterson supporting Sewell, suggesting that the premier fire Hosek instead. He accused Hosek of "caving in to Liberal hacks," and singled out Patti Starr. Rae also went after Hosek's ties to the development industry.

Rae also noted the significance: "It really means anybody who criticizes or tries to push the government to do more on housing is going to be forced out," he said. "The Metro Housing Authority becomes a cog in Ms. Hosek's bureaucratic wheel. You're either a Liberal and keep your mouth shut or you're out. It's appalling."

In 1987, Hosek was a star candidate, a former president of the National Action Committee on the Status of Women, courted by both the Liberals and the NDP. Peterson gave her the tough housing portfolio despite the fact that she had no political experience. But political scientist Graham White says she "performed poorly in the legislature. Under relentless opposition fire, she appeared uncomfortable with the rough and tumble of the House and devoid of empathy for the lot of those with housing problems, merely mouthing the platitudes and parroting the statistics supplied her by the bureaucrats."

Sewell was surprised Hosek fired him. He says he had a quiet time at the MTHA, and never saw it coming. He also says that throughout his tenure the NDP never showed any interest in the reforms he was trying to implement or what he left undone. "I can't even remember who the [NDP] housing critic was," he told his fellow columnist at NOW, Wayne Roberts, a few years later.

Sewell's friends in the newspaper business quickly revealed the direct links between Hosek and the development industry. On September 10, Michael Valpy noted that Tridel had donated to her campaign, as had Dino Chiesa, a lobbyist for Greenwin who was rumoured to be about to work for Hosek. (Chiesa soon signed a two-year $232,000 contract as an advisor with the Ministry of Housing.) Valpy said her links raised the question of whether she had been lobbied by the industry to oust Sewell because developers were very uneasy about his plans to expand public housing. He also said Rae had resorted to "overkill" by demanding her resignation because it caused the premier to defend her.

Valpy continued to track Hosek and the developers. So did *Globe* reporters Linda McQuaig and Jock Ferguson. A few days later, the paper revealed that of the $52,700 donated to her 1987 campaign, $23,447 had come from developers.

Before long, the paper trail led them to Patti Starr.

* * *

Patti Starr was raised poor, the daughter of a union leader. A profile in *Toronto Life* described how she was made fun of as a child, and was not well liked. A therapist described her as "The fat girl who gets revenge on the people who didn't invite her to the prom." She worked her way into the political backrooms by a combination of chutzpa and perseverance.

Along the way, she managed campaigns for North York Mayor Mel Lastman, and found her way onto the city's zoning commission, the ideal place to cook schemes and curry favour with developers.

The key that opened doors to her was provided through the charity circuit, which she worked skilfully. She co-headed the United Way with Rosedale millionaire Eric Jackman in 1984-5.

The Toronto chapter of the National Council of Jewish Women hitched its wagon to Starr. For almost a century, the NCJW quietly performed good works on behalf of women, children and immigrants. But with Starr at the helm, the NCJW was bound for glory. "We always had these wonderful things to do, and the grants came in," says a former Council associate. "We went from the normal motherhood and apple pie, small and invisible projects into high-profile projects that could get grants. She was very insightful in bringing the organization to that sophisticated level."

One of those high-profile NCJW projects was the Prince Charles housing development, 160 units for seniors and the disabled in North York. City councillor Howard Moscoe, a maverick New Democrat, remembers Starr at the time. "She was genuinely out to do good," he says of her efforts on the Prince Charles project. "She worms her way into everyone's heart. She's full of energy and she exudes competence." While helping usher through that project, Moscoe heard the good-humoured complaints of the project's developer, Elvio Del Zotto: "She's weaseled more out of me for this project than anyone has before."

Del Zotto understood the reciprocity of favours; his connections with Starr and the NCJW allowed him to beat out the publicly-owned Metro Toronto Housing Corporation for land allocations in North York.

With its charitable status, the Prince Charles project was entitled to over a quarter of a million dollars in provincial tax rebates. Tridel passed its $251,000 rebate over to the NCJW "for whatever purpose it chose." Tridel also paid over $100,000 in consulting fees to the NCJW for help with the housing project.

Contrary to law, a lot of that money found its way into the campaign coffers of various Liberals and Tories in 1987 — donations made by the NCJW at Starr's direction that only came to light in 1989.

Ontario Liberals headed the long list of recipients. Among them, there was $1,500 to transportation minister Ed Fulton, $1,800 to health minister Elinor Caplan, $1,000 to tourism minister Hugh O'Neill, $1,250 to revenue minister Bernard Grandmaitre, $1,000 to skills minister Alvin Curling, $1,250 to Ron Kanter, $750 to consumer minister Monte Kwinter, $350 to Lily Oddie Munro, and the list went on. It included Toronto mayor Art Eggleton, federal Liberal leader John Turner and prime minister Brian

Mulroney. All together, 25 politicians including nine provincial cabinet ministers and four back-bench MPPs got a total of almost $90,000. The Star's Thomas Walkom described it as a "financial daisy chain."

The day after the 1987 election, the Liberals rewarded Patti Starr with an appointment as chair of Ontario Place, a place where she wouldn't get mud from developers' hob-nailed boots on her expensive high-heeled shoes, and where she could hob nob with Ontario's real corporate elite. On the Ontario Place board, she found the corporate heads of Molsons, Club Monaco, Yamaha, Kodak, the Royal Bank, Coca-Cola, Pepsi, Rothmans, General Motors, Black's Photo, Irwin Toy, CHIN radio, Kellogg's, and, who else, Elvio Del Zotto of Tridel.

At Ontario Place, Starr pursued the route toward privatization that she had pushed on the board of MTHA. She cut its deficit and privatized services and shops. She introduced admissions for seniors and hiked other fees. A former manager, who left when she was appointed, said she was just fattening it up for sale. If so, the Liberal government was only following the route it had taken with other provincially-owned assets such as Minaki Lodge and the Urban Transit Development Corporation.

The Liberals were working on tenant leaders to promote small-scale "non-profits" as a viable alternative to large-scale public housing. This was a win-win situation for the Liberals, who would unburden the province from social housing, and for developers, who would build the housing and keep it in the private sector. The Liberals were forging a smooth transition to privatization until Pattigate blew it.

* * *

The digging by Valpy, McQuaig, Ferguson and others unearthed more and more dirt, linking Patti Starr, Chaviva Hosek, Elvio Del Zotto, and land developer Marco Muzzo, owner of a large garbage-hauling company who bought the Peterson family firm for $9.7 million two months prior to the 1987 campaign, and who donated over $100,000 to the Liberals that year. Given the limit on corporate donations, creative accounting procedures may have been used to do an end-run on the law.

On June 8, 1989, Patti Starr resigned as chair of Ontario Place. Two weeks later, Gordon Ashworth, Peterson's aide, resigned for accepting a free refrigerator and paint job from the Del Zottos, arranged by Patti Starr. With the trail leading directly into his office, Peterson said: "I feel like I've been kicked in the head," and launched a police probe into the incident.

Rae responded by calling for the resignations of the cabinet ministers involved. "The one decision he can make as premier is who's going to be in his cabinet. If he had any standards, he would take these steps now," Rae said, not fearing the future.

Rae and the NDP went for the lowest common denominator of scandal, treating this one as they had the others that plagued the Liberal government. He drew no distinction between Patti Starr and the incidents involving Rene Fontaine, Joan Smith, Ken Keyes, Lily Oddie Munro, Elinor Caplan and others. He was only interested in showing the special connections between the Liberals and the developers, not in showing how government boards are stacked, revealing corporate connections to the state, or the strategy of privatization.

Pattigate was not really a story of how influence gets peddled, because the elite do not work through crass bribery or small political donations. The captains of industry want integration with government through formal, predictable, legal and largely invisible channels. They don't need bribes to gain access to political leaders.

Corruption is a mark of the lack of influence, not of influence itself. Pattigate was fundamentally a distortion of how the wealthy influence the system. In the end, the inquiry Peterson launched exposed the corruption, but not the real influence. It left untouched the question of privatization, and left unaltered the connections of the corporate elite.

But the scandal seriously damaged Peterson's image. It was something that just would not go away.

Who Will Police the Police?

As had happened many times before, including the events at the Human Rights Commission, the NDP couldn't find the trail when it had a chance to make inroads with Ontario's growing ethnic communities. Another key opportunity presented itself during task force hearings to examine policing in Metro Toronto.

On December 8, 1988, a white officer of the Metropolitan Toronto Police Force shot black teenager Michael Wade Lawson in the back of the head while Lawson was driving a stolen car. He died the next day. That followed the August 9th police killing of another black man in Toronto, Lester Donaldson, in a rooming-house disturbance.

The black community, already angered by the Donaldson shooting, was predictably outraged by Lawson's killing. The police said there was no wrongdoing and refused to investigate. That only inflamed minority communities more.

The Liberal government laid charges against the officer who shot Lawson and, a week later, now five months after the actual shooting, against Donaldson's killer. June Rowlands, chair of Toronto's Police Commission, and Art Lymer, head of the Police Association, immediately criticized the government. In response as much to the police stonewalling as to the shootings themselves, the Liberals also established the Task Force on Race Relations and Policing. It was chaired by Clare Lewis, Toronto's Public Complaints Commissioner, head of the body that investigates complaints against the police.

Members of the black community were looking for radical changes in policing. Charles Roach, a black lawyer with a long record of defending victims of police abuse, said "We want a change in the system, not just a change in the colour of those who operate the system."

Against the advice of some of his staff, Rae took the unusual step of attending Lawson's funeral — something for which he was roundly criticized in ethnic communities because it appeared so blatantly opportunistic. Then in February, 1989, he made a presentation to the task force to outline the NDP's recommendations to changes in policing.

He began by quoting Sir Robert Peel, founder of Britain's police system in 1832 and the man for whom "Bobbies" are named. "The police are the public, and the public are the police," Peel said back then. Rae followed up with his own version: "When we talk about the police, we should not be talking about 'them.' We should be talking about 'us,'" he said.

This came as news to members of minority communities in Ontario, who noticed a fairly big difference between "them" and "us."

Rae himself pointed out that only 44 of 4,498 Ontario Provincial Police officers at the time were members of visible minorities. He didn't mention that only 22 of Ontario's 121 police forces had any visible minority members at all. There was one senior officer from a visible minority in the entire province. Of the 64 police forces that hired in 1988, only 12 hired minorities. Of 4,420 police officers hired in the previous four years, only 4 per cent were from minority groups.

It was not so much a problem, as police often suggested, that minorities were not looking for jobs. In 1988, minorities made up 7.4 per cent of all applicants and 2.4 per cent of those hired; by contrast, white males made up 77.9 per cent of applicants and 92.6 per cent of hired personnel.

Rae recommended an employment equity program, not just for police forces — they didn't need singling out, he implied — but for all workplaces. Police "must look to their own structures and attitudes to examine why the numbers of visible minorities are still so low," he said. Rae might have noted that minority communities in particular are well aware that the police enforce the status quo, which means in part the dominance of white power structures. Not since Irish immigrants in the 19th century joined police forces in great numbers have minority groups looked to policing as an honourable calling.

Rae made three other recommendations to the task force: enforce clear lines of police authority and regulations on the use of force; establish "a province-wide police complaints system which is independent, impartial and civilian-run;" and name an independent public prosecutor to make recommendations on criminal charges against police officers in specific cases of apparent wrongdoing.

But Rae entirely missed the point that many people in the ethnic communities and in the criminal justice system were making: that policing as practised in Ontario was racist; that it singled out blacks in particular; and that it cracked down on exactly the kind of crimes that people who are poor, powerless, unemployed and discriminated-against are most likely to commit.

The fact is, the police enforce only a small fraction of the hundreds of statutes in Ontario and federal law. The vast majority of laws fall under the jurisdiction of various inspectors: employment standards; public health laws; occupational safety requirements; agricultural regulations; consumer codes; and so on. Police officers are as unlikely to lay a charge under the Employment Standards Act as they are to enforce the Artificial Insemination of Animals Act. They lay more charges for jaywalking than they do under laws protecting the environment.

Osgoode Hall law professor Mike Mandel says: "It's a myth to think that police enforce the law. We know they have enormous discretion, and there are too many laws to enforce anyway. So it's a question of which laws they apply—health and safety, unsafe products, combines investigation, or petty theft. They usually leave the power crimes untouched." To change their priorities, according to Mandel, "you have to make police responsible to the community they're policing. That's never on the agenda, because police are there to control subordinate groups, not be controlled by them."

One of the task force members, Sher Singh, pointed out that Toronto police chief Jack Marks concocted his own scripted melodrama to press his version of policing. "On the day before he appeared before the task force," Singh said, "he released the story of a drug crackdown in Jane-Finch [a poor, mostly black neighbourhood] and 285 arrests. If you add up the time it took, the value of the drugs was shockingly small. Yet it gave the impression that this city is turning into Detroit — just to make Marks look good because he testified that morning."

Singh's observation is the kind that the NDP never made. The police systematically patrol black neighbourhoods heavily, arresting people on many minor charges, and then use their results to show that blacks commit more crime. Not only are their "statistics" misleading, they also play into racist fears in the community. This escaped the NDP's attention.

When the task force reported in early April, 1989, many human rights activists dismissed it as a white-wash, a cop-out. Instead of providing straight-forward civilian investigation of police wrongdoing or clear steps to end racist police practices, it offered multi-racial hiring policies.

In the end, the Liberal government refused to bite the bullet and crack down on police use of force or provide meaningful civilian control of investigations into police behaviour. They ignored the advice from many minority communities, the Human Rights Commission and the NDP that reforms in these areas were key.

But the NDP missed seeing that it was not a question of the colour the cop who enforced the law, but how the police colour-coded the targets of their enforcement. It would mean that as government, they had no agenda to change the culture of policing and would provoke the ire of the cops for removing the oath to the Queen and by insisting that police file reports when they drew their guns. While these measures were sensible enough in themselves, they did nothing to change the dynamic of power relationships between a para-military police enforcing the status quo and oppressed racial minorities. The backlash the NDP government received from the police showed both the results of the NDP's failure to educate people about policing and their naive expectations of police acquiescence.

The Liberals Steal the Health and Safety Agenda

On June 20, 1988, the Liberals introduced Bill 162, major amendments to the Workers' Compensation Act. Labour minister Greg Sorbara said the new legislation was intended to "ensure that workers who are permanently disabled will be treated as human beings by the workers' compensation system."

What was really at stake was an attempt by the Liberals to respond to business concerns about their spiralling Workers' Compensation Board assessments and the serious financial difficulty at the WCB. In 1988 the Board had an unfunded liability on future benefits owed, the shortfall of payments not met by revenues, estimated to be at $6 billion.

Bill 162 was meant to address those concerns. It eliminated the former pension system and replaced it with a two-part scheme, which paid a small permanent pension to compensate for a permanent disability, plus a tempo-rary "wage-loss" provision to cover lost earnings. Though Sorbara tried to put the face of humanity on the bill, workers, labour and business all knew that its real intent was to limit escalating costs.

The labour movement, the NDP, injured workers' organizations and their advocates fought the bill with fierce determination. Rookie NDP MPP Shelley Martel, who followed in her father's footsteps to win Sudbury East and become the NDP's health and safety critic, led the legislative fight against the bill. She received widespread acclaim for her detailed analysis of the legislation and her knowledge of the compensation system.

But the NDP missed an important opportunity to organize ethnic communities against the legislation. The caucus produced a great deal of material on the bill, and did a large direct-mail campaign to supporters, but it didn't reach out to Italian, Portuguese, Greek or other workers whose first language was not English. These workers were particularly vulnerable because of their high proportion of the construction industry. The party did not run articles or place advertisements in their ethnocultural newspapers, nor did it organize NDP spokespersons to appear on the variety of radio shows that had large audiences in ethnocultural communities.

On July 10, 1989, with the legislative process nearing an end on the bill, Rae called it "the most reactionary step this government has taken" and vowed "to fight It every step of the way." The NDP stalled the legislature for 90 minutes, and then voted against the bill.

Despite its apoplexy over the legislation, two and a half years after it came to office, the NDP government had done nothing apparent to lessen its impact.

* * *

But Bill 162 was only half of the Liberals' health and safety agenda. On January 24, 1989, they introduced Bill 208, the main purposes of which were to establish a joint management-union health and safety agency, and to control the rights of workers to refuse unsafe work.

Bill 208 had its beginnings during a massive work refusal at de Havilland Aircraft Canada in Downsview. Once again, it shows the hand of organized labour in attempting to control shopfloor health and safety activists and sell labour peace.

In 1986 workers at de Havilland were suffering from symptoms of a variety of illnesses, mostly skin and lung diseases and burning eyes, the result of exposure to a number of solvents and toxic chemicals, called isocyanates. After failing to get from company doctors information they thought was honest, accurate or complete, the local union invited Stan Gray to bring in doctors to examine union members. Gray's health centre provided staff doctors who knew how to spot occupational diseases and offered organizational expertise on health and safety issues.

After examining de Havilland workers, the centre's doctors diagnosed a number of cases of occupational disease that the company doctors "missed." Reporting on this for the *Toronto Star*, John Deverell wrote: "Gray's report to the union membership on the medical findings set the stage for escalating work refusals. A subsequent labour ministry inspection report confirmed substantial violations by the employer of the laws on medical reporting and control of exposure to hazardous substances."

In the face of continuing acrimony, in mid-August the Ministry of Labour wrote work orders citing de Havilland with numerous violations of the Occupational Health and Safety Act. Then the ministry refused to enforce its own orders, allowing the company to work out its own timelines of compliance. This provoked the militancy of the workers, who began work refusals that shut the plant down.

Within a week the national CAW and de Havilland came to a negotiated agreement that workers would not have to return to the job until they had been provided with adequate training and information on the dangerous chemicals they used, and until other controls were in place. The agreement excluded Gray's clinic from further involvement.

The workers were unhappy with this "settlement," and labour unrest continued. Two months later, members of the shop committee forced the union local's president, John Bettes, to declare all deals off. The local signed a separate agreement with de Havilland that brought in Gray's doctors—at company expense and on company property—as an alternative to the company doctor. All this was done in defiance of the national CAW.

Gray says the headquarters "fought tooth and nail" against the clinic being brought in, and against the whole struggle. As Deverell summed it up in the *Star*: "National CAW officials were hostile to Gray's activities and expressed this by playing down his proposals for a permanent alternative to the company-doctor system of worker medical surveillance. Bettes and his supporters, including his successor, Jerry Dias, argued that alternative medical information had been their ace in the entire situation. Without it there would have been no mass work refusal, no new worker compensation claims, and no basis for continuing pressure on the ministry and the employer for change in factory medical and hygiene practices."

Workers at nearby McDonnell Douglas, also CAW members, were experiencing even worse health and safety problems. There, in addition to solvents and isocyanates, they had problems with aluminum, asbestos and chromium. At McDonnell Douglas, the exposures were spread throughout the whole plant. In August, 1987 the local union invited Gray's doctors to examine its workers. Once again, they diagnosed many serious occupational diseases that had somehow escaped the notice of company doctors.

On November 18, 600 McDonnell Douglas workers staged a mass work refusal, sitting in the cafeteria until they got action on a series of demands. The refusals quickly spread, soon involving over 2,000 workers. The ministry cited McDonnell Douglas for more than 200 violations of the Occupational Health and Safety Act.

Again the national CAW office intervened to work out a "settlement." But the workers didn't buy it and on January 8, 1988, the union reported that "all but about 50 of the nearly 2,000 workers who exercised their right to refuse unsafe work remain off the job pending resolution of health and safety problems in the plant." For the national CAW, the situation was out of control.

The company was losing an estimated $300,000 a day. By comparison, the total of all fines levied by the government for health and safety violations in Ontario the previous year was just $150,000.

Early in the new year, McDonnell Douglas capitulated on most of the workers' demands and the workers went back to their jobs. Once again they had to fight their national union to win the right for Gray's clinic to remain involved.

The mass work refusals at de Havilland and McDonnell Douglas had two outcomes.

First, in April the government announced it would provide $3 million to start up two health and safety clinics, one in Hamilton, and the other in Toronto. These Occupational Health Clinics for Ontario Workers were set up deliberately to siphon cases away from Stan Gray's clinic, and to try to keep a lid on uncontrolled work refusals provoked by the kind of information Gray's centre provided. As one labour insider put it, "Gray was so dangerous because he was making links to workplace diseases, which are generally so hard to prove."

These clinics, though ostensibly co-ordinated by the OFL, are joint labour-management clinics, with employer representatives on the boards of directors. They are not independent clinics representing workers in health and safety struggles with management.

Second, after a series of behind the scenes meetings between labour leaders and the government, the Liberals introduced Bill 208, which clamped down on these mass disruptions by making mass work refusals much more difficult and unlikely. Bill 208 took much of the wind out of the sails of health and safety activists. This came with the blessing of almost all labour leaders.

Some aspects of Bill 208 were a step in the right direction. For example, health and safety committees were mandated for all workplaces with more than 20 workers, including in the construction industry, which had previously been exempt from these requirements. Health and safety representatives were to be trained for every workplace.

But these representatives, workers and management alike, would be trained under the auspices of a new Workplace Health and Safety Agency, a government-funded joint union-management centre. The agency gave the labour movement access to an equal share of $46 million of training money, as well as dozens of labour jobs providing training. On the funding, one labour insider quipped: "If it's a hundred, it's a bribe. If it's millions, it's a project." The pork barrel was rolled out on a red carpet.

The new agency was a recognition that the politics of health and safety training would be eliminated: workers' and management's interests were enshrined as one and the same, and labour leaders not only bought it, but encouraged it.

Stan Gray sums up the worst problems with Bill 208 this way: "They've taken things that are powers and rights that union workers ought to exercise on their own, autonomously, and they've made them exercise [them] only jointly with the agreement of the employer. Thereby they've betrayed some of the most fundamental tenets of labour. The right to refuse unsafe work, the right to educate your own members, and the right to do your own medical tests ought to be done independently."

Gray says you should "never have the employer, who is the potential criminal here, sit on the board or direct a clinic to find out the victims of that employer's violations."

But having worked behind the scenes to get the legislation, the OFL was already on side with the Liberal government on the bill. The only major spanner in the works came from OPSEU, which mounted a vigorous campaign against the legislation.

On March 28, 1989, OPSEU president James Clancy wrote to OFL president Gord Wilson to outline his opposition to the bill. "This bill represents a major change in direction in government regulation of workplace health and safety," Clancy said. "It represents a shift from reliance on legal sanctions and prosecution as an enforcement strategy to one of voluntary compliance and self-regulation, what is often referred to as the Internal Responsibility System (IRS): a policy that we in the labour movement have viewed as an excuse for government unwillingness to exercise its regulatory responsibilities in protecting workers' health....It amounts to no less than an abrogation of the government's ultimate responsibility for the formulation and enforcement of legislative standards."

Despite being long-time critics of the IRS, the NDP's initial response to Bill 208 was lukewarm. But the OFL made it perfectly clear that it wanted the bill, and the NDP fell into line. Despite concerns some caucus members expressed, the NDP not only adopted the OFL's position on the bill but also the federation's tactics.

Labour wanted the bill through quickly, without public hearings. But the Conservatives, with a strong business lobby in opposition to the bill, forced public hearings and lengthy debate in committee. When opposition mounted inside the labour movement, the OFL proposed a series of amendments to strengthen the bill and to counter business attacks. The NDP dutifully took up the fight for these amendments, but by and large they were rejected. Since organized labour had been on side from the outset, the party had little leverage in demanding improvements in the legislation.

Bill 208 finally became law on June 21, 1990.

Like other moves at the time, the bill was also a piece of the government's larger plan to rid itself of responsibilities, in this case "devolving" responsibility from its own labour inspectors to management and workers. Pauline Seville, OPSEU president Clancy's assistant, noted that: "When the government divests, it takes its responsibility and controversy out of the issue and undercuts the opposition. In that whole period, the OFL had virtually no criticisms of the government."

The one issue where New Democrats thought they could always occupy the moral high ground was on occupational health and safety. But as we've seen, the labour leadership wanted to control health and safety activists. The new management-union agency would let them do just that, and labour leaders and the NDP together had helped bring that about. Seville says that OFL chief Gord Wilson helped undercut the NDP on the one issue where it had real credibility.

Our point is not that organized labour is opposed to improved laws protecting workers' health, nor that union leaders take a cavalier attitude toward safety issues. What they have assiduously done, though, is to find ways to limit wildcat work refusals and put the lid on maverick health and safety activists. The labour brass consciously sells off health and safety to bring about labour peace — keeping its part of a bargain for which it receives a variety of returns.

Neither the Occupational Health Clinics for Ontario workers —there are now four — nor the new health and safety agency have been champions of workers' health and safety. If they were, more would be known about their successes — and the facts are that the work done in them remains largely invisible. Occupational diseases are going unrecognized and uncompensated, and workers are paying the price.

Organized labour in Ontario has willingly taken the politics out of health and safety training, given away rights that workers should exercise independently, blurred the lines between workers' interests and management's priorities, and helped limit the enforcement role of government. In all this, labour leaders brought the Ontario NDP on side to do its legislative bidding, despite the party's longstanding positions to the contrary, which were set aside with no apparent anguish.

Meech Ado About Nothing

On June 4, 1987, three weeks before his Accord with the NDP was to expire, David Peterson returned to Toronto from a marathon round of constitutional hairsplitting in Ottawa and presented another accord to the Ontario legislature. This one came from Meech Lake. Behind closed doors at the posh Gatineau retreat at the end of April, the provincial premiers and the prime minister came to an understanding that was supposed to bring Quebec into the "constitutional family." Peterson was now presenting the authoritative text.

The Meech Lake accord recognized Quebec's status as a "distinct society," increased provincial powers, contained proposals for a reformed Senate, allowed provinces to opt out of future federal programs, and required unanimous consent among the provinces for certain key constitutional changes.

On June 23, 1987, Quebec's National Assembly approved the Meech Lake accord, and the clock started to tick on the deal's three-year approval process by Parliament and all ten provincial legislatures.

Initially, Bob Rae expressed doubts about the accord. Calling the protracted discussions "essentially hypothetical questions," he noted: "I must confess to a certain amount of irreverence about this question of the Constitution," he said. "We have spent an awful lot of time in a process of national hand-wringing. Much of it, in my view, has been very unproductive. In fact, we have had a preoccupation with legal forms at the expense of real policies."

In specific, Rae seemed most concerned about Meech Lake's exclusion of native rights, and he completely rejected the notion of a triple-E Senate. In time, however, he became increasingly sanguine about the problems in the accord.

During the 1987 provincial election, all three party leaders, with different degrees of reservation, supported Meech Lake. Although many Ontarians disagreed with the accord, they had no party on their side. Once again, the New Democrats failed to stake out their own turf.

When the accord came to a vote in the legislature in June, 1988, all three parties overwhelmingly endorsed Meech Lake. Only three New Democrats opposed it. They were Floyd Laughren, who objected to the devolution of central powers, Richard Johnston, who found the process anti-democratic, and Mike Farnan, who wanted the rights of the unborn enshrined in the Constitution. A fourth MPP, Bud Wildman, would have voted against the accord because of its exclusion of native peoples, but was in his northern riding when the vote took place.

On December 15, 1988, the Supreme Court of Canada struck down Quebec's unilingual sign law. Within a week, Manitoba's new Conservative premier Gary Filmon, concerned about the protection of English-language minority rights in Quebec, withdrew Meech from his legislative agenda. Then the Quebec National Assembly voted overwhelmingly to invoke the "notwithstanding" clause to override the Supreme Court decision.

At the end of the year, the federal NDP convention chose Yukon MP Audrey McLaughlin to replace Ed Broadbent as the party's new leader. She personally opposed the Meech Lake accord, and was one of only two New Democrats to vote against it in the House of Commons. The delegates avoided a bitter split on Meech by adopting a motion to work for improvements to the accord either through direct amendment or another amendment process. The party's resolution rejected support unless there was justice for native peoples and changes to protect federal spending powers. Rae strongly opposed the motion, but did not speak to it. Immediately after the resolution passed, he went to a microphone to say that the new policy was not a repudiation of his position. His speech, in which he reiterated that Meech Lake was the key to the survival of country, was met with stony silence.

Despite his earlier reservations, by the beginning of March, 1990, Rae was completely on side. The *Toronto Star* quoted him: "The signing of the free trade agreement has already weakened our governments and helped pull us apart. The collapse of constitutional understanding will take us even further down this road."

Later that month, New Brunswick Premier Frank McKenna proposed approving Meech while separate concessions were made in a parallel accord. Fully supportive of these changes, Peterson introduced McKenna's companion resolutions favouring linguistic duality, the right of the territories to name senators and judges, and the inclusion of native peoples in future constitutional meetings.

On March 23, in Manitoba, Filmon said he wouldn't take Meech to the legislature until its flaws were fixed. Quebec Premier Robert Bourassa refused to negotiate other changes. In April, Newfoundland rescinded its earlier approval of the deal. Manitoba rejected a parallel accord.

From June 3rd to 9th, the first ministers met with Mulroney to try to hammer out an acceptable agreement. At this stage, Peterson dramatically offered to give six of Ontario's 24 Senate seats to smaller provinces to assure more equitable representation. This broke the constitutional logjam, and on June 9th the first ministers signed a new agreement calling for Senate reform, a conference on native issues every three years, and recognition that Quebec's distinct society clause did not override the Charter of Rights and Freedoms.

Two days later, Mulroney bragged that he had held off holding a conference until the last minute, to increase pressure on the first ministers. He said he had to "roll the dice." His remarks infuriated Meech opponents.

On June 15, the New Brunswick legislature unanimously approved the new, improved Meech, but in Winnipeg, things were different.

Holding an eagle feather and speaking in a barely audible voice, New Democrat Elijah Harper, a Cree Indian, refused to give unanimous consent to suspend the rules of the Manitoba legislature and debate the accord. He said he could not do so while native peoples were left out. His quiet "No" was heard clear across Canada.

Meech Lake had run dry. In Newfoundland, Premier Clyde Wells refused to bring the accord to a vote, and on June 22, the federal government declared Meech Lake dead.

On June 23, Bourassa said he would not participate in future constitutional talks. In Calgary that day, the federal Liberals elected Quebecer Jean Chretien as their new leader.

* * *

Supporters of the deal argued that this was the "Quebec round," and future constitutional talks were necessary to deal with other pressing issues. It is a mistake to see Meech Lake simply in that light.

In fact, Quebec's agenda was only a piece of the action, a high-profile piece that helped hide the federal government's objectives.

Mulroney saw Meech Lake as part of his long-range view of Canada, along with the free trade agreement and tax changes to benefit corporations and the wealthy. His agenda was one of privatization, increased powers for the Senate, and of executive federalism through the entrenched use of premiers' conferences as a way to address constitutional questions.

Critics who argued that Meech Lake weakened the Canadian government's ability to bring in new federal programs, such as universal childcare, were right. Mulroney had no intention of bringing in more national programs; Meech would make it more difficult for succeeding governments to do so even if they were so inclined.

The move to grant more powers to the Senate was a step toward increased centralization. The provinces would theoretically have more say, but only in the selection of senators. The reality was that in a parliamentary system, senators would continue to vote along party lines and not by region. Alberta Tories would vote with Ontario Tories, just as they do now, regardless of the issue. The notion of increased regional balance through the Senate was a sham.

By enshrining first ministers' meetings, Meech solidified executive federalism and ensured that key decisions would continue to be made by a select few. It perpetuated the anti-democratic, closed-door trade-offs that took place among the political elite.

Far from being a "Quebec round," the Meech Lake accord assured the continuation of Mulroney's right-wing agenda. The tragedy of the NDP's position on Meech was that it did not grasp, let alone expose this agenda. Rae, and many other New Democrats, thought they were being "nation builders."

As many people have pointed out, obsession with constitutional rights and the powers of government raises political discourse to an unnatural level of abstraction. It means that instead of talking about concrete new programs, such as a national childcare program, Canadians are consumed by discussions about the federal or provincial governments' rights to implement such schemes. Like the other parties, New Democrats got just as swept up in these abstract discussions — concerns that Rae once recognized that Canadians were not losing much sleep over.

In the end, Meech Lake came down to a single native person, worried chiefly for his own nation and for other native peoples, whose quiet No was the loudest voice in the land.

Poor Performance

In the spring of 1989, three determined groups of people from different walks of life marched from Windsor, Sudbury and Ottawa to Queen's Park to protest the shameful conditions of people living in poverty. The marches were the brainchild of anti-poverty activist John Clarke.

Clarke was head of the Union of Unemployed Workers in London, Ontario, an articulate and militant organizer with a radical British background. Early in the new year, Clarke and several other anti-poverty activists met with NDP MPP Richard Allen, the party's new social services critic, looking for help to pull together and execute the marches.

Allen, a former university professor best known for his work on the social gospel tradition in Canada, came through with organizing staff and technical assistance. Clarke credits Allen for much of the marches' success, saying that he "unquestionably put the resources in that made the vital difference." Clarke says that Allen "went to the wall on this question [of providing resources]," despite encountering "ferocious opposition from Rae" at the outset. "I saw the NDP throwing its weight behind a community mobilizing effort as quite a positive thing," Clarke says.

The marches also had the blessing of many churches, which had been speaking out against the rising numbers of poor people in their communities. Setting out symbolically on Good Friday, there was an ecumenical feel to the start of the demonstrations. Here was a perfect example of coalition-based, extra-parliamentary politics, which brought together the poor, women, the churches, the NDP and labour.

Richard Allen marched with the poor and their supporters throughout the two-week period, spending a few days on each of the three walks. The event made him a more passionate spokesperson on the issue than he would otherwise have been.

The three groups converged at Queen's Park on April 8 in a demonstration that brought thousands of supporters to the legislature to condemn inaction on poverty.

Rae spoke at the rally and appeared to take credit for the march. He recounted that Richard Allen had come to him with the proposal, and that he had said, "Go for it, Richard." But the anti-poverty activists all knew that Rae had had little to do with it, and were shocked when he gave himself so much credit. "A great number of people were enormously offended by that," Clarke says. At least one coalition group wrote a sharply-worded letter to Rae.

It was typical of Rae's relationships with social movements to try to highjack their agenda for his own ends. His particular brand of alchemy managed to turn a golden opportunity into dust. More than that, the mobilization against poverty was not an issue where a party might take political credit — as Allen had never tried to do. This was a non-partisan issue, and a non-partisan event: poverty comes in all political stripes. Rae blew that neutrality.

On the Road to Red Squirrel

September 18, 1989. Despite attempts by at least two key staff to dissuade him, and ignoring a caucus decision against going, Bob Rae arrived by helicopter near a blockade by environmentalists on the Red Squirrel Road in the heart of the Temagami wilderness area. He walked along a path through the tall pines to a bridge where the blockade was centred. The sun was blazing hot, and Wayne Roberts offered Rae his baseball cap with "Rebel" on the front. Rae declined, but told him, "I'm more of a rebel than you think."

Rae impressed the environmentalists who gathered there in an attempt to protect one of the last stands of old growth forest in Ontario. In both an impromptu speech to the demonstrators and in private conversations with them, Rae won their support. "The least I can do is share some of the risk with you," he told them. "This is it, folks, we're running out of places to make stands like this."

Rae seemed just as impressed by the dedicated environmentalists, some of whom locked themselves together, cemented themselves into the road, or had rocks piled around them to prevent further construction. Over 200 people, young and old, had made the difficult day and a half's portage from the highway. Many expected to be arrested.

The police were half a mile down the road, at the top of a huge hill. As the day wore on, it looked as if the cops were simply going to wait out the protesters, and some demonstrators began to drift away. It was mid-afternoon, and Rae and his people also prepared to leave. Then the cops got in their cruisers and drove down the hill, fifty yards or so from the blockade. The environmentalists scurried into position. Just seconds before the cops advanced, Roberts asked Rae if he was there to be arrested. "No," Rae said.

But it was too late. The police came down the hill, and as they approached, Rae took a deep breath, stepped forward, and held out his arms to be the first person taken in. He and 15 others, including Roberts, were charged that day. It was a two and a half hour dusty ride to the police station in Elk Lake, where they were booked and released.

* * *

Rae had never appeared at the blockade of Red Squirrel Road by members of the Teme-Augama Anishnabai band, though their blockade lasted for eight months in 1988. It was partly for that reason that some of Rae's advisors thought it would appear opportunistic if he showed up at the environmentalists' blockade in the fall of 1989.

Rae also failed to notify local New Democrats that he was coming. For years, northern New Democrats had been torn over the vexing triangle of demands between jobs, the environment and native rights. In May, the party's Northern Council voted to oppose any extension of the Red Squirrel Road, noting its particular concern with native land claims to the area. Ironically, the road cost more than the timber was worth. When Rae appeared at the blockade, and when he got arrested there, northerners condemned him for throwing in the party's lot with the southern tree-huggers.

Ernie Epp, president of the Northern Council and former Thunder Bay-Nipigon MP, fired off a sharp letter to Rae on September 29. He was especially critical of a statement broadcast on the radio, in which Rae indicated that in a conflict between jobs and the environment, then jobs must give way. "In the north, the economy is as fragile as the environment," Epp said later. "If a person doesn't know that about the north, he knows nothing." Epp also attacked Rae for failing to consult the riding and local unions before showing up in Temagami. He condemned Rae's arrest as street theatre, and attacked him for using the north as place to run a political morality play. Epp asked him to respect the need for a mix of environmental protection and jobs.

But if there were concerns that Rae was about to come down solidly on the side of environmentalists in the Temagami dispute, those concerns were not well founded.

According to Brian Back, head of the Temagami Wilderness Society, the NDP had shown little interest in Temagami before 1987. He says that the only time before then that the party asked a question in the legislature about Temagami was in 1986 after the International Union for the Conservation of

Nature put the Temagami area on its worldwide Threatened Areas Registry.

After the blockade, Back says the party refused to ask questions about Temagami. "For all intents and purposes," Back says, "they were silent and the government knew it; and the government knew that if we couldn't get the NDP on side, they had nothing to worry about. Since then we haven't had any illusions about the NDP."

Two other incidents confirmed Back's suspicions about Rae's fleeting interest in Temagami. Not long after his arrest, Rae told environment groups at a meeting at Guelph University that they would have to decide if they were for or against the NDP, and that, like unions, they would have to get serious about their support. "I realized right then we were finished," Back says. "It had nothing to do with whether the environment was important to protect. It was totally opportunistic."

Back was further dismayed shortly afterward when he attended a meeting between the NDP and Temagami tourist operators who wanted to protect the wilderness. The meeting included Rae, NDP environment critic Ruth Grier and northern affairs critic Bud Wildman.

Back says that Rae came in halfway through the meeting, seemed bored, and hardly spoke. Wildman attacked the wilderness society, and wondered why the NDP should support the tourist operators, especially since they didn't have the hunters and anglers, who were angry at the NDP, "on side."

"Our guys came out of there saying who the hell is this guy?" Back says. "These guys [the tourist operators], their livelihoods are at stake and Wildman attacks them for not protecting the NDP. They were so disillusioned with the NDP. It was a golden opportunity to stand up for the tourist industry. Is it our job to protect the NDP? They were so stunned."

"Until then, we thought the NDP would fight for us," Back says, but it was clear to him then that the NDP was there only for the quick hit. He says the party was just "winging it on Temagami. They were always hiding, either behind the natives or the unions."

But the NDP's outreach to the natives or the unions did not fare any better.

Union members, especially those in the IWA, were furious at Rae after his arrest, and Rae's statement that jobs should be sacrificed for the environment only made matters worse. Several unions grumbled about disaffiliating from the party, but none did.

Early in 1990, the party arranged meetings with Rae, Jack Munro, head of the loggers' union (the IWA), Gord Wilson, president of the Ontario Federation of Labour, and Gary Potts, chief of the Teme-Augama Anishnabai. They met in February and March, then Potts cancelled their scheduled April 10 meeting. Two weeks later, without so much as a courtesy call to inform Rae, Potts signed an historic deal with the Liberals.

* * *

Whoever first said that money doesn't grow on trees didn't come from the forest.

The ancient pine, cedar and yellow birch in the Temagami region fuel local homes and the local economy. Foresters in the Ministry of Natural Resources call old growth pine "forest slums," "senile" trees in need of "harvesting" before they rot. That is, their value as wood is limited by time, though it may be measured in hundreds of years.

Today's high-tech logging techniques chew up trees like there's no tomorrow. That's the problem.

In the not-so-distant past, when sawing a tree took two loggers the better part of a day, trees were carefully selected before they were cut. Younger trees, and those with signs of damage, twisting or punkrot and those on cliffs were left standing. The forest maintained some of its integrity. Not any more.

Working from aerial photographs and computers, today's "paper" foresters map out vast areas for clearcut. All trees have to be cut to two inches off the forest floor. The remains are burnt and plowed under so the minerals are exposed for seedlings. According to the provincial auditor's 1985 report on replanting, over half the seedlings planted in this way die.

The foresters discount the value the trees have to the environment and to the entire ecosystem. Because ecology has no price tag, that value doesn't add up.

The 15-kilometre long Red Squirrel Road into the Temagami wilderness was being built by the Ministry of Natural Resources to facilitate logging, and its final cost was roughly $5 million. According to the late Dieter "Duck" Buck, former woodlot and scaling manager for the Milne Lumber Company in Temagami, building the road would have salvaged at most one year's jobs for 100 loggers and saw mill operators at Milne and in Elk Lake. The cost of the road, built at public expense, was a heavy government subsidy for that lumber.

The Temagami mill had gone bankrupt in 1988, and was bought by Roger Fryer following a secret report by Premier Peterson's special assistant, Malcolm Rowan. Something in that report held the key to the government's involvement in the deal.

About the time of Rae's arrest, Wayne Roberts obtained documents from a top official at Fryer's mill. The papers would likely expose what the Liberals had committed to Fryer when he took over the bankrupt mill. Roberts offered to share those documents with the NDP, proposing that they research the material together, a project that he estimated would take about a month. The NDP research director turned him down, despite Roberts's offer to let the NDP release the information first.

According to CBC reporter Martin Chapman, toward the end of 1989 the Liberals came under pressure to make a deal with Fryer because the banks were about to foreclose on the mill. Apparently, the Ministry of Natural Resources felt that Fryer had a strong case to sue the government for non-delivery of logs — as a result of the long blockade of the Red Squirrel Road by natives and then environmentalists. The government either had to buy him out or give him access to secure logs. The banks ultimately forced the government's hand.

By turning down Roberts's information, the NDP missed the opportunity to expose whatever deal existed between Fryer and the government, and the inner workings of the Ministry of Natural Resources and the forest industry.

Behind the scenes, the Liberals were trying to work out a deal with Fryer, and with the Teme-Augama Anishnabai.

On April 20, 1990, two days before Earth Day, natural resources minister Lyn McLeod quietly signed orders in council approving cutting licenses for 27,710 hectares in the Temagami wilderness. Fryer received permission to cut 20,000 hectares — 200 square kilometres. But the big deal was still to come.

On April 23, native chiefs Gary Potts and Rita O'Sullivan signed an historic treaty with Lyn McLeod and Indian affairs minister Ian Scott, establishing "joint stewardship" over four townships in the heart of the Temagami forest, saving them from logging. The treaty recognized the sovereignty of natives and their rights as "stewards," not exploiters or managers of the land. The Teme-Augama Anishnabai have a veto on the stewardship council established by the treaty. Band spokesperson Mary Laronde noted that it respected their view "that the land is not for sale, that it belongs to people most of whom are not yet born."

At the same time, the government said it would buy the Milne mill that relied on the area for red and white pine, and shut it down. The government did not say how much it paid for the mill, but sources indicated it was in excess of $5 million.

In a separate statement later that day, McLeod announced cutting licenses for eight companies in the Temagami district, totalling just over 7,000 hectares — those signed on April 20. But she did not mention the 20,000 hectare licence granted to Roger Fryer. Those licences allow clearcutting on 87 per cent of the area covered, twice the rate permitted prior to the settlement.

Despite the joint stewardship agreement and the licences to cut, nearly 90 per cent of the Temagami wilderness area, 3,100 square kilometres, was left uncovered and still subject to land claims or logging. Only one quarter of the old growth pine was protected, though the Red Squirrel Road was a dead issue.

By announcing the treaty and licenses on the same day, the Liberals knew that attention would be focused on the historic settlement with the natives. They also cleverly neutralized the environmentalists. "The government has put us out on a limb," said Peter Quinby, a professional ecologist associated with the Temagami Wilderness Fund. "If we criticize what's going on, the public may interpret this as criticism of the natives. That was a really slick move," he said. There would be more cuts than before, but no protests.

Before disbanding to form an organization called Earthroots, the Temagami Wilderness Society worked with local tourist operators to help establish wilderness trails and provide other inducements to attract tourists and help the local economy. The TWS denounced the government for its failure to provide economic alternatives for northern resource communities. "It's a disaster for environmental politics," Brian Back said. "It's a signal to workers across the north that they better organize against environmentalists before they steal their jobs away. It's the government's job to provide support for communities to help them adjust to a new economy based on respect for the earth. Instead, all we get is political dirt."

Despite Rae's high-profile arrest, the Temagami experience was a no-win situation for the NDP. Some environmentalists felt the party sold them out, was opportunistic and not committed to their issue over the long haul. Northern New Democrats and many trade unionists were angered by Rae's apparent siding with environmentalists over jobs. And the party's discussions with the natives went for nought when Potts signed the treaty with the Liberals.

In the minds of some, perhaps no other single image so profiled Rae as a man of conviction than that arrest. But Rae didn't go to be arrested, and suffered that fate only by minutes. As in so many other instances, opportunism determined the bottom line: it would look good to appear with the environmentalists.

The day after $500 fines were set for protesters arrested more than once, the NDP refused to raise the issue in the legislature. Rae's press secretary Dean Williams told Brian Back they wouldn't pursue the matter. "Everyone thinks it's settled," Williams told him.

Star Trek: The Next Generation

After 14 years as federal leader, and six months after the poor 1988 campaign, Ed Broadbent called it quits. On March 4, 1989, he announced his resignation. The party allowed itself nine months to search the NDP galaxy and find a new starfleet commander, who would be sworn in at a Winnipeg convention in December.

The trek was notable because not a single NDP star wanted the job.

Stephen Lewis declined, as did Bob White. Nova Scotia leader Alexa McDonough said no. So did Saskatchewan's Roy Romanow. They all had other universes to conquer. It looked as if the only people to contest the nomination would be those whose household names didn't extend much beyond their own households.

Rae was interested. But early on, the party establishment and even his friends in the labour movement told him it was time for a westerner — that two Ontario leaders in a row was one too many. (This didn't stop labour delegates from lining up behind MPs Steve Langdon and Howard McCurdy, both from Windsor, when they announced.) Rae backed off.

But as fall approached and the lacklustre leadership candidates failed to impress, the calls came to Rae again, asking him to reconsider. The other high-profile non-candidate was former B.C. premier Dave Barrett, who was openly testing the waters.

The Lewis clan stepped in, in an attempt to block Barrett. It was not the first time the Lewises had tried to thwart his political ambitions. During the B.C. leadership race in 1969, organized labour solidly backed former MP Tom Berger, a labour lawyer, over Barrett. Michael Lewis organized for Berger in the leadership contest, which he won narrowly, and in the provincial election that followed, which he lost. Berger immediately resigned as leader, and Barrett took over the party, which was in disarray. Barrett, a social worker, made little attempt to placate the labour movement; the mutual dislike lingered even when he became premier in 1972. The Lewises and Barrett never buried the hatchet, and now Stephen Lewis called Dave Barrett to ask him to stay out of the race so Rae could step in and be virtually certain of victory.

Members of the Canadian Labour Congress executive, in particular Bob White, encouraged Rae's late entry. They mandated British Columbian John Fryer, head of the National Union of Provincial Government Employees and a friend of Barrett's, to call him to say the CLC wanted Rae. Fryer never made the call.

Soon after Lewis's call, Barrett announced he would run, pre-empting Rae.

Through September, Rae continued to weigh his options. Never a risk-taker, Rae did not want to jump in without an assurance of victory.

Rae's arrest in Temagami on September 18 brought criticism, but also considerable public support for taking a principled stand in favour of the environment. And although many workers were upset with him, it did not weaken big labour's support for his candidacy.

A decision was becoming more urgent as the date of the Winnipeg convention approached, and since a cross-country tour of the leadership candidates was already underway. It would be contemptuous of the process to wait for that tour to finish, and then declare.

There was widespread speculation in the Ontario caucus that Rae would go. Many people assumed that he would declare for the nomination in Broadbent's Oshawa riding and jump into the race. But Oshawa MPP Mike Breaugh let it be known that he intended to seek the federal nomination there, and would do so even if Rae decided to run.

On October 5, Rae called for an emergency caucus meeting and flew to Toronto from Thunder Bay. While his plane was in the air, most caucus members were certain that Rae wanted the meeting to tell them that he was going. The Queen's Park corridor was electric with anticipation, and in the offices, phones were ringing busily as a few caucus members lined up support for their own bids to jump into Rae's place at the head of the table even before his chair was cold. Chief among the eager contenders were Ruth Grier and Bud Wildman.

Insiders say Rae was going to tell his caucus, and then fly to Ottawa to announce his candidacy in public there. They say he changed his mind on the plane.

Rae stunned the caucus that evening by telling them he would not run. Caucus members were so surprised that they sat in silence for a few moments, then applauded. Several of them were visibly upset.

Reminiscent of the celebrated auto-insurance leak in the 1987 campaign, Robin Sears told the *Star*'s Bill Walker that Rae *would* seek the federal leadership, and the paper ran the story on its front page, causing considerable embarrassment all around.

Like so many other high-profile New Democrats who chose not to run, Rae cited family reasons for his decision. No doubt these were a legitimate factor; his wife Arlene didn't want him to run, and with his brother David's death, he was certainly feeling closer family ties. But an indisputable factor was that Rae simply did not want to chance running and losing.

With Rae out, the fight was between Yukon MP Audrey McLaughlin and Barrett. After four close ballots at the Winnipeg convention, McLaughlin triumphed. In doing so, she was helped in large measure by the Ontario establishment, including key support from the Lewises. The anti-Barrett feeling in the Lewis family still ran deep.

What We Owe Each Other

Through much of 1989, Rae worked on an extraordinarily introspective paper, the product of an emotional crisis no doubt triggered by the personal tragedies in his family. The death of Arlene's parents, his father's encroaching Alzheimer's disease, and his brother's cancer, the bone marrow transplant, and then his brother's death all forced Rae to rethink some of life's big questions.

The seeds of his thinking were reflected at the 1988 Thunder Bay convention, when he spoke of "the love we have for one another." He elaborated on this at a meeting of the provincial council that December. There he told the party: "We must combine program with inspiration, with the vision and passion that are at the heart of the social democratic ideal. Of all the political values I know there is one less talked about and understood than others. And that value is love. Not a love that is abstract or the love of the romantics. But the love we owe each other in a world that is too often cold and hostile."

By the beginning of 1990, Rae had a full-blown paper called "What We Owe Each Other" discussing socialism and linking it to "the love we owe each other." His rambling document is a psychoanalyst's delight. It is also a revelation of a personal political philosophy and the evolution of his own thinking on socialism since his days as a graduate student, when he wrote his thesis on the Fabians.

It is worth sampling some of the ideas from his remarkable paper.

Rae refused to interpret the collapse of communism as "a vindication of capitalism, or a repudiation of anything I would call democratic socialism." In that context, he wrote: "The evolutionary triumphalism of the right is as misplaced as its Marxist predecessors: the socialist ideal will not disappear. It responds to something deep and important within human nature, certainly deeper than the acquisitive spirit which is at the heart of this, and every other capitalist revival."

He said that both Nazi and Soviet totalitarianism "have shown that the collectivism of the twentieth century does not lead inevitably or naturally to the emancipation of the working class that the great leaders of the international socialist movement told us it would....The crimes and inhumanity that have been perpetuated in the name of a greater collectivist good in this century are simply too great to be ignored....They have also profoundly altered our sense of what is politically possible, and, indeed, what is politically fair and right.

"Closer to home, the most difficult challenge facing social democracy is not the short-term question of who gets what votes in an election," Rae said. "In our pre-occupation with the electoral game, we frequently choose to ignore a bigger problem: people's long-term values, their sense of how important things like community and solidarity are, in contrast to other aspirations like getting ahead, competing economically, or being materially successful."

Rae is sensitive to how he will be judged as a politician. "My own experience has, I hope, taught me a few things. The first is that I can only write in my own voice. I will let others do the labelling of me both as a person and as a politician. Some, no doubt, will be uncharitable, on both counts," he says.

Rae reveals that political problems aren't real for him unless he hears about them from an individual. "The problem of extra-billing, for example, only became real to me when a middle-aged lady came into my constituency office on Danforth Avenue in 1979 and told me her story....I have even developed a rule of thumb: if I haven't heard a real story about a problem, then it isn't a problem.

"I went into politics as a result of a simple experience: as a dispirited graduate student I only regained a sense of purpose and direction when I went to work in London, England in a housing aid project helping homeless people and young kids in difficulty with the law....

"These stories continue to give me my focus and sense of priority. At the same time, I try to make sense of all of them by relating them to my own sense of ideas and values. I am an advocate for social democracy. What I hear on the street confirms what I believe....

"I am putting these thoughts into print for one simple reason: there are stronger arguments for social and economic democracy than we realize, and we make these arguments by combining ideas and experience, by talking about values, and by telling our stories to one another."

These stories and his experience led him to expound on love. "We owe each other love, and the action that flows from that," he wrote. "We express that love in deeds, in actions, in laws, institutions, entitlements.

"Having said that, socialism is not a religion. It is no guarantor of personal spiritual happiness. It cannot protect us from the tragedies of life. Many have projected far too much onto their political faith, and are disappointed with 'everything they've ever wanted isn't enough.'"

Dismissing right-wing economics, Rae also said that "socialists have to come to terms with some critical realities as well." He rejected economic " 'planning' on its own," and wrote:

"We must see socialism as embracing a creative tension between three realities: planning, democracy, and markets. If we ignore any one of these factors, we are in trouble. If we ignore the need for sensible and practical planning by governments on behalf of the public and common interest, we become overwhelmed. We are in a housing crisis, a nursing shortage, a garbage pileup, a traffic and urban development jam; none has really been prepared for by government. We have no co-ordinated effort at planning, at thinking through the enormous changes we simply experience and try to handle from day to day."

He wrote that "capitalism's ability to 'deliver the goods' economically has been much exaggerated," but that if democratic socialism were to succeed, people would have to choose it willingly. "To inspire," he said, "socialism cannot simply be seen as about structures, systems, or strategies presented as grand plans. It must be about people, their hopes and dreams for their lives and families and not for their 'best selves.'

"When Gandhi was once asked what he thought of Western civilization, he is said to have replied 'That would be a very good idea.' I suspect that this is how many of our fellow citizens feel about the values of freedom, equality, solidarity and justice we fight for and call our vision of democracy."

Rae concluded: "It is now our turn to do the job. We must affirm and renew our values, and explain to ourselves and to others why they matter, why they are important, and how they differ from the values of others. We must apply those values as creatively and effectively as we can to the challenges of our day, either in government or in opposition, always as part of a movement for social change and economic justice. We must muster all our qualities of heart and mind in the task, unafraid of controversy, realising that we are doing what others before have done, but that we must do it for ourselves and for our generation."

* * *

The practising politician who puts these kinds of thoughts onto paper is rare. In the end, though Rae had put considerable time and thought into his paper, only a small circle of people ever saw it. The *Toronto Star*'s Thomas Walkom did a column about Rae's thinking on socialism, but otherwise it did not receive the public attention such an unusual undertaking might have.

As much as the paper is a soul-searching examination, it does not include practical economic ideas or policy — even its environmentalism is vague and preachy — and it shows no class analysis, just a set of human values by a person searching for them.

Sayonara Sears

After the NDP's federal campaign in 1988 and the sharp criticism that followed it, the relationship between campaign guru Robin Sears and Bob Rae soured. Rae's friends in the labour movement were furious with Sears and wanted him dumped. But Rae did not — not until something could be worked out. Like unions, the party tries to treat its loyalists well.

Through 1989, the working relationship between the caucus and its staff also deteriorated, and many fingers were pointed at Sears's draconian management style. Some staff members were still bitter about the heavy hand that had come down on Graham Murray in 1987. A number of key people had quit the staff, fed up with the bickering, animosity and personal nastiness that was a mark of frustration during the years of Peterson's majority. Morale was at an all-time low.

Management-staff relations declined further as the result of a bitter round of collective bargaining in which the caucus showed its true colours as bosses.

NDP caucus workers are members of the Ontario Public Service Employees' Union. Bargaining with the caucus had often been a difficult process because staff believed the party's rhetoric about a worker's role in the workplace. Though wages were generally not high, the union was well aware that the caucus did not determine its own budget, and salaries were often not the most contentious issue in bargaining. Many other aspects of its relationship with its staff were controlled by the legislative assembly and not subject to a union contract.

As a result, the workers used negotiations to extend their rights and protect their jobs.

In this round of talks the union wanted chiefly to have a say in how the salary budget was distributed, which was normal, and to clamp down on contracting out of their jobs. Another of their demands, which the union thought would be granted pro forma, was the inclusion of contract language to protect workers from sexual harassment. The union tabled the exact language that the Davis government had granted its provincial public servants a decade previously.

Members of the union's bargaining committee were shocked when management came to the table with a series of concessionary demands. These included a demand to delete all three union rights clauses in the contract and to insert one clause that would have made it easier to fire or displace long-time workers.

The union's bargaining committee at first thought these were bargaining ploys, the kind of give-away items that are traded off for the real objective. It was not the case.

The two sides concluded all the rest of the negotiations, including the wage package — which is traditionally the last issue to be settled — and the final items on the table were the union's demand on sexual harassment and management's demand to delete the three union rights clauses.

Despite the low level of staff morale, most staff were loyal to the party as a cause. Most were idealistic and committed, and always wanted to avoid embarrassment to the party. The union's bargaining committee was not at all sure it could win support for a strike over the remaining positions, and bargaining was at an impasse. To reach a settlement, the union committee proposed to drop its demand to include sexual harassment language and to delete the most innocuous union rights clause if management agreed to let the other two rights clauses stand. Management accepted.

The union team may have misread their colleagues, because when they reported the details of the tentative agreement, many of the workers were shocked at management's hard line. After a long discussion, a motion to approve the settlement passed narrowly.

The workers couldn't believe that the NDP wanted to weaken their union's rights, but they were particularly angry with caucus hypocrisy over harassment language. It was something that NDP MPPs argued for in a thousand speeches. Management's lame excuses — that they didn't want to face grievances on that issue and that workers had another avenue for complaint, the Human Rights Commission — met with as much ridicule from the staff as they had from the bargaining committee.

Everyone understood that the negotiations had been difficult, and the union had sent the appropriate signals to management that they didn't want to risk an embarrassing public confrontation on matters like this. The staff knew that even though they were not at the bargaining table, both Sears and Rae had to be aware of the nitty gritty at bargaining's eleventh hour. They must have approved management's bottom line. It only added to the bad feelings at Queen's Park.

But Sears's days were numbered anyway. In the spring on 1990, the Liberals surprised most observers when they announced that he would become the number two man at Ontario's trade mission in Tokyo, working alongside Tim Armstrong. The conduit for Sears's appointment was likely Dan Gagnier, an old friend of his who became Peterson's chief of staff after Hershell Ezrin left. Gagnier's influence with Peterson was in the midst of a meteoric rise.

As was his habit, Sears decided his parting thoughts were worthy of being committed to posterity, and he wrote and circulated "A Look Behind...and Ahead." In it he summarized what he thought were the major changes over his four-and-a-half-year tenure.

"We have a tendency to be too hard on ourselves — it comes with the turf of wanting to remake the world, I suppose," he wrote. "We focus on the perennial morale problems of an opposition political office, rather than on the creation of the best professional staff of any party office in Canada.... We agonize when we fail to dominate question period news for a day or even a week. Imagine the excuses offered by government communications officers for their failure to wipe the floor with us with resources five and ten times greater."

"It is a cruel business because excellence and hard work are not often rewarded with success and gratitude," he noted. It's easy to imagine whom he had uppermost in mind.

With that, he was gone, and many of the morale problems he referred to went with him. The *Toronto Sun*'s Michael Bennett wrote that his departure "was described as the best remedy for a democratic socialist's morale since rock 'n' roll oddball Frank Zappa started doing business with Czech president Vaclav Havel."

Televangelism Comes to the NDP

Ever since they came to power under the Accord, the Liberals had difficulties with automobile insurance. They initiated a two-year study by the auto insurance board — price tag just under $13 million — but that did little to resolve the issue or the continued popularity of the NDP's "driver-owned" insurance scheme. Those problems were compounded in the 1987 campaign when David Peterson announced that he had "a very specific plan" to deal with the insurance issue. But no such plan existed.

The Liberals also commissioned Justice Coulter Osborne to study the issue, and in April, 1988, his report, at a cost exceeding $1.6 million, rejected public auto insurance. Just two weeks later, NDP MPP Mel Swart surprised the legislature by announcing his retirement effective June 30 for health reasons. Swart had led the charge on public auto insurance, but at 68 was experiencing heart problems and was advised to step down. Peterson waited until September 23 to set a by-election date for November 3rd.

For many years, Swart had groomed his constituency assistant Mike Grimaldi as his replacement, but it became known that Grimaldi had been charged with assault by his wife, and was no longer an acceptable candidate. Into the breech stepped maverick criminal lawyer Peter Kormos, who defended his friend Grimaldi.

Kormos easily won the by-election, and Rae immediately handed him the insurance portfolio. By giving its most junior member — a person with no experience on auto insurance — this task, Rae sent a clear signal that the NDP no longer intended to give the issue the profile it had once had.

If some people are loose cannons, Kormos was a runaway multiple warhead. A defender of the downtrodden as well as unsavoury hoods, he quickly showed he had little respect for the formalities of the legislature. He exhibited a similar lack of respect for the caucus's female staff, insulting them, ridiculing them, shouting at them and occasionally threatening them.

At one point, he summarily fired a legislative assistant with over 20 years' experience over a petty matter, but was reminded of the little nuisance of the collective agreement. It was just the latest in a line of incidents that eventually resulted in the unprecedented refusal of a single caucus worker, male or female, to bid for a job opening in his office. With the consent of the union, caucus management hired temporary outside staff — which was unprecedented in the union shop.

At the federal leadership convention, a legislative intern asked Kormos who he was supporting, and Kormos replied "ABC." When asked what that meant, Kormos is said to have replied, with characteristic vulgarity, "Anybody but the cunt."

But he took to the insurance question like a hungry bear, anxious to play the bad boy to rapacious corporations and the insurance industry's well-paid lobbyists. He revelled in using the legislature's soapbox to blast the vested interests.

Shortly after he was elected, he boasted that the people of Welland expected him to be an advocate like his predecessor. Speaking of Murray Elston, the minister in charge of auto insurance, he once said: "I watch the minister really closely, and never has such a load of crap ever been unloaded in this legislature before. It should have been done out on the front lawn because at least the grass would be greener by virtue of it." On another occasion he said: "I'm going to have to grab Murray Elston and rub his nose in shit to at the very least housebreak him."

But if anyone's nose needed frequent rubbing, it was Kormos's.

At one point, during legislative committee hearings on auto insurance, the party had to make excuses for his absence. He was in his apartment nursing a hangover and a black eye from the previous night's exploits. Rae, MPP David Reville, and Rae's assistant David Agnew read Kormos the riot act.

Then on April 26 and 27, 1990, Kormos turned televangelist, preaching the homily of public auto insurance to a cable audience during an overnight 17-hour filibuster that was the longest in the history of the Ontario legislature. Like any TV marathon host, he read out telephone numbers at Queen's Park where people could phone with their pledges — in this case their insurance horror stories. Over 700 people called in, and he read out their names and described the injustices they endured. From six o'clock at night until nearly eleven the next morning, he kept it up. It was widely rumoured that he had more than adrenalin to keep him going, or that more than sheer exhaustion accounted for the wild rambling of his speech.

Kormos was given a platform, and he performed in a way that brought the phrase "beyond wildest expectations" to mind. He became a party cult hero. Despite the fact that the leader was well aware of Kormos's troubled personal behaviour and the grief his personnel problems caused caucus management, and though he was embarrassed by Kormos's unparliamentary language, Rae asked him to be the guest speaker at his York South nomination meeting prior to the 1990 campaign.

Rae may have been chagrined by the behaviour of his newest boy wonder, but he not only tolerated it — he also gave him the pedestal to shout from.

In a similar way that Rae's judgement was clouded by the inexplicable hold that Sears had over him, so Kormos, too, seemed beyond Rae's grasp.

A criminal lawyer, Kormos believed firmly in the right of accident victims to sue, a principle at odds with strict no-fault insurance and a major stumbling block in the reduction of costs as a result of huge court settlements. As the caucus's outspoken critic, he personally hijacked the right-to-sue question, and by doing so closed off the possibility of the party seriously pursuing the more far-reaching proposal of universal accident and illness insurance.

For all the attention it received and the profile it gave him, Kormos's filibuster was nothing more than a lengthy exercise in personal aggrandizement, a tale told by Kormos, full of sound and fury, signifying nothing. One month after the filibuster, the legislature passed the government's no-fault bill into law.

Although the Kormos filibuster gave the NDP the image of a fighter, like Rae's arrest at Temagami there was little substance to the impression. Kormos's all-night rant was prompted only by a sneaky last-minute move by the Liberals, who used the legislature's rules to prevent the day's customary 6:00 p.m. adjournment, forcing him to keep on speaking or to abandon his delay tactics.

The caucus was committed to public auto insurance, but couldn't get its act together about the right to sue, nor was it ready to link it with universal accident insurance — a much bolder move. With the legislation passed, public auto insurance was no longer a central plank in the party's platform. A year and a half later, the NDP government abandoned the issue altogether and then passed a barely changed version of the Liberal law.

Peterson Pulls the Plug

By the spring of 1990 the Queen's Park rumour mill peppered political conversations with the speculation of an early election. Hushed talks turned to a constant buzz that the Liberals were about to capitalize on their commanding lead in the polls by going for another term in office.

An Environics poll showed the Liberals with the support of 50 per cent of decided voters, the NDP with 26 per cent and the Tories with 24. Though the Liberals were less than three years into their mandate, it seemed that the temptation would be too great and that Peterson would pull the plug.

There were plenty of signs that spring that the Liberals were ready to jump.

On March 27, days prior to their convention, the Liberals lifted the freeze they had placed on candidate nominations. They scheduled campaign schools at the convention to train workers and prepare prospective candidates.

Just a week after Peter Kormos's full-of-bluster filibuster, on April 23 natural resources minister Lyn McLeod announced the joint stewardship agreement over 40,000 hectares of land in the Temagami wilderness with the Teme-Augama Anishnabai. Though environmentalists knew better, in the public eye the deal seemed to balance protection of the environment with protection of jobs, while offering a ground-breaking resolution of a sensitive land claims issue.

The next day, treasurer Robert Nixon brought down an election-style budget with no significant tax increases.

On May 12, Nipissing MPP Mike Harris defeated rookie MPP Diane Cunningham to become the new Tory leader, ending the lengthy "interim" leadership of Andy Brandt. Brandt, who served as his party's leader for longer than either of his two immediate predecessors, Frank Miller or Larry Grossman, was a decent but lacklustre middle-of-the road Conservative. The Tories endured the 1987-90 period in a state of shock, not quite believing that they had fallen so far from grace, and looking desperately for something to connect them to their glorious past. Brandt deserved credit for steering his fractured caucus through troubled waters. Now, with the unknown Harris, a former golf pro, at the helm, the Liberals looked to profit from his lack of experience or profile by calling an election before he had time to pull the party together.

On May 28, the Liberals passed their no-fault auto insurance bill, the last piece of their insurance puzzle. Their earlier legislation introduced a rate review board and capped rate increases, and despite the well-publicized efforts of the NDP, the insurance issue had largely blown over.

When the legislature rose on June 28, most observers thought a summer election was around the corner, and of course they were right.

On July 25, treasurer Robert Nixon openly advocated an election, but reporters questioned Peterson about the number of Liberal promises that had not been honoured. Peterson told them "I appreciate your advice," and said that there had been a high degree of compliance.

Two days later, a group of top-ranking Liberals met at the offices of public relations specialist Patrick Gossage to plan their election announcement. (Gossip between insiders said that Gossage had made his whole career on the basis of once being Pierre Elliot Trudeau's press secretary, which was "an easy job since all he ever had to do was tell the media to fuck off.") Among the group were Premier Peterson, his former principal secretary Hershell Ezrin, pollster Martin Goldfarb, personal confidante Vince Borg, campaign director and party president Kathy Robinson, and Hill & Knowlton public affairs strategist David McNaughton. There was general consensus that with the party's commanding lead in the polls, there was no way they could blow the election.

In their study of the Liberal downfall, *Not Without Cause*, party officials Dan Rath and Charlotte Gagnon describe the meeting. Peterson read a draft of a speech that made reference to the need for an agenda for a stronger economy, caring communities, and the need to move forward with social reforms. Goldfarb thought the reform message missed the mark, arguing that the middle class wanted reassurance. "People with families, especially the middle class, are extremely concerned about the erosion of their prosperity," he said. "We have to be seen to be protecting the interests of the middle class, and that means we have to reassure them." Ezrin agreed that people's anxieties were high, but Kathy Robinson nixed Goldfarb's objections, and the reform message stayed in.

But it was another aide who put his finger on the problem the Liberals would suffer throughout the campaign, one from which they would never recover. "I think that you are gonna get your nuts cut off if you don't have a good reason for going, and that you have to state it very clearly and stick to it," he said.

That good reason for going never materialized.

On July 30, Premier David Peterson sauntered into the media studio at Queen's Park and to nobody's surprise announced a fall election. He was supremely confident that on the sixth of September the voters would reward his government with another mandate. Some Liberal MPPs confided in gallery members later that they had seen polling that could mean they'd win at least 100 seats.

It was a hot, sunny, summer day. But if Peterson had looked more closely, he might have noticed that the sky was falling.

Chapter Six:
Toward the New Jerusalem:
The NDP Comes To Power

"We must earn the people's trust every single day."
— David Peterson comments on winning his majority
government on election night, September 10, 1987.

"The lesson from this election is that the public trust must
be earned....We must continue to work every day to earn it,
each and every working day." — Bob Rae sounds familiar
on election night, September 6, 1990.

Of Rats and Men

B ob Rae put on his best face and one of the four new suits he bought the
week before the election was called and stepped reluctantly, but
aggressively, onto the campaign trail.

One party stalwart who met with Rae and campaign director David
Agnew earlier that summer described Rae as "downcast." Rae told her about
his new cottage on the Rideau where he hoped to spend the summer. "We'll
be lucky to win 26 seats," he confessed. Earlier he had told Alberta NDP
leader Ray Martin that he would like to return to the federal scene.

After spending a week at his cottage in early July, he decided to quit provincial politics if he didn't improve the party's standing. "I'd have had three shots and I think that would have been my feeling and other people's feeling too," he later told Kingston journalist and former NDP staffer Jamie Swift.

As they got ready for the campaign trail, few New Democrats had higher hopes. The party's goal was to break the 30 per cent barrier in popular support and to get 30 seats, former provincial secretary Brian Harling admitted afterwards. "Less than that and Bob was in trouble," Harling says. Campaign co-chair Julie Davis, a vice-president of the Ontario Federation of Labour, agreed that winning 30 per cent of the vote was optimistic "because it's been such a psychological barrier for us."

Meanwhile, most political observers predicted an easy win for the Liberals. "I wouldn't be surprised if the Liberals win 100 seats," Wilfrid Laurier University political science professor Lev Gonick wrote. Just days after the election was called, Tory pundit Dalton Camp wrote in the *Toronto Star* that Peterson's re-election "appears assured," and called the campaign "a yawn." Of Rae he said: "Let's be serious — an NDP government tomorrow in today's Ontario?"

A very few — the NDP's Ross McClellan was among them — thought the Tories would do so badly that the NDP might just squeak through in enough seats to force the Liberals into a minority government.

"I agreed with the press assessment that the election would be a cakewalk," treasurer Robert Nixon said. "We were on a honeymoon right until a whole bunch of us were kicked in the ass."

Thinking they had the election in the bag gave the Liberals a false sense of security; they had no backup plan when things started to go wrong.

Also, because no one expected the opposition parties to go anywhere, the media gave both the New Democrats and the Tories a free ride. This was a great stroke of luck for the NDP.

Globe reporter Richard Mackie told a November 3, 1990 conference of the Canadian Association of Journalists that the media didn't take the NDP seriously and wasn't tough on Rae.

CBC TV's Steve Paikin told the same conference that few polls were commissioned because everyone expected a Liberal victory. This, too, was a break for NDP, because earlier polls would have detected the trend toward the NDP and alerted the other parties and the media. The first public poll to show the possibility of an NDP government — and a minority at that — was not published until September 1st, just five days before their election sweep.

The expected easy Liberal victory made for a different campaign and different coverage than would have been the case had the race been seen as tight from the outset.

While the NDP got off easy, Peterson's Liberals came under fire from the first minute of the campaign and were hounded by numerous protesters. Though enjoying twice the support of either opposition party at the outset, this campaign made the Liberals look wildly unpopular.

Peterson's election call was no surprise, but with two years still to go in his mandate, he was asked repeatedly why he wanted an election. He dodged these questions but finally told reporters he refused to apologize for seeking a "consultation" with the voters. The phrase didn't go over well; he apparently forgot that elections are when the voters consult the politicians.

The media jumped all over the early call. Even Peterson's normally supportive hometown *London Free Press* attacked him for it; Ottawa's *Le Droit* referred to it as "insolence electorale." It was an issue that just would not go away and that seriously damaged Peterson's image. But it was not the only worry the Liberals had.

* * *

The 1990 Ontario campaign saw the most aggressive electoral intervention by public interest groups in Canadian history. Their political involvement was a logical outcome of the flowering of coalitions during the 1980s, and represented the fruit borne of seeds planted in Canada by the peace movement during the Viet Nam war. The activism of the social movements, and the political sophistication they developed through the 1980s, had democratized the face of politics. A government could no longer rely, as Bill Davis's Conservatives had, on a silent majority.

Peterson had barely begun his statement announcing the September election when Greenpeace staffer Gord Perks sabotaged the news conference. Perks walked up to Peterson with a steel-reinforced briefcase handcuffed to his wrist, placed it on the table in front of the premier and activated a tape recorder inside. The tape played a 60-second loop condemning the Liberal government's betrayal of promises to clean up pollution, stop the Darlington nuclear reactor, ban ozone-depleting foam and reduce garbage.

Perks decided only in the last two seconds to play the tape, but says: "I just sort of felt that I had to. I just said to myself that Peterson's been wandering around with platforms and nostrums for five years while he reneged on promises that are key to our survival, and he's not going to be called to account for it unless I go up."

As the cameras scrambled to get their shots, press gallery president Gene Allen tried to get Perks off to the side. "Get the fuck out of the way, Gene," one camera operator yelled as Peterson sat in an awkward silence while the tape played on. He tried to brush off the tape's allegations, and he could not have imagined his understatement when he commented later that "It's going to be an interesting campaign."

Unfortunate for the Liberals, but a blessing for the NDP, the Greenpeace confrontation set the tone for the campaign. Perks's stunt "was like manna from heaven," campaign manager Julie Davis said. The NDP planned to come out hitting the Liberals hard and the third-party campaigns played right into their hands.

A major, if unlikely, coalition was formed at the outset by the Ontario Public Service Employees' Union (OPSEU), the Ontario Medical Association (OMA) and the Ontario Secondary School Teachers' Federation (OSSTF). Teachers, doctors and public servants all depend on the government for funding, and the three organizations were unhappy with the Liberals for their own reasons. "At first blush, it may seem a peculiar group of three musketeers," Dr. Basil Johnston, president of the OMA, acknowledged.

The campaigns waged by these three groups reinforced the impression that there was widespread unhappiness with the Liberal government. Together, the money they spent on the campaign equalled the budgets of any of the political parties, and all their resources went to undermine the Liberals.

OPSEU ran a campaign asking "Who's in Charge?" The union condemned underfunding that caused overcrowding in jails, psychiatric institutions and health care facilities. The Liberals' summer campaign was full of "barbecue smoke and mirrored sunglasses," OPSEU president James Clancy charged. The union budgeted one million dollars for its campaign intervention, not too much less than the NDP's $1.6 million budget, the Tories' $2.4 million, and the Liberals' $2.9 million.

Shortly before the election, the OMA hired former NDP provincial secretary Brian Harling to strengthen its organization and to help it overcome its isolation after the extra-billing fight. The OMA already had Paul Rhodes, former media secretary to Tory leader Larry Grossman, as its government relations officer. With Harling and Rhodes on board, the OMA showed it was looking for new ways to influence government policy, and perhaps recognized that doctors were getting nowhere by positioning themselves as reactionaries. The OMA seemed to realize it could no longer simply rely on closed-door negotiations with government, as it had done when the Tories were in office, and now it took its battle into the public arena.

The teachers, who had many years of involvement in provincial politics, considered running a campaign against the government's meddling with their pension plan, but decided against making pensions their big issue for fear that people would think they were "pampered whiners," says former OSSTF president Jim Head. The teachers already enjoyed the most lucrative pension plan in the province — with the possible exception of senior public service bureaucrats and members of the legislature.

The teachers bought newspaper ads to highlight general education issues and rented billboards with the slogan: "Spending too little on public schools is child neglect."

The OSSTF claims that more than 300 of its members worked on the federation's provincial campaign, with 900 more involved in local campaigns. It says it had as many full-time campaign workers as the Steelworkers' and Autoworkers' unions combined.

The teachers' federation targeted only 22 ridings, an indication that they thought the Liberals were unbeatable. Of the 22 ridings they concentrated on, the OSSTF-backed candidate won in 21.

The teachers didn't always rely only on simple education to bring voters on side. On election day, former OSSTF president and left-wing New Democrat Malcolm Buchanan worked with an ex-con who was out after 15 years. "If people didn't answer their doors," Buchanan said, "he'd call out: 'I'm coming in,' and go through whatever was open. Door or window, it didn't matter. He usually came out with the homeowner, ready to vote for our candidate."

Not only did they get the votes, but they persuaded people to come their way. Buchanan chuckles: "We started off by visiting everybody who had a Liberal sign, and found that many had accepted it only because it was free. They all switched after talking to us."

For Greenpeace, the decision to intervene in the election was a first, and reflected the influence of former peace movement activists like David Kraft, who had moved over to the environmental cause. Kraft and others understood the value of direct political intervention.

Greenpeace used a green minibus to shadow the Liberal tour, visiting many of Peterson's stops. On board was a giant seven-foot green rat, a symbol of Peterson's failures on environmental issues. The rat was seen regularly on television coverage of the premier's events. Greenpeace did not have the budget of the other major organizations, but still handed out over 400,000 leaflets cataloguing broken Liberal promises.

OPSEU, the OMA, the OSSTF and Greenpeace were only the largest and best-equipped organizations to go after the Liberals. There were plenty of other protests and annoyances for the Liberals. Environmentalists protested the "Temagami Chain Saw Massacre" with a giant chain saw mounted on a truck that blared chain saw noise. Anti-poverty activist John Clarke disrupted Peterson's hometown nomination meeting with cries of "Down with the poverty premier," provoking Peterson to yell back "Get a job." Television broadcasts showed Liberal heavyweights dragging Clarke from the room. Other coalitions and members of social movements also badgered the government, bringing attention to their concerns about housing, childcare, garbage and a variety of causes. They all saw the government as the vehicle for redressing social and economic problems.

By centring their attacks on the Liberals, these organizations undermined the Liberals while letting the opposition parties off the hook. "What the protesters provided was an instant flip side of whatever Peterson was saying," the *Toronto Star*'s Matt Maychack said. "So, for every punch that was delivered by the governing party, there was a counterpunch. For every punch delivered by the NDP, there was no counterpunch." The Liberals did try to mobilize the business community to weigh in on their side, or at least attack the other parties, but couldn't persuade corporations to join the fray.

It is important to note that none of the protest groups anticipated an NDP win. Their "success" may have been more than they bargained for. Doctors, in particular, can hardly have been happy with the New Democrats' victory. Confident of a Liberal win, all of the groups were trying to send Peterson a message and press their own agenda. By showing the political clout of their organizations, they hoped to force the Liberals to respond to their demands.

Similarly, the coalitions were not operating in concert with the NDP; they had not planned their campaigns with the New Democrats and they made no effort to coordinate their efforts with the NDP during the campaign. The coalitions were non-partisan; they were not front groups for either the NDP or the Tories.

Though the NDP benefitted enormously from the political intervention of these groups, their activism took place outside the New Democratic Party, not as partner with it.

In the 1990 campaign the NDP had the good fortune to be considered such a long shot that it escaped scrutiny from the media and the other parties. At the same time, New Democrats were the beneficiaries of well-executed, expensive third-party campaigns against the Liberal government.

Because so many social movements decided to intervene in the campaign, those that failed to, or consciously decided not to, stand out. Most obviously missing in action were the various ethnic communities.

Virtually all the groups that played a key role in the campaign had WASP memberships, and a high enough comfort level in society that they could take on the Liberals even though they were expected to win. This was not the case with minority groups, which — at least on an organizational level — largely stayed out of the campaign.

Some of this can be attributed to the inroads Liberals made with ethnic communities, and the access to power that immigrants were looking for. But the absence of truly disadvantaged groups from the campaign speaks to the systemic discrimination faced by members of minority groups, which lowers their spontaneous participation in the electoral process. They were the silent minorities.

The Selling of the Socialists

"We approached the assignment from the point of view of the party being a product, an idea," said Jim Ryan, a principal of Ryan MacDonald Edwards Advertising, the company hired by the NDP to package its message in the 1990 campaign. "...Seldom in Canadian politics has advertising meshed so well with the overall campaign of a party, particularly a party that has traditionally been the least sophisticated in using mass communications techniques," Stan Stutter wrote in *Marketing* magazine two weeks after the election.

The NDP was ready to try a new approach, and picked a new pollster, a new advertising agency, and a new campaign team.

And there was a new Bob Rae — the third version in three campaigns — always wearing a carefully-tailored suit that created an image that, for once, fit Rae like a glove. Neither the vaudeville piano player of 1985 nor the tough Rambob, friend-of-the-workers of 1987, Rae seemed comfortable in his new suits no matter how hot the weather. At long last he looked like the son of a diplomat and relaxed.

"...Rae has made The Suit his trademark and his statement," *Globe* columnist Geoffrey Stevens wrote just before election day. The *Toronto Star*'s Thomas Walkom also wrote that Rae's blue suit showed respectability. "Now Rae wears his suit even in the most inappropriate of situations. He still looks stiff. But he is a happy stiff," Walkom said.

Insiders attributed some of Rae's new ease to the absence of Robin Sears from the campaign. Ontario Steelworkers' leader Leo Gerard said the people were seeing "the real Bob." The *Star*'s Bill Walker wrote: "Asked whether the absence of...Robin Sears has made a major difference, Gerard smiled. 'Let's just say that he's surrounded by the right people this time and they're finally letting him be himself.'"

Janet Solberg, sister of Stephen and Michael Lewis, suggests that Sears' influence in 1987 was stifling. Apparently trying to choose her words carefully, she said: "The fact is, Robin ran [the 1987 campaign]....Robin, whether he intended it or not...It is just very difficult...He had a lot vested in his opinion. And David [Agnew] is not like that. He has no perceptible ego involved."

For its new pollster, the party chose David Gotthilf of Viewpoints Research in Winnipeg. Together with Agnew, Gotthilf began to tailor the party's message as neatly as Rae's tailored suit.

Earlier in the year, Gotthilf and Agnew had decided that the party's core vote rested at about 25 per cent of the electorate, and determined that the NDP's "universe" — that is, its maximum potential popular vote — was 40 per cent. In June, Gotthilf began extensive polling to target people in that

15 per cent gap, testing the right words and messages that would appeal to them. It was true designer socialism, niche marketing dictated not by ideas, but by opinion polls.

Yet Gotthilf wanted the NDP to deliver a class message. "There has been a perception in the NDP that somehow electoral success would come by moving to the centre, by trying very hard to appear moderate and respectable and middle class," Gotthilf later told *Kingston Whig-Standard* feature writer Jamie Swift. "I've tried to persuade my NDP clients across the country that they're better off positioning themselves as viscerally populist, very much talking in the language of class. Language like 'Make the Rich Pay' might scare some of the members of the editorial board of the *Globe and Mail,* but it plays very well with NDP constituencies...."

Gotthilf identified the deteriorating economy and the shifting of the tax burden to the middle class as key in changing people's perceptions. "Middle-class voters who might historically have identified their own economic self-interest with people who were ahead of them started to see that in the past 10 years they'd been screwed, while the people who were richer than them were taking a tax holiday. So the economic interests of the middle class in terms of its own self-perception became linked with those of the working class and the unemployed and less linked with those of the wealthy and the powerful."

Gotthilf's polling for the party and Michael Marzolini's Insight Canada polls showed that people had tangible and specific expectations of government. They wanted action on jobs, on the environment, on public safety, on taxes and on a number of other items. Far from being simply the "cranky" electorate that Brian Mulroney and David Peterson put down, and despite a decade of neo-conservative propaganda that tried to convince people that government only got in the way of initiative and progress, people wanted and expected government to be an agent of change, a force for improving their lives.

But in 1990 the Liberals could not meet that test. Their pre-election polls showed that most people could not name a single Liberal achievement, but they could name many failures. High on the list were Meech Lake, free trade and the GST, all of which were federal initiatives. The early election call also meant that a series of promises that were on the Liberals' legislative agenda were never acted upon.

Some in the party, David Peterson and Ian Scott included, attributed peoples' attitudes to the fact that the Liberals had taken on too much. Reflecting on their years in office, Scott later said: "I have learned that structural change is very hard. Governments can't do it and expect to survive. I understand now why Conservatives are conservatives. Life is much simpler if you just muddle through. Looking back, we imposed too much structural change." His comments were another version of "why the people didn't appreciate us."

The NDP's electoral strategy keyed in on two perceptions. First, the NDP would portray the Liberals as the friends of "special interests," closely linked to the wealthy and powerful members of society who had grown even more wealthy and powerful in the last decade. Second, they would attack David Peterson for a litany of broken promises.

Armed with Gotthilf's polls, the NDP hired research consultant Peter Donegan to run "focus groups," small groups of hand-picked people who fit into the 15 per cent gap the NDP was trying to appeal to.

Donegan had the focus groups draw pictures of their impressions of the parties. In one group, an illustration marked "Liberal" showed an arm with a hammer striking a little person; another drawing marked NDP just had a big question mark. Donegan's focus groups convinced him that Peterson seemed popular on the surface, but "once you dug a little deeper, you realized the electorate was really disgruntled."

People got angry as the sessions went on; they saw themselves as the NDP sees itself — as the little guy working hard and not getting to the top. Donegan decided that the campaign needed to shake people out of their complacency fast by provoking the testiness of the focus groups.

The NDP's biggest fear was another sleepwalking election, just what Peterson hoped for by calling it in the middle of summer, so it took the risk of being negative and came out swinging. Its campaign ads were designed to avoid discussion of issues and blast the Liberals. As Donegan advised his clients, voters "were scared of an NDP government. They seriously questioned whether they were really going to be any different and whether they were experienced enough to run things properly if they ever did get in. I told them they had to stay away altogether from talking about the things they would do and about the possibility of an NDP government."

The party was determined to do an "us versus them" campaign, and went to Ryan MacDonald Edwards Advertising to design the public images. It was a new Toronto agency with no political experience, but Agnew liked it particularly for its Saab automobile ads.

Working with Gotthilf's poll information and Donegan's focus group drawings, the agency developed the slogan: "Send the Liberals a letter they can't ignore," with an enormous, ragged X that was meant to cross out the Liberals as well as vote NDP. Right from the start, it was clear the NDP was running the campaign as a by-election, asking people to deliver a protest vote. Political analyst Marc Zwelling commented that it was the earliest he ever saw the NDP give up.

Ryan MacDonald Edwards developed three television commercials that deliberately blurred the line between fiction and reality. The two that were used showed a television viewer channel-hopping through a series of phoney news broadcasts, each recounting another — false — Liberal misdeed.

The agency also wrote three radio spots for the closing days of the campaign in which a narrator described David Peterson as a baseball player, swinging and missing at free trade, lower taxes, cheaper car insurance, clean water, and so on. "How many strikes 'till he's out?" the announcer wondered. The agency also scripted, but the party rejected, a radio spot with squeaking bedsprings and a voice-over: "Who's in bed with the Liberals now?"

Both the Tory and NDP ads were negative, and neither party included its own leader. All three parties spent about half their total campaign budgets on advertising. The Tories knew their own attacks on the Liberals were driving many loose voters to the NDP, but they thought they had little option if they wanted to shore up their own vote. Like everyone else, they never imagined the NDP could form a government.

The NDP advertising campaign was controversial, largely because it was based on a series of lies — the very thing Rae accused Peterson of doing. Party strategist Gerry Caplan hated the ads. "It was all lies," he complained. "I am embarrassed to have been part of it and I think it was very embarrassing for the party and I hope we never do it again. Morally they were destructive and therefore unacceptable," he said.

A former downtown Toronto NDP activist also lamented what the ads did to the party. "The party of idealism that I joined in 1970 to change the way people thought, ends this decade with a series of TV ads that simply pander to cynicism about politics," she says.

Agnew defended them on the grounds that although the facts were not correct, the ideas were important.

American ad man Phil Noble, who, according to Jamie Swift, "makes his living digging up incriminating facts about politicians for use in negative ads," was shocked by the NDP's ads. He told Swift that if he had ever made up lies like that, he would have been fired.

For its part, the media offered little scrutiny of the NDP's advertising campaign until after the election was over. The party got away with running a series of false and negative images, with only its victims, the Liberals, complaining.

Private citizen David Peterson said: "It was a low in campaigning in Canada."

The campaign confirmed that the NDP had abandoned the high road of ideas for the low road of deception. On the eve of its stunning election victory, the party that once was willing to challenge the social and economic power structures to demand universal health care and public pensions now resorted to fabricated advertising that only asked the electorate to "send a message" of anger. It was hard to know what the party really stood for any more, and people could be forgiven if they took Rae at face value when in the last days of the campaign he told approving audiences that NDP meant "No

David Peterson."

The New Democrats also had no illusions about running for govern-ment — indeed, they didn't even want people to think about the prospect. In the last week or ten days of the campaign, when their own polling showed them with an easy win, they refused to release the information for fear it would scare off the electorate. "We're sitting around in this meeting, and finally I said, 'I can't believe this,'" Julie Davis later told Swift. "It's only a group of NDPers who'd sit around a room with long faces when we find out we're in first place, saying 'Oh my God, what do we do now?'"

The party managed to avoid its own deep-seated problems of public perception, its container, by shifting the focus entirely to the Liberals. The party did not need to move to the political centre, as it had been doing for many campaigns, it simply avoided new ideas. Ironically, its only detailed platform document was proof that it didn't want to run on issues.

An Agenda for the Media

It took only minutes for Rae to make good on his first campaign promise, which was to run a "tough, direct and blunt" campaign. At his opening news conference, Rae called the premier a liar. He said Peterson "lied directly" on auto insurance and free trade, and Rae accused him of being in league with "the large and very rich private interests that have benefitted so much from the Liberal government over the past three years."

From the outset, Rae made clear that he did not intend to outline detailed policies, saying that Liberal broken promises were the focus of the NDP campaign. "I really think that people were fed up with politicians making promises they can't keep," he told the media midway through the campaign. "The public is fed up with a whole lot of promises, with 37-day promise-a-day campaigns."

Rae deliberately shifted attention from the NDP's and his own credibil-ity by fighting to ensure that the campaign would be fought on Peterson's record and the perceptions of his government. New Democrats were hoping to avoid discussion of their own weaknesses — their low credibility on economics and competence as government, for example.

For his part, Mike Harris also tried to rid himself of his greatest liability, Prime Minister Brian Mulroney. The *Toronto Sun*'s Claire Bickley wrote that at his opening news conference Harris "shed 200 pounds of fat right in front of the TV cameras."

For the first half of the campaign, Rae got away with unalloyed attacks on the Peterson government. But as time wore on, the media naturally expected the opposition parties to lay out their own proposals. More and more, Rae was being asked what he would do as premier. Finally, campaign strategists decided to release a platform, which they called "An Agenda for People." And, as the cliche goes, timing was everything.

The leaders' television debate was scheduled for Monday, August 20. The NDP campaign team knew that media attention would be focused on the debate and reaction to it for several days. So they decided to hand out the Agenda for People on the Sunday afternoon before the debate.

That afternoon, Rae spoke to a friendly crowd and then, after the event, campaign staff distributed the Agenda for People to the media. It was so low key that a Liberal spy who was sent to cover the event missed the document entirely, and reported back that nothing out of the ordinary had taken place. No reporter went to David Peterson for comment on Rae's platform.

Rae's team was worried that the media would skewer the party if all it did was criticize the Liberals, Brian Harling later conceded. "The media absolutely insists on a program," he says. "We got away with that longer than we expected." Harling admits they prepared the Agenda for People to deal with that concern. "We did it for one reason — to get the media hounds off our back." But they also wanted to deprive Peterson and Harris of the chance to say that the party was only negative.

The decision to produce the platform was made only four days before the leaders' debate, leaving just three days to put it together. Research director Chuck Rachlis led the team of researchers and insiders who drew up the list of items and made rough estimates of their cost. A party researcher says that once the list was prepared, Rachlis and campaign strategist David Reville made some cuts to save for future announcements.

The hastily-drafted Agenda included a long list of promises. The 11-page document contained a budget plan showing spending estimates of $44.506 billion for 1990-91, and revenues exceeding costs by $30 million. It was better than a balanced budget: it actually showed a government surplus. (See sidebar for details.)

Key among the provisions were a minimum corporate tax, public auto insurance, funding for 20,000 non-profit housing units and 10,000 childcare spaces a year, comprehensive pay and employment equity, and a commitment to fund 60 per cent of education costs, because the province's share had dropped below 40 per cent, with the rest of the burden falling on local property taxes.

On August 3, Rae told a Sudbury crowd that an NDP government would write its own auto insurance. "I'll say, 'Gentlemen, the door opens out. We will write insurance for ourselves. We don't need you any more.'" The next day he attacked Peterson for being a "corporate pussycat" for refusing to veto free trade, and throughout the campaign insisted there was still time to scuttle the deal. Rae also promised many times to implement a "common pause day" and crack down on Sunday shopping.

But the Agenda for People was just an agenda for the media. The party contrived it to placate them and engineered it to receive as little coverage as possible. "We managed to do it without doing it," Harling says. David Reville was even more blunt. "We, of course, had no notion that we might ever have to implement it," he admitted.

* * *

An Agenda for People

An Agenda for People included the following items:

New Taxes:

A minimum 8 per cent corporate tax, estimated to raise $1 billion a year in additional provincial revenue.

Implementation of succession duties on the "rich and super-rich," worth $190 million a year.

Tax Relief:

Elimination of income tax for people living at or below the poverty line, estimated to cost $200 million a year.
Raising the level of provincial funding of public schools to 60 per cent, at a cost of $1.5 billion over two years. Funding would come from general revenues and be shifted from property tax.

Making available up to $100 million in reduced-rate loans to farmers.

Providing personal mortgages at 10.5 per cent for 10-year terms, making $1.4 billion available, raised by a provincial bond.

Providing $40 million in reduced-rate loans to small businesses.

Other promises:

Public, "driver-owned" auto insurance "that's fair, affordable and accessible."

An improved Employment Standards Act "to increase the protection of workers facing layoffs, with a lower worker threshold, a lower years of service threshold and an extended notice period."

Establishment of a wage and benefit protection fund.

A jobs protection board to establish whether plant closures are justified.

Improved pregnancy and adoptive leave.

A new training and re-training scheme in which large employers either train their own personnel or pay a training levy.

Increasing the minimum wage over four years to 60 per cent of the average industrial wage, about $13 an hour at the time, bringing the minimum wage up to about $7.20.

Pay equity provisions to cover all women, at an estimated cost of $60 million.

Funding for 10,000 new non-profit childcare spaces and subsidies for 10,000 spaces in each of the next two years. Estimated cost: $240 million.

Employment equity legislation with "concrete mechanisms for the achievement of equality in employment."

Indexing of private pensions and assurance that pension "surpluses" belong to the members, not employers.

Increased social assistance rates estimated to cost $300 million per year.

Strict rent controls that would allow no increases for capital or financing costs.

Funding for the construction of 20,000 non-profit units a year, likely to begin in 1992, at a cost of $570 million over two years.

Introduction of "quality of care standards" for Ontario's rest and retirement homes and a doubling of the budget for the Integrated Homemaker Program — an increase of $62 million per year.

Immediate passage of an Environmental Bill of Rights.

Immediate passage of the Safe Drinking Water Act, with a goal of completely eliminating toxic chemicals from entering lakes and rivers by the year 2000. Promise of "a real zero discharge program" involving "bans and phase-outs on the use of persistent toxins in industry."

Taxes on packaging that cannot be recycled or reused.

Extension of the acid rain program and overhaul of air pollution laws "to mandate zero discharge of toxic chemicals into the air by the year 2000."

Preservation of farmland to prevent the conversion of Classes 1-3 farmland to non-farm uses and introduction of a land speculation tax "to slow the conversion of valuable farmland to other uses."

Allowing GO Transit to raise money on the bond market to finance capital costs for public transit systems in southern Ontario.

$25 million in annual funding "to train native educators and health care givers, to improve community infrastructure and to fund improvements in housing."

$400 million over two years "to promote economic development, job protection and job creation, and improved services" in northern Ontario.

$100 million a year for four-laning of the Trans-Canada Highway across northern Ontario.

Environmental Dumping

In the months leading up to the election, the NDP considered going green. Several members of the party's executive and election planning committee wanted to pick up on the ideas in the NDP's recent paper "Greening the Party, Greening the Province," in which Bob Rae himself embraced the need for new thinking about nature. (See Chapter Five) They argued that the party should centre its campaign on environmental issues.

But as the election approached, support for a green campaign diminished. At a lunch meeting to try to recruit her to run in the downtown

Toronto riding of St. Andrew-St. Patrick, Rae told prospective candidate Joyce McLean, a Greenpeace activist, that "nobody votes for issues, they vote for image." Mclean, disappointed that the party was backing away from an environmental platform, decided not to seek the nomination.

In late June, Rae and David Agnew told Brian Harling and party vice-president Simon Rosenblum that they had decided not to run on environmental issues and were opting instead for a broader campaign. Both were disappointed and disagreed. Rosenblum worried that the NDP had misled environmentalists, and that they might find it hard to take the party seriously. About the same time, one Toronto party worker tried to persuade Rae to run on environmental issues, and predicted if the party did, it might win 45 seats. Rae dismissed that speculation as wildly optimistic and worried out loud about what construction workers would think.

The party dumped its environmental platform because strategists decided to run a negative campaign and because polling showed that people thought the NDP couldn't deliver on its environmental promises, an NDP researcher close to the inner circle claims.

But environmental concerns remained throughout the campaign. One that kept coming up, and which has continued to haunt the NDP in government, was garbage, especially the question of dump sites for Metropolitan Toronto's daily mountain of waste.

On August 2nd, three days into the campaign, Rae blamed the Liberals for their failure to tackle the garbage problem, and blasted their refusal to "get tough with their friends" over returnable pop bottles. Rae said the Liberal approach to the issue, blue box recycling, "was made in the boardrooms of the pop companies." He wanted pop bottles to be sold in reusable bottles like beer, 98 per cent of which are returned, but that "would require a tough decision from the government of Ontario. More than anything else, it would require a decision that would take on industry," he said.

Meanwhile, Rae tried to present himself as the environmentalist. On August 12, he released a statement that said "...the basic challenge is whether we are prepared to examine some of our own assumptions and premises, our basic values, and assess not simply their social or economic justness, but their ecological integrity as well."

"There is an urgent, compelling need to change the society in which we live," his statement read. "A society with endless wants and the technology to satisfy them — and to create new ones — is on a collision course with a world whose resources are limited.

"We can't afford unlimited growth: Left to its own devices, it will destroy the planet and all of us who live on it. We need a different approach, an environmentally-tuned social democracy. The Ontario NDP is ready to bring that kind of democracy to this province."

But a few weeks later, on August 21, the *Financial Post* picked up on disenchantment in the environmental community with Rae and noted what was behind the NDP position. "Environmentalists are disappointed Rae has ignored the global warming and nuclear energy issues," the paper said. "Some say [their disappointment] reflects Rae's intention to make Peterson's integrity, not environment, the issue of the campaign. His attack on the blue box program, several observers say, was used to suggest Peterson is pandering to industry interests rather than as a platform to launch Rae's own initiatives."

On August 23, Rae blasted the Peterson government for permitting the dumping of toxic chemicals into the water. His statement reiterated the Agenda for People promise to enforce a zero discharge requirement by the year 2000. He also promised the NDP's Environmental Bill of Rights would protect "whistle-blowing" employees who report environmentally hazardous practices of their employers, and would give citizens the right to take companies to court. The "Bill of Rights" proposal was a triumph of style over substance. It reflected Rae's comments to environmentalist Joyce McLean that people vote for image, not ideas.

David Peterson gets Desperate

The NDP's strategy was to go on the offensive against a popular premier, try to pry open the cracks that had developed in Peterson's armour, link the government to "special interests," and repeat a litany of the Liberals' broken promises. Rae's tour was well designed for television, and employed a series of cleverly thought-out locations where his events were staged.

Like the fortuitous Gord Perks event, there was also an element of luck to Rae's TV campaign. On one occasion, for example, the NDP tour went to a Brampton school yard to protest provincial underfunding of education. As Rae made his pitch to an audience of unhappy parents and children, the cameras caught a crane depositing another school portable in the background.

Rae's first real campaign stop, on July 31, was at Ontario Place. There, Rae spoke about "this government's relationship with the development industry, its history of accepting huge corporate donations to fund its political work, and its fear of an open inquiry into those matters."

The hook, of course, was Patti Starr, appointed chair of Ontario Place by the Liberals, a socialite who made nearly $100,000 in illegal donations to various politicians, most of them provincial Liberals. Her contributions to cabinet ministers Chaviva Hosek, Lily Oddie Munro, Alvin Curling, Ed Fulton and Bernard Grandmaitre resulted in Peterson dropping them from cabinet in 1989.

The prolonged Starr scandal hurt the Liberals badly. First surfacing in early 1989, it exposed a tangled web of backroom deals, illegal contributions, powerbroking and privatization schemes. The issue dragged on and on, right through the 1990 election.

In April, 1990, the Supreme Court of Canada quashed the judicial inquiry Peterson established to investigate Pattigate. In June, Ontario's Commission on Election Finances laid a series of charges against Starr, the Toronto section of the National Council of Jewish Women (the charitable foundation she used to make the donations), the Ontario Liberal Party and several of its officers, and others. In July, facing a series of criminal charges, Starr filed a suit in the Supreme Court of Ontario against the Ontario cabinet, David Peterson, Attorney-General Ian Scott and Peterson's former principal secretary, Vince Borg. In August, with the campaign already underway, their lawyers defended them in court.

By month's end, a poll showed that 51 per cent of people thought the Liberals mishandled Pattigate. Even more damaging for the Liberals, 61 per cent thought illegal donations and corruption were widespread.

Starr's trial on criminal charges was to begin on September 6, election day. For the Liberals, there was just no escaping her.

But worse problems plagued them.

On August 15, the first day for paid advertising, the opposition parties and the social movements began to hammer the Liberals with television, radio, newspaper and billboard ads. It was just two weeks into the campaign, and the Liberals were being attacked from all sides.

Their own polling showed that they had been dropping in popularity right from the start of the campaign. According to Liberal insiders Dan Rath and Georgette Gagnon in *Not Without Cause*, Liberal campaign chair Kathy Robinson kept the bad news from Peterson and other senior party strategists. She was still operating on the assumption that their lead was too big to blow.

Robinson didn't tell others about the bad new polls until after the leaders' debate on August 20. When she did, and when the results of the debate were inconclusive, the campaign planners felt they needed something big to turn the tide. They also knew that the campaign's first public poll was due to be released later that week, and they wanted to do something positive to boost their support. When they chose their issue, it blew up in their faces.

* * *

Back in the spring, Martin Goldfarb's polling for the Liberals showed that a cut in the provincial sales tax topped the list of popular suggestions. Goldfarb argued that the Liberals should include the proposal in their early campaign announcements, noting that it fit his belief that they needed to do something for the middle class. Treasurer Robert Nixon was vehemently opposed, knowing that there was a downturn in the economy coming and, having already taken the heat for raising the tax once, he did not want to reverse himself. Others also wanted to avoid making such a move, and it was rejected.

By the time of the leaders' debate, Goldfarb was telling the campaign team that the Tories' repeated attacks on taxation were hurting. He dusted off the PST reduction and advocated it once again.

Party officials visited Nixon and told him that if the Liberals did nothing, they were going to lose, but that if they did something dramatic, they just might squeak by. Faced with a Hobson's choice, Nixon gave in. Two days after the debate, he phoned Peterson while the premier was on the campaign bus to Cornwall, and gave the go-ahead. At the planned campaign stop, Peterson announced a 1 per cent reduction in the PST effective January 1. "To the extent that we can, we are attempting to soften the blow of the GST," he said. (The federal Goods and Services Tax was scheduled to take effect on the same date.)

Both Peterson and Nixon tried lamely to convince the media that the timing of the tax cut had nothing to do with the election. Others saw it differently.

Mike Harris said the announcement was "the most shameless attempt to buy an election ever foisted on the people of this province," but still he welcomed the reduction. Rae said: "I think David Peterson has made the biggest miscalculation of his career."

The tax cut had been so hastily announced that the Liberals didn't have their lines straight, and Peterson and Nixon gave different answers to questions about how long the tax would remain reduced. Rae denounced the move as "bribery" and said that Peterson was "not even trying to buy people's votes any more. He just wants to rent them for a few weeks."

Newspapers blasted the move as cynical opportunism. "This move tarnishes the Liberals' responsible fiscal record and ultimately undermines their very credibility," the *Toronto Star* editorialized. Columnist Thomas Walkom said Peterson's "audacity is shameless."

Nixon knew they had made a mistake. "We should have done it [announced the reduction] while we were riding high rather than when we were hanging on to the last straw," he said later. "Reporters would look at it and play up that 'These guys are dead.' And they were right."

* * *

The tax cut announcement was one of many strokes of good fortune the NDP received during the campaign. At the time of the announcement, the NDP was stalled in the polls. The blast the Liberals took for their tax ploy gave the NDP a giant boost. An Environics poll released August 28 showed the NDP catching up fast. The poll, the first one made public during the campaign, put the Liberals at 40 per cent, the NDP at 34, and the Tories at 23.

But the media continued to dismiss the New Democrats. The next day, *Globe* columnist Robert Sheppard wrote: "Bob Rae for premier of Ontario. C'mon, gimme a break." The *Star*'s Thomas Walkom even doubted that the Liberals would lose their majority government.

NDP pollster David Gotthilf said the poll had a significant impact. "A lot of people still view voting as going to the track: they've got a record to sustain," he told Swift. "The idea of voting is not to vote for the candidate they like best, but to vote for the winner. Within four or five days after that poll our numbers were going up every day. It was like nothing I've ever seen before."

At first even the NDP didn't believe the polls. New provincial secretary Jill Marzetti later admitted that the first polls showing big gains came three weeks before the end of the campaign. The results were kept among a handful of top strategists until their polling showed them consistently in the lead, and only then were the numbers shown to any other insiders.

The first public poll to show the NDP in the lead came on September 1st, just five days before election day. An Angus Reid-Southam poll had the NDP ahead with 38 per cent, the Liberals trailing with 34, and the Tories at 24. Nonetheless, Liberals, New Democrats and the media still found an NDP win hard to believe. In the Liberal camp, desperation set in, while the Rae started to tone down his tough rhetoric and tried to sound more responsible.

"Rae is no longer the hard-hitting, aggressive campaigner who began the election," the *Toronto Star*'s William Walker wrote. "He even seems to be going easier on the premier."

Rae also tried to allay business fears of an NDP government. He indicated the minimum corporate tax — the number one item in the Agenda for People — would indeed be minimal, and he passed off the NDP's plan to introduce an inheritance tax as a simple closing of a loophole.

Compare Rae's attempts to downplay fears of the NDP with a radio address made by Tommy Douglas just three days before his Saskatchewan party formed the first CCF government in Canada. Douglas said: "This is no time for the timid and the weaklings who are willing to sell themselves and become apologists for big business. These are times that call for men of courage and women of vision to strike a blow for our economic emancipation. Every vote for the CCF is another link broken in the chains of our economic servitude. The time has come for each of you to take sides."

While Rae pulled back, Peterson went off the deep end. "I believe the

NDP would lay waste to this economy," he warned. "This is not a by-election. This is a general election," Peterson reminded voters, trying to raise fears of an NDP win. "They will kill businesses, they will kill jobs, and they will kill our economy," he said. "My friends, we cannot have everything we fought for destroyed by the socialist philosophy."

Many observers commented that Peterson had sunk to the old "red scare" to warn people off the NDP. But his attacks were not so much redbaiting as they were a vain effort to raise people's fears about the NDP's economic competence. He was trying to push the familiar button that the NDP couldn't run the corner store, much less the province of Ontario.

But he was surely desperate. The Liberals could see the writing on the wall. Campaign strategist David McNaughton commented that by then, "you had to get pictures of Bob Rae with rams or sheep. By that point in time, if you didn't say something pretty outrageous, it wasn't going to be reported at all."

While Peterson was trying to remind people of their own deep-seated fears of the NDP's ability, his inflammatory rhetoric helped to undermine his own credibility badly. When Peterson was at the height on his popularity in 1987 and 1988, he appeared unusually non-partisan, as well as fair and reasonable. These impressions were key parts of his own "container."

The early election call made Peterson look manipulative, crassly taking advantage of a big lead in the polls. Why else would he hold an election with more than two years left in his mandate? The constant reminders of an "unnecessary" election helped undermine that image of impartiality, and branded him a politician like all others.

The hammering he took during the campaign by the opposition parties and the social movements further shook people's confidence in that fair, reasonable and non-partisan leader. That was compounded by the cynical, vote-grabbing tax cut. In the last days of the campaign, when Peterson resorted to scare tactics, when he spoke of the election as "war" and the NDP as laying waste to the economy, and when he talked about children going hungry under an NDP government, he only served to destroy people's impressions of him further. His desperation showed and people reacted badly to it — ironically, the more so because of his previous high standing on these scores.

In the first minutes of the campaign, Gord Perks from Greenpeace set the tone for confrontation by sabotaging Peterson's news conference; in its last days Peterson was his own worst enemy.

An Academy Award-Winning Performance

As the campaign came to a close, most observers clung to the belief that when it actually came time to mark their X, many people just wouldn't be able to bring themselves to vote NDP. Despite the polls, even most New Democrats did not expect to win.

Bob Rae himself admitted that: "I never believed that we would form the government, even during the last week of the campaign. I really didn't." In a stunning about-face from the 1985 campaign, when he whined to the party's provincial council that he lost because he was not introduced as "the next premier of Ontario," this time he said: "All the times I was introduced...as the 'next premier of Ontario,' and everybody would dutifully applaud. I mean, give me a break. Nobody believed it — I didn't."

Not expecting to win, the NDP never put in place a transition team, not even in the last days. The key people were working flat out on the campaign.

The first time New Democrats met to discuss a decision they would have to make as government was on the afternoon of election day, when a small group gathered in the Toronto home of Gerry Caplan to figure out what to do about Toronto's Olympic bid. At the meeting were Rae, Agnew, Caplan, Stephen Lewis, Julie Davis and David Reville. They quickly decided that an NDP government would approve the bid, for which the Peterson government had agreed to cover any deficit. That could amount to one billion dollars — the entire amount the NDP expected to raise from its minimum corporate tax.

Then it was off to prepare for the celebration.

* * *

Rae watched the returns with his wife Arlene in a suite in the Skyline Triumph hotel.

From the moment the returns started to come in, the size of the NDP victory was shocking. At 8:35, just half an hour after the polls closed, the CBC decision desk announced an NDP majority government and anchor Steve Paikin, a bit given to hyperbole, called it "the story of the century."

Bob and Arlene phoned their daughters. The youngest, Eleanor, wondered: "Daddy, does this mean you're the boss of the Liberals?" Lisa, the middle child, wanted to know: "Daddy, does this mean you're going to clean up the lake?"

* * *

Delirious New Democrats packed the Rae campaign's victory party at La Rotunda, an Italian banquet hall on Dufferin Street. The returns piled up. At the end of the night, there were 74 New Democrats going to Queen's Park, an incredible leap from the 19 they had elected in 1987. Peterson's Liberals fell from a record 95 seats to just 36. The Tories elected 20, up from 16.

Commenting for the New Democrats on CBC television, Richard Johnston said: "The onus on us not to disappoint is very weighty." Gerry Caplan, on CFTO, seemed as surprised and awed as anyone else as the early results came in, and kept wondering if the popular vote was enough for the NDP to win — right up to the moment when the majority government was declared.

In London, an ashen David Peterson appeared briefly before a stunned and sombre audience. The former boxer said: "A man is judged not for getting knocked down, but for not getting up again." He warmly thanked his supporters and resigned as party leader. Peterson was probably relieved to have lost his own seat, which meant he would not have to lead a rump of dispirited Liberals from the opposition benches.

Then, to the deafening chant of "Pre-mier Bob! Pre-mier Bob!" the first-ever CCF or NDP premier-designate of Ontario made his way to the podium in La Rotunda, smiled, waved, smiled some more and then blew the moment.

Rae started off with an Academy-Awards-style speech, thanking most of the people to whom he was related by blood or marriage, and bringing family members onto the stage. He treated the NDP victory as a personal triumph wholly in keeping with the image politics he had waged. It may have been a night to celebrate Rae's victory, but those who waited patiently for the coming of democratic socialism to Ontario saw no sign from him that their patience was rewarded.

Rae failed to capture the spirit of the victory, the jubilation that New Democrats clear across Canada were feeling that night. He did not suggest this was a new beginning or the end of politics as people knew it. He did not utter one Hallelujah. He did not say that at long last the poor, the disenfranchised, or even ordinary workers finally had a government that would give them hope or power.

In the middle of his speech he did remember to "pay special tribute in my heart tonight to David Lewis and Tommy Douglas" and to the others who had the courage to represent their cause and movement.

Then the first nominally socialist premier of the province quickly reassured everyone that it would be business as usual. Noting that the province faced economic difficulties, Rae said: "I can tell you I deeply realize as a premier who now has obligations to all the people of the province and not just to members of my party,...we have to work with all the sections of the community to build confidence in the future of our economy and confidence in the future of our society. And I can tell all the citizens of the province I am determined to work with everyone, with everyone, to make sure that that is exactly what happens for the benefit of all the citizens of the province of Ontario."

These, of course, were codewords to the business class. Relax, he was saying. We will not be as bad as you fear. Trust us.

Card-carrying New Democrats might also have heard between the lines that Rae, not the party, was going to be in control. His remarks were a clear signal that he would not consider NDP policy binding on his government.

How Did it Happen?

Was Rae's 1990 victory a triumph of a decade of NDP moderation? Does it show that the party's lack of new ideas, its intolerance of dissent, its faulty relationships with the labour and social movements, ethnic communities and the media, its failure to develop practical economic solutions, and its other faults were not real problems? Does the election vindicate the party's approach to politics under Rae's leadership?

In one way, of course, it does. The NDP was elected, and so in the most literal sense it either overcame these problems or they proved not to be insuperable problems in the first place.

But the answers are not so simple.

New Democrats may have recalled the message that Tommy Douglas gave them in 1983, on the 50th anniversary of the signing of the Regina Manifesto, a small part of which we have reprinted at the opening of this book. "Don't give up conviction for success," Douglas said. "Don't ever give up quality for quantity. In a movement like ours, we're not just interested in getting votes. We are seeking to get people who are willing to dedicate their lives to building a different kind of society."

In the final analysis, the 1990 election was neither a triumph of the NDP's moderation nor the logical outcome of a well-designed NDP strategy through the 1980s. In large measure, the party was in the right place at the right time and benefitted from a political harmonic convergence.

The New Democrats vaulted into power in Ontario in the fall of 1990 for a variety of reasons. Peterson's early call undermined the people's perceptions of him as a fair, reasonable premier and cast his lot with all other cynical, rotten politicians. During the campaign, the pestering he received from social movements and organizations like OPSEU, the OSSTF, the OMA, Greenpeace and others seriously damaged the government's credibility. The Liberals' huge lead and anticipated easy victory meant that the media — and the electorate — did not give the opposition parties the scrutiny they might otherwise have received.

The NDP's stunning majority was achieved with just 37.6 per cent of the popular vote — a huge increase over its previous levels, to be sure, but nonetheless the first majority government in Ontario with less than 40 per cent of the vote. The NDP won many seats where the traditional Conservative vote fell off and allowed the NDP to come up through the middle. The fringe parties, most of them right wing, received 6.5 per cent of the popular vote — an uncommonly high total. They siphoned more votes from the Liberals and Conservatives than from the NDP and, given the narrowness of some contests, helped New Democrats get elected.

But of course there were changes in the society and economy that were part of a longer trend through the 1980s that created a set of conditions that made it easier for people to cast their ballots for New Democrats.

One of those is the quickening rate of change and its attendant diminution of loyalty, a willingness on the part of people to part company with past allegiances with greater ease than ever before. People move in and out of jobs, homes and relationships with an equanimity that was unheard of just two generations ago.

The same goes for political parties. Rarely do we hear someone say today that they're voting Conservative because "my grandfather was a Tory, and my father was a Tory." On election night, former Ontario Conservative leader Larry Grossman said that not long ago about 60 per cent of the people could be relied on to vote for the party they had voted for previously; now that was down to about 20 per cent.

The *Globe*'s Jeffrey Simpson wrote: "Politics is now like a vast Turkish bazaar through which the electorate passes, haggling with the political vendors, assuming the vendors are in it for themselves, threatening to go elsewhere if the price is not right, and demonstrating that customer loyalty means next to nothing." But Simpson pointed out that their mercurial nature continued after the purchase. "In this bazaar," he continued, "a political vendor who at least temporarily seems to believe in his product — somebody who has core values and ethical integrity — stands a fair chance of making a sale. But soon after the sale, the shopping begins again."

Futurist John Kettle, philosopher of the "Big Generation," says that people of the baby-boom age are better educated and have more information than their predecessors; as a result they are more free to think for themselves and less susceptible to group pressure. "They think of government the way people think of insurance companies," he says. "Does it pay off when I have trouble? How much does it cost? If I don't like it, I'll switch."

Kettle says that Big Generation men and women find corruption very offensive because they believe in merit rather than connections. Their geographical mobility divorces them from communities, and they don't know neighbours who owe their jobs to a kind politician. They react badly to patronage and were upset by the Patti Starr scandal.

Kettle points out that Big Generation members have no loyalty to the NDP's ideology and no commitment to its mandate. Their attitude is: "If we don't like them, we'll throw them out."

Political analyst Marc Zwelling agrees that this shift is important. He, too, says voters were not committed to the NDP's platform, and that the NDP's relationship with the people is "not a mandate but a blind date."

On election night, pollster Allan Gregg expressed a similar view that people had not voted for the NDP because of its ideology. He hinted, in fact, that they had voted for it despite its ideology. Gregg said the NDP benefitted from not being either Liberals or Tories. "It had nothing to do with socialism, but about attitudes to politics," he said.

Insight Canada's post-election poll determined that of the nearly 38 per cent of voters who opted for the NDP, over one-third were new supporters of the party. Their report claims that "83 per cent of the NDP's new support came from negative reactions to the Liberals."

University of Toronto political scientist Stephen Clarkson thinks that people did have an understanding that the NDP would be more interventionist than the other political parties, but that it did not deter them from voting for them. "The welfare state and big government are not out of fashion," Clarkson says. "It was a pro-governing but anti-government vote." He rightly points out that all the pressure groups wanted more government intervention, not less.

The *Globe's* provincial affairs columnist Robert Sheppard wrote that the Liberals made a mistake in the 1987-90 period by thinking that Ontario wanted a caretaker government, not an activist one. Thus he, too, ascribes to the notion that people still think government plays a valuable role in their lives.

Some people blamed the Liberals' defeat on Meech Lake, the constitutional deal that collapsed just one month before Peterson hit the election trail. Liberal pollster Martin Goldfarb, whose sage advice convinced them to announce the provincial sales tax reduction, said Meech caused the defeat because people wanted their politicians to deal with the economy, free trade and the Goods and Services Tax, while David Peterson was wrapped up with national unity.

But if Meech Lake caused David Peterson political damage it was probably not because he was overly interested in unity questions to the detriment of other issues. More likely, the Meech Lake episode did hurt Peterson because it lumped him in with politicians making backroom deals in a closed process. People reacted badly to the symbolism of Meech: Mulroney, Peterson and the others closeting themselves away to make a deal that could not be amended in a process the public did not like. Television coverage of Meech solidified the Mulroney-Bourassa-Peterson axis, much to Peterson's detriment.

Though in the 1990 campaign the Liberals tried to tie Mulroney like an albatross around Mike Harris's neck, he was as much a liability for the Liberals. "Mulroney and the huge disgust he's created for all politicians destroyed the Liberals," Richard Johnston said. "In a funny way, the Tories weren't hurt by Mulroney as much as the Liberals were." Ontarians wished they had a federal election to get at Mulroney; they took it out on Peterson instead.

As we have pointed out, federal issues tend to weigh heavily in Ontario. The failure of the constitutional deal and renewed questions of Quebec's status were only one part of a summer of discontent that included native demands, best exemplified by the tense and bitter standoff with the Mohawks at Oka, and a number of environmental struggles. These gave people an uneasy impression that their social fabric was fraying at the edges; that insecurity may have steered them toward a party that seemed caring and committed to them.

Finally, the declining economy and changing consumer trends served to hurt the Liberals and benefit the NDP.

In a study on "The Consumer of the '90s" prepared for its clients by the advertising firm Saatchi and Saatchi, the authors argue that by the end of the 1980s people were turning away from high-speed and high-tech yuppie materialism and returning to slower, tried-and true comforts. They identify the watchwords of the 1980s as "new, future, state-of-the-art, leading edge, fast-track, me," while those of the 1990s will be "comfort, enduring, real character, health, high-touch, surefooted, us."

They say consumer attitudes, for example, are: "Give me products and services which I can trust, so I don't have to think about them any more." "I want sound advice and good, reliable information from people how genuinely care about me, my lifestyle, my values and the world I live in."

The trends that Saatchi and Saatchi identify in their October, 1989 study suggest the possibility of a consumer-type move toward the NDP. Other economic changes also played into the NDP's hands.

Economically, if Ontarians felt worse off in 1990, they were. In 1990, average after-tax income was below the 1980 level, according to Statistics Canada. This ended a long run of steady growth: after-tax income, in real terms, increased 27 per cent in the 1950s, 34 per cent in the 1960s and 22 per cent in the 1970s.

Much of the stagnation through the 1980s was caused by the sharp downturn in the decade's first years, and people began to make up some of that decline in the late 1980s. But taxation significantly bit into those gains.

In 1980, the average family paid taxes of $7,300. That dipped to $7,100 in 1982, but jumped to $9,600 in 1989.

Because after-tax income over the decade showed no growth, while taxes took a big hike, people were right in believing that the increased taxes they paid only maintained the status quo. They were not getting their money's worth out of taxes, and they were further angered by the new GST. The message that Mike Harris delivered about Liberal tax increases fell on sympathetic ears. So did Rae's arguments about corporate taxation. Middle-class people felt they were bearing the largest burden of taxes, and they were right.

In the immediate pre-election period, there were signs that the economy was in serious trouble. The number of layoffs and plant closings in the first six months of 1990 were more than double those of the previous year: 14,000 jobs lost in 97 complete or partial closures in 1990, compared to 6,500 lost jobs in the same period in 1989. In July, the *Globe* reported that employment was down 49,000 since November, 1989. The Toronto unemployment rate jumped from 3.9 per cent in June, 1990 to 6 per cent in July. In Windsor, the July rate was 8.3 per cent. The NDP's Ross McClellan noted that: "[Peterson] expected the recession wouldn't hit until the fall, and missed the fact that it's already hit."

The NDP was fortunate that the campaign was waged on the Peterson government's record. This diverted attention from its own low credibility on economic issues. Because of the cynicism with politicians and the fact that Peterson helped undermine his own credibility with voters, enough of the electorate obviously felt that it was time to give the New Democrats a chance, and perhaps that they could be no worse than any of the others.

"I'd like to say the NDP won because of its great policy positions," former provincial secretary Brian Harling said. "But it was more a case of voters scared by a style of politics — political sleaze where voters were lied to and manipulated."

Yes, Deputy Minister

The day after the election, Rae announced that Stephen Lewis would head the NDP's transition team. With the exception of Lewis, the same people who ran the campaign shifted gears and began to prepare for office.

Burned out from the 37-day campaign, they took no time off to charge their batteries or reflect calmly on the task ahead of them. Unlike the Liberals in 1985, who brought in a team of experienced administrators — some of whom had few ties to the Liberal party — to facilitate their transition to government, the NDP relied entirely on its own tried-and-true people. "It was simply inconceivable that anyone other than a long-time, highly-activist New Democrat, well-known to the Queen's Park insiders and trusted by them, could serve on the [NDP] transition team," political scientist Graham White wrote.

White says that members of the transition team later recognized their inexperience was a liability: "...not only were [the NDP transition team members] generally ignorant of the workings of the Ontario government, but only Stephen Lewis had any significant experience with large bureaucratic operations."

At the outset, the transition team was knocked for a loop: about 10 days after the election, treasury officials met with Rae, David Agnew and Floyd Laughren and told them the NDP government would inherit a $700 million deficit based on a "no-change scenario" — that is, if the government made no new decisions. When outgoing treasurer Robert Nixon learned that his bureaucrats had told the new government about the deficit two days before they told him, he hit the roof.

News of the deficit floored the New Democrats, who reacted to it in campaign mode by insinuating that the Liberals had known about it all a-long. They wondered what other evils they would find. When the NDP started to grumble about the deficit, treasury officials rushed over to Rae's office to tell him to shut up. He was making the international money market — already upset over the NDP win — even more nervous.

With a touch of school-boy naughtiness, the New Democrats called themselves the "transmission team," and joked that the first company to be nationalized would be Mr. Transmission.

The "transmission team" had a hard time shifting gears from election mode. Chuck Rachlis, the caucus research director, confirmed later that the key transition workers thought in a partisan way about everything. Despite this partisan thinking, they clung to the view that the apparatus of the state was neutral — that its bureaucrats simply reflected the ideology of the government in power.

They had thought so little during all their years in opposition about how the state functioned that in many ways they were ignorant of its complexities and benignly accepted its administrators. Lewis gushed after meeting with chief public servant Peter Barnes, that he had "learned more in two hours" about the process and functioning of government bureaucracy than in all his years in the legislature.

The New Democrats were so unaware of the inner workings of the state that Rachlis went off to the legislative library to get an organizational chart of the government. Later, key New Democrats studied the chart, occasionally wondering out loud, "What do you suppose *these* guys do?" Historian Des Morton confirmed the party's long-standing ignorance when he wrote: "Since 1971, when Stephen Lewis's threat to become Ontario's next premier spooked business into loading Tory coffers, the NDP has tried to sneak up to power. Part of the camouflage was wilful ignorance of public administration. Few New Democrats thought about government, and few of those few entered the circle of power in 1990."

In the first days after the election, Rae said that as the son of a public servant, "I understand well their sense of professionalism and their sense of public service, and it's that sense of professionalism and public service that, as premier, I want to draw on." One of Rae's first decisions as premier was to rubber-stamp the re-appointment of nine deputy ministers whose contracts expired in August.

When challenged with evidence that the public service was likely to undermine them, Agnew confirmed Rae's high-school civics view: "We expect at the end of the day, when government makes a decision, that the bureaucracy will respond. That's their job."

As Graham White wrote: "Among members of the transition team — as among New Democrats generally — it was widely presumed that once the content of policy was settled, the process of implementing and administering it was straightforward and required little attention from the political decision-makers."

Despite mutual distrust and suspicion between the incoming New Democrats and the senior public service, the NDP was sending signals to the deputy ministers and other key bureaucrats that the advice they had provided to the Liberals could simply be fine-tuned, if necessary, to meet the needs of an NDP government. It was one of the first signals that the NDP course would not be a radical departure from that of previous governments.

One theory holds that a new government needs six months to find its sea legs and the washrooms before it can make changes in the public service; another holds that if a government doesn't make changes in its first six months, then it becomes captive of the state. The NDP showed that it believed in the first theory; the results show that the second came true. Rachlis said they didn't move senior public servants in the initial period because they were too busy getting themselves organized to really think about how to run a government.

"We mistakenly assume that the bulk of government process proceeds from the cabinet down through," says one well-placed insider familiar with the workings of government. "But the bulk is incremental adjustments and refinements that in terms of bureaucratic organization goes from the middle up." He says that: "Unless you have a definite view and are prepared to take risks, you essentially become a captive."

Lewis and others, including former Saskatchewan premier Allan Blakeney, proposed that the cabinet office be structured following a model used in Saskatchewan, employing a so-called "Red Secretariat." This organization puts in place an umbrella group of senior advisors responsible for reviewing broad policy initiatives from all the ministries. It serves as a check on the bureaucratic administrators, helping provide overall policy direction and ensuring that the government's plans get priority.

Rae's team rejected the notion of a Red Secretariat, according to Rachlis, because they didn't like the optics of a big, costly cabinet office. They also turned down a suggestion that the premier's office appoint someone specifically to provide liaison with the social movements — a key role in keeping contact with powerful and influential coalitions.

One of the most important functions of the transition team was to find key staff members for the ministers' offices. As part of their "political staff," ministers all have an executive assistant, a legislative assistant, and a number of policy assistants. These roles are crucial in helping ministers understand issues and avoid political quagmires.

To find the people for these jobs, the NDP called once again upon the Lewis family, asking party president Janet Solberg to use her extensive contacts. Solberg used her personal address book and made dozens of phone calls, inviting people to work for the government — despite the fact that the new government was receiving 3,000 resumes a week. As the mountain of resumes piled up, many went unanswered for months. The NDP weeded them out largely on the basis of party involvement.

Solberg's list was extensive, but selective on the basis of party loyalists. Boasting that "I *am* the establishment," she was looking above all for people the government could trust. "It went without saying that anyone considered for a position in a minister's office had to be a member of the party faithful," Graham White wrote. He quotes one transition team member: "It was reassuring to offer jobs to people we knew." It was a natural, simple reflection of the NDP mindset to hire on the basis of loyalty, and it assured a cadre of yesmen and yeswomen in key jobs. In addition, the people they hired usually had no government experience and many, as members of social movements, had fought openly with public servants prior to the election.

Solberg concentrated on finding executive assistants, not knowing who the cabinet ministers would be, nor how many. "I really pushed very hard to have all the people in place [by the time the government was sworn in]," she told Jamie Swift, "but that didn't happen, partly because nobody understood what happened to a cabinet minister the moment they became one, and partly because we wanted the flexibility to hire more visible minorities and women."

The ministerial executive assistants Solberg found were well aware that they had been recruited and hired by the Premier's Office, and were responsible primarily to it, not to the minister with whom they were eventually placed. Many of these executive assistants in turn hired other staff, and so the chain of obligation was extended. This helped undermine the ministers.

Solberg could not find enough assistants for the ministers, and Rae insisted on reviewing hiring decisions personally. After they were sworn in, many ministers had to function either without their key staff, or with bureaucrats in the political roles, because the process was taking so long.

Some of the more powerful ministers went ahead and hired people they knew and trusted, thumbing their noses at the agonizingly slow process centred in the Premier's Office. Environment minister Ruth Grier, for example, was stuck with a ministry personnel director as her executive assistant for a month because Rae wanted someone from the Manitoba Ministry of the Environment to take the job. Grier finally hired Mary Lewis, one of her close friends, for the job. Other ministers engaged in power struggles with Rae over staff; some won, some lost.

Rae's re-appointment of the deputy ministers and the slow start in placing key staff allowed the bureaucracy to assert itself, especially with the very inexperienced ministers. Not a one had cabinet experience, of course, and of the 26 ministers, 12 had not served a day in the legislature. That made them especially vulnerable to the bureaucracy. Swift wrote that: "Such confusion [during the transition], coupled with the inexperience and the surprise victory — and reinforced by Bob Rae's natural caution — meant that the new government was initially vulnerable to the innate inertia of the civil service." Confusion was the key word of the transition team. Several weeks after the swearing in, CBC radio reporter Gerry McAuliffe ran a tape of an unanswered telephone, sound bite of the new regime.

In the early days, one deputy minister told a cabinet minister that he couldn't — or wouldn't — prepare a set of proposals the minister had asked for, and told the minister that the government would only be there for four years, while his was a lifetime career. The minister did not relieve the deputy of his responsibilities.

Another cabinet minister, frustrated that the same old recommendations kept coming up, insisted that every list of options the deputy provided include "nationalization without compensation." At least not all of the ministers lost their sense of humour.

Is Anybody Here an Economist?

It was the first time treasurer Floyd Laughren's key political staff were to meet with senior treasury bureaucrats, the most grey of the grey public service. Simon Rosenblum, a long-time friend and close associate of Laughren's, was hired as a policy advisor, and he gave some thought to just how he would establish himself with the bureaucrats.

Rosenblum was a key leader of the party's left wing during the 1970s and early 1980s, who, like Laughren, favoured nationalization of re-source industries and other key sectors of the economy. He once wrote: "Government now must either play ball with the corporations or find itself faced with a corporate 'investment strike.' (Corporations can always exert their freedom not to reinvest their capital or to invest in some other country.) Only public ownership of the commanding heights of the economy can change that." Rosenblum was also well-known in NDP and peace movement circles as a fierce anti-Communist.

Before he introduced himself, Rosenblum was preceded by his col-league Riel Miller, who rattled off a long list of academic credentials, including his doctorate from the London School of Economics and his work with the OECD in Paris, to which he later returned.

Then it was his turn, and Rosenblum told the following story:

After the Cuban revolution, Fidel Castro gathered around him his trusted advisors and launched into one of his famous hours-long speeches. As Castro went on and on, some of the more exhausted revolutionaries started to nod off. Eventually, Castro said it was time to choose a finance minister. "Is anyone here an economist?" he asked.

Rousing himself from his dozing, Che Guevera shouted exuberantly, "I am! I am!"

"Good," Castro said, "then you're the finance minister."

Guevera was shocked. "But I don't know anything about economics," he complained.

"You just said you were an economist," Castro replied.

"'*Communist.*' I thought you said, '*Communist,*'" Guevera said.

Rosenblum paused, and smiled. You could have heard a pin drop.

Commencement at Convocation Hall

Though at first the New Democrats thought they could take office on September 24, they soon realized that there was too much to put in place before that day. They settled on October 1st.

Like all premiers, Rae was faced with the difficult chore of naming his cabinet, a problem compounded by the fact that so few in his caucus had political experience. Not only that, but Rae did not even know some of the people he named to cabinet. He was also playing a very hands-on role in the hiring of ministers' staff while trying to learn the ropes.

The day before the swearing in, Harry Rosen's Bloor Street store reportedly sold several $1,000 suits to ministers-in-waiting. Insiders say they were steered there by the dapper David Agnew.

Faced with a huge problem of who to invite to the swearing in and agonizing over who to leave out, the transition team took Gerry Caplan's advice and arranged to hold the ceremony in the University of Toronto's Convocation Hall, which holds about 1,700 people.

There, on a crisp fall afternoon, hundreds more people than could be accommodated inside milled around outside to get a glimpse of their new government. Those lucky enough to have received an embossed invitation from the Queen's representative were allowed inside, where they scrambled to find seats.

The Toronto Intergenerational Choir, a chorus of children and seniors, was on stage as people arrived, and they promptly began to sing. Their singing was lively and warm, matching the generosity of spirit and deeply-felt emotion that washed over the crowd. Many had waited a lifetime and licked a million envelopes, and could hardly believe their eyes.

Then two regimental guards with glistening ceremonial trumpets approached stage right to herald the arrival of the lieutenant governor and the incoming ministers of the crown. Their fanfare was drowned out by thunderous applause and an enormous cheer when Rae walked on stage behind Lincoln Alexander.

Alexander, the first black person ever elected to Canada's House of Commons, was a member of Joe Clark's government that fell on December 13, 1979 when Rae moved his non-confidence motion on Clark's budget. That day helped launch Rae's career as a giant killer. Now a beaming vice-regal Alexander looked at Rae's broad grin and said to the crowd: "I've seen that smile before; watch out for that smile." He was as caught up in the emotion as anyone else.

Rae introduced his cabinet, 26 members, 11 of them women. It was the largest number of women in any government in Canada. With the exception of Treasurer, a post reserved for veteran Floyd Laughren, the key posts went to women: health, education, social services, environment and energy. Another woman was chair of the Management Board of Cabinet, a pivotal portfolio responsible for monitoring government spending.

This government had a new face. Only three lawyers were in the cabinet: Rae, Attorney General Howard Hampton, and Peter Kormos, who was given responsibility for bringing in public auto insurance. Marion Boyd, the new minister of education, had run a women's shelter in London before defeating David Peterson. Ruth Grier, the former environment critic, became its minister. Evelyn Gigantes was minister of health. Newcomers Zanana Akande, a black school principal and former schoolmate of Lewis and Caplan, was named social services minister, and Peterborough's Jenny Carter became minister of energy. The caucus included steelworkers, autoworkers, hospital workers, and a number of people from the social movements.

When Rosario Marchese was sworn in as the minister of culture and communications, one of his children broke the decorum by shouting out, "All right, Daddy!"

It was just that kind of day, when rules were broken and people choked back tears of joy for a dream come true.

PART THREE
The NDP In Office

T wo and a half years into the NDP's mandate, Ontario New Democrats still have strong emotions about their government. But now they are angry and disappointed as the government betrays its principles and sells out its supporters. The CCF started off in 1933 with a promise to eradicate capitalism; the Ontario NDP in 1993 is governing as if it is hell bent on eradicating democratic socialism.

This book goes to press shortly after two April 1, 1993 by-elections, when the NDP won barely more than 8 per cent of the vote in one seat which it held, and in another where local NDP riding association members were so angry they prevented the nomination of a candidate.

The public sector union brass is meeting with the NDP to work out a "social contract," a government euphemism for concessions. At the same time, the government announces it will eliminate 11,000 public sector jobs and slash billions of dollars in public spending. Some union leaders, who are traditionally among Rae's most ardent supporters, are calling for his resignation. The rank and file is so fed up that workers are disaffiliating from the party, and when a worker at one union protest shouts "Bring out the rope!" his cry is met with an enormous burst of laughter and applause.

Deepening scandals reach into the Premier's Office. Cabinet ministers resign in disgrace. Rebellious caucus members openly campaign against the policies of their government.

In the face of all this, Rae increasingly centralizes power in his own office. The circle of people he feels he can trust draws tighter and tighter. The government feels under seige from every corner, and, for the first time in its history, the NDP cannot smash its internal critics. They are everywhere.

Though the NDP's mandate still has two years to run, it is not too early to show that each of the ten themes we have identified prove that the problems that have long plagued the NDP continue to do so.

1. No New Ideas

> "Is there any other point to which you would wish to
>   draw my attention?"
> "To the curious incident of the dog in the
>   night-time."
> "The dog did nothing in the night-time."
> "That was the curious incident," remarked Sherlock
>   Holmes. — Sir Arthur Conan Doyle, *The Return*
>   *of Sherlock Holmes.*

As Sherlock Holmes knew, the evidence of things that do not appear when they should can be as telling as those that appear when they should not. And as he might have said, while it is singularly difficult to offer evidence of things that do not exist, it is still possible to determine the impact of their absence. Even the great detective would have a hard time finding new ideas in the NDP government.

If New Democrats had promised no departure from the status quo, it would be unfair to criticize them for offering nothing new. But re-reading speeches given by members of the NDP caucus when they were in opposition, some of them now members of cabinet, brings to mind the warning on movies that any similarities between actual events and those depicted are purely coincidental.

From the outset, Rae acknowledged that it was much easier being in opposition than in government. In a speech to a group of young corporate presidents in January, 1991, Rae asked them to imagine themselves working for a company for a long time, always opposing what their bosses were doing, "and suddenly the entire board of directors of the company and all the senior management just resigned and said, 'Here you are, Harry, you think you can do a better job, go ahead.' It's a little daunting, I don't mind saying that."

As much as any party leader ever has been, Rae is an ideological chameleon, adopting new stripes to blend in with his surroundings until he became comfortable with his own reflection. Like all animals in camouflage, he wants to be invisible to his predators.

Ontarians have been dismayed by the NDP's failure to put forward new solutions to the province's growing problems. The government's lack of new ideas is a reflection of its intellectual timidity, its lack of commitment to real social change, and its inability to set priorities.

As we have discussed, the reasons for the NDP's lack of new ideas are many: its intolerance of dissent, which drives out ginger groups; its continual reliance on a small group of trusted insiders, which creates a cadre of yesmen

and yeswomen; and its poor and distrustful relationships with social movements and minority groups, which limit its vision and its practical experience
dealing with nitty-gritty problems. The policies it does have, countless
resolutions routinely passed at party conventions, have been left in the party's
back rooms as the government proved itself unwilling to maintain its
principles or stick to its guns in the face of political and corporate opposition.

With the party in power, new forces put even more pressure on the NDP
to conform with the status quo. In contrast to its many years in opposition,
the NDP government has a vested interest in promoting social harmony. It
has no desire or motivation to draw into relief the sharp divisions between
rich and poor, black and white, male and female. Exacerbating social tensions
is rarely the goal of government. This makes it more reluctant to challenge
the systemic problems faced by people across Ontario. There has been no
new balance in the imbalance of power and the recession, for which the NDP
has proposed no new remedies, has left many people worse off than before.

The NDP's first throne speech was a time for Ontario's first democratic
socialist government to lay out a new social vision. Like most throne
speeches, it lacked specifics. More to the point, it failed to present an
alternate view of Ontario. It was no clarion call of changed priorities.

The budget deficit pales in comparison with the intellectual deficit about
how to deal with it.

Faced with a deep recession, the NDP government has see-sawed
between two classic options of traditional economics: spend and save your
way out.

In its first budget, the NDP appeared to be trying to spend its way out,
stimulating the economy with public spending while the deficit skyrocketed
to $9.7 billion.

But as the chief economist of the Conference Board of Canada, who
praised the budget, pointed out, only $640 million of the deficit reflected
new expenditures, while the rest could be attributed to decreased revenues
and ongoing commitments. Even the widely-touted $700 million in
spending on public works was taken right off the Liberal shelf.

In that budget, the NDP government did make a conscious choice not
to lay off public servants or eliminate government programs, things other
governments might have done, but its approach can hardly be seen as
innovative. It soon became clear that poor economic forecasting, not left-
wing economic principles, underlay their efforts at pump-priming. When
the economy continued to decline, the NDP had no other tool and quickly
fell back on orthodox old-party economics. By early 1993 the government
had announced massive public sector layoffs.

Even earlier, the government had announced billions of dollars of
spending cuts; it delayed spending, postponed the implementation of new

programs, and said it was looking to sell off government assets. In actively promoting the sale of government property, the NDP turned its back on a basic principle of its philosophy, which was that public assets should be held for the common good. Instead, the government looked to privatize its assets, something the NDP always condemned Liberal and Conservative governments for doing.

While tough times may have prevented the government from implementing costly remedies, the recession offered a chance for the NDP to expose the ways that international capitalism was failing. It was a time to lay out a new economic direction. Instead, the NDP relied on big public works projects — the sewer socialism of the 1930s.

The NDP turned a blind eye to its own revenue-increasing plans, putting off a study of tax reform to its new Fair Tax Commission. When the Commission issued its report more than two years into the NDP's mandate, the government said it would take more time to review the proposals. Finance minister Floyd Laughren specifically rejected the imposition of wealth and inheritance taxes — which he and the NDP had advocated for many years — and made no move to introduce the minimum corporate tax he had promised in the election.

In February, 1993, the NDP announced it would establish three new Crown corporations, which would oversee the development of highway and rapid-transit systems, new water and sewage treatment facilities, and disposition of government properties. This shift in administration has two purposes: to eliminate, on paper, the existing and growing debt in those areas; and to facilitate the further privatization of public services.

Because Crown corporations keep their own financial records, separate from those of government, their liabilities don't appear in the government's deficit. Thus, Ontario Hydro's staggering $34 billion debt does not appear on the government's books. By shifting accounting to them, the new Crown corporations allow the government to paint a rosier picture of its deficit. That picture will be illusory.

New Crown corporations might be a novel idea if they expanded the public sector into new areas, but these three are simply a restructuring of services already performed by government. They are not a signal that the NDP is looking for increased public participation in society — quite the opposite. They are a mechanism for removing citizen and government influence over highway maintenance, public transportation, sewage treatment, and so on. The new Crown corporations just open the door to increased privatization and contracting-out of services previously performed directly by the provincial government. These notions are normally anathema to left-wing parties.

In thinking about economic restructuring, the NDP has not moved to facilitate the participation of non-traditional organizations in the economy: non-profits, co-operatives, or community-based businesses, for example. Because these newer forms of economic management are structured differently from traditional, profit-making corporations — they are more democratic, less reliant on capitalism's share-owner profit makers and locally-based — they fit with social democratic economic philosophies. The NDP was eventually badgered into moving to extend some temporary tax breaks to co-ops, but otherwise has done little to encourage their development.

Nor has the NDP shown much interest in the growing number of "ecopreneurs" — environmentally-friendly businesses and services, many of which are on the cutting edge of innovation. At a time when the economy is restructuring, when continued growth is being challenged and the future of our environment is at risk, the new ideas of ecopreneurs should be especially welcome. In particular, they should be welcomed by a party less tied to the traditional capitalist infrastructure. The NDP's lack of business friends is partly its own doing.

* * *

The issue that obsessed the premier during the early part of his first term was constitutional affairs. Here, too, Rae accepted traditional solutions and processes, and again, the NDP brought few new ideas to the table.

Rae quickly abandoned his early idea about convening a constituent assembly of provincial legislators and native leaders to discuss new constitutional proposals. In the end, the discussions that culminated in the Charlottetown accord were limited to the first ministers and four native leaders. Rae jumped on the constitutional bandwagon, singing from the same songsheet as all other first ministers, passionately supporting an unamendable deal.

In thinking about a new constitutional formula, Rae offered no new forms of participatory democracy; his suggestions did not bring government closer to the people, correct the systemic under-representation of women and minorities in parliament or address the over-representation of traditional political parties.

One potentially innovative measure Rae pushed hard for was the inclusion of a "social charter" into the Constitution. Such a charter would have provided a "guarantee that basic national values and principles are maintained," Rae said. Rae saw it as a means to ensure that governments would abide by such fundamental values as universal health care, education, adequate social assistance, protection of the environment, and so on. Theoretically, it would also would have assured that governments fund these programs.

But Prime Minister Mulroney and other premiers, including New Democrats Mike Harcourt and Roy Romanow, argued that a social charter would give the courts too much power by allowing them to determine levels of adequacy, accessibility, and so on. Rae backed off.

In the end, a social charter was included as a separate piece of the Charlottetown accord, and for Rae, this was one of the key reasons to support the deal. But the accord specifically set aside the social charter as a section that could not be appealed to the courts. It was nothing more than a set of unenforceable principles, not worth its weight in words.

Rae tried to turn the 1991-92 round of negotiations into a "Canada round," with something for everyone instead of a repeat of Meech with just something for Quebec. But once again, the NDP had nothing new to offer.

As it had done for many years, the Ontario NDP refused to recognize that Quebec is the homeland of a francophone nation. It hoped to solve the constitutional riddle by conferring the status of a "distinct society" upon Quebec, though still treating it as a province much like the others.

Rae negated the option of Quebec's sovereignty and also made it clear that there was no caving in to Quebec's demands for fuller autonomy. He also refused to keep his long-standing promise to Ontario's francophone minority to make French an official language in the province.

Because provincial leaders refused to recognize Quebec's status as a nation, they forced massive decentralization on the rest of Canada so their own provinces could have similar powers. The Ontario NDP, long a supporter of a strong federal government, supported a constitutional deal that would have tied the federal government's hands in many areas.

In a grandstand, eleventh-hour gesture, Rae acceded to western demands for a triple-E — elected, equal and effective — Senate. In doing so, he astounded his own constitutional advisors, who had no inkling that he was about to reverse Ontario's long-held position.

In buying into the triple-E Senate, Rae made it impossible to use Senate reform to redress real political imbalance in the country, which is not between the provinces but among the people of Canada. The Senate proposal Rae begged Canadians to accept would have slammed the door on innovative suggestions to use the Senate to assure the representation of women, natives and other ethnic minorities, and disabled people in parliament.

In the fall of 1991, Rae said: "The next six months, the next year, is perhaps the most critical period this country has faced since it was born." Just before the October 26, 1992 referendum, as Canadians became increasingly exasperated with the attention given to the constitution at the expense of the economy, Rae suggested that the worst thing for the economy would be for the Charlottetown accord to fail.

On that day, a majority of people in six of the ten provinces and a majority of native people rejected the deal. Despite his dire threats about the collapse of Canada, Rae commented on referendum night: "Life will go on. The country will go on."

Two days after the resounding No vote, the dollar rose, the prime rate dropped, and the Toronto Stock Exchange rose 300 points.

* * *

The economy and the Constitution are examples of only two major areas where Bob Rae's NDP has shown it has no new ideas. If this has disappointed people, it's because they had expectations. New Democrats led them to believe that they had novel solutions and new approaches.

Before the 1980s, the CCF/NDP had a solid record of launching programs with such popularity that other governments had to imitate them, and which subsequent governments wouldn't undo.

In the 1940s, the federal CCF was the first Canadian political party to propose legislation for universal pensions. In 1947, the Saskatchewan CCF government, representing the poorest province in the country, brought in universal hospital insurance. The Saskatchewan NDP government was the first provincial government to introduce dental care for children, the right to refuse unsafe work, and public fire and automobile insurance. Manitoba's NDP government was the first to introduce legislation prohibiting discrimination on the basis of sex, religion or nationality, the first to introduce legislated equal pay for work of equal value, and universal pharmacare for seniors. The British Columbia NDP was the first provincial government to introduce rent controls, a Department of Housing, and anti-strikebreaking legislation.

The most recent of these initiatives took place almost 20 years ago. Historians will have a hard time making up a comparable list for Bob Rae's government.

NDP historian Des Morton has called Rae's government "conservative progressive." Thomas Walkom said the NDP was on its way to becoming another liberal party. "Perhaps that's good," Walkom wrote. "Perhaps it is valuable to have three parties which are more or less the same, rather than just two. But we'll miss the NDP. It seemed like such a good idea at the time."

2. The No Dissent Party

The No Dissent Party traditions of the NDP have plagued the relations between Rae, along with his central staff, and all elements of the party and government: the cabinet, caucus, and the party itself.

Right from the start, Rae became the disciplinarian of the NDP obedience school.

The message was clear when Rae left Hamilton Mountain MPP Brian Charlton out of his first cabinet. Charlton, a former energy critic, made the mistake of speculating in public after the election that an NDP government might give away energy-efficient refrigerators and shut down nuclear plants. His musings preceded government discussion, and though he was in line with NDP policy and a caucus task force report on Ontario Hydro, Charlton was punished for speaking out of turn. Highly respected in the opposition NDP caucus, Charlton was the only incumbent MPP not to get a cabinet position.

Charlton learned his lesson. When he replaced Peter Kormos in cabinet and later took over as energy minister, his more radical notions had long since been left by the wayside.

Cabinet ministers themselves were not exempt from being called on the carpet. In December, 1990, Hamilton West MPP Richard Allen, the Minister of Colleges and Universities, and Etobicoke's Ed Philip, Minister of Transportation told Hamilton NDP aldermen that the controversial Red Hill Creek expressway would not be built. Rae took Allen and Philip to task for discussing cabinet business outside the inner circle. This was apparently not what Rae had in mind when he promised an open government, and when Allen and Philip publicly apologized for their transgression, it sent a message about the limits of consultation with constituencies.

These housebreaking lessons show that Rae intended to keep his caucus and cabinet colleagues on a short leash, and to make sure they knew who was boss.

Rae quickly centralized power and control in his office. In future, the Premier's Office would approve all public statements, even those of cabinet ministers.

Former MPP David Reville, who became one of Rae's advisors after the election, told *Maclean's* magazine that a lot passed through the tight controls. "There is a perception that if a minister wants to fart," Reville said, "they need approval from the Premier's Office on the timing of the fart, the quality of the fart and the frequency of the fart. But in fact, there's a lot of room for ministers to promote their own agendas." His windy statement offended the sensibilities of the premier's team, as well as many other people, and quickly undermined his influence in the office.

Staff in the Premier's Office and in the ministerial offices also realized the lessons of obedience. The NDP's old Lewis gang hired only people they knew and trusted, and it was obvious that many people were hired more for their loyalty than for their abilities. The government thus created its own talent shortage.

Rae's insistence on reviewing all key staff placements, an agonizingly slow process, helped paralyse the incoming government. That paralysis also contributed to it becoming captive of its deputy ministers, just one ironic consequence of the application of the loyalty test.

Surrounded by yesmen and yeswomen not given to differing with their masters, the premier and his ministers did not always get the best advice. The sounding board echoed only their own voices.

In terms of the government's relations with the party, Rae sent signals right from his victory statement on election night that he no longer felt bound by party policy. Thinking of himself as "Everybody's Premier," Rae made it clear to party members that he was going to listen carefully to other voices. He started to draw a line in the sand between party policy and government policy, and between the party and the government itself. Dissent in the party would be dismissed simply by ignoring party policy.

How different his behaviour was from that of Tommy Douglas's Saskatchewan CCF government in 1944. As head of the first socialist government elected in North America, Douglas tried to find a way to keep the government true to its democratic principles and accountable to its party.

"Before we took office," Douglas said, "we discussed how we would keep the government and the party on parallel lines — social democratic governments in almost every country in the world start out together but end up going in different directions. We amended the [CCF] constitution to require the setting up of a Legislative Advisory Committee by the provincial council. It would report back to the council, which reported back to the convention...."

"After conventions, the Legislative Advisory Committee went over the resolutions that had been passed with the cabinet, before each session. We had to account to them. If we couldn't do things in full, we had to justify the changes."

Douglas even discussed upcoming provincial budgets with the party's provincial council, and came under real criticism from the opposition. "Of course the Liberals and Conservatives said the party was running the province...." Douglas recalled. "But I said: 'This is not just an ordinary political party. This is a democratic socialist movement — not just socialist, but democratic. And the people are going to have some input.'"

No such efforts were ever made in Ontario.

In the past, the NDP lured new members by convincing them they could develop and influence policy, and it tamed their ideological fervour by arguing that convention resolutions were important because they would become government policy if the NDP were ever elected.

Now that it has formed a government, the NDP will no longer have to maintain that fiction. It is clear, as it will be to any Ontario New Democrat in future, that NDP policy is written on water and is subject to the tide of public opinion, much as it is in other political parties.

It did not take long for the government to draw the line between itself and party policy. In March, 1991, at the NDP's first post-election convention, delegates overwhelmingly affirmed their support for the party's long-standing call for the abolition of university tuition fees. This came at the same time that the financially-strapped government was raising tuition fees. Minutes after the resolution carried, Rae went to the mike to explain that his government was not bound by the convention. Youth delegates issued angry leaflets and cartoons lampooning Rae.

But by the 1992 convention, party members had been tamed. Rae told them that compromise was the quid pro quo for holding power, and delegates sat by as the government trashed long-held policies.

The difficult relationship between the government and the party also showed up when the party tried to distance itself from government. In the face of a strident anti-NDP campaign by the business community, the party tried to whip up the troops in defense of the legislation. A party campaign with the rhetoric at full blast counter-attacked big businesses just when the government was trying to make connections with the capitalists. A party fund-raising letter that said "big business is out to stop us" was repudiated by an embarrassed industry minister Ed Philip, who said: "I can tell you that big business is not out to stop us."

No policy reversal was more high-profile and controversial than the abandonment of the party's stand on public automobile insurance. Former MPP Mel Swart, the party stalwart who championed the issue before he stepped down for health reasons, was furious with Rae when he sold out on the issue. Swart, who had nominated Rae at the leadership convention in 1982 and could not be dismissed as a radical, wrote a seven-page letter to the party's provincial secretary, with copies to Rae and many others, blasting the move. He stopped just short of resigning from the party.

In early 1993, Swart made a presentation to a legislative committee holding hearings on auto insurance. Not wanting him to speak out, the NDP members tried to block Swart's televised appearance, and when that failed, they did their best to minimize his time in front of the cameras. Swart was so angry over the policy reversal that he admitted that if he had it to do over again, he would not nominate Rae as leader.

His public statement brought this response from party president Julie Davis: "It bothers me. I understand his terrible sense of disappointment, but I have a hard time understanding the personal attacks. I don't think he has had these conversations face to face with the premier."

What she was really saying was that Swart ought not be taking on the government in public. It is an insistence on privacy; the implication is that it would have been okay for Swart to meet with Rae and tell him he was disappointed, but not to voice his concerns in the media. Party members owe the government their silence.

That same crack-down on the right of party activists to go public manifested itself at the party's March, 1993 provincial council meeting. There, the NDP environment committee was censured for writing to Ontario Hydro chairperson Maurice Strong to congratulate him for halting the re-tubing of the Bruce nuclear power station. The committee was slapped on the wrists and instructed to write a second letter to Strong, indicating they were not speaking for the party, though policy favours a phase-out of nuclear power.

As ongoing policy reversals provoked anger and criticism among New Democrats and their traditional allies in the social movements, and as a series of petty scandals heaped ridicule on the government, dissent became even more unwelcome. The government felt besieged by friend and foe. Unwilling as ever to admit it might be doing something wrong, the NDP circled the wagons.

A joke made the rounds at Queen's Park in the government's second year. One of the many regular groups of visiting school children was sitting on the wide red-carpeted main staircase, fussing and talking as a photographer set up for their group photo. A legislative guide was with them. Just then, Rae came walking down the corridor, muttering to himself. "Quiet!," the staff member hushed the children. "Quiet! Can't you see there's a cabinet meeting in progress?"

In February, 1993, when the government issued a series of major announcements over a two-week period, it was Rae, and not the cabinet ministers, who made the statements. There was no notion of decentralizing the government, or of having anyone other than the premier spread its message.

Perhaps the most key of those announcements was a restructuring of the cabinet. The NDP dropped a number of minor ministries, combining their function with other ministries, and reducing the number of cabinet members. Rae also created three "super ministries" of finance, economic development, and education and training. Heading them were Floyd Laughren, Frances Lankin, and Dave Cooke, respectively.

Indicative of his centralization of power, Rae did not bring his three new "super ministers" into his confidence about the reorganization until he had already made up his mind to do it. Rae did not discuss the merits of the restructuring with his most powerful cabinet colleagues, not even with Laughren, his treasurer and deputy premier.

The spate of major announcements Rae made that February had to compete with stories on three well-publicized caucus dissenters: Peter Kormos, who continued to defy the government over its reversal on public auto insurance, Dennis Drainville, who publicly disagreed with the government's plan to introduce casino gambling, and Mark Morrow, a Kormos acolyte.

The caucus debated kicking the difficult Kormos out, but decided against it. The others were also under careful scrutiny.

Dave Cooke was forced to defend a written document that surfaced outlining disciplinary steps for dissenting caucus members. It included the loss of caucus positions and other legislative perks, and the threats were not to be taken lightly. Lincoln MPP Ron Hansen had already been dropped as chairperson of the Finance and Economic Affairs Committee after voting against the government's tobacco tax on second reading. (There are tobacco farmers in his constituency.) He got the job back after he voted in favour of the tax on final reading.

While a government has reason to expect that its members will agree with its main policy initiatives, the NDP was caught in the untenable position of disciplining its members for adhering to party policy after the government had abandoned it. When the disgruntled Kormos was asked if he might cross the floor of the legislature, he quipped: "Why should I cross the floor when it seems the government has already done it?"

Ironically, it is easier to crack down on dissenters when the party is in opposition, since the government doesn't want to be seen as brutal or vindictive toward its own caucus members — especially when it is they who are abiding by party policy. The dissenters are subject to pressure from their constituents, which outweighs their guilt and loss of perks.

A big part of the problem has been the lack of consultation between the cabinet and caucus.

Backbenchers complained that they were rarely given an opportunity to have input into key government decisions, and were treated like mushrooms: kept in the dark and fed bullshit. They were there only to vote as the government wanted, to support the government no matter what it did, and otherwise keep quiet.

Backbenchers bitterly resented this because, as MPPs, they expected to have some real input into public policy. Now, as caucus members, they found themselves shut out of the process. Not only is no dissent allowed, but often there is even no discussion. Rae will make the decisions and everyone else will go along.

A good example of Rae's intolerance of other opinions came during the last stages of the constitutional discussions.

From the outset, Rae opposed ratification of the constitutional package by referendum, feeling a referendum was too divisive. He preferred leaving it to the provincial legislatures and parliament to approve the deal. To many people, this smacked of elitism. The politicians got locked into a referendum, however, because Quebec's Belanger-Campeau commission mandated that the province hold a referendum by October, 1992. Both the tactic and the timing of the federal referendum were determined by Quebec's timetable.

Rae was intolerant of dissenting voices during the debate. It was as if he simply couldn't understand how people could possibly disagree with something he and the other premiers had worked out.

When the voters in Quebec resoundingly rejected the accord being pushed on them by their political masters, Rae arrogantly complained: "You could have produced anything at all, the Ten Commandments, the Sermon on the Mount all combined, and they [Quebecers] would have said it was not good enough".

Rae expressed his contempt for the views of ordinary people in another way. Three days before the referendum was held, Rae told *Toronto Star* journalist Thomas Walkom that he was worried about the anti politician flavour of the debate, as if corrupt politicians were preventing the perfect deal. "You know, trust is a two-way street," Rae said. "We're trusting people in this referendum with exercising their sound judgement." Sound judgement in this case meant agreeing with him.

When former prime minister Trudeau criticized the Charlottetown accord, Rae blasted Trudeau as mean-spirited, destructive, antiquated and an egotistical has-been out to destroy Canada. Rae dismissed people on the No side as "peddlers of illusions, snake-oil salesmen who are dreaming in technicolour."

Rae went on television on the night of October 23 to push the Yes side, as did the leaders of Ontario's opposition parties. He wasn't concerned about the No forces being denied equal time. "That's not my problem," he said. "Three political parties are all responding and that arrangement has been worked through and if the No committees want to purchase time they can do it." As long as the political parties got to speak, why should other groups?

* * *

For the government, the consequences of its intolerance of dissent are many. Because he trusts only a few individuals, Rae is forced to centralize power unrealistically and unnecessarily. The self-censorship exercised by loyal staff limits options and advice, and the exclusion of cabinet ministers and backbenchers from meaningful input creates resentment. The open, new style of government Rae promised has failed to materialize.

3. Selling out the Social Movements

No one could remember it ever happening before: members of an NDP riding association so angry that they refused to allow the nomination of candidate. But in early 1993 the gay and lesbian community in downtown Toronto's St. George - St. David riding twice blocked attempts to nominate a candidate in the race to replace the retiring Ian Scott. Eventually provincial secretary Jill Marzetti was forced to use a provision of the NDP constitution and appoint a candidate.

The gay and lesbian activists, who make up the core of the riding association, were furious with the government over its failure to follow through on an early promise to extend spousal benefits to same-sex couples. It was one of the government's first commitments, yet two and a half years later it still had not been acted upon. Attorney-general Marion Boyd told gay and lesbian activists that she personally was fighting for homosexual couples in cabinet, but that Rae was blocking the initiative because he feared a backlash in rural Ontario. Rae is still caught in his notions of private morality and doesn't — or won't — recognize that the legitimacy of same-sex relationships is a matter of public policy.

Frantic behind-the-scenes negotiations took place, imploring the gay activists to let the nomination go through, but memories of the NDP sellout of gay rights in 1981 are long. The riding refused the nomination, and when a candidate was appointed, voted to contribute just $1 to the campaign.

This open split with the government caused a great deal of embarrassment for the NDP, but it was just one of many indications that the social movements think the NDP has sold them out.

The bitter reaction in the gay and lesbian community is not what Rae had in mind when, at the beginning of his term, he told progressives not to become complacent with the NDP in office. Speaking to the Law Union two weeks after becoming premier, he said he knew how the political and corporate elites could force their ideas onto the political agenda, and said he did not want to be left at the mercy of society's traditional power-brokers.

Rae, who received a standing ovation from the Law Union members, told them: "We want to change the political culture of government in this province so that it doesn't see a demonstration outside the window as something to run away from."

One week later Rae spoke at a Greenpeace-sponsored demonstration at Queen's Park. His warm reception was an indication that the environmentalists felt they finally had a friend in the premier's office. "Queen's Park is a people place," he told them. "It's a place for demonstrators. It's a place for the public — not just a place for the lobbyists and private interests."

Environment activists sent Rae a letter reminding him of his campaign promises. Now the premier said he did not believe in "shopping lists" from supporters. Greenpeace's Gord Perks said: "We do not believe in having a honeymoon with someone who is going to run away and leave us."

At the beginning of November, one month into his term, childcare activists met with Rae and praised his good intentions and promises to create 10,000 new childcare spaces, though Rae refused to affirm his election promises. Janet Davis, president of the Ontario Coalition for Better Child Care, said she was satisfied that the government would live up to its commitments.

But two short years later, the length of time it took for Rae's hair to go from blond to gray, the *Globe* headlined that "Activists Feel Betrayed by NDP." This was even before the gay rebellion in St. George.

Kerry McCuaig, executive director of the Ontario Coalition for Better Child Care, complained: "People really feel used. I don't think the government comprehends the anger that's there." Gord Perks told reporters: "There were some people in the environmental movement who believed this government would deliver all kinds of wonderful things. They've been disappointed." Political science professor Fred Fletcher said the government was being "hacked to death" from the left and the right.

Across the social movements, anti-poverty, childcare and equal pay supporters, the disabled, environmentalists, students and even organized labour, activists condemned the NDP for its betrayal of their causes. People were angry, disappointed, sold out. Rae, who for years was out fighting for "ordinary Canadians," seems to think of himself no longer even as an advocate, just a mediator. He told the *Star's* Derek Ferguson: "I now insist that when I'm faced with a number of advocacy groups being present from one perspective or another, my simple, short answer to them is: I won't see you unless your opponents are in the room with you."

But by the fall of 1992, most of the movements, which had been patient at the outset, were beginning to fight back. "We want to see the kind of policies that we elected the NDP for," said Daina Green, of the Alliance for Employment Equity. Three major environmental groups suspended relations with the government over frustration with delays on Great Lakes pollution. An emotional protest by disabled and mentally handicapped people took place at Queen's Park. The deaf community, backed by NDP MPP Gary Malkowski, staged rallies to press for their demands. Hospital workers erected a guillotine in front of the legislature. Rae was not sticking his neck out for these groups.

It is important to step back and recall the culture of the NDP that frequently attracted activists from these groups, and caused them to pin their hopes on the New Democrats, more than any other party.

Progressive groups actively look to governments for solutions to social problems. They don't turn to the anarchy of the marketplace, and they know that individual good intentions or charitable donations will never surmount the obstacles to or provide adequate funding for the programs they want to see put in place. Most of those initiatives, such as childcare, social assistance, protection of human rights, nuclear disarmament, public transportation, energy conservation, prevention of sexual assault, anti-racist and anti-sexist education, etc., require aggressive public policy. Progressive social movements are involved in politics precisely because they see politics as the best — and in many cases, only — place to achieve their goals.

For decades, many social activists have thought their best hope was with the New Democratic Party. They have very often, but by no means always, been NDP members and, through its councils and conventions, have helped shape party policy. They brought their ideas, their commitment, their money and their hard work to the NDP. The culture and propaganda of the party led them to believe that an NDP government would be committed to its platform, and their reward for their expertise and dedication would be the implementation of their programs.

At the same time, getting the NDP to share their goals was often a difficult battle. The Ontario NDP frequently fought the social movements from within, sold them out when the going got tough, or used them opportunistically. We have recounted some of the most important of those struggles: on abortion, gay rights, workers' health and safety, tenants' rights, protecting the Temagami wilderness, and others. While many activists remained within the NDP to fight the good fight, others were frustrated and angry.

For its part, the NDP never fully trusted the social movements. Several dynamics were at play.

First, before the NDP came to power, a prospect that seemed remote, the social movements lobbied and worked with Conservative and Liberal governments. This gave them a relationship with the NDP's political foes that the party was uncomfortable with.

Second, the NDP was unwilling to be a player in a coalition because it could not control the political agenda. The party could work with some activists on a personal level, but it was suspicious of their organizations because it could never be certain of their demands or tactics.

Finally, the NDP knew that many key players in the social movements were not New Democrats. Many were to the left of the party, and the NDP continued to fear communist tendencies. Other activists were Liberals. Some groups, especially the peace movement and the churches, were non-partisan, and welcomed the participation of members from all political backgrounds. The NDP found it hard to work with them.

So when the NDP came to power, it had long but checkered relationships with a great many social activists who had an expectation that the NDP would implement the platform they had helped write. At the same time, it often had a poor relationship with the social movements as organizations.

For the activists who had remained loyal to the party, the NDP's unexpected victory was the opportunity of a lifetime. Some were hired for jobs in ministers' offices, where they thought they could have a direct role putting their ideas into practice. Activists who were more suspicious or cynical waited for the NDP to prove itself.

Of all the groups and constituencies pushing for social change, it is probably women who have fared best from the NDP. The government passed legislation ensuring court-ordered spousal support payments would be paid; it improved parental leave; provided funding for new childcare spaces and subsidies and conversion of for-profit centres to non-profits; funded new sexual assault centres, increased funding for existing services and launched extensive advertising programs on sexual assault; increased access to abortion services and provided emergency funding after the Morgentaler clinic was bombed; and introduced legislation eliminating the time limits for filing cases of sexual assault.

But many women's activists are fed up with the NDP government for its failure to follow through with announcements it had made. In October, 1990, for example, Rae promised that the government would go ahead with its pay equity program even if it cost millions of dollars. "The fact that women are underpaid is a fact that needs to be changed in our society," he said. The government admitted it did not know how much pay equity would cost, and confessed that the $60 million publicized in its Agenda for People would cover only the 80,000 women employed directly by the government. The government trumpeted pay equity legislation for a further 420,000 women, but then put the entire program on hold.

The same was true for employment equity, where an early commitment to legislation resulted in delay after delay. In April, 1993, employment equity activists quit the government's advisory committee in anger and frustration over the government's failure to implement its legislation.

Many women still harbour resentment over Rae's flat-out support for the Charlottetown constitutional accord, believing that it would have diminished the rights of women and made national social programs impossible.

Opposition to the Charlottetown accord was led by the National Action Committee on the Status of Women, whose president, Judy Rebick, had long been aligned with the NDP.

NAC's main objections fell into three areas: The premiers had dropped all provisions for proportional representation in the Senate, which would have assured representation of women, natives, ethnic minorities and other under-represented groups; existing guarantees for women in the Charter of

Rights and Freedoms appeared to be weakened by the so-called "Canada Clause", which appeared to override the Charter; and the right of provinces to opt out of federal programs would mean the end of a national childcare program and would threaten existing social programs. Women were also concerned that the rights of native women in their own communities might not be protected under the vague provisions for native self-government.

Rae dismissed NAC as an "interest group," and said it was wrong of the organization to disagree with the constitutional proposals. Rebick, who was familiar with being on the wrong side of Bob Rae, responded: "Why he turns on us — in a way that most women aren't turning on us even if they don't agree with us — is because it's the ego thing. It's the men saying, 'Where do you women get off telling us what to do?' It's this male, macho politics where you can't have a civilized debate because your ego's at stake."

Rebick told reporters: "What we're saying is that we represent the interests of women, and the interests of women are being violated by this accord. If we don't stand up and say it, who's going to say it? That's our job."

The rift between women and the NDP grew into a serious one during the entire period leading up to the referendum on October 26, 1992. Women once again felt shut out of the process, and were presented with an un-amendable fait accompli.

For the NDP, this was a crucial group to lose. NAC says the NDP sold out its principles by abandoning voiceless minority groups ignored in the deal. One NAC spokesperson, Lorraine Gautier, suggested publicly that traditional NDP supporters were so mad they might vote for the Reform party, which also opposed the deal.

Anti-poverty activists are also bitterly disappointed with the NDP's performance, citing the enormous gap between the government's rhetoric about the poor and homeless, and what it has actually done.

Noting that "a traitor is worse than an enemy," anti-poverty activist John Clarke has repeatedly blasted the government for its inaction. "If Rae and his ministers think that the recession is giving them a rough time, they should see what's happening to the unemployed, the hungry, the homeless and the poor," a flyer at a demonstration organized by Clarke's coalition read. Gerard Kennedy, head of the Daily Bread Food Bank, wondered: "Maybe there's something in the insulation [at Queen's Park] that gives off blandness."

Following recommendations of the Thomson commission, the Liberal government introduced a program that allowed recipients of social assistance who found jobs to retain most of their additional earnings. The working poor could apply under the same program to receive supplemental social assist-ance. In mid-1992, the NDP imposed a three-month waiting period before recipients who found jobs could keep most of their salaries, and eliminated the eligibility of the working poor for the program entirely. The changes were expected to save the government between $30 and $60 million.

In early 1993, Rae's musings about the need to transform welfare infuriated anti-poverty activists. "My own view about welfare...is that simply paying people to sit at home is not smart," Rae said. The *Globe's* Martin Mittelstaedt noted that it was a remark that "would not have seemed out of place delivered by Ronald Reagan or Margaret Thatcher."

But Michael Shapcott, once a prominent New Democrat now with the Social Planning Council of Metropolitan Toronto said: "A system that overtly or covertly tries to get people to work...assumes a character flaw in those on welfare, when in fact the real problem is that there are no jobs."

A leaked government document proposed sweeping changes in social assistance, including workfare proposals, mandatory "volunteer" work as a condition of receiving benefits, and requiring some elderly and disabled recipients to look for jobs.

Ruth Mott, a Toronto NDP member and community activist, said she was "shocked and devastated" by the government's report. "The fact these ideas were even down on paper is a complete betrayal of everything we've ever worked for," Mott said.

Some cabinet ministers quickly repudiated the government's rhetoric. The social services minister of the day, Marion Boyd, said it was "unlikely" that the report's controversial recommendations would be approved. Treasurer Floyd Laughren indicated he would oppose any program that denied people social assistance. "There are not enough jobs out there for everybody now," he acknowledged. "So it would be silly to be punitive at a time when there aren't enough jobs for everybody who wants to work."

But the damage was done. The *Star's* Kelly Toughill called it "a startling about-face for the New Democratic Party."

Shapcott pointed out that by 1993, most of the people on welfare and the homeless had become completely resigned to the reality that the NDP was no different. "They've lost the will to fight," he says.

In the environmental movement, things are no better. There, activists are furious over the government's mishandling of the mounting problem of garbage, the continued dumping of toxic wastes into the air and water, and by the NDP's foot-dragging on the reduction of nuclear energy.

In its first budget, the NDP introduced a "gas-guzzler" tax on the sale of new vehicles with poor gas mileage. But under pressure from the Autoworkers' union and the automobile industry, the NDP gutted the tax just two months later.

Environmentalists complained that the new tax did not do what it was intended to do because it simply taxed cars, not the use of those cars. A family with a big car pollutes less than one with two cars that drives more, for example. They wanted an increased tax on gasoline itself, since that's the only way to relate taxation to consumption.

In principle, environmentalists want green taxes earmarked for environmental solutions, so the public is aware of environmental costs and consequences, and so the taxes are not just another grab by government. They can point to the fact that less than 20 per cent of Ontario's former $5 tire tax went to tire recycling; the rest went into general revenue. Meanwhile, the government still does not know what to do about the mountains of used tires.

An Inside Job

On April 12, 1991, an environment coalition called a news conference to demand the resignation of Marc Eliesen, deputy minister of energy, for his role in backing Ontario's big corporate power users at the expense of conservation efforts. Eliesen had long-time NDP connections stretching back to his days as the federal party's research director in the Broadbent era.

A few days later, energy minister Jenny Carter's assistant Paul McKay, a former activist who used to introduce himself as "the environmentalist in Carter's office," met with the Greenpeace anti-nuclear unit. McKay arrived with a blue-suited public servant with a southern-U.S. drawl, and read from a prepared statement denouncing Greenpeace for taking part in the news conference and for its attacks on Eliesen. The deputy was, after all, a family man who could find himself out of a job, McKay reminded them.

There was no dialogue with Greenpeace and no request for suggestions, just a lecture on "environmentalism as if ethics mattered." With the public servant in tow, Greenpeace members held their tongues.

At the end of the meeting, to remind him of his roots, they presented McKay with a framed photograph of him perched on a platform when he occupied a tower at Darlington in 1981. McKay blushed.

Exactly one week later, the NDP named Marc Eliesen the head of Ontario Hydro. Before long, McKay quit his job at the ministry.

Environmentalists are also well aware that while the bottom has fallen out of the blue box recycling market, pop companies, which helped launch the program as a means of avoiding strict laws on returnable containers, are getting a free ride. Despite a legal requirement of 30 per cent of sales in returnables, sales hover around 10 per cent while the government "consults" with the industry.

Despite its loud noises in opposition, the NDP has been unable to resolve the mounting problem of garbage. In 1992, lawn signs proclaiming "Dump

Grier, Not Garbage" — a reference to the former environment minister — festooned suburban lawns north of Toronto, communities on the hit list for a dump for Metro's garbage.

Ontario Hydro has a $34 billion deficit, while the province's largest industrial power consumers are shifting to co-generation to produce their own electricity. Some of these companies, as well as many municipalities, are pushing to get off Hydro's power grid entirely. Hydro would have to give permission to give up its power monopoly, but won't. To reduce its deficit Hydro needs to sell more power in an era when people are pushing for conservation.

Meanwhile, the NDP's long pledge to shut down nuclear generating stations suffers the same moratorium the government imposed on new nuclear plants. The Bruce nuclear station operated at just over 50 per cent of capacity in 1992, while coal imports for coal-fired plants rose to $868 million. Burning that much coal produces more carbon dioxide emissions than all cars in the province do.

The New Democrats continued to build the second phase of the Darlington station despite their moratorium; the price tag has passed $14 billion but Phase Two has not yet produced a single watt of energy.

Inside government, two stories show how difficult it has been for NDP staff to get things done.

At a meeting of the Coalition for a Green Economic Recovery with Ministry of Environment officials, one person congratulated the ministry for using recycled photocopy paper. A member of the premier's staff said: "Gee, I wish I could get some; I've been trying for six months." One environmentalist wondered why he was trying to get the NDP to change the world when the premier's office couldn't change to recycled paper.

On another occasion, solar engineer Greg Allen told a ministerial executive assistant that the bureaucrats in the environmental section of the Ministry of Government Services were telling contractors not to worry about green specifications, and to do things as they always had done. The EA's response was: "Well, we'll see about that! I'll be sending them a memo!"

While proving itself bankrupt of new ideas to deal with garbage, nuclear energy, toxic wastes and other environmental issues, the NDP has alienated environmentalists by rejecting the dozens of green ideas they have put before the government. Some of these ideas are as simple as giving away rain barrels instead of spending billions on new sewers; expanding the use of private composting bins and setting up composting centres to avoid hauling waste that could be turned into a resource; or hiring people to deliver and install simple water-saving devices. At the same time, the government has funded Bay Street consulting firms instead of providing seed capital to launch environmental products or conduct research into renewable energy or environmentally-friendly consumer products.

Right across the broad spectrum of social activism, people are angry. Their expectations of an NDP government were high, though their relations with the party were often strained. Now they feel let down and sold out. But some of it is their own making.

Buoyed by the euphoria of the NDP win, leaders of the social movements immediately decided not to pressure the government. They were confident the NDP would implement its policies, and sure that their own concerns would be dealt with.

As a result, the social movements slipped quietly from the streets into the back rooms. To a certain extent they were welcomed into the hushed corridors of power: the government hired from their leadership and established task forces, held hearings and invited activists to meetings. Leaders of the movements bought into endless rounds of consultation and compromise, discussion and delay. Due partly to their own limited resources, they were hijacked by government.

Leaders of the movements not only had unrealistic expectations of the NDP's willingness to implement change, they committed a cardinal sin of activist politics: they backed off the very mobilization that had given them a degree of influence in the first place.

Their failure to use their organizational and educational skills also meant they were not at work creating the political space that the NDP could move into. They allowed themselves to be co-opted and consulted to death, while the government stalled action on their demands.

Some groups and people were quicker to realize this than others, but their failure to press their agenda where it was most effective — in public — has proven to be an enormous mistake.

4. Still Polishing the Labour Brass

No one was smiling more broadly on election night, 1990, than Ontario's labour leaders. Like so many others, most of them thought the NDP victory was a too good to be true. It was CAW secretary-treasurer Bob Nickerson who began the chant of "Pre-mier Bob! Pre-mier Bob!" at Rae's victory party that night. Not a drinking man, Nickerson couldn't applaud when Rae entered the room because he had a beer in each hand.

The one-hand-washes-the-other relationship between labour leaders and the NDP elite was well established, and the labour brass had every reason to believe an NDP government would come through for them.

By the end of 1992, a few key labour leaders were speaking in public about their disappointment with the government, and some even called for the resignation of Pre-mier Bob. Rank and file union members were signing petitions to disaffiliate from the party and the CAW's largest local voted to quit the NDP.

This grim picture was made worse by the province's debt crisis. With a deficit estimated at $17 billion, the NDP was looking for ways to slash as much as $7 billion in costs. Rumours persisted that foreign money-lenders were getting ready to lower the boom.

But some treasury officials and other economists pointed out that the government could not afford to take that much money out of the economy without causing serious problems. One treasury insider said the government had "no real understanding that it can't have it both ways. You can't go on a big deficit reduction scheme without the consequences. They're not thinking about what happens when you suck billions out of the economy."

In the spring of 1993, the government launched into "social contract" negotiations with the public sector labour brass, consistent with its approach of bringing in the leaders to solve problems and quiet the rank and file. The NDP was desperate to convince labour leaders of the seriousness of the government's deficit situation, get them on side, and sell a package of concessions. It also hoped that unions would contribute some imaginative and flexible new ideas such as shorter work weeks, altered work schedules, reorganized workplaces, etc., that would reduce the government's wage costs and might avoid layoffs.

In return, some union leaders representing workers in the broader public sector, such as hospitals, were hoping that the government would agree to centralized bargaining. This would simplify their jobs, reduce the costs of servicing their members and make it easier to represent their workers. (OPSEU has more than 350 locals; CUPE has over 700.) The unions knew that a Liberal or Tory government would never agree to centralized bargaining, and, having virtually given up on the prospect of the NDP government being re-elected, were anxious to press that demand before the next election.

For the government, the stakes were enormously high, and it had little to trade off. It could not promise job security and it hardly wanted to impose wage rollbacks or massive layoffs on tens of thousands of workers with an election not far off. It needed creative solutions, and these were hard to come by from a government with little imagination, and from a labour movement with a long history of intellectual laziness.

The NDP desperately hoped a solution could be worked out. But the government was preparing legislation and weighing other options to impose on over 900,000 broader public sector workers if the "social contract" bargaining failed.

For their part, the unions' initial positions seemed to offer little flexibility or imagination. Some offered reactionary solutions: CUPE's Hydro workers wanted the government to forge ahead with the re-tubing of the Bruce plant. Teachers advocated scrapping de-streaming. OPSEU said the government could save some money by stalling its planned decentralization.

The risk for unions is great. Walking away from the bargaining simply allows the government to sell their intransigence to the public, yet unions will have a hard time swallowing concessions. Many observers think the government is simply setting them up for a fall, demanding cutbacks they know the union leaders will never agree to. But the consultation process itself, an unlikely event during a Liberal or Tory regime, shows that the NDP hopes to trade off on its special relationship with labour leaders.

* * *

Organized labour was not disappointed when Rae expressed caution on election night and said he would work "with everyone," an olive branch extended to the business community. Labour, after all, worked with business every day. "No government can address all our grievances and be re-elected four years later," Ontario Federation of Labour president Gord Wilson said. "That doesn't mean we're backing off our agenda. It just means a longer term agenda."

Labour leaders were prepared to be patient. "This is the first friendly government we've faced," Wilson said. "Everything has changed. Now it's no longer a matter of making militant speeches." Organized labour felt a sense of responsibility and thought it would be more than a bit player in the decision-making process. "We've been handed the ball," the OFL leader said.

New Democrats and labour leaders remembered, in their own way, the one-term NDP government of Dave Barrett in British Columbia in the early 1970s. Relations between Barrett's government and labour were not good —labour supported his rival, Thomas Berger, for party leader, and the two sides never buried the hatchet. The interpretation Ontario labour and NDP leaders put on Barrett's defeat was that labour had been too impatient, had pushed too hard, and broke ranks in public. They were determined not to make that mistake in Ontario. At the outset, the labour leadership would be quiet and patient, and they played a big role in stifling dissent in the early days of Rae's mandate.

Just one month after the NDP was sworn in, a leaked OFL strategy document surfaced that reflected the key role labour expected to play in the government. "The labour movement seeks to be involved in the process of policy formation in a way that is sustained, intensive and at a high level," the paper said. "The involvement which we are seeking therefore goes well beyond what is usually connoted by such terms as 'consultation' or 'access.'"

Here immediately were signs of the quid pro quo. Organized labour would be patient, supportive, tone down its rhetoric and moderate its demands. In return, it wanted the NDP government to give it special access and move on labour's top priorities.

The special relationship between the labour brass and party leaders convinced them they could work out their agenda in the back rooms. By deciding to avoid public debate, they closed the door on the option of using their organizational strengths to create a public demand for change. Organized labour decided not to lead the charge or do public education that would give the government space to move into. It was a crucial strategic error, but it reflected the party's close relationship was with labour leaders, not working people.

Despite the media outcry and business concern over the leaked document, organized labour did get some access and influence. One example was the government's reversal of the gas guzzler tax it brought down in its first budget, quickly removed after public objections and behind-the-scenes intervention from the Autoworkers' union.

Another example was provided a few days before Rae made his unusual televised state-of-the-collapsing-economy address on January 21, 1992. Rae went on the air to discuss the hard times and announce transfer payments of just 1 per cent to hospitals, municipalities, school boards and universities. In fact, only days before, Rae planned no increases at all, until he met privately with a handful of the province's labour leaders.

In a meeting that included Gord Wilson, OPSEU president Fred Upshaw, and CUPE president Judy Darcy, Rae outlined the government's plans for no increase and met furious resistance. Darcy, whose union represents municipal and other workers in the broad public sector, was especially angry.

As a result of the meeting, the government shifted $160 million from a proposed employee adjustment fund — enough for the 1 per cent hike — and Rae announced the meagre increase.

But organized labour did not get the high-level and consistent involvement in decision-making that it wanted and, outside the Ministry of Labour, hardly had any influence at all. There were no labour policy experts in the Premier's Office, for example, and the only high-profile labour leader to join the government's ranks, Rae's friend, former CUPE leader Jeff Rose, was assigned to constitutional issues.

* * *

The private sector unions had a friend in Bob Mackenzie, a former Steelwork-ers' Union staffer, the party's long-time opposition labour critic. But just five days after he was sworn in as labour minister, Mackenzie said: "I've said many times the job should be minister *for* labour, not minister *of* labour,...but I guess I'm softening." As part of Mackenzie's new "neutrality" and the squeaky-clean image the government was trying to present, Rae forced Mackenzie to give up the union card he had carried proudly since he was a boy in steeltown Hamilton. To our knowledge, no former minister of labour had been compelled to give up membership in the Albany Club, Granite Club, or a chamber of commerce.

Mackenzie's preoccupation during the NDP's first two years in office was a set of changes to the province's labour code — changes that would address the labour movement's concerns and make organizing easier. The reforms themselves were surprisingly bland and simply borrowed from time-tested laws elsewhere in Canada, and even from Ontario's public sector. Nevertheless, they raised business objections to a fever pitch and seriously undermined the relationship the government was trying to establish with the business community.

Unions had been hard hit by the massive restructuring that took place in Ontario through the 1980s. The number of well-paying manufacturing and resource jobs in Ontario declined dramatically, and union membership fell 6 per cent between 1982 and 1990. Most new jobs were in the low-paid service sector, where the many small workplaces, fast employee turnover, and high percentage of part-time workers makes union organizing notoriously difficult and servicing the membership extremely expensive. Organized labour estimated it had to sign up 35,000 new members a year just to stay even with plant shutdowns, but was only managing about half that number.

When the ministry's first discussion paper on the labour reforms was released in the early fall of 1991, the OFL was on side. The government can't "just pander to a special interest group," Gord Wilson said. But Mackenzie said he "ran into a buzz saw with my cabinet colleagues," who pushed him to toughen the legislation.

At the same time, ordinary workers were getting frustrated with the NDP. To many of them, the New Democrats had come down on the side of natives, gays, women, the environment and visible minorities. Labour's rank-and-file wondered when it would be their turn. This message was getting through to labour leaders, and in turn to Mackenzie, who decided to go for broke.

But the business community went for the jugular.

Conrad Black, always good for a dose of Marxist rhetoric when the left has long abandoned it, wrote: "It is nothing less than the truth to say that the provincial government plans a union usurpation of the means of production, expropriation without compensation....This is not the co-operation of which the premier has spoken, other than in the sense that a corpse co-operates with its embalmer; this is legislated conquest. In strictly economic terms, it is communism, the economic dictatorship of the proverbial prole-tariat."

A new discussion paper released in November, 1991, reflected a change of heart by the government, which dropped 12 of its original 60 proposed amendments. The *Globe* noted that the NDP was "taking the muscle out of the law" in a bid to conciliate business; the labour movement complained that the reforms were short of what it wanted and attacked business for its hysteria.

But for the next twelve months the business hysteria continued. Two major coalitions came together, Project Economic Growth, with 350 corpo-rate members, and the More Jobs Coalition. Both waged expensive cam-paigns to force the government to withdraw the legislation. Part of the problem was business' complaint that it had no consultation with the government.

Business concerns on this score reflected two realities. One was the NDP's lack of contacts and credibility with business, and its incompetence in knowing how to make links with the corporate heavyweights. The other was the fact that business was used to getting its way from sympathetic Conservative and Liberal governments, and did not know how best to press its case with the New Democrats.

Experienced government relations people realized the fury of the busi-ness campaign broke a cardinal rule of lobbying: give your adversary some room to manoeuvre. "The rhetoric and tactics of the various business lobbies organized to fight labour-law reform seem to ignore this dictum," wrote *Lobby Digest* magazine. But the broadside assault continued.

The party apparatus of the NDP responded in defense. Provincial secretary Jill Marzetti wrote: "Big business lobbies are trying to take our province away from us....Their goal is to discredit and destroy our elected government....They are throwing a collective temper tantrum because in the election of 1990 they didn't get their way."

The *Financial Post*'s Diane Francis wrote, speaking of the government: "These unionists must simply be stopped."

Even though business overplayed its hand, it did succeed in watering down the bill, and, more generally, in scaring the NDP off other reforms. The price the NDP paid for bungling the labour reforms so badly was that the government lost the nerve to do anything else confrontational.

On November 6, 1992, the labour law reform bill passed 67 to 49. The premier was absent for the vote; he was in Asia trying to drum up invest-ment.

* * *

Over the course of the two-year process that brought the labour law into being, the NDP made some major tactical blunders and missed an opportunity to help workers most in need of labour reform.

The government was caught in a difficult balancing act between the demands of its friends in organized labour and its attempts to mollify an angry business community. When the bill was passed into law, union leaders felt they didn't gain much; business still complained bitterly.

The NDP postponed the question of sectoral bargaining, the best hope for unorganized workers in the service sector. Sectoral bargaining, which is in place in some employment sectors in Quebec, Australia and several European countries, allows unions to negotiate a basic contract with groups of employer representatives on an industry-wide basis. Salespeople in the retail sector, domestics, or waiters and waitresses in the hospitality business, for example, can be assured certain wages, benefits and working conditions.

Sectoral certification, another piece of the puzzle, provides automatic union recognition and guarantees minimum standards of wages and benefits to all workers in their particular industry. Unions are not obliged to go into every workplace to sign up individual workers. This makes organizing and representing workers in small workplaces possible and affordable.

Though pressured by organized labour to allow sectoral bargaining, the government deferred the idea to a study group, where it can be studied to death. The workers most in need of union protection were left out in the cold.

The women's community felt the labour changes, as they were, would not help working women. In August, 1992, the National Action Committee on the Status of Women complained: "It is extremely unlikely that even if all of the proposals are implemented, women and visible minority workers will benefit to any extent."

The NDP tried to sell its labour reforms on the basis of increased co-operation between workers and management; this new relationship would supposedly increase productivity. This was an ironic sales pitch in the face of the bitter fight the business community was putting up.

Surprisingly, in the course of pushing the legislation, union leaders did not practice the bipartite approach they advocated. "The OFL was really quite drunk with power," said one member of the government team reviewing the bill. "It never occurred to them to sit down with business and work out a consensus, using the NDP's power as a lever. It didn't occur to them because they were in power, and, by gosh, the party was going to deliver."

"If the government had done that [forced unions and business to sit down together], they could have sold just as much and no one would have been in a frenzy," said one leader of a major business lobby.

The NDP also failed to use its clout with labour to discuss ways to rationalize union representation, pressuring them to specialize in particular groups of employees so they develop expertise and make both organizing and representing workers easier.

Two years of controversy so bitter that the NDP backed off reforms in other areas, and little to show for the working people most in need of protection.

* * *

In what passed for an industrial strategy, the NDP government also spent millions of dollars to prop up jobs at Algoma Steel in Sault Ste. Marie and the de Havilland Aircraft Company in Downsview. The government's close ties to the Steelworkers' and Autoworkers' unions helped keep these companies going.

Early in 1991, Dofasco announced that it was writing off its $713 million in debts for the troubled Algoma Steel and leaving town. At risk were about 5,500 jobs and hundreds more in the community that depended on Algoma as its major employer. The NDP established a committee of management, union and government representatives to try to save Algoma; both the union and management praised Rae's efforts at bringing the two sides together.

Within a year, a proposal was agreed to that would see management and workers own 60 per cent of the company, with the balance held by the banks and other creditors. The provincial and federal governments gave $100 million in loan guarantees, as well as providing for the early retirement of 1600 workers, who would collect from a special pension fund estimated to cost the taxpayers about $50 million. The workers gave up $2.89 an hour in wages as well as reductions in other benefits.

Dofasco had decided it was cheaper to write off its investment than to try to make the company profitable. It was looking to bail out of integrated steel production and invest in a specialty mini-mill in the U.S. Algoma had lost money in eight of the previous 10 years, including $190 million in 1991 and $74 million in 1992. The company's main product, steel rails, was in oversupply. Dofasco had invested $380 million in producing pipe for the oil and gas industry, just as the boom in that market ended. Its third product, structural steel, was being produced better and cheaper at small specialty mills in the United States. Despite these factors, the union waged a four-month strike in 1990.

Industry analysts and Algoma managers expected the decline in the steel industry to continue. One prominent industry analyst said that the Algoma deal was "nothing more than a giant make-work project and a senseless drain on the taxpayers." Even Jack Ostroski, chair of the Steel local at Algoma, said: "We've turned a bankrupt company into a gold mine for our senior citizens," and worried about the unlucky younger workers who "own a piece of the Titanic now."

Despite the government money and reduction in workers' wages, the biggest North American experiment in worker ownership started out with a debt over $300 million, in a chronic money-losing company in a depressed industry.

Not knowing what else to do to save the community, the NDP thought it was worth the risk. The government's decision to save de Havilland Aircraft cost even more money.

Saying it had never made a profit in the five years it had owned de Havilland, its parent, the Boeing Corporation, put the company up for sale in 1990. It was close to finalizing a deal with a French-Italian consortium in mid-1991, but the federal and provincial governments were concerned that a foreign owner would buy de Havilland to shut it down. They tried to find a Canadian buyer.

In the fall of 1991, as the cash-strapped NDP looked to sell off provincial assets, the Montreal-based Bombardier Corporation bought Ontario's profitable Urban Transit Development Corporation. That deal paved the way for Bombardier to step in as the buyer of de Havilland.

The *Financial Post* said: "The NDP government has finally found an industrial strategy, and it's called Bombardier." The *Post* also noted that Bombardier specialized in taking over troubled companies, paying rock bottom prices and getting government money in exchange for promises of jobs. In the de Havilland deal, Bombardier put up $51 million for a 51 per cent share, and the Ontario government pitched in $49 million for 49 per cent. The NDP also provided $260 million for restructuring, research and development, and paid Boeing $70 million. Ottawa provided $230 million in assistance, and forgave $13.1 million in loans. The provincial and federal governments also set aside a $300 million reserve to cover Bombardier's losses in the first four years. In April, 1993, de Havilland announced a two-month summer shutdown, the first in its 65-year history.

The de Havilland deal is a sign of the NDP's interest in keeping the best-paying industrial jobs afloat in companies where the workers belong to the unions closest to the NDP.

The government also gave scarce public money to automakers. Chrysler Canada's $500 million investment in Windsor came with $30 million for training, and a promise to allow Chrysler to co-generate its own power — something it had previously denied to the cities of Kingston, Sudbury and Windsor. Ford's $2.2 billion for its plants in south-west Ontario came with 34 million training dollars.

"To the extent that governments need to be paying for training and retraining, one might think that a preference should go to helping workers in dying industries who are suddenly and surprisingly thrown out of work with skills that have no market value," the *Globe*'s Terence Corcoran wrote. "The auto industry handouts not only assist companies that do not need adjustment assistance, they assist profit-making firms where workers are already enjoying the highest wages and benefits in the land and the richest job security packages in the private sector." The subsidies amounted to nearly $8,000 per worker at Chrysler and Ford; at de Havilland, the costs per job were much higher.

Labour leaders were fully supportive of these corporate grants. Under other circumstances, they used to complain that the corporations did not pay their fair share of taxes.

* * *

The labour brass took good care of themselves through the newly-established bipartite Workers' Health and Safety Agency, the training body set up by the Liberals' Bill 208.

The agency opened in 1990, just months before the NDP election. Its co-chairs were long-time OFL water-carrier Paul Forder and employer representative Bob McMurdo. The two were paid $105,000 apiece to administer the Agency's operations.

Two years after the agency opened, it still had not trained a single worker, and labour and employer appointees to its board were fighting over how much training the workplace health and safety reps mandated by the legislation would get. Labour leaders "are more interested in power and control of funds than worker health," Ian Howcroft of the Canadian Manufacturers' Association complained. Though understandable from a business point of view, his comments echoed complaints among health and safety activists about the fact the agency would become a pork barrel.

That's just what it seemed when *Toronto Star* journalist John Deverell revealed extensive nepotism in the hiring of agency staff. These included Gord Wilson's daughter, Susan; OPSEU president Fred Upshaw's daughter, Charlotte; Lyle Hargrove, brother of now CAW president Buzz Hargrove; Loretta Michaud, wife of CAW staffer Gerry Michaud; and the son of former OFL chief Cliff Pilkey's partner. The salaries for their jobs ranged from roughly $45,000 to $60,000.

Organized labour responded angrily to these charges. Pilkey said: "You want us to hire people off the street, people we don't even know?" Upshaw complained: "I'll be damned if my daughter should be discriminated against for a job opening simply because I'm OPSEU president." Upshaw didn't have anything to say about people being discriminated against because they lacked the necessary relatives. The controversy gave "labour relations" a new spin.

Embarrassed, Rae and Mackenzie launched an investigation, which the government quietly shelved.

In October, 1992, the agency board reached a decision on training. According to the *Star*'s Leslie Papp, it was "rammed through...by labour directors and a minority of business directors. That broke with an earlier practice of having a consensus of labour and business sections."

Forder, boasting that it was a "proud day," was pleased that "Now we have no more deadlock." Five of the nine business reps on the board resigned, and they demanded the resignation of co-chair Bob McMurdo.

Though the agency clearly wasn't working as intended, labour minister Mackenzie just appointed new employer reps. The agency, which was already spending almost $7 million a year, was finally about to start to train workers.

There was no discussion in the labour movement over the perils of joint health and safety training with the boss. As far as the labour leaders were concerned, that question had been resolved. Joint training was a way to cool out health and safety activists and buy labour peace. In 1992, the CAW, which had established its showplace education centre in Port Elgin as a facility that would not allow joint programs, voted to allow joint health and safety training there.

* * *

In the union ranks, workers were furious with the NDP government. They complained that they had busted their asses for years on behalf of the NDP, and wondered what they had to show for it. The policy reversals on public auto insurance and Sunday working were the lightning rods, but workers were also angered by the NDP's appeasement of business, the failure to tax corporations or the rich, and by the general bungling. The message was getting through to the labour heavyweights that the troops were unhappy.

At the outset, the labour leaders had been patient. They feared if the NDP moved too far, too fast, it would be a one-term government. But as time went on, and the NDP's popularity plummeted, labour leaders began to realize they should get whatever they could from the government before it was defeated.

Behind the scenes, labour leaders were telling the New Democrats just how angry their workers were. And because no leader can afford to be too far from his or her membership, they also realized that they were going to have to go public with some of their complaints.

The first labour leader to do so was new CAW chief Buzz Hargrove, who took over from Bob White when White became head of the CLC in 1992. In December of that year, Hargrove reported to the CAW Council on "worker frustration."

Saying he was wrong to have initially supported the government's change of heart on public auto insurance, and calling it a "defeat of the government," Hargrove said the reversal "gave the corporate world the confidence that they could defeat or at least control the economic agenda of the government while they continued to attack the government on equality issues. The Rae government responded by trying to diffuse the criticism of the corporate world by more and more talking the language of the Business Council on National Issues and the language of the right-wing government in Ottawa. Its programs, policies and public statements were full of rhetoric on competitiveness, partnership, restraint, cutbacks and how you give incentives to business as the key to economic renewal."

Hargrove criticized the government for its "refusal to challenge capital," and said Rae "has not put in place a credible alternative around which to mobilize party and labour activists."

He spelled out a lengthy list of proposals that the government should move on. He suggested they be funded by an "Ontario Development Bond," which would be a war bond for the battle against unemployment and poverty.

Hargrove said he understood the constraints the government felt itself under, and appreciated what it had done. "But one point is becoming increasingly clear," he said, "we cannot simply leave politics to the government we elected. Governments will stray unless they are held accountable. If we take the idea of social democracy seriously, then we have a *responsibility* to criticize this government, challenge it, make demands on it, mobilize for it, and — yes — sometimes mobilize against its direction....We have to forcefully say to our friends in government that there *is* an alternative."

Hargrove's criticisms stung the NDP. If the government was losing support from such a key ally, then it was truly losing its base.

In March, 1993, Bob White called for a meeting of labour leaders with the NDP premiers of Ontario, Saskatchewan and British Columbia, and federal leader Audrey McLaughlin.

"The labour movement, nationally and provincially, is going through a change," White said. "We keep talking about building a broad-based social movement to counter the corporate agenda, regardless of who is in power. We believe it is fundamentally important to get [New Democrats] elected in as large numbers as possible, but even with NDP governments the labour movement and social groups must push for change....We will be around, as a labour movement and as social-action groups, after the NDP governments have been defeated as well. We have an obligation to our members."

Within a matter of days, when Ontario Hydro announced layoffs of 4,500 workers, most of them CUPE members, Rae called Hydro's move "courageous." An angry Sid Ryan, president of CUPE's Ontario Division, called on Rae to return to social democratic principles or to resign. But within another week, the government was talking openly about laying off up to 18,000 public servants in a major cost-cutting move. This sparked the outrage of OPSEU president Fred Upshaw, who to that point had been a quiet NDP supporter, and whose union had recently negotiated a job-protecting collective agreement in exchange for wage increases well below inflation.

In 1991, members of his union challenged Upshaw as a government toady, to which he replied: "If this is being in bed with the employer, then don't wake me up." Two years later, in the midst of a tough union re-election campaign, he said: "If I knew two years ago what I know today, I would not have voted for Bob Rae."

The NDP government had lost support of the rank and file, and was now losing the support, even in public, of the labour leadership.

5. No Lunchbucket Economics

In its second budget the NDP government announced a new three-part "jobsOntario" program to stimulate investment, train workers, and build new homes. One aspect of the overall program, a three-year, $1.1 billion training fund, was "designed to train and provide work for up to 100,000 people on social assistance or whose Unemployment Insurance has run out." It would also provide skills upgrading for up to 80,000 employed workers.

It did this by granting employers $10,000 for each new worker hired. In the first year of the program, 14,000 jobs had been provided, less than half of the target, and the ministry responsible couldn't say how many people placed in the program were actually working. As the first year wound up, the government decided to spend an additional $1.5 million to advertise it to prospective employers.

The initiative reflected the ad hocery of job training in Ontario, a total absence of labour market planning, and a reliance on private employers to hire untrained workers for a $10,000 subsidy when their own costs would far exceed that amount.

The program was also a clear indication that the New Democrats have shown a disappointing but predictable lack of hands-on economic ideas.

On the government's second anniversary, James Laxer wrote: "Two years into its term, most people in the province still have no clear idea what a social democratic approach to the economy involves. Rae and his ministers cannot decide whether they want to promote neo-conservatism with a human face, or whether they represent an alternative to the orthodoxy of the last decade....For too long, the government has delayed mobilizing the public on behalf of a new vision of the economy. The better future that social democrats have long promised cannot be realized by a government whose leaders are more comfortable hiding behind daily crises than pointing the way to a genuine alternative."

Laxer, the former Waffle leader who went on to become the federal party's research director, left Ottawa in a blaze of controversy when he published *Rethinking the Economy* in 1983. (See Chapter Three.) In his book, Laxer blamed the New Democrats for outdated economic beliefs, something he saw come to fruition with the Ontario NDP. He said the NDP rejected some methods of government intervention in the economy because they might scare off voters, and dismissed others because they might turn off party activists. "Most of the time the party advocates none of the tools needed in an actual industrial strategy," he said.

At the time Laxer's book was released, John Fryer, long-time New Democrat and president of the National Union of Government Employees, said: "We are united on platitudes and shibboleths. When it comes to real answers, we fall short."

Fryer and Laxer — and many others — were saying that the NDP lacked the kind of practical economic ideas that we have described as "lunchbucket economics."

The late American socialist Michael Harrington, well-respected in NDP circles, wrote in *The New Left* that the political left-wing should not just be in favour of more and better economic planning, it must be for "the transfer of power to men and women at the base, to 'ordinary' citizens." But there has been little evidence of this in Ontario. John Sewell, former mayor of Toronto, who was appointed by the NDP to examine housing policies, said of his political bosses: "If they weren't going to empower a different set of people, what were they going to do when they got in power?"

But NDP stalwart Gerry Caplan put his finger on the problem when, in a review of the federal party's 1984 election campaign, he noted that polls showed people didn't expect the NDP to have to deliver. "Few [people] expect us to form a government," he said then. "We are admired because we can be counted on to fight for ordinary Canadians, not because we are expected to implement certain policies. We are respected because we are seen to be fighters for, not planners of."

Caplan, who is credited with coining the phrase that people think the NDP "can't run the corner store," was not suggesting this was a good thing, just that it was true. Now, of course, the NDP is in charge of Ontario.

A great many people have blamed the recession for the NDP's inability to deal with the economy. They let the NDP off the hook, arguing that hard times prevent the party from implementing its many good economic ideas, whatever they might be. It is true that a cash-strapped government's options are more limited those riding an economic wave. But as NDP historian Des Morton pointed out: "The NDP came to power at a terrible time, when Ontario was finally paying the price for free trade, resource depletion and an abysmal record in job training, applied research and industrial modernization. But did the NDP think it would win only when Ontario was booming? If the NDP did not want to win in 1990, it should have told someone."

In fact, social democratic parties have always argued that their philosophies were specifically designed with the poor in mind. The recession gave them an opportunity to prove that in times when they most needed it, the disadvantaged could count on the NDP.

But Rae's NDP has been simply unable to make Robin Hood economics work. Why is the NDP so lacking in practical, win-win economic solutions?

* * *

In February, 1993, Rae captured two weeks of headlines about his government's new economic agenda, and said the plan would create 100,000 jobs. He managed this by announcing government spending that sounded big but totalled only six tenths of one per cent of provincial revenues, $330 million a year for ten years.

The government's new plan relied on large-scale public works projects and depended on private investors and user fees for such investments as new highways, sewage and water treatment, and real estate and telecommunications corporations. If the computer-linked high-tech communications proposal sounded new, the others were traditional depression-era public works projects that put the government on the cutting edge of yesterday's technology.

Perhaps memories of the Depression and the Dirty Thirties, when the CCF got its start, have left the NDP with a legacy of economic problem-solving that is based not so much on re-distributing income as looking for ways to make the economy grow, and trying to ensure that the poor get a greater share of the new wealth. NDP economics are dependent upon a growing pie, not a differently-shared pie.

Like Oliver Twist's gruel, this "Please, sir, I'd like some more" approach seems only humane and just. But at a time when the economic pie is shrinking, and at a time when environmentalists in particular are making the case that our society cannot continue to grow endlessly, the NDP has nothing new to offer.

The NDP must also confront a powerful North American ethos, driven by attitudes in the United States, that taxes are simply money taken away from people, not money that provides them with services or redistributes wealth. In the U.S., where billions of tax dollars disappear into the military-industrial complex every year, there is little to show for and much to resent about taxation. Americans' attitudes toward taxation might be very different if they saw their money used to provide health services, education, adequate pensions, public transportation, housing, child care, jobs and other benefits. That attitude spills over into Canada.

Through the 1980s, neo-conservatism played to this resentment of taxes, trying to convince people to look to the market, rather than the state, as the guarantor of their economic well-being. The NDP must be prepared to challenge this notion, but it has failed to do so.

While rightly pointing out that the tax burden is unfairly distributed, the NDP makes its pitch to working- and middle-class people that their taxes are too high — not just in relative but in absolute terms. In appealing to their desire for lower taxes, the NDP plays to the belief that taxes are a social evil. At the same time, it reinforces the reality of private wealth and public squalor. People resist taxes that go to things they cannot see or, perhaps even worse, that go to someone else.

Whether in opposition or in government, the NDP seldom made the case for the social benefits of taxation, and what those revenues should best be used for. Now, as government, the NDP finds it difficult to persuade people that the social programs and public services they depend on require a greater level of taxation not just from the rich and the corporations, but from working people as well.

As we have discussed elsewhere, the NDP has deep roots in the prairie social gospel tradition, a Protestant attempt to bring the social teachings of Jesus into everyday life. These roots give the NDP an ethical foundation that serves as another source of its failure to develop practical "lunchbucket" economic ideas. It's why Bob Rae talks about "fairness," but not about class, gender or race exploitation.

In fact, New Democrats have come so far from the notion of a class analysis that they are astonished at how hard the capitalists fight for their own interests.

In the face of its mounting deficit, the NDP has also failed to explain to people why the growing debt is a problem — not for right-wing reasons, but as a measure of any government's ability to make economic decisions. Specifically, the government has yet to go public about the power of international capital, and how the province's ability to direct its economic future is restricted by foreign money-lenders. The government has never attempted to rally nationalist sentiments in an attempt to gain control of our economy by mobilizing local resources.

To counter the right wing's dogma of the supremacy of the marketplace, to overcome people's resistance to taxation, to find new ways not just to distribute new income but re-distribute existing wealth, and to mobilize local capital to deal with Ontario's economic crisis, the NDP needs to politicize economics. It needs to develop common-sense, every-day notions of what the state can do to improve people's lives and make them share more equitably in society's riches.

* * *

The incoming NDP government was shocked to learn, even before it took office, that it was about to inherit a $700 million deficit. Within months, and before the NDP had made any major spending decisions, the deficit had climbed to $2.5 billion.

In no time at all, the government sent signals that it was backing off its agenda. Journalist Jamie Swift wrote: "The revolution of falling expectations had begun, setting the tone for the new government's first months in office. From that point on new ministers would begin prefacing remarks with a few sober sentences that almost inevitably contained the figure $2.5 billion. Rae intoned darkly about 'the new realities of the '90s' and his choices between 'cod-liver oil and cough syrup' rather than 'strawberries and cream or creme caramel.'"

His government's first budget, brought down in April, 1991, reflected the collapsing economy with a deficit skyrocketing to $9.7 billion. It included $700 million in public works spending, a plan the outgoing Liberals had in the works. The government hoped the spending would help to kick-start the economy.

One year later, Laughren's second budget relied on conventional measures to limit government spending in an attempt to control the deficit. As Thomas Walkom wrote: "The transformation of the Ontario NDP into a centre-right government has been wondrous to behold. It has been swift and shameless."

Back in 1984, differing from Ed Broadbent about the need to control deficits, Rae said: "I have never regarded deficits as the central issue. The central issue is what steps need to be taken to get the economy moving. I think that discussions about deficits are really red herrings."

This was no longer the case. By early 1993, the entire government was consumed by the province's deficit. At the end of March, senior treasury advisors presented an unprecedented series of mandatory briefings for caucus staff to explain just how bad things were. Among the dire forecasts was the warning that international money-lenders were about to drop Ontario's double-A credit rating, and were already charging interest at the rate of single-A.

But official estimates of the government's financial picture varied wildly. As recently as mid-1992, treasury projected the 1995-96 deficit would decline to $4.1 billion; in early 1993 it was predicting it would be $18.3 billion instead.

The *Globe*'s Richard Mackie wrote: "Anything that will show that the NDP government is working to boost the economy is played up by the Premier's Office. Other government activities are either shifted to the background or given a twist to emphasize their economic aspects. As a result, welfare reform is talked about as 'getting people back to work.' Education reform becomes 'better preparing people to enter the work force.' Building roads becomes 'upgrading the transportation infrastructure to better serve industry.'"

But the fixation on the deficit did not impress a number of economists and left-wing academics.

In an editorial in the *Canadian Forum*, Duncan Cameron cited John Hotson from the Committee on Monetary and Economic Reform, and wrote: "Electing an NDP government that is unwilling to use all of its powers to fight recession and unemployment is like electing the Green Party and being told they can't do anything about the environment. The three NDP provincial governments must break the logic of debt bondage that is being used to constrain their actions against unemployment."

Yet still there were no new ideas. Rae scared anti-poverty activists by using the language of the right-wing about welfare reform. He moved to privatize water, sewage, roads and highways — long a bulwark of positive socialist examples of public control. He described Ontario Hydro's pending layoff of 4,500 workers as "courageous." He said the public service was as slow-moving and outdated as the Spanish Armada, and talked about public servants "with quill pens." And he prepared public servants for massive layoffs, perhaps as many as 18,000, after having signed a collective agreement with the union that gave below-inflation wage increases in exchange for job security.

"At Queen's Park, Mr. Rae's musings led people to joke that his nickname needed to be changed from 'Comrade Bob' to 'Conrad Bob,'" Mackie wrote, a reference to the ebullient capitalist Conrad Black.

Looking at both the big picture, the NDP was ignoring the advice of left-wing economists about government spending instead of deficit control. Looking at the smaller details, the NDP wasn't listening to practical suggestions coming to it from a wide range of people.

* * *

In the spring of 1992, the Coalition for a Green Economic Recovery presented the government with 29 proposals for a "green" budget. These were the kind of lunchbucket ideas the NDP needed to create jobs, improve the environment, and save money on big-ticket items.

The coalition urged the government to hire 15,000 students to deliver backyard composters during the summer of 1992. They cited a Durham region study that showed that "the cost of diverting a ton of 'wet waste' to free backyard composters...is $23.11 a ton." Collecting and dumping the same material costs municipalities over $200 a ton. The program would have paid for itself.

The coalition suggested the government hire 20,000 people to deliver free rainbarrels for homeowners to hook to their eavestroughs. Saved rainwater used for lawns and gardens would reduce the load on urban sewage systems. It, too, would have paid for itself from savings from an expanded sewage system and reduced use of expensive treated water.

The coalition also suggested the government employ 20,000 people to deliver and install simple water conservation equipment. Devices such as water-efficient showerheads, faucets and toilet-dams would significantly reduce the amount of water used. Based on estimates from the Potomac Water Conservation Authority, Metro Toronto might save $180 million a year in water bills and sewage treatment. The program would have paid for itself within a year.

Other people had other ideas.

Michael Porter, author of *Canada at the Crossroads: The Reality of a New Competitive Environment*, a study widely circulated and welcomed within the senior ranks of government and the public service, wrote that governments infrequently produce change by being a sophisticated buyer, or by creating an early market for new products. He advocated that Canada play a more direct role in that kind of economic growth.

But when the government introduced a law requiring bicycle riders to wear helmets, there was not a single helmet manufacturer in Ontario. The government had no plans to encourage an industry to supply helmets to a ready market of tens of thousands of bicycle riders.

Before abandoning the idea to the private sector, the NDP advocated public auto insurance, but never talked about one of the best ways to control escalating insurance costs: getting a grip on the high cost of parts and repairs. The NDP had no plans to reduce parts costs by intervening actively in the parts supply market, either as a mass purchaser or by working with Ontario's automakers and parts suppliers to rationalize supply. As every vehicle owner knows, replacement parts cost many times more than original parts. At the same time, the government showed little interest in attempting to regulate the repair industry by setting rates or establishing British Columbia-style estimate centres to determine what the government would pay for accident claims.

Energy specialists urged Ontario Hydro to launch programs to lease energy-efficient equipment whose initial high purchase cost deters consumers. Hydro has long leased home water heaters; activists wanted it to make available equipment like compact fluorescent bulbs, solar water heaters or home retrofit insulation packages, paid for over time, just as hydro stations are.

On a larger scale, some activists suggested that the NDP should employ construction workers, either directly or through private contractors, to improve the energy efficiency of private homes with the use of improved insulation, new windows, or conversion from electric heat to gas furnaces, for example.

Tens of thousands of workers with a variety of skills could be employed for many years, and the province would benefit enormously from reduced energy demand. Construction jobs the province would lose by not having to build, or by cancelling the construction of electrical generating stations would more than be replaced by the people employed to retrofit homes. The money not spent building the generating stations could be used to employ those workers.

People from the social movements and the labour movement offered a wide variety of ideas to the government. No doubt some of those ideas would not have worked. But many would have. Some would have been expensive: building public transportation or alternatives to traditional water-treatment plants, and retrofitting homes. Others would have been cheap: handing out compost bins, rain barrels or shower heads. But it didn't matter — the government wasn't listening.

In the spring on 1993, anti-poverty activist Michael Shapcott described the split that had developed in the social movements. "There are two factions," he said. "One group is busy writing detailed programs and policies because they think the NDP doesn't know what to do. But there's a growing number who think that it's not that it doesn't know, but that it's not committed."

But it was not as if the government had not been flooded with ideas. Its failure to develop practical, lunchbucket economics is perhaps the government's biggest failing. It is its most inexcusable.

6. Romancing the Working Class

For decades the NDP has positioned itself as the champion of the working class, underpaid and overworked, unrewarded and overtaxed. New Democrats reach out to this audience through the big industrial unions, and they've stuck to their line even as society and the economy changed dramatically. Those changes hit those traditional blue-collar workers, the people the NDP thinks of as its core support, hardest.

In the late 1940s, about 60 per cent of Canadian workers had jobs manufacturing goods. By the early 1990s, 70 per cent of jobs were in the service industry. Between 1975 and 1990, about 40 per cent of new jobs were part time, which meant not only low wages but no benefits. Most of those new jobs were in the service sector: it accounted for 90 per cent of new jobs since 1967. These factors also combined to result in a decline in union representation.

In the fall of 1991, Statistics Canada confirmed what most people already knew: families were no better off at the end of the 1980s than they were when the decade began. While after-tax income had increased 27 per cent in real terms in the 1950s, 34 per cent in the 1960s and 22 per cent in the 1970s, most people barely broke even during the 1980s.

People's wages increased slightly over the decade, but their taxes also went up. In 1982, the average family paid taxes of $7,300; those increased to $9,600 in 1989. Canadians could be excused for thinking that they were paying more for less.

Middle-income families bore the financial brunt of the combination of these factors. These people were typical of the industrial manufacturing elite represented by the Steelworkers' and Autoworkers' unions, the private sector unions with the closest links to the NDP.

Workers in jobs represented by those unions were also among the hardest hit by the restructuring that is taking place in the Ontario economy in the 1990s. Between March, 1990 and March, 1991, Ontario lost 226,000 jobs; 200,000 of them were in manufacturing.

The lost jobs, higher taxes and generally bleak economic picture were factors in people's unhappiness with the Peterson government, which they blamed for doing nothing to deal with the economy. People who had never voted NDP before became more receptive to the NDP's appeal to make the rich pay, and to its message that the Liberals were beholden to "special interests" whose interests were not their own.

But once in office, New Democrats found themselves trapped by the deepening recession and paralysed by a combination of a lack of breathing space and a lack of imagination to solve the worsening economic crisis.

The NDP clung to its romantic notion of the downtrodden worker, people who now own their own homes, cottages, boats, recreational vehicles and skidoos, but who still have to worry about putting their kids through college and paying their mortgages. The NDP's attachment to its romantic image of the working class steered it away from proposing the kind of legislation that would have best served the truly disadvantaged.

Perhaps nowhere was this romantic notion of the struggling worker in need of their paternal help more true than with the NDP's long fight over Sunday shopping.

David Peterson's Liberal government was hounded by the issue of Sunday shopping, and its attempts to make the law more flexible were met with fierce resistance by the opposition New Democrats. Rae was at his sanctimonious best — or worst — over the affects that Sunday shopping would have on families across the province.

When solicitor-general Joan Smith introduced changes to the Retail Business Holidays Act in April, 1988, Rae threatened a major legislative battle. "What the [Peterson] government is proposing is not fair, it is not right, and is offensive to literally thousands of families in this province," Rae said. "It is going to represent a hardship and a burden on working people and their families....I want to tell the government...[that its members] are going to have a fight on these measures such as they have never seen in their political careers before."

Reminding Smith that she had opposed Sunday shopping before becoming solicitor-general, Rae said he felt "an enormous sense of sadness" when he heard her speak on the issue now. Then, without fear of having to eat his words, Rae said: "Those of us who have been involved in politics and watched the wonders of the effects of power on some can hardly be surprised. One becomes, if not cynical at least sceptical, in observing the varieties of human behaviour in this regard, but when somebody says one thing as a private member and then turns around as a cabinet minister and says the opposite, I think something is wrong with respect to telling it straight and telling it like it is." The Sunday shopping fight was the toughest battle the opposition NDP took on during the Peterson years.

But the NDP could never explain what made retail workers so special. Tens of thousands of people in other jobs commonly worked on Sunday — people in hotels, restaurants, foundries, mines, hospitals, gas stations and automobile assembly lines, as well as the government's own workers in jails, institutions and parks, for example. In the mid-1980s, the Canadian Autoworkers' Union negotiated a ground-breaking contract with Northern Telecom that provided hundreds of jobs on a steady weekend shift — ten hours on Saturday and ten hours on Sunday — for 40 hours' pay.

The nature of work was changing, and so were social values. People wanted to shop on Sundays, and among those who favoured it most were single parents and people in the middle-income bracket.

The fight against "Sunday working" was led by the churches and by the United Food and Commercial Workers' union, which represents thousands of workers in food stores across Ontario. In the 1990 election, the UFCW produced campaign material that urged its members to vote NDP. "A vote for any other party will guarantee that you and your family will be working on Sundays," it said. A staunch NDP ally, the UFCW thought it could count on the party.

But once elected, the NDP caucus was badly split on the issue. Polls showed a big majority of single parents, union households and people who worked irregular hours supported Sunday shopping. Enforcement was also a problem, with thousands of charges pending, tying up police forces and the courts. Municipalities didn't want the province closing down stores, and when the Ontario Municipal Board approved Windsor's declaration of the entire city as a tourist area, it made a farce of provincial restrictions.

The government's intended introduction of new Sunday shopping laws met with one delay after another as the New Democrats tried to sort out what to do. A year after taking office, the NDP brought in its first Sunday shopping bill, but the proposed legislation still left it to municipalities to determine tourist areas according to provincial guidelines, and it included a widely-ridiculed provision that allowed any "interested citizen" to ask the courts to shut down a store. The government amended the bill to allow stores to open on Sundays in December for Christmas shopping, and passed it in November, 1991.

But the law didn't last long. Pressure from retailers, municipalities and shoppers kept up.

In May, 1992, the party's provincial council held an emergency meeting to discuss the issue. Fearing another reversal of party policy, OFL president Gord Wilson said: "Like I just told the labour caucus [labour delegates to the council], at times we make mistakes as to who we elect to represent our views within the NDP."

Another delegate warned: "If we yield to public opinion, we may as well be Liberals. If we yield to business, we may as well be Conservatives. If we yield to the leader, we may as well be Reform. How do we rally the troops if we don't carry out our policies?"

The council reaffirmed the party's opposition to Sunday shopping by a margin of about 9 to 1. Sensing that the government was about to approve open Sundays anyway, party president Julie Davis, the OFL's secretary-treasurer, put a novel spin on the controversy. The NDP was upholding its promises, she said, because it promised to be "open, accessible and accountable, and that is what the government is trying to do."

Ten days later, the premier stood in the legislature and announced that the government would allow wide-open Sunday shopping.

"This has not been an easy decision," Rae said. "I have often stood in my place on both sides of the House to argue in defence of a common pause day on Sunday, and restricted access to Sunday store openings. Experience, and a change in public attitudes in recent years, have combined to persuade me that such legislation, however well intended, is extremely difficult to enforce fairly, and runs up against a growing sense that many people want to shop on Sunday and are increasingly impatient of rules and regulations that prevent them from doing so." Having been defeated in the NDP sweep, Joan Smith was not in the House to hear this.

The Sunday shopping issue — from unyielding opposition to eventual capitulation — shows the NDP's reluctance to recognize that the nature of work has changed. The key to protecting employees from greedy bosses is not to keep stores closed on Sunday, which protects only retail workers and denies people who want to shop, but to write legislation that guarantees all workers premium pay and the right to refuse Sunday work. Invariably looking at the bottom line, stores and other businesses won't open on Sundays if the cost of staying open is too great. The same protection should be available to workers in any job.

Ironically, another major policy reversal made this issue even more difficult for the NDP government. Early in 1992, word leaked out that the NDP was considering opening casinos in the province. Desperate for revenue, the NDP was considering all its options.

Allan Fotheringham wrote in *Maclean's* about the awkward position this put the government in, especially for Rae, whom he called "Premier Prude." Fotheringham said: "Elected on a platform promising that he was not just like the rest of the politicians, that he was actually going to change the imbalance between the privileged and the unwashed, he is now dissipating his government's schedule and energy by trying to hold back the tide of public opinion. Until recently, Rae's government could be accused only of amateurism, ad hocery, righteousness, fumbling and idealism. That was until recently. With its plans for gambling casinos, slot machines and off-track betting, it can now be quite rightly be called hypocritical as well. To stand on the Bible and shield us from a commercial Sunday while welcoming the roulette wheel is a stand too ludicrous to maintain."

* * *

At the start of 1993, some of the unionized workers to whom the NDP was romantically attached started to leave the party. The issue made headlines when the CAW's largest local, workers at the Oshawa General Motors facility, voted in March to disaffiliate.

Some of the media created the inaccurate impression that the Oshawa workers were unhappy with the NDP for its policy reversals on issues such as Sunday shopping and public auto insurance. In fact, the problem was that many workers were equally unhappy with the NDP for its intended equity reforms. They thought the government's employment and pay equity proposals threatened their seniority rights, although they did not — not to mention their white, male hegemony. One shopfloor leaflet complained about the NDP's allowing natives to fish and hunt out of season. Some opponents of affiliation were landlords who opposed the NDP's rent control law.

But while the ringleaders were easily dismissed as right-wing Tory or Reform party backers, the support they gathered could not be discounted so readily. A vote on March 4 to withdraw support for the NDP passed 553 to 337. The anti-NDP faction claimed to have 8,000 signatures on a petition, and a referendum vote among the local's roughly 20,000 active and retired workers was scheduled for May.

The Oshawa workers, members of CAW Local 222, were always a thorn in the side of the union brass. The local was one of the stingiest, most reactionary sections of the union, beset with fierce infighting between two rival factions, neither of which was supportive of the union's national leadership or its progressive policies.

Far from being downtrodden workers, most members of Local 222 regularly make $60,000 to $80,000 a year, and many are paid more than that. They are the industrial labour aristocracy, pulling in pay that puts them at the top of the blue-collar workforce.

Before disaffiliation, the local contributed between $30,000 and $40,000 every year to the federal NDP; the province's share was about one-quarter of the take. Across Canada, roughly 740 union locals are affiliated, bringing in just over $600,000, or about 10 per cent of the party's national finances. The Ontario party, with about 200,000 affiliated members, gets about $150,000.

Organized labour's problem was not that there were pockets of well-to-do right-wing workers who wanted no part of the NDP, but that the NDP's traditional supporters could not be mobilized to take on the fight. They had simply become too disappointed with the NDP to be willing to confront the anti-NDP faction.

After the Oshawa vote, the *Globe's* Virginia Galt wrote: "The disenchantment of the left wing in the labour movement is more of a threat to the NDP than the unhappiness in labour's right wing, which is one of the reasons CAW chief Buzz Hargrove said he recently went public with some of labour's concerns. He felt that if the problems were not resolved, the NDP would lose crucial support and labour would again be saddled with governments far less sympathetic to unions."

Local 222 was not the first to leave the party and go home early. Another CAW local, at Budd Automotive in Kitchener, left the NDP late in 1992. Other union locals also faced disaffiliation campaigns, including the large CUPE Local 1000, which represents Ontario Hydro's nuclear energy workers, and whose average wage is roughly $65,000. They, too, are not the downtrodden.

The NDP's romantic notion of working people sends mixed messages to its potential voters. On the one hand, it backs the labour movement, the core of its traditional support, many of whose workers are reasonably well off, and who share middle-class values and aspirations. On the other hand, the NDP embraces reforms — like pay and employment equity and increased social assistance — that are, for the most part, targeted at an entirely different class of person in society.

As government, the NDP's attempts to bring these reforms into being, even though stalled, are causing them grief among the people the New Democrats like to think of as their own. Because the NDP is naive about its romancing of workers and takes them for granted, the government doesn't even bother to organize and educate about the need for its reforms.

7. Colour Blind

At the 1992 NDP convention, a youth employment counsellor asked MPP Zanana Akande how the government's new black-oriented $20 million summer job creation program would target black youths. "No one seems to have a problem identifying us when they want to shoot us," she said. "It seems to me they can use the same identification skills when they want to employ us."

Though Akande's remarks provoked outrage in some circles — Conservative leader Mike Harris demanded that she apologize "to every police officer in the province" — she was only echoing an attitude felt in the black community. Polls showed that blacks felt they were more likely to be the victims of police violence and discriminated against in the justice system than white people were. For his part, Rae half-heartedly defended Akande, saying her remarks were "blunt and provocative," but that they were a symptom of the frustration in the black community. "Certainly I don't think it's directed at the police," he said, as if someone else were doing the shooting.

Rae had long misunderstood attitudes between the police and the black community. In his presentation to the Task Force on Race Relations and Policing in 1989, he posed the improbable case that the two sides should not think about "us and them." In an interview shortly after becoming premier, he said: "I mean, one of the things that has to break down is the sense that there's the police and then there's the black community. In a society like ours, we can't afford to have that sort of a distinction."

He misunderstood not just the feelings black people have toward the police, but the degree of racism among police and in the white community in general. An 18-month investigation launched by the Metro Toronto Police Services Board into bias on the force found no evidence of institutional racism, but its author, auditor Allan Andrews, said that: "There is a definite bias in the way some of the officers enforce the law." Andrews said police officers "develop feelings" toward the groups they most come in contact with, and that this "bias is evident in their feelings against minorities."

In the spring of 1992, racial tensions took a new focus.

On April 29, a jury in suburban Simi Valley, California, home of Ronald Reagan's presidential museum, acquitted four white Los Angeles police officers of excessive force in the arrest of Rodney King. Coming after millions of North Americans watched an amateur videotape of the officers beating the living daylights out of King, the acquittal provoked the worst riots in modern America.

Three days later, Metro Toronto constable Robert Rice shot and killed 22-year-old Raymond Lawrence in a pre-dawn drug bust. Police say Lawrence confronted Rice with a knife and was shot twice in the chest. He was the eighth black person shot by police in Toronto in the previous four years, and the fourth to die.

On May 4, Toronto's Black Action Defence Committee organized a demonstration at the U.S. consulate to protest the acquittals in the Rodney King case. The peaceful action moved to police headquarters to protest the shooting of Lawrence.

After that, things got out of hand. On Yonge Street, a mixed crowd of white and black youths gathered, smashing windows and looting stores. When it was over, over 100 stores suffered $250,000 damage and more than $100,000 in stolen property. The police said the riot was not racially motivated, and it was clear that the Defence Committee had tried to calm the crowd.

Within days, Rae asked Stephen Lewis to investigate the roots of the disturbance, gave him a broad mandate, and asked him to report quickly.

Lewis reported in a 37-page "Dear Bob" letter on June 9, making recommendations about the criminal justice process, policing, employment equity, education and training, relations with government, and community development.

His one month study convinced him that "what we are dealing with, at root, and fundamentally, is anti-Black racism." He pointed out that while other minority groups also suffer discrimination, blacks were clearly the "primary target" of racism in Ontario.

"If I've ever felt two solitudes in my life," Lewis wrote, "it's the apparent chasm between the Metropolitan Toronto Police and many representatives of the Black community." Lewis made a number of specific recommendations about policing, including support for the filing of a report whenever police draw their guns.

He also told Rae that all minority groups saw employment equity as "a kind of cause celebre." "They see it as the consummate affirmation of opportunity and access. With the possible exception of education, nothing is so important," Lewis said.

He also told Rae there was "great concern about the progress of the government's intended employment equity legislation. It can't be introduced soon enough. And there may be no other explicit legislative initiative which will mean so much to establishing a positive climate of race relations in the minds of every single minority grouping...." Lewis suggested the legislation should be in place "as early as possible in 1993."

Lewis's most vague recommendation was in the area of community development. Recognizing that his sense of the solution was "impressionistic," he wrote: "If we are ever to rid this world of so much of the poverty and despair to which vulnerable communities are subject, then we simply must develop bold — even daring — economic and social policies. A new race relations construct might be just the place to start." But the best he could suggest in this context was that his proposed Anti-Racism Directorate "work with representative minority constituencies to fashion an unprecedented community development plan which incorporates the many proposals and ideas that never seem to be examined by others."

A *Globe and Mail* editorial said Lewis's report was bereft of new ideas; Lewis responded that the paper's comments were "fatuous in the extreme" and that they showed "a complete lack of understanding about the diversity of the community....But I expect that of the *Globe and Mail*," he said.

A syndicated column by Robert Fulford dismissed the report as "intellectually impoverished." Fulford said that the report "...treats black people as objects. They are entirely blameless (white racism is the only problem mentioned) and they are not called upon to do anything at all. Bad things have been done to them in the past (the report implies) and now good things will be done to them. They do not act, they are acted upon. This is the ultimate in white condescension."

But the black community was cautiously optimistic that the report might lead to the kinds of changes it had been talking about for years. "Lewis was only pulling together things that people in the black community were saying all along," says one black NDP activist. "There was nothing new in that sense."

Rae said he would move on the recommendations quickly, and in fact some of the suggestions Lewis made were put in place, including shifting all complaints of racial discrimination by police directly to the Police Complaints Commission instead of the local police force, and the announcement of a sweeping inquiry into racism in the criminal justice system. But in many other areas the province has not moved with dispatch. "There's unhappiness now [in the black community] about the slowness of implementation," the NDP activist says. "Not much has been done on some of the more substantive recommendations of the report."

A major frustration is with the government's employment equity plans.

Though the NDP said employment equity was one of its top priorities, and despite the fact that Rae had introduced a private member's bill in 1990, the government did not present legislation until the end of June, 1992. Its bill rejected legislated hiring quotas and settled for goals and timetables established by employers; it also gave companies up to three years to file plans. At the same time, the exclusion of companies with fewer than 50 workers means the law will have no impact in the very places where most new jobs are being created.

The bill was to receive second reading in December, 1992, but did not. Second reading was then planned for the spring 1993 session, while the law's regulations were being drafted by a select group of deputy ministers. According to one supporter: "There's a fear that because the deputies are drafting the regulations they won't be tough enough....It's unfortunate, but I'm not expecting too much."

Members of advocacy groups, who had already seen the legislation as a significant retreat from Rae's own bill, quit the government's advisory committee in April, 1993, over frustration with the delays.

The NDP has put a great deal of stock in its employment equity package. But it is clear that even if the legislation is passed soon, and even if its provisions are strict enough to achieve the desired goals, employment equity is of limited practical value when companies are not hiring.

Supporters still argue, however, that employment equity is helpful for sensitizing employers and in cases of promotions. They also want the legislation in place before the expected upturn in the economy when employers start to hire new workers. The recession gives employers time to put their plans in place.

Politically, the delay has meant the if NDP does proceed with employment equity, its implementation will come during an election period, when the government will be more sensitive to the law's opponents. Many of those people are working- and middle-class white men who fear their own jobs, and the future employment of their sons, are in jeopardy.

The government took enormous heat for moving on one of Lewis's more inconsequential suggestions: that police officers should file reports when they draw their guns. Metro Toronto's overwhelmingly white, male police, who already saw themselves as victims in the NDP's support for visible minorities, staged a month-long protest against the government in the fall of 1992. The NDP looked weak as the police thumbed their noses at the government and eventually accepted the filing requirement, and in return won the right to carry more deadly guns. The government also agreed that the reports on drawn guns could not be used in disciplinary matters.

The underlying weakness of Lewis's report is indicated by his vague language around community development. Lewis's recommendations are basically assimilationist; he argues that changing social institutions to make them less racist, and educating and training black people so they have more opportunities are the answers to redressing systemic discrimination. In these ways, he suggests, minority groups will become better integrated into Ontario society and hence more equal.

His report is more concerned with institutional modifications than with empowering the black community or strengthening existing cultural bonds. The NDP bought into this model; it is far easier to shift around institutional accountability than it is to find new ways to weave minority groups into the fabric of society. The NDP's approach mirrors politically-correct liberalism: treat people politely, but don't transfer power.

"The black community was generally supportive of the government in the start," one activist says, "but that's gone now." The feeling is that there are a lot of good intentions, but little action.

* * *

The NDP government also failed to score points with Ontario's multicultural community on account of its determined support of the failed Charlottetown constitutional accord.

Women and visible minorities pointed to the supremacy of the "Canada clause" over the Charter of Rights and Freedoms as a mechanism that would curtail the rights of groups without power.

Lawyer Anne Bayefsky wrote that there was "no governmental obligation whatsoever" to promote racial, ethnic or gender equality in the constitutional package. She called the deal "a shameful retreat from human-rights standards that Canada touts as of paramount importance all over the rest of the world."

In the *Toronto Star*, writer Andrew Cardozo noted: "The power structure as outlined in the accord (and consequently in the Constitution) will serve only to maintain the hegemony of 'the founding peoples' and respond to some needs of aboriginal peoples. For the others, they will be kept in their place — in the constitutional outhouse. For minorities, it's a wretched situation," Cardozo wrote.

Rae, who signed important agreements with native people in Ontario shortly after becoming premier, supported the provisions of the accord granting self-government to natives. But the deal was completely vague about just what self-government meant, left open the specifics to future negotiations, transferred no resources, money or real power to native people, and specifically rejected use of the term "sovereignty."

As negotiations were drawing to a close, some native leaders suggested that they should go back to their people for discussion. As the *Toronto Star*'s Rosemary Speirs recounted one late-night incident: "Bob Rae was sitting at an Apple computer, typing new wording into the native constitutional agreement, aiming to satisfy the concerns of Quebec Premier Robert Bourassa." Ovide Mercredi, chief of the Council of First Nations, was watching over Rae's shoulder, and at one point suggested that they sleep on it. "Are you nuts?" Rae said to Mercredi. The constitutional pressure cooker that Rae said must be avoided was up to full steam.

The deal Rae so heartily endorsed missed an opportunity to improve representation of minority groups in two other key areas. First, by opting into triple-E Senate reform, Rae missed the opportunity to use a reconstituted Senate to increase the representation of women, natives and ethnic people in parliament. Second, the Constitution perpetuated over-representation in the House of Commons of rural areas at the expense of urban areas, where most minority communities are centred.

Finding a way to accommodate other premiers was more important than finding a way to include minority representation.

* * *

Just three weeks after taking office, Bud Wildman, the minister responsible for native affairs, gave land for reserves to six northern Indian bands who had been squatting on the land for decades. The government also agreed to fund $2 million in programs.

In May, 1991, the NDP signed a historic joint-stewardship agreement with the Teme-Augama Anishnabai, recognizing the natives' right to "equal membership with the province on a board overseeing resource development in four townships in the Temagami region...." The rights the province recognized went beyond those held by most native bands in Canada.

A year and a half later, the government and the Teme-Augama Anishnabai agreed to enter into "substantive negotiations" on a "treaty of co-existence." Native chief Gary Potts said: "In the 116th year of our struggle for justice the government of Ontario has taken a very positive step towards bringing to a close this chapter of colonialism...which has caused so much pain to the Teme-Augama Anishnabai...."

But not all natives were so pleased. Native spokespeople complained that the government's focus was only toward natives living on reserves, people who amounted to only 30 per cent of the native population in Ontario. "Off-

reserve native peoples are now worse off than we were two years ago, because
the provincial government has accepted the bands' claim that they represent
off-reserve status Indians," said Charles Reid, a Metis lawyer.

* * *

In other human rights initiatives, the NDP did not fare so well.

In the summer of 1991, ombudsman Roberta Jamieson blasted the
backlog of complaints at the Human Rights Commission, saying that the
"unreasonable" and "oppressive" delays were so bad that the commission was
not doing its job. She noted that many complaints were taking years to hear
— some as long as eight years.

The Human Rights Reform Group also condemned the commission as
a failure and demanded that the government form a task force to investigate.
Six months later, in March, 1992, the NDP announced that a review would
be headed by human rights lawyer Mary Cornish.

When Cornish's task force reported in July, it said the commission was
so flawed that it should be totally overhauled. Their 234-page report with
88 recommendations said the government should take responsibility for
hearing discrimination complaints away from the commission and turn them
over to new community Equality Rights Centres.

Nearly a year later, little had changed at the Human Rights Commission.

* * *

In other areas the NDP's unwillingness to move on initiatives has frustrated
Ontario's multicultural communities.

One area where the government could make a significant advancement
for minorities, and improve Ontario's skills base at the same time, is with
foreign-trained people. In his report, Stephen Lewis pointed out: "The
classic argument that there are large numbers of people now in Ontario, who
come from a variety of cultural backgrounds and countries, who have
professional or trades accreditation in their country of origin which is not
recognized in this province, is undoubtedly valid. And there's something
faintly perverse in not establishing a system where language difficulties could
be overcome, or academic deficits compensated for, or additional technical
proficiency acquired."

Lewis vaguely called on the government "to expand its commitment to
developing a system" to allow foreign-trained people to work in their fields.
But there has been no progress.

The government also promised to de-stream Grade 9 and eliminate
other barriers to access to education. The NDP had long opposed the

streaming of students into one of the advanced, general or basic streams, and it was well-known among educators that the system discriminated against the children of working-class and ethnic families. The report by George Radwanski commissioned by the Liberal government showed that the drop-out rate among students in the advanced stream was 12 per cent, but was 62 per cent in the general and 79 per cent in the basic streams.

As the government forged ahead with its plans, opposition mounted in the teachers' federations. In November, 1992 the Ontario Secondary School Teachers' Federation called for the resignation of education minister Tony Silipo, a former chairperson of the Toronto Board of Education.

When Rae restructured his cabinet in February, 1993, Silipo was shifted out of education, and replaced by Dave Cooke. Cooke immediately backed off the commitment to destreaming, suggesting that the province and school boards might not be ready for the government's September, 1993 deadline. Cooke, who said the government was still committed to full destreaming by 1996, also refused repeated requests to release a 750-page report on 64 pilot projects.

Lewis addressed the question of education in his report, and spoke of the need for more multiculturalism and anti-racist education. At about the same time, two Los Angeles gangs, the Bloods and the Crips, produced their own report on the education needs of their black, inner-city community.

The Bloods and Crips demanded higher education standards in low-income areas, higher salaries to encourage teachers to work there along with the removal of teachers who don't do a good job, mandatory after-school tutoring for poorly-performing students, and a basic curriculum with English and writing skills, math and science. They made no mention of multicultural sensitivity.

Writing in the *Globe* on the striking differences between the Lewis/ NDP approach and the Bloods and Crips' approach, former educator Andrew Nikiforuk said: "It seems that what well-meaning and well-educated liberals think is right for working people and the poor (formulas on multiculturalism) often bears little resemblance to what these people value: a strong grounding in the rudiments of learning."

Nikiforuk concluded: "Although Mr. Lewis evoked the spirit of equal educational opportunity by calling for more resources to be delivered into the hands of educators who make a living on multicultural programs, the street gangs demanded the very reverse of the equality doctrine. Spend money directly and spend more of it, said the gang report, on those youngsters whose abilities are such that they are least likely to develop their minds in laissez-faire schools. And spend these funds not on policies that highlight differences and may heighten tensions, but on developing the highest standards of teaching and learning."

* * *

Despite what seem to be good intentions and a legitimate commitment, poor relations with ethnic communities through its years in opposition have hampered the NDP government's ability to make inroads with and advances on behalf on Ontario's minority population.

8. New Democrats in Liberal Clothing

In opposition, the New Democrats wistfully longed for the day when politics in Ontario would polarize between themselves and the Conservatives, leaving the Liberals out of the picture. New Democrats always imagined they would fare well in this new politics of the left and right.

At the same time, the NDP refused to recognize that the Liberals are Canada's champion ideological chameleons, adapting with remarkable ease to a changing political environment. It was much easier, though generally untrue, for the NDP to lump the Liberals in with the Tories as a right-wing party of big business.

In both these ways New Democrats drank their own bath water; they not only thought of these positions as vote-getting propaganda for public consumption, they came to believe them themselves.

Now in government, the Ontario NDP has proven to be what many people worried it would be: a party of the political centre much like the others. Defying the laws of both physics and politics, the NDP has occupied the same space at the same time not just as the Liberals but often as the Conservatives as well.

Ideologically, it has been the New Democrats — not the Liberals —who have failed to distinguish themselves from the other parties. As we have shown, in 1985, when the NDP made up its original list for negotiation with the Liberals over the Accord, it started with almost 100 items on which the two parties had substantially the same position. It whittled those down to 40 or so, which formed the basis of the agreement.

With the NDP in office, it is difficult to name a single position on which it differs substantively from the Liberal opposition or from the Peterson government, including its eventual stands on auto insurance, Sunday shopping, rent control, housing, education, pay or employment equity, or even its labour legislation. And as always, it is the duty of the opposition to oppose, so the Liberals disagree with NDP legislation in principle without disagreeing on the fundamentals.

Under attack for its own policy reversals and the mistakes of its members, the NDP has been unable to launch any kind of offensive against its opponents. (New Democrats used to complain that no one paid them any attention, now they're sorry that no one will leave them alone.) In fact, the NDP has virtually ignored the Liberals since the 1990 election. It has been so preoccupied with its own problems that it has simply given the Liberals an open field.

Despite the fact that during the government's term in office, the Liberals have had three interim leaders followed by Lyn McLeod, who has failed to capture the public's fancy, the NDP has not been able to paint them as a party of incompetence, of muddled politics, or as a party tied to business. In fact, it's the NDP that is muddled and incompetent, and is desperately trying to forge links with business.

By failing to distinguish itself from the Liberals, the NDP has allowed the Liberals to continue to occupy the political centre. For the Liberals, there is a marginal dilemma in this. They cannot attempt to out-flank Mike Harris's Conservatives on the right, nor will they try to out-manoeuvre Rae's NDP on the left. With policies so much like those of the NDP, the Liberals' only option is to portray themselves as more effective managers than the New Democrats. By comparison, that should not be too difficult to do, and the public has a short memory.

But the Peterson government itself had deficits in four of its five years in office, despite a growing economy and despite 30 to 40 tax increases, depending on how you count them. The Liberals added over $9 billion to the provincial debt, which will look like chicken feed by the time the NDP is finished, but which still tarnishes the Liberal image as effective managers. Now Lyn McLeod predictably says she would be tougher than the NDP in cutting government spending.

Once the public's honeymoon with the NDP ended, the then-leaderless Liberals zoomed to the top of the polls. They have remained solidly in first place for a year and a half. The by-election results on April 1, 1993, in which the NDP got just 8 per cent of the vote in two Toronto seats can hardly be discounted as a simple protest.

Yet the New Democrats continue to downplay the Liberals as a political force. In early 1993, with the federal Liberals at 49 per cent in the polls and its own support near 10 per cent, the NDP was still making plans to go after soft Liberal support in the next federal election. Ontario party president Julie Davis said: "The Liberal party is the largest free-standing parking lot in the world. The one thing they have going for them is they are everybody's second choice." In the jargon, she meant that people were "parking" their votes with the Liberals until the election came. She didn't explain why the NDP seemed to be stalled in the garage.

On the first anniversary of McLeod's narrow leadership win over Murray Elston, the *Toronto Star*'s Derek Ferguson wrote: "While the Liberals have a new chief, the renaissance in policy has yet to come. So far, the only concrete change has been a new logo launched last month." The logo has a waving red flag with a white trillium, and is meant to symbolize movement. The problem is, no one knows in what direction. Again, the NDP has been unable to capitalize on that apparent lack of focus in the Liberal party.

Meanwhile, the Liberals continue to walk both sides of the street. McLeod had her outreach department organize anti-dumping rallies in greater Metro Toronto in order to pick up an NDP crowd, though the Liberals don't say what they would do with the mountain of garbage. And, while the Liberals complain that the NDP is padding the deficit, McLeod says she would cut deeper into government spending.

It is twilight for Rae's government, and the chickens are coming home to roost. The NDP is still trapped in its wishful thinking that the Liberals would go away, and that politics would polarize between themselves and the Conservatives. Only then would the New Democrats look more progressive. And since the NDP has been unable to distinguish its policies from those of the Liberals, the next provincial election is not likely to be fought on ideological grounds, but on turf where the NDP is especially vulnerable: competence and credibility.

The NDP will not be able, as it did in 1990, to run a campaign asking for a protest vote against an apparently popular government. In the next election, the opposition parties and the media will be scrutinizing the NDP's record.

9. Media Ogre

> "I've never had any favours from the media. I've never been
> a media favourite or had the support or the endorsement."
> — Premier Bob Rae, quoted in the *Globe and Mail,* Nov.
> 28, 1992

How soon they forget. Bob Rae, darling of the Ottawa press gallery, the man the media said "gives good clip," the man who won the Ontario NDP leadership on the basis of the media exposure he received as the federal party's finance critic, says the media never did him any favours.

Rae could not have become premier without their help. The media, which gave David Peterson his movie-star image in the 1987 campaign, gleefully reported every attack on him in the 1990 election and — by their own admission — gave Rae an easy ride. Just as surely as the media helped make Peterson, they helped make Rae. And just as surely as they helped undo

Peterson, they are at work on Rae.

The media likes to make stars, and once the stars are elevated to heavenly heights, likes to help them fade. It gives the media power, and it's an old story. The media made the careers of people as diverse as Pierre Trudeau, John Turner and Bob Rae, and before long, set upon them.

Like many politicians, Rae figures the media owe him something, namely good coverage and plenty of it. They should also get off his back. Two days after he told the *Globe* that the media never did him any favours, the *Toronto Star* reported: "Rae said he could not recall any other government being subjected to the degree of scrutiny that his has."

Rae, who was born and bred into politics and is a student of history, might have brought the Nixon administration after Watergate into mind. He might have recalled how the media went after the long parade of Brian Mulroney's scandal-ridden cabinet ministers or the fantasy-land Vander Zalm government in British Columbia. Rae might especially have remembered the way the media tore into the Ontario Liberals over the Patti Starr affair, with stories lasting nearly two years.

Rae's comments are not a reflection of his poor memory but of his paranoia.

Ironically, for a person whom the media helped create, Rae has had poor relations with the press gallery since his first days at Queen's Park. We have discussed some of those encounters and the party's failure to develop a sensible and workable media strategy while in opposition. Now in government, the New Democrats have fared even worse.

All governments rely on the media to deliver their message. But the media does far more than disseminate information. The media — in particular television, since it depends on government authority figures as spokespersons — also creates the impressions people have of politicians. Television's watchful eye shows when government figures look confident, in control and informed or when they appear defensive, badgered and confused. For a government, having a good working relationship with the media is crucial.

Governments have a far greater opportunity to control media coverage than opposition parties do. A government picks the issues it wants to give priority to; sets the legislative agenda; has an army of bureaucrats to churn out press releases; trots out cabinet ministers to announce government policy; hands out countless grants, awards and other accolades; and can solicit advice from an enormous number of public relations experts in the ministries and the ministers' political staff to decide the government's "spin" on issues. On top of all this, the government, unlike the opposition, determines the timing of these actions. This allows the government to highlight one issue or event or bury another.

That makes it sound a bit too simple, because opposition parties and sometimes journalists themselves try to undermine the government's agenda, with varying degrees of success. But without question, a government has far more resources at its disposal and far more control over political issues than its adversaries do.

The NDP government feels under attack, the victim of a media owned by large, right-wing corporations that don't want to upset the traditional power structures and so won't cover it fairly. The right-wing Mulroney government, on the other hand, always thought it was under attack by left-wing journalists who disagreed with its ideology. From their own perspectives, government can't win.

The culture of opposition to dissent within the NDP has very deep roots and widely spreading branches. The party's reliance on a small group of trusted insiders, characters in a long-running soap opera, is part of that culture. So is the NDP's sense that everyone is out to get it, including the media. Like the party's dissenters, journalists who cross the NDP are not to be trusted.

Feeling beleaguered, the NDP went so far as to stage a rally in its own defense, on June 1, 1992. Billed as "Whose Ontario Is It?," the rally featured a number of prominent New Democrats and party supporters who blamed the media and the business community for trying to take their government away from them.

Speaking at the rally, party heavyweight Gerry Caplan, who has access to half a million readers through his weekly column in the *Toronto Star* and appears regularly as a commentator on CTV, referred to media giant Maclean Hunter, which owns *Maclean's*, the *Toronto Sun* and the *Financial Post*, as "the real ringleaders" who are "overtly out to destroy this government." He singled out right-wing columnists Diane Francis and Barbara Amiel, and complained that the *Globe and Mail* "treats our government as if it's a bunch of nincompoops in short pants."

In mid-1991, Rae's principal secretary, David Agnew, told the *Globe*: "We're doing a lot of things people would like. They don't get a lot of attention."

In an article for the party's 1992 convention booklet, former provincial secretary Michael Lewis, now a staff member with the Steelworkers' union, noted that at union meetings, workers complain two-to-one about auto insurance, taxes, government scandals, casinos and the lack of a strategy to deal with the recession. "It's not surprising when you consider that we all get our information from the morning paper, what we see on TV and what we hear on the radio. But the media rarely tries to tell the whole story," Lewis wrote.

At the same convention, party members told of a story going around

Queen's Park about Rae's dog. It was said that Rae invited a number of reporters to watch his talented pooch walk across the water when Rae threw a stick into the lake for it to fetch. The NDP said the headlines would read: "Bob Rae's Dog Can't Swim."

Disturbed by their media coverage, the New Democrats launched their own "Ontario NDP Media Response Network," a volunteer group whose purpose was to "monitor print and broadcast media and report on unfair or poor coverage of the party and government." The group would then write letters, circulate articles to newspapers and encourage calls to phone-in shows "in order to get out the good news on our government."

This paranoia of media coverage, the sense that the government is getting a bad deal, comes naturally to a party that thinks nothing could be its own fault. It's linked to the party's intolerance of dissent and to its deep sense of righteousness. Why blame yourself when you can blame the media?

This manifests itself in different ways. One prominent television reporter says Rae's press secretary, Peter Mosher, would send him notes in the legislature about his coverage of the government. "If they thought this was going to make me turn into a propagandist for them, they were wrong," he says. Mosher's assistant, Laurie Stephens, wrote a letter to the president of Canadian Press after CP ran a story critical of Rae for appointing long-time ally Tim Armstrong to a $1,000 a day contract as an advisor.

At the outset, inexperienced cabinet ministers were scared of the media. Solicitor general Mike Farnan shut the door on a TV reporter. Energy minister Jenny Carter waved her hands in front of her face as she backed away from journalists, saying she didn't want to talk. Social services minister Zanana Akande also refused to talk outside a cabinet meeting — and all this happened in just the NDP's first two weeks in office.

One former executive assistant says that top ministry staff used to meet once a week with Norm Simon, the government's first spin doctor, to discuss media strategy. "It was an alcoholics anonymous experience," the EA says. "My story is worse than yours. But they just talked about how the press got it wrong, not about how to get their message out."

He says the problem "was that self righteous edge: 'Who are they to criticize us? We can't expect them to do anything for us.' And of course it was a self-fulfilling prophesy."

We have already mentioned that the NDP government had no public relations person in the treasury ministry when the government brought down its first budget in 1991. It was two months later when the *Toronto Star* reported that Laughren had just "decided to deliver his most spirited defence of the April 29 budget just as an anti-government campaign appears to be gaining momentum."

In British Columbia, the NDP government elected in 1991 learned from the Ontario mistake and consciously scripted a well-planned media strategy. There, "a masterly media campaign over the past few months has helped mute the criticisms that are bound to be levelled at the B.C. government's first budget," wrote the *Star*.

In advance of his first budget, B.C. finance minister Glen Clark called in press gallery reporters to meet with senior ministry officials, who briefed them on the government's financial picture, including how the previous Social Credit administration had cooked the books. Then an economics firm showed how the federal government's monetary policy was adversely affecting B.C. Clark also held pre-budget briefings for business, labour and community groups that were public and open to the media. By the time Clark presented the budget, the media was by and large sympathetic. As a result of the generally understanding coverage the government received, there was no outcry from the business or labour communities, nor from the public when the budget was delivered.

Unlike the Ontario experience, the British Columbia government consciously gave the media access and information and brought them on side. In B.C., the government paid as much attention to how it was going to sell its first budget as to what was in it.

But it is not always so easy for governments to control the agenda, especially when things go off the rails. This has certainly been the case with the Ontario NDP.

Foolish scandals and rookie mistakes took the bloom off the NDP government right from the start. For the media, this was a golden opportunity to attack the holier-than-thou attitude Rae displayed so self-righteously from the opposition benches. It was time to pay him back. Journalists liked nothing better than confronting Rae about his ministers' transgressions, in large part because Rae had promised a government more pure than any group of human beings could be.

The worst example — dare we say "to this point"? — of a gross mistake in misjudging the media and attempting to manipulate it came during the so-called "Piper affair."

To recount the complex history briefly, the mess began with an inquiry into sexual abuse at the Grandview School for Girls in 1973. Will Ferguson, then an 18-year-old student counsellor, allegedly helped a resident, Judi Harris, escape. She claims that the two had sex. Ferguson categorically denies these charges. In a remark worthy of Tory patriarch John Crosbie, Will Ferguson joked that he must have been real good in bed if she could remember it twenty years later.

When Ferguson's involvement in the Grandview School situation became public in February, 1992, he resigned as Rae's minister of energy pending an investigation. Harris, for her part, initially said Ferguson had done nothing wrong and bore him no grudge. But the business turned into a mess when Ferguson and Harris later filed suit and counter-suit, and Ferguson obtained a copy of Harris's criminal record.

In the early afternoon of November 17, 1992, Ferguson met briefly with John Piper, Rae's communications advisor, in Piper's office. Piper was a well-respected NDP insider and friend of Bob Rae, the person Rae chose to travel to Tokyo with Floyd Laughren to meet with the International Olympic Committee immediately following the NDP's victory. He had reluctantly left his job with the government affairs firm of Hill and Knowlton when he was asked to move into the Premier's Office in 1991. Ironically, his role was to improve the NDP's relations with the media and consequently to boost its image with the public. Piper was a quintessential backroom boy, an advisor to many campaigns and a valued strategist who never personally sought the limelight.

Ferguson gave Piper a copy of Harris's rap sheet, claiming it was a public document. Piper asked Ferguson what he thought should be done with it, and Ferguson suggested he give it to the media, specifically to *Toronto Sun* reporter Anne Dawson, who had written several articles on the issue. Not thinking, Piper at once called Dawson, with whom he thought he had a good relationship, and invited her to his office.

In a meeting that lasted only minutes, Piper offered Harris's record to Dawson, explaining that it was a public document easily obtained from the court in Owen Sound. Dawson said if it was a matter of public record, she would get it herself, and left without taking the document.

Three days later, the *Sun* ran a front-page story on Piper's attempt to smear Judi Harris. The delay in reporting the incident is curious. Dawson is an experienced reporter, and she must have known she had a bombshell. As this book went to press, Dawson refused to comment on the incident, or say why the *Sun* held the story for three days.

At a regular morning meeting on November 20, the day the *Sun* story broke, Piper met with cabinet secretary David Agnew, his deputy secretary Michael Mendelson, and policy advisor Ross McClellan. Piper briefed them on what happened, identified Ferguson as the source of Harris's record and immediately resigned. (Agnew and McClellan deny that Piper told them where he got the document.) Piper also apologized publicly for the embarrassment he had caused the premier.

Rae was on his way back from a trip to the Far East when the *Sun* story broke. Asked at the Vancouver airport if he had discussed the incident with Piper, Rae said flatly: "No, and I won't be." Rae instantly cut Piper off like a dead limb.

On March, 4, 1993, the Ontario Provincial Police cleared Piper of any criminal wrongdoing. The next day, Piper, who had gone into exile following his resignation, held a news conference and apologized again for the grief that he had caused. He had made a terrible mistake, he realized it, and tried to show his regret. The one thing he did not do was name Ferguson as the source of Harris's rap sheet.

This sorry affair showed that even victims of sexual abuse were not immune from the NDP's readiness to smear its opponents. The NDP had lost its ethics, and was just in the spin business.

Though the newspapers, especially the *Toronto Sun*, had a field day with the messy business, they have not really explored the motivations behind Piper's apparently unaccountable attempt to smear Judi Harris. To understand why someone as experienced as Piper would do something so unconscionable, it's necessary to understand the culture of the NDP.

Piper's government and his friend Bob Rae were being attacked and ridiculed by the media. The economy was going down the tubes and the NDP seemed unable to stop it. Cabinet ministers were being caught figuratively and literally with their pants down. The New Democrats, on whose behalf Piper had dedicated a lifetime, had finally come to office, and everything was going wrong. Now a former cabinet minister, Will Ferguson, was under investigation for an ancient incident, an investigation that was dragging on and on, and Ferguson was desperate to have his name cleared.

Two key elements explain Piper's behaviour. Most important is the New Democrats' siege mentality, the sense that the NDP was a blameless victim, unfairly attacked from all sides. Under the circumstances, many party loyalists would do almost anything to point the finger the other way. When faced with dissent, smash the dissenters. When faced with opposition, smear the opponents, for above all, the party can do no wrong. Piper seems to have become so caught up in the siege mentality that he lost his judgement.

The other factor is the loyalty test itself. With Ferguson practically begging him to help, Piper lost track of the bigger picture. Piper never warned Ferguson how inappropriate it was for the government to be involved in a such a smear. In fact, Piper never took the time to think through what he was doing when he offered Judi Harris's rap sheet to Anne Dawson. Neither Piper nor Ferguson seems to have sensed in advance that it would look as if the NDP government had its own Nixon-style enemies list.

Much as it was central to the whole Piper affair, the media also generally ignored how Bob Rae handled himself in this sordid business. It tells much about the man.

From the very start, Rae completely distanced himself from Piper, his friend and confidante. When asked about the incident on his return from Japan, Rae did not say that he had only been told about the *Sun* report and had not had a chance to talk with anyone, including John Piper, about it. His initial public position was that he would not discuss it with Piper, and he didn't.

Months later, when Piper planned the news conference to clear his name, Rae attempted to stop him. Rae personally phoned Piper's close friend, University of Toronto vice president Gordon Cressy, and asked him to dissuade Piper. That attempt failed. Then Rae's office tried to block NDP MPP Zanana Akande from formally sponsoring the news conference in the Queen's Park media studio. She refused to back down.

In Rae's eyes, Piper had become a non-person. A big part of the explanation for Piper's behaviour was his loyalty to the NDP and to Rae personally. But for Bob Rae, that loyalty is not a two-way street. As in Piper's case, even a lifetime of dedication to the NDP was not enough.

* * *

"Bob Rae's Revolution"

If the NDP thought the media was out to get it, they must have had eerie feelings about the *Maclean's* magazine cover story on September 14, 1992. Headed "Bob Rae's Revolution," the article and accompanying photos were subtly designed to send a chill up the spines of Maclean's middle-class white readers.

The nearly full-page colour photo that ran with the article's lead was of a large crowd of mostly black people at an anti-racism rally at Queen's Park. Many of those in the front of the photo had their fists raised in a "black power" salute.

The article said the NDP's "declared aim is nothing less than to change the distribution of power and redress what the government perceives as deep-seated social injustices" in Ontario. It quoted University of Toronto professor Michael Bliss, who expressed reservations about the government's employment equity plan. "I think they are raising the awareness of race and sex almost to a fever pitch," he said. *Maclean's* also quoted Canadian Civil Liberties lawyer Alan Borovoy, who said: "It is not acceptable for any individual white or man to be made to suffer for the sins committed by other people."

The article used the phrase "so-called visible minorities" and cited problems in the U.S. with affirmative action programs. It also worried about rights and benefits extended to gays and lesbians, and ran a photo of gay lawyer Michael Leshner with his partner Michael Stark, both smiling with their foreheads touching.

> Another photo of a police officer holding a man to the ground was subtitled "picket line violence;" the article worried about the government's labour law changes.
>
> At the end, it quoted Rae's determination to forge ahead regardless of public opinion: "There are those who don't like it. But there is always going to be resistance to social change, particularly when we ask some people to share power," Rae said.
>
> It concluded with a veiled threat of the NDP's willingness to "dictate" in the face of opposition: "In fact, in many cases, the government is prepared to go beyond mere requests for co-operation by dictating the terms of a new order — one that would place Ontario in the front lines of a social revolution."

Over the course of its first few years, the NDP government tried several different tacks in its relations with the media.

At first, cabinet ministers were instructed to be accessible. Then, as mistakes mounted, Rae centralized more and more power in his own office, and became the government's spokesperson on the vast majority of issues.

In 1992, after the defeat of the Charlottetown constitutional accord, in which Rae invested so much personal energy, the strategy changed noticeably. Rae became more distant and abrupt with the media, backing away, refusing to be interviewed, giving curt answers that the media resented as rude and indifferent.

In early 1993, Rae switched to the Bill Clinton approach.

His office booked him onto radio and television shows so he could reach out to the people directly, without the filter of the Queen's Park press gallery. "It's a sign that they feel they've got to control the media environment a lot better than they have," said Michael Nolan, a professor of journalism at the University of Western Ontario. Nolan acknowledged that it was a way for Rae to avoid "the tough questions" that he was regularly being asked.

In March, Rae played the piano and sang a blues number on the CBC's Ralph Benmergui show, with his approving wife Arlene Perly Rae in the audience. Wearing a blue shirt without jacket or tie, this was the Rae equivalent of Clinton's famous saxophone performance on the Arsenio Hall show. Rae chatted briefly with Benmergui and admitted that if he were a better performer, he would prefer it to being premier. "In politics, you can go from hero to zero in thirty seconds," Rae said.

Both Rae and Benmergui were so low in the ratings that people wondered which one would be cancelled first.

Rae also answered phone calls from rock and roll buffs on Toronto radio station Q107 and appeared on the city's 24-hour sports station, The Fan.

Nolan said the strategy has its risks. "What they're trying to do, of course, is put him on the offensive....You've got to make sure you don't lose the dignity of the office. It is not a panacea and if it looks at all contrived, it can be disastrous."

The NDP was confusing image with substance. It was trying to warm up the premier and bring him, in a milieu outside politics, directly to the people. As it had done with the three different images the party created for Rae in the 1985, 1987 and 1990 campaigns, it was looking to overcome the negative impressions people had of him as a leader. And, once again, it was looking to the media — the same media that Rae said did him no favours — to deliver the new package. It was, as Yogi Berra would say, deja vu all over again.

The NDP was still making the mistake of working on image, rather than attempting to tackle the more deep-seated impressions people have of New Democrats, the last of its ten deadly sins.

10. A Reuseable Container

Long before the NDP's election, most Ontarians had a set of general impressions and ingrained beliefs about the party: what we've called its "container." Most people had a sense that they knew what the NDP was all about, and, whether those impressions were true or not, they were as good as true if most people believed them.

The key aspects of the NDP's "container" included the following perceptions: Ontarians thought New Democrats were good on social issues and were the champion of the underdog. They also gave the NDP credit for being a party of principle, one committed to its policies even though people might not agree with a number of them. In addition, NDP leaders, including Bob Rae, often scored high marks for trustworthiness and integrity.

But Ontarians also worried that the NDP "couldn't run the corner store." It was a party of left-wing ideas, closely — perhaps too closely — tied to the labour movement and antagonistic toward big business.

Because people's impressions are ingrained, it's not easy for a political party to change its "container." That's why parties usually work at the simpler aspects of political renewal: changing the image of their leaders or the leaders themselves, coming up with a fresh set of election promises, or just attacking their opponents without articulating their own platforms.

But once elected, Rae's NDP government quickly reinforced the worst aspects of its container and set about destroying the most positive ones.

In short order, it was obvious that the NDP government had no intention of sticking to its principles, and it entered into a long string of policy reversals. Peoples' worst fears that the NDP couldn't run the corner store were realized, and it became apparent that the government had no new ideas to deal with the deepening economic crisis. The government of morality and integrity Rae promised fell apart in a continuing round of scandals. Rae single-handedly destroyed people's sense of the party's compassion for the poor when he mused about forcing people on welfare to find jobs that others in his government quickly pointed out did not exist. He alienated working people and labour leaders when he called Ontario Hydro's planned 4,500 layoffs "courageous" and when the government speculated about cutting up to 18,000 public sector jobs.

In no time at all, people simply didn't know what the NDP stood for The government lurched from confusion to chaos to collapse with a swiftness and totality that was breathtaking. The catalogue of policy reversals and ministerial scandals and that smashed the NDP's container is too long to list here, and we suspect that the list is far from over. Later historians will have to take up that challenge. For us, it is important to note the that those reversals helped destroy the government's credibility and the people's faith in it.

At the outset, expectations were high. Writing in the *Kingston Whig-Standard* one month after the NDP victory, Dudley Hill, MPP Fred Wilson's campaign manager, said: "...Some of us have waited all our lives for this moment, sustained by a belief in social democracy and its adherents. I believe that the legacy of this government will be a renewal of faith in the political process and a lessening of voter cynicism."

Hill's comments were representative of the confidence and euphoria that surrounded the NDP's election. That didn't last long.

Five weeks after being sworn in, the NDP allowed the $1.1 billion sale of Consumers' Gas to British Gas PLC. Rae had argued as recently as March, 1990, that "We think it should be a public utility, publicly owned," but the government made no effort to find a Canadian buyer.

The *Toronto Star* editorialized: "The decision sends two clear messages: one to foreign investors that it will be business as usual and the other to Ontarians that they were sadly mistaken if they thought this government would live by its word....The NDP spent a long, long time in opposition making the case that when foreign investors own Canada's industries, they call the shots. But with his first chance to act in the interest of Ontarians, Rae has turned decades of NDP economic nationalism upside down."

Early in 1991, treasurer Floyd Laughren announced that the government had shelved its 1990 election platform, the Agenda for People, which other New Democrats had candidly admitted the NDP had no expectation of ever having to carry out. Again the *Toronto Star* wrote: "Broken promises will not be easily forgotten — or forgiven — by people who were told that cynicism was the exclusive domain of Liberals and Conservatives."

In March, 1991, the NDP put its long-standing promise to implement a minimum corporate tax on hold, saying it would be studied for three years by the newly-appointed Fair Tax Commission. When asked what had changed, Laughren said: "We didn't have experts before, quite frankly." When Laughren raised traditional sin taxes on booze and cigarettes while leaving corporations and the wealthy alone, workers wondered how the NDP's tax policies were different from any other party's.

In April, social services minister Zanana Akande announced that it would be impossible to eliminate food banks during the government's first term. Environment minister Ruth Grier confirmed that she didn't know how to enforce the NDP's firm commitment that a minimum of 30 per cent of pop sales would be in refillable containers. She had repeatedly blasted the Liberal government for its inaction on the law, and now the best she could do herself was have "extensive discussions" with the industry. When frustrated industry representatives pressed for a conclusion, Grier threatened to make a decision. Party policy to eliminate university tuition fees conflicted with a tuition hike while construction proceeded on the Darlington nuclear generating station, also contrary to party policy.

Before his first year in office was up, Rae admitted in a *Maclean's* magazine interview: "Even if there is something that has been in your program for a long time, if you reach the conclusion that it is not in the public interest to do it, then you have a responsibility to say, 'I've changed my mind.' That is the sole test — not what was in your program 10 years ago, or what you said in a speech in 1985. You end up disappointing some people who worked for you. And you have to say, 'I'm sorry.'"

Just a few weeks later, he told the *Globe*: "I think that the rhetoric of politicians has frequently exceeded the expectations of the public....What the public now wants is action from politicians that's more in keeping with their expectations."

Rae was saying that politicians — including himself, presumably — were in the habit of making exaggerated promises that the public didn't expect them to keep. If that were true, the public would not have been demanding that governments keep their promises. Rae based his 1990 campaign on the fact that David Peterson had "lied directly" to the people, and now he was saying that politics only means having to say "I'm sorry."

No reversal was more dramatic and controversial than the sellout of public automobile insurance, an announcement Rae made on the first anniversary of the NDP's victory. Furious New Democrats mailed in their party cards and puzzled Ontarians finally began to understand that Rae's government was prepared to backtrack on even its most high profile policies.

An NDP backgrounder on the issue showed just how much the government had turned its policy on its head. "We are also looking at one-stop shopping," it boasted, "enabling consumers to purchase their insurance and renew their licences at the same time and place. This would improve service to the public." Instead of this happening at government offices, the NDP was considering privatizing the issuing of licences. The turnaround was spectacular.

The auto insurance announcement not only undermined the government's credibility, but it set in motion a rebellion led by caucus bad boy Peter Kormos and supported by party arch-loyalist Mel Swart. When Swart said that if he had it to do all over again he would not nominate Bob Rae for leader, the party and the public knew the depths of dissatisfaction within the NDP.

"Could the Ontario NDP run in the next election or ones after that on the issue of public auto insurance?" Swart wrote in a leaflet defending the policy. "Of course not! No one would believe us! For sure our credibility is decimated on this issue and its effect spills over on other issues."

Swart's leaflet clearly pointed to the electoral problem the NDP would now face. "The NDP was elected to power because the public expected us to be different," it said. "They believed that we were a more grass-roots democratic party. They expected us to keep our promises. They thought we would put the public good ahead of wealthy vested interests. They thought that we have the political courage to proceed with our program, even though they may have disagreed with some of our policies. Now, all those beliefs are in shambles. There's no doubt that we are paying a heavy price with disillusioned and angry NDP members and an electorate which now feels that we play the same old political games as the other parties."

Two other major policy reversals also undermined the government's credibility.

Its total capitulation on Sunday shopping angered the labour leadership and, in particular, members of the United Food and Commercial Workers' Union, which campaigned vigorously for the NDP on its policy of banning Sunday working. Another policy that Rae had fought tooth-and-nail for over a period of years simply went down the chute.

At the same time, the government advocated opening gambling casinos. A small group of key cabinet ministers floated the idea early in 1992; by April, the cabinet approved the idea and in May announced it would set up a casino that year.

One minister confided that the cabinet approved casinos by only one vote, and the majority decision was simply imposed. No attempt was made to reach a consensus. The minister responsible for casinos, Marilyn Churley, admitted publicly: "Yes, I think it's fair to say we made a decision without having all the information we needed."

The NDP caucus had only one 45-minute information-style discussion of casinos and was never asked for its opinion before the announcement approving casinos was made. That infuriated MPP Dennis Drainville, who launched his own offensive against both the idea of casinos and the process that excluded caucus members from decision-making.

The *Globe* wrote: "Coming from the same purse-lipped bunch that says 'never on Sunday' to acts of commerce between consenting adults, this latest proposal offers further evidence of confusion over the dividing line between public and private morality."

Rae opposed casinos as recently as 1990. "The casino plays on greed," he said in the legislature then. "The sense of the ultimate chance, the hope against hope that the spin of the wheel or the shoot of the die will produce instant wealth, instant power, instant gratification. The work ethic, 'steady as you go,' appears alongside as fundamentally boring, goody-two-shoes values." His treasurer, Floyd Laughren, opposed not only casinos but also lotteries, and said in 1990 that "essential services should be funded by the tax system of this province, not through games of chance."

Plain and simple, the government was so desperate for revenue that it was willing to take odds on any scheme, including casinos. Now Rae hoped that the spin of the wheel would produce instant wealth for Ontario.

"When a government encourages its citizens to gamble in order to produce revenue," Thomas Walkom wrote, "it is admitting defeat. It is saying that society is no longer able, in an open and democratic way, to tax itself for the services it wants. It is conceding that government has lost the moral authority to convince taxpayers that, if they want public goods such as roads and health care, they must be willing to pay for them."

If any party should have been willing to fight for the principle of fair taxation to provide government services, it should have been the NDP.

But as the economy continued its decline, the public's belief that the NDP didn't know how to run the corner store proved itself in spades. We discussed above the NDP's lack of practical, lunchbucket economic ideas. We've shown how a general lack of imagination left the government unprepared to try novel economic strategies proposed by others. Instead, it relied on traditional bailouts at Algoma and de Havilland, provided millions of scarce public dollars to Ford and Chrysler, sold off some public assets and considered privatizing many others, invented new Crown corporations that would implement user fees, such as tolls on roads, and, finally, proposed wage rollbacks and massive layoffs in the public sector. The NDP was only doing what Tory and Liberal governments before it had done, actions which the opposition NDP roundly condemned.

Sam Gindin, chief economist and assistant to the president of the Canadian Auto Workers' Union, lamented that the government was attempting to cater to the priorities of the business community, and that "demoralizes the base" of the party. "Once you decide you have to pacify capital," Gindin told the *Globe*, "there is a whole set of things that follow from that. The more timid you are the more they are encouraged to attack you."

Gindin said it was the federal Conservatives who had been "much more class conscious and ideological, and it's the NDP that's trying to be pragmatic."

The overriding economic pragmatism came directly from Rae, who was never a democratic socialist and was never ideologically grounded. Rae's own intellectual meandering, best exemplified in his personal "What We Owe Each Other" testimony, made him comfortable with American-style neo-liberalism.

"Rae began an intellectual journey when he took office two and a half years ago," Walkom wrote in early 1993. "He left opposition as a social democrat with doubts, one who was trying to piece together what it means to be a socialist in the late 20th century. It's not simply that Rae has shifted to the right. That shift has been obvious since the first weeks of his government. What was not clear then was where he would stop. In his first year of office, Rae proved himself a better liberal than the Liberals, shedding long-held NDP policies such as public auto insurance in the interest of what he called pragmatism. Now, at the mid-point of his five year term, he has signalled he is willing to become a better conservative than the Tories."

* * *

The other big problem of Rae's government that destroyed the public's confidence in New Democrats was the long series of embarrassing scandals that plagued the NDP from the outset. The mostly petty scandals were especially problematic because Rae had promised an open, honest government free of conflict of interest. He even forced labour minister Bob Mackenzie to give up the union card he had carried since he was a young man in order to avoid any appearance of conflict.

In his first days in office, Rae kicked out caucus member Tony Rizzo when it was revealed that Rizzo's construction companies violated labour laws by avoiding payment of over $8,000 in union benefits. Rizzo was already under fire for receiving free architectural work from a company he helped get lucrative city contracts, and had been in the centre of a controversy for making a $700 campaign donation to a political opponent several days after the opponent quit the race. On leaving the caucus, Rizzo said: "It's a squeaky-clean government and has to remain a squeaky-clean government."

But the only thing squeaking was the NDP as it went off the rails.

Kormos was dropped from cabinet in March, 1991 after he appeared as a *Toronto Sun* Sunshine Boy. The *Sun* held the photo for weeks and used it in the middle of International Women's Week when, as the consumer minister, Kormos announced a crack-down on sexism in beer advertising. A year later, an unrepentant Kormos appeared in a Florida-based "Bachelor Book," a so-called "male-order" catalogue.

The scandals mounted. Health minister Evelyn Gigantes resigned. Solicitor-general Mike Farnan was embroiled in controversy, as was social services minister Zanana Akande. Farnan was dropped in the first shuffle. Women's minister Anne Swarbrick and northern development minister Shelley Martel offered to resign but Rae refused their resignations. (Rae originally accepted Martel's and then reversed himself). Martel was later the focus of opposition calls for her resignation for months; she took a lie detect-or test to prove she was telling the truth when she said she had lied about allegations concerning a Sudbury doctor. The *Toronto Star* editorialized: "After first claiming the moral high ground, [the NDP government] has sunk to the lowest levels of political morality....Rae's personal integrity may be beyond reproach, but his political morality may now be beyond recovery."

Akande resigned after being found guilty of charging illegal rents. Energy minister Will Ferguson quit over allegations of sexual improprieties at a school for girls where he worked twenty years previously. Tourism minister Peter North quit after offering a job to a Toronto barmaid with whom he had a widely-publicized and ludicrous affair which apparently involved them sleeping together without having sex. North refused to wear a condom, saying it wasn't necessary because he was faithful to his wife; the irony was not lost on his companion.

Carlton Masters, the man Rae appointed as the province's agent-general in New York City, resigned in the face of allegations of sexual harassment and caused considerable embarrassment to the government when he demanded that the report into his conduct be made public. Toronto's black community stood by him for the most part, and awarded him the prestigious Harry Jerome award despite the controversy.

Then, in the spring of 1993, the scandals reached into the heart of Rae's own office when his media specialist John Piper resigned after trying to give the criminal record of the woman involved in the Will Ferguson affair to a reporter. Rae's cabinet secretary David Agnew, and advisors Ross McClellan and Michael Mendelson reportedly knew that Ferguson gave the criminal record to Piper, yet Rae continued to deny any knowledge of the mess.

"They're being hoisted on their own petard over ethics in government," said University of Toronto political scientist Nelson Wiseman. "That's why there is special glee in the opposition and the media over this." On a TV-Ontario public affairs show, Rae admitted: "I think I'm paying the price, probably, for 10 years of sanctimony in opposition."

The government of integrity that Rae promised utterly disintegrated. An early 1993 Environics poll showed that only 16 per cent of Ontarians thought Rae was providing more honest government than David Peterson, while 38 per cent said Rae's government was less honest. Sixty-six per cent said they felt less favourable toward Rae than they did two years previously.

He had set the standards himself, buying into the notion that a "good" government was not necessarily one that kept its promises and implemented policies most beneficial to its citizens, but one that was "clean" and free of scandal. Ultimately, the long list of scandals reflected not just on those individuals, but on the entire New Democratic Party. In future, people would no longer believe that as politicians, New Democrats were any more pure than any other.

"No Mistakes Planned"

The following transcript of a phone conversation with a spokesperson from "NDP headquarters" appeared in the *Toronto Star's* "*eye*" tabloid on January 14, 1993:

eye: We do a thing every week called Rolling eye, which is a bit of a satiric thing, and we got a lot of mileage out of some of the mistakes that some of the NDP cabinet made, you know, the North thing, the Piper thing, all those things, and there hasn't been a mistake like that for a while. We're sort of running out of things to write about (NDP spokesperson begins to laugh). Do you know when we could expect the next mistake? NDP spokesperson: (laughing)...(big pause)...No, I don't. No mistakes planned.
eye: Are they on holiday? Are things changing? Because when stuff like that happens, it's excellent for our section, we have a lot of stuff to write about.
NDP spokesperson: (continues laughing) Yes, no doubt (trying to compose herself). No, there are no mistakes planned.
eye: So, you're not really expecting any mistakes in 1993?
NDP spokesperson: Well, people are human, people make mistakes.
eye: Ah, yes.
NDP spokesperson: They're not planned.
eye: And you have no idea when we would be able to look forward to the next one?
NDP spokesperson: (giggle) No.

---

* * *

In its first two and a half years in office, Rae's government managed to undermine the positive aspects of the party's container: that it was a party of principle committed to its policies, that it was different from the other parties, that it cared most about ordinary Canadians, and that it was a party of integrity and trustworthiness. At the same time, Rae's government reinforced the worst aspect of its container: that it didn't know how to manage economics.

The end result is that people no longer trust New Democrats. No one believes they will stick to what they say they stand for. Rae's government, and principally Rae himself, has destroyed the public's belief in social democrats not just as people with a different set of ideals, but as people with the integrity to implement them.

It is hard to imagine what reasons the New Democrats will give for asking people to vote for them again, and harder still to imagine why people would believe them.

* * *

The political fallout from Bob Rae's government is far more than a trail of broken promises and a legacy of petty scandal.

Rae's term in office has caused NDP supporters to lose faith in a set of values that let them hope the world could be a better place if social democrats were in government.

People can live with disappointment, but not without dreams. They can live with failure, but not without hope. Rae's government has shattered even this, and there are no easy ways to put it right.

Now people have to start to build all over again, find a new faith, and dream new dreams.

Appendix

On May 28, 1985, Liberal party leader David Peterson and NDP leader Bob Rae signed *An Agenda for Reform: Proposals for Minority Parliament*, which came to be known popularly as the "Accord." This is the complete text of that agreement.

An Agreement for a Reform Minority Parliament

On May 2, 1985, the people of Ontario created an opportunity for change after 42 years of Conservative government. We are determined to accept responsibility for bringing about that change.

During the election campaign, both the Liberal and New Democratic Parties advanced significant public policy and legislative reform proposals. These proposals contained many elements in common, which are outlined in the attached documents.

In the interests of making minority government work, we are committed to a program of public policy reforms which will improve the quality of life for everyone in this province. We are also committed to legislative reforms designed to improve public access to and information about the legislative process in Ontario.

It will take time to achieve these objectives. We have agreed on the need for a period of stability during which this program can proceed.

Should the Lieutenant Governor invite the Leader of the Liberal Party to form a Government, this agreement will be for two years from the day that the Leader of the Liberal Party assumes the office of Premier.

It is understood that the traditions, practices and precedents of the Ontario Legislature are that individual bills are not considered matters of confidence unless so designated by the Government.

We undertake the following:

1. The Leader of the Liberal Party will not request a dissolution of the Legislature during the term of this agreement, except following defeat on a

specifically-framed motion of non-confidence.

2. The New Democratic Party will neither move nor vote non-confidence during the term of this agreement.

3. While individual bills, including budget bills, will not be treated or designated as matters of confidence, the overall budgetary policy of the Government, including the votes on supply, will be treated as a matter of confidence.

(Signed by David Peterson and Bob Rae)

Document 1

Legislative reform

Legislation on freedom of information and protection of privacy.

Reform of the House by strengthening and broadening the role of committees and individual members and increasing public involvement in the legislative process. Select Committees will be established to investigate the commercialization of health and social services in Ontario and to study and report on bilateral environmental issues affecting Ontario.

Changes to broaden the powers of the Public Accounts Committee and the Provincial Auditor to cover current and proposed expenditures and to reiterate the authority of the Committee to direct investigations of all aspects of public spending.

Establishment of a Standing Committee on Energy to oversee Ontario Hydro and other energy matters.

Establishment of a Select Committee on procedures for appointments in the public sector to recommend changes in the system of recruitment and selection of public appointees.

Election financing reform to cover spending limits and rebates, at both the central and local campaign level.

Redefinition and broadening of the rights of public service workers to participation in political activity.

Electronic Hansard (television in the Legislature).

Document 2

Proposals for action in first session from common campaign proposals, to be implemented within a framework of fiscal responsibility.

Begin implementation of separate school funding.
  - Release present draft legislation immediately.
  - Introduce legislation upon a Liberal government meeting the legislature and refer to Committee for public hearings.

Introduce programs to create employment and training opportunities for young people.

Ban extra billing by medical doctors.

Proclaim the sections of the Environmental Protection Act dealing with spills.

Reform Ontario's tenant protection laws, including:
  - Establishment of a rent registry.
  - Establishment of a four per cent rent review guideline.
  - Inclusion of the provisions of Bill 198 as a permanent part of the Residential Tenancies Act.
  - Extension of rent review to cover post-1976 buildings.
  - An end to the $750 a month exemption from rent review.
  - Introduction of a rent review procedure to deal with costs-no-longer-borne by landlords.
  - Introduction of enabling legislation to permit demolition control by municipalities.

Introduce legislation for equal pay for work of equal value in both the public and private sector.

Include a first contract law in Ontario labour legislation.

Introduce reforms to the Occupational Health and Safety Act including toxic substances designation and regulations to give workers the right to know about workplace hazards.

Continue the pre-budget freeze on ad valorem gasoline tax and establish an inquiry into gas price differentials between Northern and Southern Ontario.

Wind up the Royal Commission on the Northern Environment and obtain release of all working papers and reports.

Provide full coverage of medically necessary travel under OHIP for residents of Northern Ontario.

Document 3

Program for action from common campaign proposals, to be implemented within a framework of fiscal responsibility.

Affirmative action and employment equity for women, minorities and the handicapped and expansion of the role and budget of Human Rights Commission to deal with workplace and housing discrimination.

Establishment of an Ontario housing program to fund immediately 10,000 co-op and non-profit housing units, in addition to those provided for under federal funding arrangements.

New enforceable mechanisms for the control of pollution to enable Ontario to deal effectively with acid rain and to establish the principle that the polluter pays.

Reform of services for the elderly to provide alternatives to institutional care and a reform of the present nursing home licensing and inspection system.

Reform of job security legislation, including notice and justification of lay-offs and plant shutdowns and improved severance legislation.

Farm financing reform, including low interest loans for farmers.

Workers' compensation reform.

Private pension reform based on the recommendations of the Ontario Select Committee on Pensions.

Reform of day care policy and funding to recognize child care as a basic public service and not a form of welfare.

An independent audit of Ontario's forest resources, and additional programs to provide for on-going regeneration of Ontario's forests.

Index

Copy for back cover

When Bob Rae stepped into the brisk, sunny afternoon on October 1, 1990, Ontario's first NDP premier carried with him a generation of NDP commitments and the bright promise of hopeful expectation, shining in the eyes of New Democrats who thought they would never live to see the day.

Giving Away A Miracle is a lively, behind-the-scenes account of how and why those hopes were dashed. It explains why the Ontario NDP's failures cannot be blamed on hard economic times or inexperience but on the deep-seated flaws in NDP history.

The authors:
Long-time New Democrats George Ehring and Wayne Roberts were leaders of the NDP's left wing and senior union staffers in the 1980s. A labour historian, Roberts is the author of books on the Energy and Chemical Workers' Union and the Ontario Public Service Employees' Union, and writes on Queen's Park for NOW magazine. Ehring is a former vice-president of the Ontario NDP and a former legislative assistant at the NDP caucus. He writes on labour and politics for Our Times.

Copy for back cover

When Bob Rae stepped into the brisk, sunny afternoon on October 1, 1990, Ontario's first NDP premier carried with him a generation of NDP commitments and the bright promise of hopeful expectation, shining in the eyes of New Democrats who thought they would never live to see the day.

Giving Away A Miracle is a lively, behind-the-scenes account of how and why those hopes were dashed. It explains why the Ontario NDP's failures cannot be blamed on hard economic times or inexperience but on the deep-seated flaws in NDP history.

The authors
Long-time New Democrats George Ehring and Wayne Roberts were leaders of the NDP's left wing and senior union staffers in the 1980s. A labour historian, Roberts is the author of books on the Energy and Chemical Workers' Union and the Ontario Public Service Employees' Union, and writes on Queen's Park for NOW magazine. Ehring is a former vice-president of the Ontario NDP and a former legislative assistant at the NDP caucus. He writes on labour and politics for Our Times.